THE S. MARK TAPER FOUNDATION

IMPRINT IN JEWISH STUDIES

BY THIS ENDOWMENT

THE S. MARK TAPER FOUNDATION SUPPORTS

THE APPRECIATION AND UNDERSTANDING

OF THE RICHNESS AND DIVERSITY OF

JEWISH LIFE AND CULTURE

The publisher gratefully acknowledges the generous contribution to this book provided by the Jewish Studies Endowment Fund of the University of California Press Foundation, which is supported by a major gift from the S. Mark Taper Foundation.

Two Nations in Your Womb

Two Nations in Your Womb

PERCEPTIONS OF JEWS AND CHRISTIANS
IN LATE ANTIQUITY AND THE MIDDLE AGES

Israel Jacob Yuval

Translated from the Hebrew by
Barbara Harshav and Jonathan Chipman

UNIVERSITY OF CALIFORNIA PRESS

BERKELEY   LOS ANGELES   LONDON

University of California Press, one of the most distinguished
university presses in the United States, enriches lives around
the world by advancing scholarship in the humanities, social
sciences, and natural sciences. Its activities are supported by
the UC Press Foundation and by philanthropic contributions
from individuals and institutions. For more information,
visit www.ucpress.edu.

University of California Press
Berkeley and Los Angeles, California

University of California Press, Ltd.
London, England

© 2006 by
The Regents of the University of California
First paperback printing 2008

All biblical quotations are taken from the Revised
Standard Version of the Bible.

Library of Congress Cataloging-in-Publication Data

Yuval, Israel Jacob, 1949–.
    [Hakhamim be-doram. English].
    Two nations in your womb : perceptions of Jews
and Christians in late antiquity and the Middle Ages /
Israel Jacob Yuval ; translated from the Hebrew by
Barbara Harshav and Jonathan Chipman.
        p.   cm.
    Includes bibliographical references and index.
    ISBN: 978-0-520-25818-1
    1. Rabbis—Germany—Biography.   2. Jewish
scholars—Germany—Biography.   3. Judaism—
Germany—History.   4. Jews—Germany—History—
1096–1800.   5. Germany—Ethnic relations.   I. Title.

BM750.Y8813   2006
296.3'960902—dc22   2005032842

Manufactured in the United States of America

17   16   15   14   13   12   11   10   09
11   10   9   8   7   6   5   4   3   2

For Esther
and for our beloved children,
Shlomit and Yoel Greenberg
Naomi
Shira

In memory of my beloved mother,
Hedva Yuval (Klara Kofler)
Vienna 1922–Jerusalem 2005

A lover of knowledge and wisdom
Uprooted from her homeland and family
She immigrated to the Land of Israel in 1939
And she took root and filled the land (PSALMS 80:10)

CONTENTS

ILLUSTRATIONS

THE CREATION OF THIS BOOK BEGAN as an afterthought, continued in a stormy and bitter polemic, and concluded with a still, small voice.

This book was born during the summer semester of 1992, when I was a visiting professor at the University of Trier at the invitation of my friend, the noble-hearted Professor Alfred Haverkamp. During a walk around the city with my wife, Esther, and our three daughters, Shlomit, Naomi, and Shira, we came across the enormous Roman basilica—one of the most important and beautiful attractions of the city. While standing at the foot of this imposing structure, I removed from my briefcase the Hebrew chronicle by Solomon ben Samson describing the First Crusades and read the description of what happened at this place in 1096. At that time the Jews of the city bastioned themselves within the basilica, planning to throw both their children and themselves from this tall building in order to avoid their forcible conversion to Christianity. The building imposes on the visitor a feeling of imminent and real fear. The basilica at Trier is the only place in all of Germany, among those described in the Hebrew chronicles of the Crusades, that has survived, and there is no place more appropriate to exemplify this awesome tragedy, that of parents wishing to kill their own children.

This was a rare occasion, one in which my profession as historian and my duty as father coincided. The question that the father within posed to the historian within was a pointed one: What can motivate sane people to kill their own children, to hurl them to such a cruel death? I am certainly not the first person to raise this question, but I may well be the first Israeli historian to read his children the chronicle of 1096 at the foot of the basilica in Trier. This unmediated encounter with the site of the historical event, in the company of those who could have been its helpless victims, aroused within me strong feelings, which texts alone do not always succeed in arousing.

This book is an attempt to answer that question—a very partial attempt, I must admit. It does not answer the question of what motivated the martyrs themselves, who killed themselves before managing to tell the next generations why. What remain are the explanations of the survivors, the words of those who were not killed or who did not kill themselves, who became apostates, or were simply lucky. Are they allowed to speak in the name of the victims? It would seem not; yet history is written by the survivors, not by those who are lost, and these survivors left behind explanations and theories that a modern person finds difficult to accept. The descriptions of the Jews' behavior during the First Crusade—their suicides, the killing of their close relatives, and the murder of children by their parents—ought to arouse not only historical curiosity but also ethical puzzles, among both Jews and Christians. In this book I wish to argue that this behavior—that is, its retrospective interpretation by the survivors—is related to messianic ideas that were widespread among Ashkenazic Jewry during that period, ideas that linked the spilled blood of the martyrs with the avenging of their blood at the time of the future Redemption. Kiddush Hashem (Sanctification of the Holy Name) was considered a kind of restorative response to the hardships of the Exile, because it was thought to hasten the Redemption and thereby played a role, at the very heart of Jewish apologetics, in regards to the subjugating and dominant Christianity. This argument seeks to explain the intensity of Ashkenazic martyrdom, its unique ceremonies, and its immediate response to the challenge of the Crusaders.

Study of the central significance given to martyrdom among Ashkenazic Jewry and its location at the center of its confrontation with the Christian milieu led me to examine the similarity between the acts of those Jews who performed acts of murder with certain ritual characteristics and the widespread accusation in Western Europe almost one generation after the First Crusade: that Jews were carrying out ritual murder of Christians with messianic motivations and in order to hasten their Redemption. It is self-evident that alongside the external resemblance there is also a substantive difference: the Jewish martyrs killed their loved ones, while those fabricating the stories accused them of murdering Christians. This comparison took me in one fell swoop from the history of facts to the history of mutual images.

As a member of the generation born after the Christian-Jewish polemic in its old form had come to an end, I naively thought that there was nothing insulting in this comparison, for history is also a series of optical illusions and demonic images. It was in this spirit that I began to write my first paper on this subject, published in the journal *Zion* in 1993. But the reactions to the article were something completely different. What was originally intended to be just another esoteric research article quickly became a confrontation involving multiple participants. A double issue of *Zion* (1994) was devoted to the subject. My article and the reactions to it were even covered in the Israeli and international press. One of my harshest critics did not hesitate to conclude his review with the following sentence: "This article is of the type that it would have been better had it never been written; and once written—it would have been better had it never been published; and once published—it would have been better had it been forgotten as quickly as possible." Thus, I found myself unintentionally hitting some very raw nerves.

After things calmed down, between 1995 and 1997, I was able to expand on my original viewpoint and to base it on some new sources, to examine other periods, and to raise new questions. Thus was this book born. Parts of it were published in various forums, mostly in Hebrew, while others were published for the first time in the Hebrew version of this book. The weaving of old articles into a new book enabled me to reexamine several of my initial statements, to correct them, to update them, and even to retract some of them.[1] But in principle I have not recanted my fundamental theses and have even added new ones, which are now presented here.

The completion of the book was accompanied by a sense of relief, since alongside the words of criticism, I found more and more people, particu-

---

1. Two critical reactions to my article appeared in the United States: R. Chazan, *Medieval Stereotypes and Modern Antisemitism* (Berkeley and Los Angeles, 1997), 75–77; David Berger, "From Crusades to Blood Libels to Expulsions: Some New Approaches to Medieval Antisemitism," Second Annual Lecture of the Victor J. Selmanowitz Chair of Jewish History (New York, 1997), 16–22. I accepted several of the points raised by the two of them and corrected this book accordingly. Other arguments are based on misunderstandings, and here too I saw fit to correct the text to avert such errors. Yet other points I rejected, but I prefer not to use the present forum for polemical purposes.

larly among younger historians, who were willing to evaluate my approach sympathetically. In truth, what in 1993 was still considered by many a radical and controversial innovation was, by the time I finished the book in 1999, a view shared by at least three other scholars. Historians Ivan Marcus, Mary Minty, and Willis Johnson also felt, each in his or her own way and without knowing each other, that the story of the accusations of ritual murder had to be told in relation to the ideology of Kiddush Hashem.[2] Of course, this does not imply that they are fully in agreement with everything said in this book.

This book is thus a further link in the infinite chain of historical interpretations that emerge over time, in which each generation retells its ancient tribal stories. I hope that my contemporaries and I will have the strength not only to articulate our viewpoint with courage but also, when the time comes, to listen with humility and patience to "revisionist" interpretations of the next generation of researchers, whose day is yet to come. For one generation passes and another comes, and history always changes.

———

A book of this type cannot be written without the support of devoted and loving friends. Even though I can enumerate here only a partial list of their virtues, I wish to express my full and total gratitude. First of all, I would like to thank Oded Irshai, with whom I have come a long way, since the days of our innocent youth when we took the straight and easy route, through the tortuous and narrow paths of teaching and research. He, along with Immanuel Etkes and Ora Limor, were the first critical readers of my work. Their wisdom, their extensive knowledge, and their good sense all left their mark on many pages of this book. Richard Cohen and Elchanan Reiner were unstinting in their advice, help, and encouragement in bringing the book to completion. Amnon Raz-Krakotzkin gave abundantly of

---

2. I. Marcus, "Hierarchies, Religious Boundaries, and Jewish Spirituality in Medieval Germany," *Jewish History* 1 (1986): 23 n. 27; M. Minty, "Kiddush Hashem in the Eyes of Christians in Mediaeval Germany" [in Hebrew], *Zion* 59 (1994): 209–66 (an abbreviated English version appeared as "Responses to Medieval Ashkenazi Martyrdom (Kiddush ha-Shem) in Late Medieval German Christian Sources," *Jahrbuch für Antisemitismusforschung* 4 [1995]: 13–38); W. Johnson, "Before the Blood Libel: Jewish and Christian Exegesis after the Massacres of 1096" (master's thesis, Faculty of History, University of Cambridge, 1994). Johnson had planned to present this innovation in his master's thesis, but my Hebrew article appeared in print at the same time. In his modesty and generosity he chose to revise his thesis topic.

his support and love. Yaakov Guggenheim, a perceptive scholar and Renaissance man, always knew how to add a bit of spice and wit. And finally, last and most beloved, to the four women in my life: my wife, Esther, and our three daughters, Shlomit, Naomi, and Shira. It was all because of them and for their sake.

This book is dedicated to the memory of three precious souls whom I never knew: my grandmother and grandfather, Sarah and Jacob Kofler, and their daughter, Hella Kofler, who were en route from Vienna to Palestine during the Second World War. Help came too late, and they were caught and murdered by the Nazis. Their images and their fate were before my eyes throughout the writing of this book.

Jerusalem 1999

THE ENGLISH TRANSLATION OF THIS BOOK is based on the first Hebrew edition, which was completed in 1999 and published in 2000. Since the translation was subject to considerable delay, I decided not to change anything in the translated version, apart from correcting several technical errors. The English edition thus reflects the state of research and my knowledge of it up to the year 2000.

The basic premise of this book is that the polemics between Judaism and Christianity during the first centuries of the Common Era, in all their varieties and nuances, played a substantial role in the mutual formation of the two religions. Here I am referring not only to an explicit and declared polemic, but to a broad panorama of expressions that include, particularly from the Jewish side, allusions, ambiguities, denials, refutations, and at times also internalization and quiet agreement. The literary-exegetical method required by this approach is very similar to that implied by Daniel Boyarin, who has articulated his positions a number of times in recent years.[1] I share with him the recognition that Jewish culture conducts a very circuitous and complex

---

1. Daniel Boyarin, *Dying for God: Martyrdom and the Making of Christianity and Judaism* (Stanford, 1999); Boyarin, *Border Lines: The Partition of Judaeo-Christianity* (Philadelphia, 2004).

conversation with its mirror image, Christianity. Nonetheless, in my view it is still too early to summarize the historical picture that emerges from the method of literary reading that is common in the most recent research.

The breakthrough attained through the hermeneutic novelty of this kind of literary interpretation has subverted and even refuted a number of historical conceptions of the previous generation—for example, the assumption that the Babylonian Talmud, which allegedly took shape in a non-Christian environment, was not concerned with Christianity. Another example pertains to the relationship between Rabbinic literature and early Christian literature. Literary criticism has upset the place of honor that in the past was given almost automatically to Rabbinic literature as the "source" of the New Testament.

Despite the fact that only a few years have passed since the publication of the Hebrew edition of this book, scholarly literature has been enriched by numerous publications relating to the relations between Jews and Christians against the background of anti-Jewish violence during the First Crusade in 1096—a subject that occupies a central place in this book. I wish to mention in particular the works of Susan Einbinder,[2] Robert Chazan,[3] Jeremy Cohen,[4] Simha Goldin,[5] Haym Soloveitchik,[6] and Shmuel Shepkaru;[7] the collections of papers edited by Anna Sapir Abulafia,[8] Yom Tov Assis, and others;[9] and Alfred Haverkamp,[10] Michael Signer, and John van Engen.[11]

2. Susan Einbinder, *Beautiful Death: Jewish Poetry and Martyrdom in Medieval France* (Princeton, 2002).

3. Robert Chazan, *God, Humanity, and History: The Hebrew First-Crusade Narratives* (Berkeley, 2000).

4. Jeremy Cohen, *Sanctifying the Name of God: Jewish Martyrs and Jewish Memories of the First Crusade* (Philadelphia, 2004).

5. Simha Goldin, The *Ways of Jewish Martyrdom* [in Hebrew], (Lydda, 2002).

6. Haym Soloveitchik, "Halakhah, Hermeneutics, and Martyrdom in Medieval Ashkenaz," *JQR*94, no. 1 (2004): 77–108; 2: 278–99.

7. Shmuel Shepkaru, "From After Life to Afterdeath: Martyrdom and Its Recompense," *AJS Review* 24 (1999), 1–44; Shepkaru, "To Die for God: Martyrs' Heaven in Hebrew and Latin Crusade Narratives," *Speculum* 77 (2002): 311–41.

8. Anna Sapir Abulafia, ed., *Religious Violence Between Christians and Jews: Medieval Roots, Modern Perspectives* (New York, 2002).

9. Yom Tov Assis et al., eds., *Facing the Cross: The Persecutions of 1096 in History and Historiography*, (Jerusalem, 2000).

10. Alfred Haverkamp, ed., *Juden und Christen zur Zeit der Kreuzzüge* (Sigmaringen, 1999).

11. Michael A. Signer and John van Engen, eds., *Jews and Christians in Twelfth-Century Europe*, (Notre Dame, IN, 2001).

The Hebrew chronicles concerning the Crusades—the most significant historical source for understanding Jewish martyrdom—have recently been republished in a new critical edition with a detailed introduction on the history of the text and extensive commentary by Eva Haverkamp.[12]

Since the publication of this book in Hebrew, several of its major theses have become part of the discourse in the field. One thesis relates to the existence of a mutual dialogue between the Jewish Passover following the Destruction of the Second Temple and the celebration of the Christian Easter. From this was born an attempt to interpret certain passages in the Passover Haggadah as reflecting a hidden polemic with Christianity. A similar approach was taken by Etienne Nodet, in an article that I overlooked while preparing the Hebrew edition, and which deserves to be included in any future discussion of this issue.[13] Judith Hauptman has stated: "Yisrael Yuval has claimed that the Seder and the Haggadah were created at Yavneh,"[14] whereas in her opinion, the Passover Haggadah was composed later. But nowhere have I claimed that the Haggadah in its extant form was created during the generation of Yavneh. My only explicit statement pertaining to the date of composition of the Passover Haggadah was aimed at refuting a view widely held in the previous generation, according to which the Haggadah dated from the Second Temple period. I see no reason to enter into debate with those who date the creation of the Passover Haggadah even later, such as Clemens Leonhard.[15] Such clarifications are important in studying the history of the text but less so in evaluating the historical context in which there arose the need among Jews to confront Easter, a context that changed very little during the first centuries C.E.

---

12. Eva Haverkamp, *Hebräische Berichte über die Judenverfolgungen während des Ersten Kreuzzugs* (*Hebraeische Texte aus dem mittelalterlichen Deutschland*, vol. 1; Monumenta Germaniae Historica and the Israeli Academy of Sciences (April 2005).

13. Etienne Nodet, "Miettes Messianiques," in *Messiah and Christos: Studies in the Jewish Origins of Christianity Presented to David Flusser on the Occasion of His Seventy-Fifth Birthday*, ed. I. Gruenwald, S. Shaked, and G. Stroumsa (Tübingen, 1992), 119–41. By contrast, Sagit Mor, in her study of the Passover Haggadah ("The Laws of Sacrifice or Telling the Story of the Exodus?" [in Hebrew], *Zion* 68 [2003]: 297–311), did not consider the Christian context.

14. Judith Hauptman, "How Old Is the Haggadah?" *Judaism* 51 (2002): 5–18.

15. Clemens Leonhard, "Die älteste Haggada; Übersetzung der Pesachhaggada nach dem palästinischen Ritus und Vorschläge zu ihrem Ursprung und ihrer Bedeutung für die Geschichte der christlichen Liturgie," *Archiv für Liturgiewissenschaft* 45 (2003): 201–31; Leonhard, "Die Ursprünge der Liturgie des jüdischen Pesach und das christliche Osterfest," in *Dialog oder Monolog? Zur liturgischen Beziehung zwischen Judentum and Christentum*, ed. Albert Gerhards and Hans H. Henrix (Freiburg im Breisgau, 2004), 151–66.

More reactions were elicited, as was to be expected, by another thesis first proposed in an article and now in this book: namely, that suggesting a possible connection between the murder of Jewish children by the martyrs of the First Crusade and the accusation made by Christians that Jews performed ritual murder, mostly of children, at Eastertime. The list of those opposed to this thesis did not grow any shorter after the publication of the Hebrew book.[16] In contrast, this thesis received unexpected support in an article published in 2001 by Lee Patterson of Yale University,[17] although he presented it as his own theory, without noting that it was first published in my 1993 paper.[18] Nevertheless, Patterson thereby joins the list of scholars for whom this thesis seems reasonable.[19]

I am grateful to the project editor, Ms. Suzanne Knott, and to the manuscript editor, Ms. Mimi Kusch, from the University of California Press for their excellent work on the English version of the book.

I had the privilege and the pleasure to work with Ms. Shuli Schneider-

---

16. For an extensive picture of the polemic aroused by the theses in my book, see Rainer Walz, "Die Debatte über die Thesen Israel J. Yuvals," *Aschkenas* 9 (1999): 189–232. This polemic was also summarized by Michael Toch, *Die Juden im mittelalterlichen Reich* (München, 1998), 134–38. An analysis of the positions in terms of a broader perspective was presented by Amnon Raz-Krakotzkin, "Historisches Bewutsein und historische Verantwortung," in *Historikerstreit in Israel. Die "neuen" Historiker zwischen Wissenschaft und Öffentlichkeit,* ed. B. Schäfer (Frankfurt and New York, 2000), 151–80. Johannes Heil ("'Deep enmity' and/or 'Close ties'? Jews and Christians before 1096: Sources, Hermeneutics, and Writing History in 1096," *Jewish Studies Quarterly* 9 [2002]: 259–306) disagrees with the gravity with which I depict the Jewish enmity toward Christianity. A skeptical position toward my suggested explanation for the appearance of the accusation of ritual murder was also put forward by Christopher Ocker, "Ritual Murder and the Subjectivity of Christ: A Choice in Medieval Christianity," *Harvard Theological Review* 91 (1998): 154–59.

17. Lee Patterson, "'The Living Witnesses of Our Redemption': Martyrdom and Imitation in Chaucer's Prioress's Tale," *Journal of Medieval and Early Modern Studies* 31 (2001): 507–60.

18. On p. 530 he writes, "It may well be that the charge of ritual murder—which first arose in England in the late 1140s and early 1150s in relation to William of Norwich—was a response to the massacres and the attendant acts of ritual slaughter of Jewish children by their parents during the Second Crusade of 1146." To this sentence is attached footnote 90, which makes no reference to earlier research literature, and ipso facto not to my Hebrew paper on this subject, in which I proposed this explanation and discussed it at length. My paper is only mentioned once, in n. 116, far from that quotation. Patterson also erroneously confuses the Second Crusade (for which there is hardly any recorded evidence of Kiddush Hashem) and the First Crusade, of 1096. I would conjecture that his disregard of my paper derives from his lack of knowledge of the Hebrew language.

19. See preface to the Hebrew edition, n. 2, p. xiv.

man on the final draft of the translation. The book benefited from her sharp mind and crystal-clear thinking.

The translation of the Hebrew book has been ably accomplished by Rabbi Jonathan Chipman, who is not only an expert translator but also a scholar in his own right. His translation was accompanied by astute comments, and he suggested substantive corrections. My thanks to him from the bottom of my heart.

ONE

Introduction

Et Major Serviet Minori
(And the Elder Will Serve the Younger)

THE THEMATIC FRAMEWORK

This book is intended to be a study of the reciprocal attitudes of Jews and Christians toward one another, not a history of the relations between them. I do not intend to present a systematic and comprehensive description of the dialogue and conflicts between Jews and Christians, with their various historical metamorphoses. My sole purpose is to reveal fragmented images of repressed and internalized ideas that lie beneath the surface of the official, overt religious ideology, which are not always explicitly expressed. My objective is to engage in a rational and open discussion of the roles played by irrationality, disinformation, and misinformation in shaping both the self-definition and the definition of the "other" among Jews and Christians in the Middle Ages.

The book revolves around three pairs: Jacob and Esau, Passover and Easter, Jewish martyrdom and blood libel. The first pair is typological, that is, it uses an existing narrative system based on the Scriptures and charges it with the later conflict between Israel and Edom, Judaea and Rome, Judaism and Christianity, a conflict between chosen and rejected, persecuted and persecutor. This involvement with the question of who is chosen and who is rejected, who is "Jacob" and who is "Esau," reflects a process of self-definition as well as, ipso facto, a definition of the other, the persecutor and rival. The tension evoked by this typology is one between subjugation, suffering, and exile, on the one hand, and dominion, primogeniture, and victory, on the other. For Christianity, it is viewed as the tension between the Old Testament and the New Testament; for Judaism, it is that between Exile and Redemption. The first two chapters and the final chapter of this book concern this issue.

The second pair deals with the two most important holidays in Judaism and Christianity, Passover and Easter. Both holidays share the conceptual premise of being based on ancient tales about a deliverance in the past and the promise of deliverance in the future. Although this confrontation has a long history, it will not be told here. Our discussion will be limited to exposing points of friction between these two festivals on three levels. The first level is a description of the denial of the rival ceremony by means of overt or covert polemics; the second is a description of the appropriation of specific ritual elements taken from the rival religion, along with a change in their ideological content; the third, a description of misunderstandings in which the ceremonies of one religion are misinterpreted by members of the other religion so as to confirm the latter interpretation to the world of the observer and interpreter. These motifs will be discussed in chapters 2 and 5.

The third pair—martyrdom and blood libel—leads us deep into the world of reciprocal images. Here we shall attempt to confront concrete Jewish suffering with the world of messianic imagination. Imagination and hallucination were designed to offer compensation and reward for the flaws and deficiencies of reality, but they also played an important role in the revised shaping of reality—not only of Jews but of Christians too. The acts of the Jewish martyrs in Germany during the Crusades express not just their despair but also their hopes, and the Christian spectators not only witnessed the deeds themselves, but they also noted the ideology of those who performed them. Thus, a vicious circle with tragic consequences was set into motion. This complex circle is described in chapters 3 and 4.

Both religions interpreted themselves through pairs of typological biblical characters. The one is youthful, beautiful, spiritual, righteous, and, most important, triumphant and powerful; the other is old, ugly, wild, wicked and, most important, defeated and humbled. The polemic is two-sided and direct and recognizes only one alternative. Such was the world of Jews and Christians during late antiquity until Islam appeared as a third religious option, and such was the situation in Europe throughout most of the Middle Ages. Unlike in the Muslim countries, where Muslims, Christians, and Jews lived together, interreligious conflict in Europe tended to be bipolar: hence the propagandistic power of pairs such as Cain and Abel, Isaac and

Ishmael, Rachel and Leah, Ephraim and Manasseh—and of course, of Jacob and Esau.

I have therefore chosen to focus on the typological conflict between Esau and Jacob, which relates to interpreting the past, to understanding the present, and especially to grasping the nature of the blessing for the future: "and the elder will serve the younger." In the Middle Ages Jews and Christians argued about their common biblical past as well as about the present—their beliefs and religious praxis—but essentially the argument turned on the future, on messianic faith and on what was expected at the End of Days. Both Jews and Christians were deeply devoted to their faith, and it was unlikely that opposing interpretations of the rival religion would undermine it or instill doubt in their hearts about either the mythic past or the concrete here and now. Nevertheless, there was considerable mutual uneasiness about the unknown future. For medieval people, the future was the age of the Messiah, and the messianic realization of the blessing given to Jacob by Isaac was understood not only as a promise for a glorious future but also as a stirring up of terror about days to come. What was awaiting them in the new world order? Who would be raised up, and who would be brought down? Which one was the "elder" who would serve the "younger"?

The typological meaning of Jacob and Esau's story intersects the relationship between Christianity and Judaism from its inception down to our own day. Thus, before approaching this historical tale itself, we must first undertake a brief literary analysis of its biblical source. I do not intend to engage in a rigorous philological description of the meaning of the scriptures in question or of the various interpretations of the story by Christians, Jews, and modern scholars; rather, I shall attempt to read it simply as literature, free, as much as possible, of interpretive tendencies, whether traditional or modern. The aim of this introductory discussion is to understand what it is about this primordial story of Esau and Jacob that has made generation after generation squeeze themselves into it, seeking in it a hint of themselves and of their future.

THE EARLY TYPOLOGY: *ESAU ID EST EDOM*

From the outset, the story of the twin brothers does not augur well. Even before they are born, God informs their mother, Rebecca: "Two nations are in your womb." The twins' struggle in the mother's womb causes her suffering, and the difficult pregnancy heralds a difficult history: "Two peoples, born of you, shall be divided; the one shall be stronger than the other, the elder shall serve the younger" (Gen 25:23). Unlike the covert rivalry between Isaac and Ishmael, the hostility for Esau expressed in the Bible is overt and steeped in harsh memories of love, hate, and fear. The biblical narrator certainly wished to cope with the political reality of his day, in which the brother-nation Edom was the rival of the kingdoms of Judaea and Israel, and therefore he imposed the resentments of the present on the embryonic, dim, mythic past.[1]

Like Cain and Abel, Esau and Jacob were full brothers, unlike Ishmael and Isaac, who shared the same father but not the same mother.[2] The greater the consanguinity, the more intense the quarrel. Isaac was the first of Abraham's descendants to be born in the Land of Israel. An immigrant, Abraham feared that his son would take a wife from among the local women. Hence, he called his servant and instructed: "You will not take a wife for my son from the daughters of the Canaanites, among whom I dwell" (Gen 24:3). Abraham sent his servant to what seemed a most unlikely place: to the home of his forebears in Aram, which he had forsaken many years earlier, following God's commandment: "Go from your country and your kindred and your father's house" (Gen 12:1). Now he wishes to connect his son with the same circles he had left.[3]

1. See Ze'ev Weissman, "National Consciousness in the Promises to the Patriarchs" [in Hebrew], *Mil'et* 1 (1983): 9–24; Weissman, *Mi-Ya'aqov le-Yisrael* (Jerusalem, 1986), 86–89. For the polemical intention of the present story to cover up the sins of Jacob and to cope with the ancient traditions that criticized Jacob's actions, see Yair Zakovitch, "Jacob's Heel" [in Hebrew], *Sefer Dr. Barukh Ben Yehuda* (Tel Aviv, 1981), 121–44. This interpretation is opposed by Moshe Garsiel, "Literary Structure and Message in the Jacob and Esau Stories" [in Hebrew], *Hagut be-Miqra* 4 (1983): 63–81. For a position that rejects the existence of any covert polemics in the Jacob and Esau story, seeing it as a literary fiction devoid of any historiographical pretension, see Thomas L. Thompson, "Conflict Themes in the Jacob Narratives," *Semeia* 15 (1979): 5–26.

2. Weissman, "Diverse Historical and Social Reflections in the Shaping of Patriarchal History" [in Hebrew], *Zion* 50 (1985): 7, notes the difference in family structure between the story of Jacob and that of Abraham and Isaac—a monogamous family structure in the former as opposed to a polygamous one in the latter. This difference was one of the factors that led Weissman to see the traditions of the Jacob narrative as having a different and more ancient origin than those of the Abraham and Isaac narrative. For an assessment of Weissman's position, see Alexander Rofé, "History of Tradition and the Creation of the Jacob Cycle" [in Hebrew], *Tarbiz* 56 (1987): 593–97.

3. Rofé thinks this episode reflects the atmosphere in the period of Ezra and Nehemiah and the opposition to mixed marriages with the indigenous inhabitants of the land: "An Enquiry into the Betrothal of Rebekah," in *Die Hebräische Bibel und ihre zweifache Nachgeschichte: Festschrift für Rolf Rendtorff zum 65. Geburtstag* (Neukirchen-Vluyn, 1990), 27–39.

The success of the servant's mission leads to another separation in the family and produces another departure from the ancestral homeland in Aram to the land of Canaan. This time the one who goes is Rebecca, who also prefers an unknown land and even a foreign bridegroom to her homeland and to living in her mother's house. When asked if she desires to join Abraham's servant and to part from her family, she answers with one Hebrew word: *Elekh:* "I will go" (Gen 24:58). Abraham went to the land of Canaan by God's decree; Rebecca goes there at the bidding of her heart.

Unlike Abraham and Sarah, Isaac and Rebecca are thus partners from two different lands. Perhaps the great split that will tear their sons apart has its origin in their parents' story. The initial encounter between Rebecca, a young maiden from Aram, and Isaac, a middle-aged man, takes place in a field. Rebecca arrives at the fields of the Negev after a fatiguing journey riding on a camel, anxiously awaiting the first meeting with her future husband. She knows very well where she is coming from, where she is going, and whom she is to meet, whereas Isaac, the intended bridegroom, does not know anything about what is to occur: "And Isaac went out to meditate in the field in the evening" (Gen 24:63), as was his habit. While people are returning to their homes, he goes out to the field, not knowing who is approaching him. Rebecca knows what awaits her, but Isaac knows nothing.

It is then that the first encounter takes place: "And he lifted up his eyes and looked, and behold, there were camels coming. And Rebecca lifted up her eyes, and she saw Isaac" (Gen 24:63–64). They both raise their eyes, they both see something, but Isaac does not see Rebecca, he only sees camels, while Rebecca sees Isaac right away. Isaac sees, but does not comprehend. Does Rebecca? When she sees Isaac, she "falls off the camel"—that is, alights from it, waits for the man coming toward her, and asks the servant: "Who is the man yonder, walking in the field to meet us?" And the servant answers, "It is my master." So she took her veil and covered herself (Gen 24:65). Isaac walks idly, aimlessly in the field, while Rebecca takes pains to find out who is standing before her. When she hears that he is indeed her intended husband, she covers her head, in a sense disappearing into her demure identity.

Now we come to a second dialogue, between the servant and Isaac, and the presence of Rebecca covered by her veil seems to fade away. "And the servant told Isaac all the things that he had done. Then Isaac brought her into the tent of Sarah his mother, and took Rebecca, and she became his wife; and he loved her. So Isaac was comforted after his mother's death" (Gen 24:66–67). Two characters, who have thus far played a peripheral role in the story, here take center stage. One is Isaac, who though he is forty years old, is led to his marriage by his father, with the help of the servant. The second is Sarah: even though she has now been dead for three years, her spirit still dominates her son. In contrast, the two main characters in the story of Isaac's marriage, Abraham and Rebecca, who had been proactive, now disappear. The servant reports on the success of his mission, not to Abraham, but to Isaac, evidently because Abraham was no longer alive. As for Rebecca, who had received the servant generously and actively when he came to Aram and had boldly decided to go to a new land and a distant family, now becomes merely a bland substitute for the dead mother. Her identity seems to have been swallowed up, and from now on her place is in the tent of her mother-in-law.

This tension between Isaac, the man of the field, and Rebecca, hidden in the tent, is a metaphor for the dualism between two characters and two symbols. The field is the arena of one who lives in nature, in the open, while the tent is a symbol of enclosure and innocence. But despite her enclosure, the one who sees clearly is Rebecca, while Isaac's eyes grow dim. Rebecca, who acts surreptitiously between the folds of the closed tent, sees more clearly than her husband, the man of the open field.

This difference between the field and the tent involves another dimension as well. Isaac was the first farmer among the Patriarchs. While for the classical Rabbinic Sages his image is that of a spiritual man, one who became blind because of the tears that the ministering angels shed on him during the Binding,[4] one who went out to "meditate" in the field to pray and to reflect,[5] his character in the Bible is completely different. Isaac sows and brings forth a blessing from his toil "and reaped in the same year a hundredfold" (Gen 26:12). He quarrels with the local Philistine farmers about water. He wanders little, and God even forbids him to leave the land in time of famine. He is completely connected to the land and to his labor on it. Unlike his wife, his mother, and his father—all of whom were immigrants and nomads, either herders or traders—he was born there. The tent is the symbol of transience and alienation, the dwelling of the exile and the nomad, while the field indicates fixity and attachment to place.

The difference between the parents sets the scene for the difference between the children, the twins who struggle with one another. From Isaac,

4. *Gen. Rab.* 65.10, ed. Theodore-Albeck (Jerusalem, 1965), 719.
5. *Gen. Rab.* 60.14, 654–55.

the man of the field, Esau is born: "Esau was a skillful hunter, a man of the field," while from the mother, who sits in the tent, "Jacob . . . a mild [or: simple] man, dwelling in tents" is born (Gen 25:27). Thus Isaac loves Esau, while Rebecca loves Jacob. Esau is referred to as the "older son" of Isaac (Gen 27:1), while Jacob is simply "the son" of Rebecca (Gen 27:6). The parents' characteristics are magnified in their children: from Isaac the farmer, who quarrels with the local residents over water rights, is born Esau, who lives by the sword (Gen 27:40) and who mobilizes a band of soldiers to greet Jacob (Gen 32:6).[6] In contrast, Jacob, at the scent of danger, prefers to flee for his life and go into exile in a distant land. Esau is the hunter who subsists on wild animals, while Jacob is sustained by the homely meals that his mother prepares for him in the tent.

The selling of the birthright takes place after Esau returns home "from the field . . . famished" (Gen 25:29). The field disappoints him, and Esau is left hungry. He sells his birthright for homely food—"bread and pottage of lentils" (Gen 25:34)—and the birthright passes from the man of the field to the man of the tent.[7] But Isaac is unaware of all this. He is blind and lives in the past. Before he dies he asks Esau to "go out to the field, and hunt [him] some game" (Gen 27:3) so that he may bless him. Rebecca overhears. She, who sees the open field clearly, also hears clearly between the folds of the tent. When Esau goes out to the field to hunt venison, she proves her superiority and quickly prepares food for Isaac from her flock. Thus Jacob gains the birthright reserved for the firstborn, after his father smells him and finds that his odor "is as the smell of the field" (Gen 27:27). Both Esau and his father, Isaac, are portrayed as gluttons, willing to sell a birthright or a blessing for a favorite food.[8]

The theft of the blessing and the transformation of the young Jacob to the favored son bring down Esau's wrath on Jacob. Jacob flees, retracing his

6. The expression "four hundred men with him" alludes to an army battalion. See A. Shapira, "Jacob and Esau: A Polyvalent Reading" [in Hebrew], *'Iyyunei Miqra u-parshanut* 4 (1997): 270–72. According to Yoel Bin-Nun, "The Yitzhak Stories" [in Hebrew], *Megadim* 25 (1996): 68–70, Esau's army was intended to defend his homestead.

7. According to V. Maag, "Jakob-Esau-Edom," *Theologische Zeitschrift* 13 (1957): 418–29, the earliest layer in the narrative of Jacob and Esau reflects a tension between hunters (Esau) and shepherds (Jacob) who dwelled alongside one another in the northern part of the Land of Israel, in Gilead and Bashan. At the time of David, and as a result of the conquest of Edom, another, southern, layer was added, which identified Esau with Edom, and the typology of the Jacob-Edom story became a national one.

8. Zakovitch (n. 1, p. 4), 130–31.

mother's footsteps back to her home and her family, but he thereby cuts himself off from his own family and goes into exile. There, in a foreign land, he marries his wives and sires his children (except for Benjamin, his youngest). Jacob arrives in Aram as a chosen son and returns as the head of a chosen family, father of the twelve tribes. This transition, from chosen son to chosen family, takes place specifically in the Aramaean exile, far from the Promised Land, just as the transition from chosen family to chosen people occurs in the Exile of Egypt. Jacob is "a wandering Aramaean" (Deut 26:5), that is, an exile in Aram, who inherits the Land of Israel and evicts Esau from it. After twenty years of exile, God commands him to "return to the land of [his] fathers and to [his] kindred" (Gen 31:3). Not "go from your country" (Gen 12:1) as told to Abraham or "I will go" (Gen 24:58) as proclaimed by Rebecca, but "return"—the return of an exile to the land of his forefathers. Abraham was a stranger in the land of Canaan, Isaac was a native son who never left the land, while Jacob returns to "his homeland" from exile.

Perhaps the Bible's intention here is to say that the Land is given in perpetuity not to the stranger who settles in it or to the local "man of the field," but only to the exiled son who returns to it. Indeed, Isaac's blessing of Jacob is only realized at the end of the story of Jacob and Esau. After Jacob returns, he buys "the piece of land on which he had pitched his tent" (Gen 33:19) in Shechem. Now Jacob too has bought a field in the land of Canaan. This action is followed by a description of Esau's departure from the land, and the Bible does not mince words in describing the heaviness in Esau's abandonment of it: "Then Esau took his wives, his sons, his daughters, and all the members of his household, his cattle, all his beasts, and all his property which he had acquired in the land of Canaan; and he went into a land away from his brother Jacob. . . . So Esau dwelt in the hill country of Seir: Esau is Edom" (Gen 36:6, 8). By contrast, later on it says of Jacob: "Jacob dwelt in the land of his father's sojournings, in the land of Canaan" (Gen 37:1). Thus the promise was fulfilled: the separation between the brothers is accomplished, and the land becomes Jacob's.

The entire story may be read as a covert polemic with a counternarrative containing opposite territorial claims, designed to create a mythic history in order to justify a contemporary political reality. The narrator's ideology bases a claim to ownership of the Land of Israel on a divine promise, while denying opposing claims of local residents or their neighbors over the Land. The essential motif in the biblical claim to the Land is the superiority of the one who returns from exile over the native, since the foreign settler comes by dint of divine promise, not of original holding or rights. Thus we have a denial of autochthony as the basis for any claim to the Land.[9] Jacob and his descendants are described as destined to be lords of the land, while Esau and Ishmael are to serve as their subjects—a reality fulfilled at the time of the First Temple after the subjugation of Edom by David.[10] At the end of the First Temple period, during the Babylonian rule over the kingdom of Judaea, Edom took advantage of this opportunity and ruled over the border regions of Judaea in the northern Negev and thereafter was considered a treacherous brother deserving of the harshest revenge and punishment.[11]

The biblical polemic with Edom is also reflected in the story of Hadad the Edomite, King Solomon's great enemy (1 Kgs 11:14–25). The story of Hadad's life contains motifs clearly reminiscent of the history of Israel in Egypt and of the life of Moses. Like Moses, who was born and saved after Pharaoh had ordered that every male son born be thrown into the Nile, Hadad was also saved from the slaughter of all the males in Edom during the period of David's conquest (1 Kgs 15). Hadad fled to Egypt via Midian, much like Moses, who returned to Egypt from Midian. Pharaoh greeted Hadad with blessings and even gave him land on which to live, like the land of Goshen given to the Israelites. Hadad was raised in the home of Pharaoh, where he married Pharaoh's sister-in-law, who bore him a son, Genubath (in Hebrew: "the stolen one")—a name reminiscent of the words of Joseph: "for I was indeed stolen out of the land of the Hebrews" (Gen 40:15). Hadad, who was "of the royal house in Edom," thereby enjoyed an additional degree of status in the Egyptian royal house, like Moses, who was adopted as a son by Pharaoh's daughter. After Hadad learned of David's death, he turned to Pharaoh and asked him: "Let me depart, that I may go to my own country" (Gen 21)—an echo of Moses's repeated request "Let my people go" (Exod 5:1 and passim). Hadad's request was also not initially granted: "But Pharaoh said to him: 'What have you lacked with me that you are now seeking to go to your own country?" And like Moses, Hadad was also insistent: "And he said to him, 'Only let me go'" (Exod 22).

Yair Zakovitch explains that this resemblance reflects the wish to present

---

9. Compare Y. Levi, "A Territorial Dispute in the Land of Israel in Ancient Times" [in Hebrew], in 'Olamot nifgashim (Jerusalem, 1969), 60–78.

10. 2 Sam 8:14.

11. Isa 34:5–7; 63:1–6; Ezek 25:12–14; Obadiah.

the story of Hadad as an inverted parallel to the story of Jeroboam ben Nabath (1 Kgs 11:26ff.), who was also seen as a kind of "second Moses."[12] In his opinion, the story of Hadad is the work of scribes from Judaea, who wished to deny Jeroboam any resemblance to Moses. To that end, the story of Jeroboam was superimposed on a secondary personality—Hadad. I suggest reading the story of Hadad as echoing a rival Edomite tradition, according to which Hadad was considered the national savior from subjugation to David, who was compared to Pharaoh. The biblical author had no difficulty in accepting this tradition, since it furthered his goal: to present Hadad as appointed by God to be the "adversary against Solomon" (1 Kgs 14)—that is, as a way to punish Solomon for his forbidden love of Pharaoh's daughter, as a kind of measure for measure. The very existence of a rival Edomite story to the story of Moses may be seen as an expression of the widespread enmity between the sons of Jacob and those of Esau—rival sons competing for the same territory and the same ancestral heritage.

THE LATE TYPOLOGY: *EDOM ID EST ROMA*

Our proposed reading of this biblical story suggests that the later typology, identifying Edom with Rome, did not come out of thin air but was based on the biblical typology identifying Esau with Edom. The emergence of this later typology is presumably the result of the disappearance of the Edomites—the concrete element for whom the biblical typology was originally invented. But the decisive event leading to the creation of the new typology was the destruction of the Second Temple in 70 C.E., in whose wake a far-reaching change occurred in the meaning of the terms Esau and Edom. For the Jews, the quarrel between Jacob and Esau ceased to be a story of a territorial quarrel between neighboring tribes and was instead converted into a conflict of messianic dimensions between Judaea and Rome. As soon as Edom became synonymous with Rome, all prophecies of future revenge were shifted in one fell swoop from Edom to Rome, along with the expectation of its fall and ruin at the End of Days.

During the first centuries of the Common Era, Edom was synonymous with pagan Rome, and the biblical drama between Esau and Jacob, with its charged symbols, was interpreted as an allegory and a prophecy of the

12. Yair Zakovitch, *"And You Shall Tell Your Son . . . "*: *The Concept of the Exodus in the Bible* (Jerusalem, 1991), 87–97.

ongoing conflict between Judaea and pagan Rome. According to this conception, there can be no peace between the two nations: "If this one is full, that one is destroyed."[13] Rabbi Akiba seems to have been the first to understand Edom as a metonym for Rome. He interpreted the verse "a star [*kokhav*] shall come forth out of Jacob" (Num 24:17) as a prophecy alluding to Bar Kokhba, because the subsequent verses continue: "Edom shall be a dispossessed. . . . By Jacob shall dominion be exercised, and the survivors of a city be destroyed" (Num 24 18–19), in which the "city" is interpreted as Rome.[14]

Yet since there were other opinions on this point, it behooves us to return to the verse "two nations are in your womb." The Masoretic version reads here *ge'im* (גאים) rather than *goyim* (גוים; "nations"), and the Sages interpreted this unusual spelling as an allusion to pride (גאים; i.e., "proud ones")—that is, both brothers, and their respective nations, Judaea and Rome, are proud. Although proud brothers are indeed likely to clash, according to this Midrash, calm prevails between them: "Two proud nations are in your womb: this one takes pride in his world, and that one takes pride in his world—Hadrian among the nations, and Solomon in Israel."[15] Each nation prides itself on the myth of a model leader in the distant past. Another Midrash of a more contemporary bent depicts the emperor of Rome, Antoninus, and the Patriarch Rabbi Judah Ha-Nasi as models of brotherhood: "'Two nations *(goyim)* are in your womb.' [This verse has been interpreted as follows]: Do not read *goyim* [nations], but rather read *ge'im* [proud ones]. Rav Yehudah said in the name of Rav: This refers to Antoninus and Rabbi [i.e., Judah ha-Nasi] from whose table neither radish nor horseradish nor cucumber was ever lacking, in either summer or winter."[16] Abundance is a sign of greatness, and the leader of the Jews in the Land of Israel is portrayed here as an equal partner to his friend, the emperor of Rome.

This harmonious perspective was common during the third century C.E., when tension between conquering Rome and subjugated Judaea had slackened, and before Rome became Christian. At that time the status of the Patriarch reached its peak, with the claim that he was a descendant of the

13. *b. Meg.* 6a.
14. *j. Ta'an.* 4.8 (68d).
15. *Gen. Rab.* 63.7: 685; H. Freedman and M. Simon, eds.; *Midrash Rabbah*, translated into English, (1939; repr. London, 1961), 561.
16. *b. Ber.* 57a; *b. 'Avod. Zar.* 11a.

Davidic royal house. For a moment it seemed as if this self-delusion would be strong enough to soften the permanent opposition of the Jewish nation to its subjugation to Rome and to its lack of political sovereignty.

Another exegete interpreted the verse "two nations are in your womb" rather differently. He read the Hebrew *shnei* (two) as *senu'ei* (hated): "Those hated of the nations are in your womb: all the nations hate Esau, and all the nations hate Israel."[17] At that time a strange solidarity existed between Rome and Judaea: both were hated. The preacher may have sensed a similarity between the triumphalist imperialism of Rome and the universal messianic aspirations of Judaism. It is doubtful whether there was any other time in history when Jews were willing to share their sense of persecution with another nation, let alone with Esau.

But the early fourth century and the Christianization of Rome marked the end of this openness and the hope of cooperation. The hostility between the two "brothers" prevailed over their fraternity and was carried over into the raging channel of tense relations between Christianity and Judaism, a turgid stream that persisted in its course throughout the Middle Ages. Henceforth, the Jewish identification of Edom with Rome carried a double meaning, both religious and political. There were some who called the Christian Church by the name of Edom, while there were others who saw that name as a metonym for the empire itself and for the Roman-Byzantine state. Edom thus became the last mythological foe of Israel until the End of Days—changing its identity, name, time, and place but always known by the ancient and threatening name: Edom.

Yet for Christians the names Jacob and Esau carried the opposite meaning: Jacob was the prototype of the Christians, the true Children of Israel, while Esau was the archetype of the Jew, the elder brother who loses his birthright to his younger brother, the Church.[18] The source of this notion appears in Paul's epistle to the Romans, where he speaks of the election of Israel in the flesh, as opposed to that of Israel in the spirit:

> For not all who are descended from Israel belong to Israel, and not all
> are children of Abraham because they are his descendants; but "Through
> Isaac shall your descendants be named." This means that it is not the
> children of the flesh who are the children of God, but the children of the

17. *Gen. Rab.* (n. 15, p. 11).

18. For a comprehensive survey of Christian exegesis, see Klaus Thraede, "Jakob und Esau," *Reallexikon für Antike und Christentum* 16, (1950–2004): 1118–217.

promise are reckoned as descendants. For this is what the promise said, "About this time I will return and Sarah shall have a son." And not only so, but also when Rebecca had conceived children by one man, our forefather Isaac, though they were not yet born and had done nothing either good or bad, in order that God's purpose of election might continue, not because of works but because of his call, she was told, "The elder will serve the younger." As it is written, "Jacob I loved, but Esau I hated."[19]

Just as Paul wished to extend the status of Israel to uncircumcised Christians, he also required the election of Isaac and Jacob, on the one hand, and the rejection of Ishmael and Esau, on the other, as proof that even within the same family there can be a rejected older brother alongside a chosen one. His proof is made up of two stages, the second one stronger than the first. The first is the rejection of Ishmael and the election of Isaac. Both were sons of the same father, but only one of them was chosen; hence, not all fleshly sons are necessarily sons in God. But this is a weak proof, since Ishmael's rejection may be explained by the argument that he was not the son of the legitimate wife. Therefore, there was need for a second proof, that of Jacob and Esau—both of whom are twin sons of the same parents. Moreover, the rejection of the one did not occur after his birth or because of his evil deeds, but before his birth. Hence it is the divine promise, and not the ethnic-biological pedigree, that determines the status of the chosen one.

This view appears in the writings of Christian authors from the second century on: the author of *Epistle of Barnabas,* Justin Martyr, and Melito of Sardis.[20] In the writings of all three authors, the typological identification

19. Rom 9:6–13. And cf.: Gal 4:21–31; Heb 12:16–17. Whether it was Paul himself who believed that the Jews had been rejected as a chosen people or whether it was a later interpretation of his doctrine remains an open question. See John Gager, *Reinventing Paul* (Oxford, 2000).

20. *The Epistle of Barnabas* 13: "And the Lord said to her [i.e., Rebecca]: two nations are in thy womb, and two people in thy belly, and one people shall overcome a people, and the greater shall serve the less. She ought to understand who is Isaac and who is Rebecca, and of whom he has shown that this people is greater than that people." The homily alludes to the typological significance of the prophecy to Rebecca, "two nations are in your womb," and immediately thereafter turns to a discussion of the symbolic meaning of Jacob's blessing to Joseph's two sons, Ephraim and Manasseh. Jacob crosses his hands, placing his right hand on the head of the younger, Ephraim, and his left hand on that of the elder, Manasseh—a sign of preference of the younger over the elder (Gen 48:13–19). The equation, Rachel = Church, Leah = synagogue, appears in the writings of Justin Martyr, once again in order to show that the younger is more beloved. But he adds a new insight to the equation Jacob = Christianity: "Ja-

implied in the story of Jacob and Esau is still implicit, with the emphasis on the Pauline idea of election, that children by the flesh are not necessarily children of divine promise. Irenaeus was the first to make the typological identification of Esau with the Jews and Jacob. He maintains that the verse "two nations are in your womb" alludes to two nations that are to arise from the same father: the Jews and the Christians:

> [Jacob] received the rights of the firstborn, when his brothers looked on them with contempt; even as also the younger nation received Him, Christ, the first-begotten, when the elder nation rejected Him . . . [Jacob] suffered the plots and persecutions of a brother, just as the Church suffers this selfsame thing from the Jews. In a foreign country were the twelve tribes born, the race of Israel, inasmuch as Christ was also, in a strange country, to generate the twelve-pillared foundation of the Church.[21]

Irenaeus goes on to compare the events of Jacob's life to those of Jesus's, but the strongest analogy between Jacob and Jesus seems to be the persecution and suffering experienced by both. In light of Irenaeus's words, the famous homily in the Passover Haggadah on Deuteronomy 26:5, "a wandering Aramaean was my father" (which we will discuss in detail in the next chapter), has an especially interesting ring. The Haggadah suggests an alternative reading of the Hebrew verse, which would translate as "an Aramaean would have destroyed my father," that is, Laban, the Aramaean, wanted to make Jacob perish. Irenaeus's typological move is clearly continued by the Church Fathers of the third century—Cyprian, Origen, and Tertullian.[22] The Christians countered the Jewish equation of Jacob = Jews, Esau = Rome, with the opposite equation: Jacob = Christians, Esau = Jews. It is noteworthy that these parallel systems of identification emerged at the same time.

---

cob was hated for all time by his brother; and we now, and our Lord himself, are hated by you and by all men" (Justin, *Dialogue with Trypho*, sec. 134). Compare this exegesis with the one cited above (n. 17): "All the nations hate Esau, and all the nations hate Israel." Melito of Sardis explains the identification of the Jews with Edom by the fact that they were reddened with the blood of Jesus (Gerson D. Cohen, "Esau as Symbol in Early Medieval Thought," in *Jewish Medieval and Renaissance Studies*, ed. A. Altmann [Cambridge, MA, 1967], n. 43). A similar idea is found in a Jewish Midrash on Esau: "'ruddy' . . . for he was filled with blood, yet he hated the blood of circumcision" (*Midrash ha-Gadol, Bereshit,* 439).

21. Irenaeus, *Adversus Haereses,* 4.21.

22. Tertullian, *Adversus Judaeos,* chap. 1; Cyprian, *Testimonia,* 1.19, 20; Origen, *Hom. In Gen.* 12.3, cited by J. Danielou, *Origen,* trans. W. Mitchell (New York, 1955), 164.

Even before the Christianization of the Roman Empire, Christians saw the Destruction of the Temple and the subjugation of the Jews to Rome as proof of the fulfillment of the blessing "the elder shall serve the younger."

In contrast to the Jewish interpretation of the figure of Esau, Paul's use of the figure of the younger, chosen brother as opposed to the older, rejected brother is natural and obvious, since it is intended to grant the status of chosenness to the new, non-Jewish believers. Turning Esau into the prefiguring of pagan Rome provokes a number of difficult questions. First, Esau, like Jacob, is a Semite; how then could the Sages see him as patronymic of Rome, he who is among the sons of Japheth? Second, Rome had already received a different typological identification in the writings of the Judaean Desert sect: namely, the Kittim. Why was this identification abandoned, and how did it fit with the new identification? Third, what led Jews in the second century c.e. to consider Rome a "brother?" What did such a kinship have to do with the dreary reality of the Destruction of Jerusalem and the Temple? Fourth, there are those who think that, since the Edomites were accused of participating in the Destruction of the First Temple,[23] they were identified with Rome, who destroyed the Second.[24] Yet, in fact, the Idumaeans (identified with the biblical Edomites) fought vigorously alongside the Jewish Zealots in the Great Roman War.[25] How was it possible within one or two generations to forget the Idumaeans' alliance with the rebels against Rome, instead turning them into a metonym for the empire against which they fought?

In a paper surveying the image of Esau in Jewish and Christian exegesis, Gerson Cohen described the Christian and Jewish moves as parallel developments, traveling on two independent tracks: "The new Christian usage of Esau did not originate as a retort to the Jews, but rather as a taunt inspired by the apostle Paul's Epistle to the Romans [9:6–13], quite without regard to—or probably, even the vaguest knowledge of—what the rabbis were saying about their pagan Roman overlords [31]." Yet in the previous section Cohen discusses the increasing difficulty of the Jews in coping with the political reality of Christian rule after the fourth century. How could the success of Christianity and its earthly dominion be explained while identifying it with Esau, the rejected brother, who was meant to be subjugated

23. Ps 137:7.
24. Moshe D. Herr, "Edom," *Encyclopedia Judaica* (Jerusalem, 1972), 6:379.
25. Josephus, *Jewish Wars*, 5.249ff.

to his younger brother, Jacob? In fact, Christian propaganda, according to Cohen, could strike back: "Christian typology had appropriated the very symbols that provided the substance of Jewish eschatological theory and had turned them against the Jews [30]."[26]

In other words, Cohen distinguishes between the ancient exegesis, of Paul and the early Church Fathers, which developed as an internal position, and the later Christian exegesis of the early Middle Ages, which carried on a lively dialogue with Jewish symbolism. Cohen rejects out of hand the possibility that Paul had already adopted Jewish eschatological symbols regarding Jacob and Esau. Why? Simply because the Jewish identification of Esau with Rome did not emerge until the early second century, just before the Bar Kokhba Revolt, as quoted above from Rabbi Akiba, who lived about three generations after Paul. Thus, Cohen states that the Jewish eschatological identification that emerged just before the Bar Kokhba Revolt had nothing to do with the Pauline move that preceded it and was formed entirely against the backdrop of the hostile relations between Jews and Romans after the failure of the Great Revolt. Hence, Cohen sees the development of the parallel Christian exegesis as an internal tradition, originating in the writings of Paul.

But the opposite parallelism, between Christian and Jewish exegesis, cries out for clarification. Does it exist merely by chance? Is there not a mutual affinity between the Christian claim that the Jews are Esau and the Jewish claim that Esau is Rome? Is it really plausible to assume that in this great debate concerning each side's identification with Jacob, the issue of the counteridentification of the "other" as Esau did not arise? The possibility should be considered that the Jewish identification with Jacob emerged from internalizing the Christian position and confronting it. Cohen treats the identification of Esau in its messianic context, and here his position that the Jewish exegesis came earlier is plausible.[27] Yet, the identification of Esau has another, more basic context that arises in early Christian writings: the question of election. On this topic, Pauline thought seems to have preceded

---

26. Cohen (n. 20, p. 13), 19–48.

27. Many scholars think that the first expression of this can be found in 4 Ezra 2:6, 8, about one generation before Rabbi Akiba: "From Abraham to Isaac. For from him sprang Jacob and Esau, but Jacob's hand held the heel of Esau from the beginning. The heel of the first age is Esau; the hand of the second is Jacob." Yakov Licht understood Esau as a symbol of this world and Jacob as a symbol of the World to Come; see *Sefer Hazon 'Ezra* (Jerusalem, 1968), 35. But Michael E. Stone, following many scholars, thinks that Esau is Rome, the final

that of the Sages and even to have caused the latter to defend itself. Posing the problem of election in the center of early Christian doctrine and the attempt to deny Judaism its position as the natural heir of Jacob and Israel (*Verus Israel*) necessitated a Jewish response that stressed its identification with the biblical Jacob. Such a Midrash, dealing directly with Paul's arguments, appears in *Sifrei Deuteronomy:*

> "For the portion of the Lord is his people" [Deut 32:9]. A parable. A king had a field, which he leased to tenants. When the tenants began to steal from it, he took it away from them and leased it to their children. When the children began to act worse than their fathers, he took it away from them and gave it to the original tenants' grandchildren. When these too became worse than their predecessors, a son was born to him. He then said to the grandchildren: "Leave my property. You may not remain therein. Give me back my portion, so that I may repossess it." Thus also, when our father Abraham came into the world, unworthy [descendants] issued from him, Ishmael and all of Keturah's children. When Isaac came into the world, unworthy [descendants] issued from him, Esau and all the princes of Edom, and they became worse than their predecessors. When Jacob came into the world, he did not produce unworthy [descendants], rather all his children were worthy.[28]

The implicit claim in this Midrash is rather surprising. The author sees fit to deprive Abraham and Isaac of their position as chosen sons and to see them as tenants simply because of the defective offspring that came from them. His position may be understood in the context of Paul's claim that Abraham—father of many nations—is the typological father of the new converts to Christianity, for he was chosen even before he was circumcised. Considerable similarity exists between this parable and that of the vineyard owner and the tenants in Matthew 21:33–44 (Luke 19:9–19). The son of

kingdom, in whose wake shall come the Kingdom of Jacob; see *Fourth Ezra: A Commentary on the Book of Fourth Ezra* (Minneapolis, 1990). This view is also found in *Midrash ha-Gadol* to Gen 25:26, ed. M. Margolies (Jerusalem, 1947), 441. Cohen (n. 20, p. 13), 21, thinks that Jacob and Esau represent historical cycles as well as specific kingdoms, being paradigms of the love and hatred of God.

28. *Sifrei Deut.*, sec. 312, ed. L. Finkelstein, 353; English: *Sifre: A Tannaitic Commentary on the Book of Deuteronomy*, trans. R. Hammer (New Haven and London, 1986), 318. And see the analysis of this Midrash in E. Mihaly, "A Rabbinic Defense of the Election of Israel," *HUCA* 35 (1964): 103–35; M. Derret, *Studies in the New Testament* (Leiden, 1978), 2:92–98.

the vineyard owner (Jesus) is killed by the tenants (the Pharisee and Sadducee establishment), who wish to control the vineyard (Israel). The owner of the vineyard (God) punishes the tenants and destroys them and gives the vineyard to other tenants (the nations). The view expressed in *Sifrei* is the opposite of that in Paul and the Gospels.[29] It claims that Jacob is the elected one, the last and final one, since none of his sons is rejected. The Jewish preacher goes on to talk of Israel being *segula* (a treasure), that is, an everlasting election—unlike Paul's claim that the election of Jacob and the rejection of Esau from the womb prove that the firstborn is not necessarily the elected one.

Hence, the issue of Esau's identity is clearly tangential to the debate over the identification of Jacob, in which the Jewish position is reactive and defensive. The propaganda of post-Pauline Christianity, which depicted Christians as the heirs of Jacob, was also a successful and painful claim regarding the identification of the persecuted brother: it is the Jews who are the older brother, and as such they persecuted the early Christians. Even after Christianity became the majority religion, the original trauma documented in the New Testament did not disappear. The Jewish response, which persisted in identifying the Jews with Jacob, probably found it difficult to determine the identification of Esau, the pursuing and dangerous older brother.

Yet if we assume that the Jews internalized the troubling Christian typological exegesis, we may understand how the conquering and subjugating Rome wound up as the mythic heir of Esau and Edom. Jacob represents a double fate: suffering and persecution at the hands of his brother in the present, alongside the promise for the future that the persecuting brother would lose his position and become a slave to Jacob. This picture corresponded to the position of the Christians before and after the Destruction of the Temple and to that of the Jews only afterward. The rivalry between Jews and Christians was over the identification of the persecuted one, and consequently over the identification of his persecutor.

Thus, after the Destruction of the Temple, Jewish apologetics faced a se-

---

29. On the similarity between the two parables, see David Flusser, *Yahadut u-meqorot ha-Nazrut* (Tel Aviv, 1979), 181–83; cf. David Flusser, "Two Anti-Jewish Montages in Matthew," *Immanuel* 5 (1975): 36–37. According to D. Stern, *Parables in Midrash* (London, 1991), 190–97, the "son" in the Gospels is not Jesus but John the Baptist. Yet this is certainly not how the parable was understood in early Christian literature, and the Jewish Midrash counters that interpretation.

rious challenge: How could it claim that the Jews were still the beloved children of God even after his Temple had been destroyed? To meet this challenge, they needed to relate to the adversary's menacing slogan and turn it around. The Jewish response was that the promise, "the elder shall serve the younger," had not yet been fulfilled. Present reality was temporary, and Isaac's blessing on Jacob would be realized in the future, in the time of the Messiah, when Rome, which now subjugates Jacob, shall perish. The choice of Edom as the metonym for Rome is thus a forced response on the part of the Jews to the Christian exegesis about the nullification of the Jewish nation's election following the Destruction. This should not be seen so much as a direct polemic with Christianity, but rather as an apologetic explanation of Judaea's subjugation, using religious language that at that time was conventional and widespread among both Jews and Christians.

This dialogue between Christian critics and Jewish apologetics is expressed in a sermon of Ambrose of Milan, who also thought that the dissimilarities of the sons originated in the different natures of the parents. The maternal Rebecca is bound to the gentle younger son, while the stern Isaac is associated with the strong and rugged son and recognizes the older son's natural right of primogeniture. The father grants honor, the mother gives love:

> Accordingly, Jacob received his brother's clothing, because he excelled the elder in wisdom. . . . Rebecca presented this clothing as a symbol of the Church; she gave to the younger son the clothing of the Old Testament, the prophetic and priestly clothing, the royal Davidic clothing, the clothing of the kings Solomon and Ezechias and Josias, and she gave it too to the Christian people, who would know how to use the garment they had received, since the Jewish people kept it without using it and did not know its proper adornments. This clothing was lying in shadow, cast off and forgotten. . . . The Christian people put it on, and it shone brightly.[30]

An opposite interpretation of Esau's garment is found in a Jewish Midrash: "Rabbi Aha said in the name of Rabbi Huna: Esau, the evil one, is destined to put on his cloak and dwell with the righteous in the Garden

---

30. Ambrosius, *De Jacob et via beata*, 2.9.2, in *Fathers of the Church* (Washington, 1972), 65:150–51.

of Eden in the Time to Come. But the Holy One blessed be He will drag him out and throw him out of there."[31]

Both the Jewish and the Christian exegeses dispute the symbolic meaning of Esau's garments. Ambrose views the garments in the same way that he views Esau himself: a symbol of the old covenant that was superceded. The Jew sees in these same garments an allusion to Esau's deceitfulness and his attempt to adopt a borrowed identity and to impersonate a righteous Jew; and only God can recognize his deceit.

THE CONCILIATORY APPROACH OF MODERN RESEARCH

Following the line of typological thought of earlier generations, which understood the deeds of the fathers as an omen for their sons, we may perhaps learn something from the conciliatory end of the quarrel between the two brothers. Unlike other pairs of brothers in Genesis, whose rivalry ended in murder (Cain and Abel) or exile (Ishmael and Isaac), Esau and Jacob knew how to forgive one another and to make up after decades of jealousy, separation, and exile. When Jacob returned from exile to the land of his fathers, Edom goes back to being the brother of Israel.

The Christian-Jewish debate that started nineteen hundred years ago, in our day came to a conciliatory close. Throughout the centuries, the Christian side based its argument on two fundamental assumptions. The first was that the physical existence of the Jews within Christian society had to be guaranteed; the second, that the Exile of the Jewish nation and the destruction of its religious and political center in the Land of Israel were punishment for the Crucifixion. These two basic assumptions collapsed within a single decade. In 1945 the Christian world learned of the horrors and scope of the Final Solution, and in 1948, the State of Israel was established. The murderous outburst of Nazi anti-Semitism stood in clear contrast to the Church doctrine of tolerance formulated by Augustine, within whose boundaries the traditional debate with the Jews was possible. In one fell swoop, the anti-Jewish position of Christianity became reprehensible and illegitimate, among other reasons because the Church was accused of being indirectly responsible for that lethal outburst

---

31. *j. Ned.* 3.8 (38a); Eng. trans. by Jacob Neusner, *The Talmud of the Land of Israel, 23, Nedarim* (Chicago, 1985), 66. For this homily and its relation to the Jewish-Christian polemic over the identity of Jacob and Esau, see M. Simon, *Verus Israel* (London, 1986), 187–89.

of hatred against the Jews. The establishment of the State of Israel and the renewed political sovereignty of the Jewish nation made the Christian exegesis of exile and destruction irrelevant. And indeed, within twenty years, Pope Paul VI visited the Holy Land and, on October 28, 1965, Vatican Council II adopted a declaration *(Nostra Aetate)* on the relation of the Church to non-Christian faiths, which included a "Jewish paragraph" removing guilt for the Crucifixion from the Jews and recognizing their status as a "chosen people."

Ours is thus the first generation of scholars that can and may discuss the Christian-Jewish debate from a certain remove. This book is hence the product of a postpolemical age, a fact that makes it easier to publicly declare things that were once discussed in whispers in private chambers or known only to a chosen few. This book could not have been written by my mentors at the Hebrew University, who were trained in Europe between the two world wars. Just as the scholarship of previous generations is bound by the framework of their perspectives, this book too presents, at best, what my generation can do. It ought not be surprising, therefore, that we, who stand on the shoulders of the previous generation, can and do see the other side—the dialogue and the tacit agreements—better than they could.

Of course, the old historical scholars also paid a great deal of attention to the presence of parallel phenomena in Judaism and Christianity. But they tended to concentrate more on shared social or theological aspects and to balk at touching on shared systems of religious symbols and ceremonies. These systems were considered the very heart and soul of religious uniqueness, and as such they were generally deemed off-limits in comparative discussion, since they posed a threat to the notion of religious and cultural uniqueness. The old Jewish historical scholars tended to adhere to the dogma of the authenticity of Judaism and were deeply fearful of parallel moves that were likely to present Judaism as adopting rival symbols into its world. In this book, I have tended to seek dialogism rather than "authenticity." The dialogical affinity of one culture with its environment does not necessarily impair its uniqueness or authenticity. Specifically, in Ashkenazic Jewry, previously considered a bastion of closure and loyalty to its internal religious tradition, there developed a profound affinity, albeit one mixed with hatred, with its sister religion, Christianity.

From here there follows another basic assumption of this book: that whenever we find a similarity between Judaism and Christianity, and we do not have grounds to suggest a shared heritage, we may assume that it is indicative of the influence of the Christian milieu on the Jews, and not vice versa, unless it may be proved that the Jewish sources are more ancient. The reason for this assumption is quite simple: minority cultures tend to adopt the agenda of the majority culture. True, from a theological perspective relations between the two religions were even and balanced, but the historian cannot ignore the relative and completely different dimensions distinguishing the two sister religions. Judaism certainly played an important role in shaping Christian self-awareness in medieval Europe, since the Jew helped define the boundaries of the "other"; however, Judaism's influence on determining the religious and intellectual agenda of the period is not to be overestimated. The Jews always tended to occupy an important place in Western consciousness, far beyond their real weight. However, cultural, economic, social, and political agenda was dictated by the majority to the minority, and not the other way around.

This willingness to accept the one-way influence of Christianity on Judaism as a plausible working hypothesis also reflects a different cultural starting point from that which was used in older research, which tended to emphasize Jewish "authenticity."[32] The dialogic position sees Jewish life in Christian Europe as involving the absorption and internalization of many values of the environment, along with its body language, ceremonies, and holy time. The uniqueness of Ashkenazic Jewry, which constitutes the main focus of this book, is also inherent in that interaction. Whereas the Jews of Spain were only one element in a varied and heterogeneous milieu, the Jews of Ashkenaz were the only alien element in an otherwise rather homogeneous environment. Belonging to the only minority requires the creation of barriers—and indeed, on the level of open discourse, Ashkenazic Jews created a world that was extremely estranged from Christians. Yet it was precisely this intensive sojourn in the shadow of a dominant religion that provided the strongest exposure to the majority culture, which even the highest barriers could not block out.

32. This approach is evident, for example, in Yitzhak Baer's work; see my paper, "Yitzhak Baer and the Search for Authentic Judaism," in *The Jewish Past Revisited: Reflections on Modern Jewish Historians*, ed. D. N. Myers and D. Ruderman (New Haven, 1998), 77–87. It is not my intention to belittle the enormous achievements of Baer, who succeeded, perhaps more than any other historian, in identifying parallel phenomena in Judaism and Christianity, although precisely for that reason he tended to ascribe the similarity with Christianity to Jewish influences on Christianity, and not vice versa. An extreme example of the "authentic-seeking" approach is Ezra Fleischer; see, for example, his "Early Hebrew Liturgical Poetry in Its Cultural Setting (Comparative Experiments)" [in Hebrew], in *Moises Starosta Memorial Lectures*, ed. Y. Geiger (Jerusalem, 1994), 63–97.

But one may also raise the following question: If Christian influence on Judaism was indeed considerable, why are there relatively few differences between the practices of Ashkenazic Jewry and those of Jews from such Muslim centers as North Africa or Babylonia? In the final analysis, the basic religious ceremonies and texts of these two Jewries are quite similar. My answer to this question is quite simply that the Christian influence on Jewry did not first emerge in the Middle Ages. Like the Jews of Christian Europe, the Jews in Muslim lands inherited a religion whose historical formation had already taken shape through the rejection of the alternative offered by Christianity to the crisis of the Destruction of the Second Temple. The confrontation with Christianity lies at the very heart of Midrashic and Talmudic Judaism,[33] which deal intensively with a renewed self-definition of who is a Jew and what is Judaism, as part of determining the reverse definition—namely, who is not a Jew. It was essential to define this in relation to those who wished to see themselves as Jews and were rejected by the Sages of the Mishnah and the Talmud because of their belief in the messiahhood of Jesus. Self-definition is an extensive and open process, one based not solely on automatic denial, but also on absorbing new religious ideas, ceremonies, and symbols from the outside. The processes of appropriation and the struggle over that which is appropriated characterize the world of anti-Christian polemic during the Rabbinic period. In the Middle Ages, however, the tendency of mutual denial came to dominate.

Three examples exemplify this process, each pertaining to one of the foundations of religious life: holy place, holy time, and holy text. "Mount Zion," known today to every Jew and Christian as the name used for the upper city of old Jerusalem, was originally a Christian (or Jewish-Christian) term that originated as a way to expropriate the holiness of the Temple Mount following the Destruction of the Temple and to transfer that holiness to an alternative mountain, the traditional site of the tomb of King David, the

---

33. On the basis of this assumption, we should rely on the classical work of Hermann Strack and P. Billerbeck, *Kommentar zum Neuen Testament aus Talmud und Midrasch*, 4 vols. (München, 1922–28), but in a form diametrically opposed to theirs. The many parallels between the Talmud and the New Testament are not necessarily a result of the influence of the cultural world represented by the Talmud on the New Testament, but rather the opposite. The relation between the New Testament and Talmudic literature is discussed by Geza Vermes, "Jewish Literature and New Testament Exegesis: Reflections on Methodology," *JJS* 31 (1982): 361–76. Vermes is a New Testament scholar who seeks to justify the benefit of comparison with Talmudic literature but in the process of doing so rejects the likelihood that the world of the Sages was directly influenced by the New Testament.

prototype of Jesus.[34] Yet Jews also used and still use the name "Mount Zion," apparently without sensing the absurdity of it, even though it was originally the name of the Temple Mount. They accepted the Christian identification, because their polemic with Christianity was built not only on denial but also on the absorption and acculturation of traditions, names, ceremonies, and symbols.

The same holds true for the development of the holidays. There is room to suppose—and far more research is required on this important question—that Jewish liturgical time was profoundly influenced by Christian liturgical time. Passover is the focus of this book and will be discussed in detail later; for the moment, this principle can be easily demonstrated by examining the status of the Jewish festival of Shavu'ot in relation to Pentecost. The new significance given to Shavu'ot by the Talmudic Sages, as the holiday celebrating the Giving of the Torah, emerged after the description of the descent of the Holy Spirit to the apostles on the fiftieth day after the Crucifixion, as related in Acts 2. If this is not a one-sided influence, only a parallel development can explain this similarity of conceptions, in which Mount Sinai and Mount Zion (where the Holy Spirit descended on the apostles)—that is, the Old Testament and the New Testament—contest one another.[35] Particularly famous is the Midrash about how God courted the nations and offered them the Torah, and about how all of them refused, except for Israel.[36] This legend expresses an acute competition with the Christian claim that the new Torah was taken from Israel in the flesh and given to Israel in the spirit.

The Sages' ban on writing down the Oral Law may be also explained in

34. Ora Limor, "Christian Sanctity—Jewish Authority" [in Hebrew], *Cathedra* 80 (1997): 31–62; Y. Zafrir, "Zion—The South-Western Hill and Its Role in the Development of the City of Jerusalem During the Byzantine Period" [in Hebrew] (PhD diss., The Hebrew University of Jerusalem, 1975), 6–7.

35. Compare Gal 4:24–26. On the parallel development of the holidays, see Moshe Weinfeld, "The Uniqueness of the Decalogue and Its Place in Jewish Tradition," in *The Ten Commandments in History and Tradition,* ed. B. Z. Segal, trans. G. Levi (Jerusalem, 1985), 40–44.

36. *Sifrei Deut.* sec. 343, ed. L. Finkelstein, 395–97: "When the Holy One blessed be He appeared to give Torah to Israel, it was not only to Israel that He appeared, but to all the nations. First He went to the children of Esau. He said to them: Do you accept the Torah? They said to Him, What is written in it? He said to them: 'Thou shalt not kill.' They said, the whole nature of those people and their father is a murderer, as the Bible says, 'the hands are the hands of Esau' (Gen 27:22), and 'by thy sword shalt thou live' (Gen 27:40). He went to the children of Ammon and Moab . . . He went to the children of Ishmael . . . when the Holy One blessed be He saw that it was thus, he gave it to Israel."

a similar manner.[37] This ban seems to be a conscious, thoroughly ideological response to the fear that the Oral Law would be universalized and expropriated from its internal Jewish context, as happened to the Written Law when the Hebrew Bible was translated into the Septuagint and canonized by Christianity. This suggestion, explicitly raised in a late Midrash that will be discussed in chapter 2,[38] implies that the Sages were well aware of the threat posed by the competing sister religion. It is hard to imagine a more convincing explanation for this unprecedented phenomenon, in which a culture with such a deep commitment to learning insists on preserving a specifically oral framework, unless we assume that it was motivated by a struggle for the very existence of that culture.

It is no wonder, then, that the distinctions between Ashkenazim and Sephardim in the Middle Ages cannot be reduced simply to the difference between the Christian environment and the Muslim one, because Judaism in Muslim lands in the Middle Ages was also a continuation of a long-standing anti-Christian tradition that defined its religious identity through the denial of the alternative option. To be a "Jew" meant, in the most profound sense, to adopt a religious identity that competed with Christianity, and vice versa. Or, to adopt the formulation of the late Jacob Katz, the veracity of one religion depended on the negation of the other.[39]

Thus, one cannot accept the claim that the Jews of Muslim lands were exempt from a confrontation with Christianity. On the contrary, the most ancient anti-Christian Jewish polemic was written in the Muslim countries,[40] because the urgent need to struggle with the Christian alternative also arose in those areas, even during the pre-Islamic period. Likewise, in the Persian-Sassanid Empire and in its Zoroastrian religious milieu, Christianity presented an unparalleled challenge to the Jew.[41] As we shall discuss

37. *b. Gittin* 60b: "Teachings that were given to you orally you are not permitted to transmit in writing." And: "The Holy One blessed be He established a covenant with Israel only on the basis of the oral teachings." *Tanhuma, Ki-Tissa* 34:27: "The Holy One blessed be He says to the nations of the world: You claim that you are My children, but I know that only those who know My secrets are My children. Where are His secrets? In the Mishnah, which was given orally," and similarly elsewhere.

38. *Tanhuma, Ki Tissa* sec. 34.

39. Jacob Katz, *'Et lahqor ve-'et lehitbonen* (Jerusalem, 1999), 54.

40. D. J. Lasker and S. Stroumsa, eds., *The Polemic of Nestor the Priest*, 2 vols. (Jerusalem, 1996).

41. See N. Koltun-Fromm, "A Jewish-Christian Conversation in Fourth-Century Persian Mesopotamia," *JJS* 47 (1996): 45–63.

later, the sequence of legends about the Destruction of the Temple specifically in the Babylonian Talmud is characterized by a covert anti-Christian polemic, unlike the versions in the Jerusalem Talmud, in which the anti-Christian motifs are weaker and far more muted. The Byzantine government obviously exerted considerable pressure on the Jews of the Land of Israel, but this does not contradict the intensity of the polemics conducted by the Nestorian Christians and the Jews in Babylonia. It is therefore probably no coincidence that the only non-Jewish work cited in the entire vast literature of the Talmud and Midrash—and of all places in the Babylonian Talmud—is the New Testament.[42]

THE MOTHER, THE DAUGHTER, AND THE SISTER

The polemic in question is not necessarily direct and explicit. In the introduction to the earliest known anti-Christian work, the polemic of Nestor the Priest, the editors, Sarah Stroumsa and Daniel Lasker, note: "Despite evidence of a Jewish interest in Christianity, a review of the Jewish polemical arguments during the first eight centuries of the Christian era demonstrates that the daughter religion was not a central concern of the Jews."[43] This view faithfully represents the central trend of scholarship in this field, as demonstrated by a statement of Anna Sapir Abulafia: "Any consideration about relations between Judaism and Christianity must begin with an obvious point. Christianity is a daughter religion of Judaism and as such it draws much of its validity from the very sources that Jews have always claimed as their own."[44] And David Berger wrote:

> The corpus of early Christian works directed against Judaism is, as we have already noted, rather extensive. Anti-Christian works by Jews, on the other hand, are virtually nonexistent before the twelfth century. One reason for this disparity is that Jews had no internal motivation for writing polemics against Christians; in times or places where Christianity was not a threat, we cannot expect Jews to be concerned with a refutation of its claims.[45]

42. *b. Shabb.* 116a-b.

43. Lasker and Stroumsa (n. 40, p. 25), 14. And cf. A. Limor, "Judaism Looks at Christianity: The Polemic of Nestor the Priest and *Sefer Toldot Yeshu*" [in Hebrew], *Pe'amim* 75 (1998): 109–25.

44. Anna Sapir Abulafia, *Christians and Jews in the Twelfth-Century Renaissance* (London, 1995), 63.

45. David Berger, *The Jewish-Christian Debate in the High Middle Ages* (Philadelphia, 1979), 7.

In contrast, in an article on Christian influences on the Zohar, Yehuda Liebes wrote: "The nature of Christianity as a daughter-religion (or, rather, a sister-religion) of Judaism, an alternative interpretation of a common scriptural tradition, made it all the easier for the two religions to influence one another."[46] Indeed, there seems to be good and sufficient reason to revise the view that grants Judaism the status of mother religion. First, the term *daughter religion* is problematic insofar as it relates to the status of Christianity in relation to Talmudic Judaism, seeing that both are daughter religions of biblical Judaism, which was centered on the Temple before its destruction in 70 C.E.[47] The dispute over which of them is more authentic in its claim to succession is a subject for theological debate, and it is doubtful whether the historian (especially one who is a Christian or Jew!) should take a position in such a dispute. Second, precisely because the challenge posed by Christianity to post-Temple Judaism was so demanding, a search for direct and explicit polemics cannot suffice. There are, in fact, no extant polemical compositions prior to the ninth century, but the field of polemics is far broader than the specific literary genre bearing that name. If we tune our ears to listening to more hidden tones, rustlings of subtle hints intended to counter the claims of "heretics" will reach our ears.

Classical scholarship frequently tended to examine the relations between Christianity and Judaism through the literature of direct and explicit polemics. But polemical literature deals with professed theology, and its purpose is to sharpen the points of friction between the two religions. Even the harshest and most scathing polemics require a common language and shared presuppositions regarding the point of departure of the debate. Hence, beneath the ideological and emotional tensions, we can identify hidden and more complex layers of mutual recognition, cooperation, and great cultural similarity. Moreover, not everything we identify today as "Christian" was necessarily understood as such by medieval people. The "Christian" language of ritual and ceremony of the majority culture may have been considered by the minority culture as a neutral and universal language that might be "Judaized" and subsequently incorporated into Jewish ritual.

The assumption that, despite the official and explicit ideological barriers,

46. Yehudah Liebes, "Christian Influences in the Zohar," *Immanuel* 17 (1983–84): 43.

47. This has already been noted by A. F. Segal, *Rebecca's Children: Judaism and Christianity in the Roman World* (Cambridge, MA, 1986). Among recent studies that identify the depth of the common liturgical and polemical language of Jews and Christians is L. A. Hoffman, *Covenant of Blood; Circumcision and Gender in Rabbinic Judaism* (Chicago, 1996).

the Jewry of Christian Europe internalized the language and the textual world of their environment is increasingly confirmed by recently published studies. Some of them shed a different light on the character of Ashkenazic Jewry. Ivan Marcus, for example, recently showed how Jewish rites initiating a child into his school studies were clearly influenced by Christian ceremonies.[48] Jeremy Cohen has demonstrated how figures from the New Testament, Christian liturgical motifs, and even Crusader values, penetrated tales of Jewish martyrdom in 1096.[49] And Elliot Horowitz has indicated the strong attraction the Jews felt for the Cross and the important subconscious role it played in the system of Jewish symbols, far beyond that which studies of the previous generation would lead us to imagine.[50] This tendency to rebut the opponent while internalizing his symbolic world also follows from Ora Limor and Elchanan Reiner's studies on holy places in Judaism and Christianity.[51] These studies convincingly demonstrate a clear, one-sided influence of Christianity on Judaism. The "rediscovery" of the Holy Land by the Jews of Christian Europe in the twelfth century, the formulation of the settling of the Holy Land, and the pilgrimage to the Land as important religious obligations—all these are clear expressions of the spirit of the age, the age of Christian Crusaders who were stirred to set off to a distant and almost forgotten land.

We seem to be confronting a genuine revision in our historical understanding of the mental world of the Jews who lived in Christian countries in general, and in Ashkenaz in particular: no longer a closed and suspicious Jewish society, but one that succeeded in maintaining, alongside the hos-

---

48. Ivan G. Marcus, *Rituals of Childhood* (New Haven, 1996). In other publications as well Marcus describes the process as "inward acculturation" of the world of Christian symbols within Judaism.

49. Jeremy Cohen, "The Persecutions of 1096, from Martyrdom to Martyrology: The Sociocultural Context of the Hebrew Crusade Chronicles" [in Hebrew], *Zion* 59 (1994): 169–209.

50. Elliot Horowitz, "Medieval Jews Facing the Cross" [in Hebrew], in *Yehudim mul ha-Zelav: gezerot TTN"W behistoriyah uvehistoriographiyah*, ed. Y. T. Assis et al. (Jerusalem, 2000).

51. Limor (nn. 34, 43, pp. 24 and 26); Elchanan Reiner, "From Joshua to Jesus: The Transformation of a Biblical Story to Local Myth: A Chapter in the Religious Life of the Galilean Jew," in *Sharing the Sacred: Religious Contacts and Conflicts in the Holy Land*, ed. A. Kofsky and G. G. Stroumsa (Jerusalem, 1998), 223–71; Limor, "A Jewish Response to the Crusades: The Dispute over Sacred Places in the Holy Land," in *Juden und Christen zur Zeit der Kreuzzüge*, ed. A. Haverkamp, *Vorträge und Forschungen*, herausgegeben vom Konstanzer Arbeitskreis für mittelalterliche Geschichte 47 (Sigmaringen, 1999), 209–31.

tility, a lively and open dialogue with the Christian milieu.[52] In this context, the extremist religious pietism of the Ashkenazic Hasidism may also be seen as a kind of internalization of the world of Christian values, which may also account for their mighty effort to defend themselves against its influence. As Jeremy Cohen has noted, "What is common to Jewish and Christian culture in the Middle Ages is just as impressive as the appeals of members of those cultures to alien values outside their culture. That is, those cultures were more complex than is usually supposed, and the channels between the two were always open in both directions, even in times of crisis and conflict between them."[53]

The widespread image, in research and among the general public, of Ashkenazic Jewry as being cut off from the Christian milieu, reflects two very modern points of view. One expresses the influence of the modern urban metropolis, whose dimensions and density are radically different from the tiny dimensions of the medieval city. Modern people have no difficulty imagining minority groups living in closed ghettoes, maintaining their own internal subculture and subsociety, zealously preserving their uniqueness. In the bastion of ultratraditional Orthodoxy in Jerusalem's Meah Shearim quarter—which is certainly as intolerant as a typical medieval city—stands the Church of Saint Peter of the Finnish messianic congregation, and those ultra-Orthodox Jews going to their *stiblach* (little prayer houses) do not have a clue about what is going on within the church right under their noses, and vice versa. But this kind of mutual alienation found in modern cities could not have existed in the intimacy of the medieval city. The assumption that human beings living in such compact and dense neighborhoods, practically on top of one another, in a city whose tumult consisted of human voices and not automobiles would not recognize or know or hear what was happening beyond the walls of their houses is implausible. The burden of proof rests on anyone who argues that. In this respect as well we

52. This has long been recognized by art historians such as J. Gutmann, "When the Kingdom Comes: Messianic Themes in Medieval Jewish Art," *Art Journal* 27 (1967–68): 173–75; Gutman, "The Messiah at the Seder: A Fifteenth-Century Motif in Jewish Art," *Raphael Mahler Jubilee Volume* (Tel Aviv, 1974), 29–38. But this view has not been adequately accepted among historians, perhaps because the place of art in the everyday life of Ashkenazic Jewry has not been fully clarified. Or perhaps art is still considered a non-normative manifestation of Jewish religious life in the Middle Ages.

53. Cohen (n. 49, p. 28), 205.

need to change our point of departure and assume—as long as it has not been proven to the contrary—that religious ceremonies and texts used by one side were known to the other.

Another consideration that led past scholarship to consider Ashkenazic religious culture as closed and immune to outside influences was the modernization and Westernization of Jewish identity. For both modernizers and traditionalists, the Westernization of the nineteenth century is understood as involving an abandonment of the old religious tradition. The religiosity of the Middle Ages is perceived by them as a reflection of contemporary Orthodoxy. As a result, religion has become identified with the rejection of Westernization. Paradoxically, it was in the more open and secular and less Christian world of the nineteenth century that religion was assigned the function of preserving the old world, sealing itself off from the temptations of its surroundings. But medieval religion was entirely different. Its function was not only to preserve the old world but also to offer a dynamic cultural framework that would absorb and express changing ideas and ideals. Religion in the Middle Ages did not turn its back on its environment, language, or symbols but, rather, it wished to incorporate them all. From this there followed its willingness to assimilate the spirit of the age, through its ability to plant a new seed in the guise of an ancient husk, as in the Talmudic saying that "whatever innovation a veteran scholar may introduce was already told to Moses at Sinai."

All this should not blur the distinctions between then and now. Insofar as cooperation did exist between Jews and Christians, it proceeded mainly in the subconscious realms of the culture. During the Middle Ages there was no ideology of cooperation and mutual respect, no declared and conscious tolerance for the "other" and his culture. The "other" certainly had an influence, and his presence was threatening. Even if the houses of Jews and Christians were very similar, they were separated by an invisible wall of hostility. By contrast, in recent generations we have seen an increased awareness of the common perspectives of different cultures and of the way in which human beings perceive the "other" living among them. It is this awareness that gives hope for greater tolerance and understanding in relations among individuals, communities, and nations.

TWO

Rome or Jerusalem

The Foundations of Jewish-Christian Hostility

SINCE ITS CONQUEST BY THE ROMANS in 63 B.C.E., Judaea, along with all the other nations of the East, was subjected to a hitherto unknown form of political subjugation. In the past, the nation of Israel had at one time or another fought with many other nations, near and far, but the Roman conquest initiated a new era: one of unending confrontation with a global empire. For the people of those generations, it seemed as if the rule of "eternal" Rome would go on forever. Hence, as the subjugation of Judaea intensified, so did the tendency to identify Rome with the Fourth Kingdom of the Book of Daniel, that which would precede the coming of the Messiah. In this way the deliverance of Judaea became dependent on the annihilation of Rome. The Destruction of the Temple, God's sanctuary, in 70 C.E. reinforced the view that Jerusalem could not be rebuilt until Rome was destroyed.[1]

---

1. *b. Meg.* 6a: "If someone says to you that both Caesarea [i.e., Rome] and Jerusalem have been destroyed, do not believe him; if he says that both are flourishing, do not believe him; if he says that Caesarea has been laid waste and Jerusalem is flourishing, or that Jerusalem has been laid waste and Caesarea is flourishing, you may believe him; as it says, 'I shall be replenished, but she is laid waste' (Ezek 26:2): if this one is filled, that one laid waste, and if that one is filled, this one is laid waste." For the view that makes deliverance dependent on the annihilation of Rome, see M. Hengel, *The Zealots: Investigations into the Jewish Freedom*

Once Rome became Christian, in the fourth century, the language of the struggle changed. The political struggle with the empire gave way to a religious debate between Christianity and Judaism. For both religions, the idea of messianic divine vengeance was one of the cornerstones of religious thought.[2] Christianity saw the Destruction of the Temple as a manifestation of God's vengeance for the Crucifixion of his Son; Jewish Exile and subsequent subjugation were accordingly interpreted as revenge by the "Savior." The Jewish explanation for the Exile was "because of our sins we were exiled from our land"; it was impossible to ignore the opposing Christian claim that "because of your sins, you were exiled from your land." Jews and Christians argued over what brought about the destruction of Jerusalem: a petty, almost ridiculous incident, as Jews believed, or the Crucifixion of Jesus. Just as the Church accused the Jew of the "original sin" of the Crucifixion, so did the Jew charge Rome, and by extension the Church, with the "original sin" of the Destruction of Jerusalem and the Temple. Rome, which is Edom, was guilty of the Destruction, and its guilt will extend till the end of time, until the messianic healing comes to the Jews suffering in Exile. The intensity of the polemics between Christians and Jews determined central issues in Jewish messianic doctrine.[3]

The language in which these ideas are expressed in traditional religious literature, particularly in the Midrash and the Talmuds, is that of typolog-

---

Movement in the Period from Herod I until 70 A.D. (Edinburgh, 1989), 302–12. On the role of the Destruction of the Temple in the political and religious polemic between Judaea and Rome, see H. Schwier, *Tempel und Tempelzerstörung: Untersuchungen zu den theologischen und ideologischen Factoren im ersten jüdisch-römischen Krieg (66–74 n. Chr)* (Freiburg, 1989), 330–62. The author proposes the interesting thesis that there was a connection between the burning of the Capitol in Rome in December 69 and Titus's decision to burn the Temple in Jerusalem in the summer of 70. With his act, Titus wanted to prove the superiority of Jupiter over the God of Judaea and to attain political legitimacy for the Flavian regime. The author suggests that the revolt of the Diaspora in 115–117 be seen as a Jewish attempt to avenge the Destruction of the Temple. And cf. S. Heid, "Auf welcher Seite kämpft Gott? Der Anspruch Jerusalems und Roms auf die Waffenhilfe Gottes in frühchristlicher Apologetik," *Zeitschrift für Kirchengeschichte* 104 (1993): 1–22.

2. On the idea of eschatological vengeance in Scripture, see H. G. L. Peels, *The Vengeance of God* (Leiden, 1994), 132–234.

3. On the Destruction of the Temple as a decisive factor in the shaping of Rabbinic Judaism, on the one hand, and of Christianity, on the other—especially regarding their respective messianic doctrines—see Itamar Gruenwald, "From Priesthood to Messianism: The Anti-Priestly Polemic and the Messianic Factor," in *Messiah and Christos: Studies in the Jewish Origins of Christianity, Presented to David Flusser*, ed. I. Gruenwald, S. Shaked, and G. Stroumsa (Tübingen, 1992), 75–93. On Jewish messianic expectations of the destruction of Constan-

ical legends, myths, allegories, and ceremonies. In this chapter we shall attempt to trace the meanings of this language. While a comparative examination of explicit religious ideas tends to reveal and to emphasize the difference between the two religions, the language of symbols and ceremonies reveals the common means by which both religions were able to elucidate and refine their independent identities. This common language should not mislead us into thinking it constituted any sort of closeness between the religions. To the contrary: hostility and rivalry demand a common language for formulating diametrically opposed positions, because conflicting conceptual messages can only be conveyed through symbols understood by both sides.

THE SONS OF EPHRAIM AND THE SON OF JOSEPH

The connection between revenge and deliverance is clearly visible in the Talmudic legend about the sons of Ephraim. This legend tells of the sons of the tribe of Ephraim who erred in calculating the time of the Redemption during the Exile in Egypt, left Egypt too soon, and were killed by the Philistines of Gath. Later, when the time came for the Israelites to leave Egypt, "the Holy One blessed be He said: If Israel see the bones of the sons of Ephraim strewn on the way, they will return to Egypt" and therefore turned them toward the desert.[4] The following addition appears in a Midrash: "What did the Holy One blessed be He do? He took the blood of the sons of Ephraim and dipped His garments therein, as it were, for it says: 'Why is thy apparel red?' (Isa 63:2). The Holy One blessed be He said: I will not be comforted until I avenge myself of the crime against the sons of Ephraim, as it says: 'And God was not comforted' (Exod 13:17)."[5]

Louis Ginzberg already noted the typological meaning of this legend as an allusion to the Messiah son of Joseph who will precede the Davidic Messiah and die in a war.[6] According to Ginzberg, the legend of the Ephraimites'

---

tinople, the heir of Rome, see Oded Irshai, "Historical Aspects of the Christian-Jewish Polemic Concerning the Church of Jerusalem in the Fourth Century (in the Light of Patristic and Rabbinic Literature)" [in Hebrew] (PhD diss., The Hebrew University of Jerusalem, 1993), 1:167–68.

4. *Mekhilta de-Rabbi Yishma'el, Beshalah*, 76–77; *b. Sanh.* 92b and parallels.

5. *Exod. Rab.* 20.11.

6. Louis Ginzberg, "Eine unbekannte jüdische Sekte," *MGWJ* 58 (1914): 159–77, 395–429. Scholarly literature on the figure of the suffering/slain Messiah/prophet is vast. For the most

premature exodus from Egypt generated the figure of the Messiah-son-of-Ephraim-son-of-Joseph,[7] the penultimate Messiah who is destined to die in the eschatological war preceding the coming of the final Messiah, the son of David:

There is no real biblical basis for the legend of the sons of Ephraim who left Egypt too soon.[8] According to the literal sense of the Bible, Ephraim did not emigrate from Egypt but remained in the Land of Israel, and was the local founder of his tribal inheritance.[9] Apparently it was not the Rabbinic legend that invented the figure of the Messiah son of Joseph but, to the contrary, the midrash was shaped as a retrospective typology after the figure of Messiah son of Joseph had already emerged. The appearance in tannaitic literature of the independent figure of the Messiah son of Joseph may be ascribed to the political reality following the Destruction, when captive Judaea was no longer able to cope militarily with the power of Rome. At that time, the belief developed that a Messiah from the tribe of Ephraim, the leader of the ten tribes, would redeem Judaea from the yoke of Rome. These hopes were expressed in the Midrash: "By whose hand will the kingdom of Edom fall? By the hand of the one anointed for war, who shall be descended from Joseph. . . . We have a tradition that Esau will only fall at the hand of Rachel's descendants."[10]

---

recent summary, see Michael Fishbane, "Midrash and Messianism: Some Theologies of Suffering and Salvation," in *Toward the Millennium: Messianic Expectations from the Bible to Waco*, ed. P. Schäfer and M. Cohen (Leiden, 1998), 57–71.

7. According to Joseph Heinemann, the tradition concerning the death of Messiah son of Joseph developed following the Bar Kokhba Revolt in an attempt to preserve the figure of Bar Kokhba as a messiah; see Joseph Heinemann, "The Messiah of Ephraim and the Premature Exodus of the Tribe of Ephraim," *HTR* 68 (1975): 1–16. And cf. David Berger, "Three Typological Themes in Early Jewish Messianism: Messiah Son of Joseph, Rabbinic Calculations, and the Figure of Armilus," *AJS Review* 10 (1985): 141–64; Yaakov Blidstein, "The Ephraimite Exodus from Egypt: A Reevaluation" [in Hebrew], *Jerusalem Studies in Jewish Thought* 5 (1986): 1–13.

8. The biblical verses cited in the Midrash (Hos 9:13; 1 Chr 7:21) seem to be merely references. The exegesis on the biblical verse "God did not lead them by way of the land of the Philistines" may relate to the following verse: "And Moses took the bones of Joseph with him" (Exod 13:17, 19).

9. Alexander Rofé, "The Family-Saga as a Source for The History of The Settlement" [in Hebrew], *Eretz-Yisrael—Archaeological, Historical and Geographical Studies* 24 (1993): 188, and bibliography there.

10. *Gen. Rab.* 79, ed. Theodor-Albeck, p. 1274, and the parallels cited there; see *b. Bab. Bat.* 123b: "Esau's seed is only delivered into the hands of Jacob's seed."

The appearance from afar of a Jewish army commanded by the Messiah son of Joseph is linked to the hope that the Kingdom of Israel would be restored, including the return of the ten tribes.[11] The northern warrior messiah is destined to die in battle and make way for the Messiah son of David, representative of the kingdom of Judaea and of present Jewry. Assuming that the legend of the sons of Ephraim who ascend from Egypt was indeed created in retrospect, as a typological justification for the Messiah son of Joseph, the addition in the Midrash concerning avenging the blood of the sons of Ephraim contains a clear messianic meaning, as a message to all those killed in the wars of deliverance, that their blood will be avenged. The avenging of their blood, God's "consolation," was a condition for those leaving Egypt to come into the Land of Israel, and will be so before the final deliverance, the return to Zion.

The Rabbinic theory of two messiahs, the Messiah son of Joseph and the Messiah son of David, was the development of a viewpoint that was widespread during the Second Temple period. In the pseudepigraphical *Testaments of the Tribes* one finds the opinion that the Messiah will come from the seed of Levi and the seed of Judah,[12] while the writings of the Qumran sect include an expectation of two messiahs, the Messiah son of Aaron and the Messiah son of David.[13] Not a single source from the Second Temple period mentions the Messiah son of Joseph. There is, however, one exception: Jesus, son of Joseph. This descent of Jesus from a man named Joseph did not elicit any discussion in early Christian literature and may be treated

---

11. On the belief in the existence of the ten tribes, see Josephus, *Ant. Jud.*, 11.133 ("until now there have been ten tribes beyond the Euphrates"); *m. Sanh.* 10.3 ("The ten tribes shall not return again . . . so said R. Akiba. But R. Eliezer says: Like as the day grows dark and then grows light, so also after darkness is fallen upon the ten tribes shall light hereafter shine upon them"). And cf. Acts 26:8; James 1:1; 4 Ezra 13:39–52 ("for the most high then wrought wonders for them, and stayed the springs of the River until they were passed over"; see R. H. Charles, *The Apocrypha and Pseudepigrapha of the Old Testament in English* (Oxford, 1913), 619.

12. M. Z. Segal, "The Origin of King Messiah" [in Hebrew], *Tarbiz* 21 (1950): 129–36.

13. Shemaryahu Talmon, "Waiting for the Messiah: The Spiritual Universe of the Qumran Covenanters," in *Judaisms and Their Messiahs at the Turn of the Christian Era*, ed. J. Neusner, W. C. Green, and E. S. Frerichs (Cambridge, 1987), 111–37; H. W. Kuhn, "Die beiden Messias in den Qumrantexten und die Messiasvorstellung in der rabbinischen Literatur," *Zeitschrift für Alttestamentliche Wissenschaft* 70 (1958): 200–208; Yaakov M. Grintz, *Peraqim betoldot Bayit Sheni* (Jerusalem, 1969), 125–30. For earlier allusions to Messiah son of Joseph, see G. H. Dix, "The Messiah Ben Joseph," *JTS* 27 (1926): 130–43; C. C. Torrey, "The Messiah Son of Ephraim," *JBL* 66 (1947): 253–77.

simply as a biographical fact. The double and problematic attribution of Jesus to Joseph (Mary's husband, but not Jesus's father) and through him to David corresponds to his double origin: he is a Galilean born in Judaea. A certain tension existed between the biographical facts (being the son of Joseph and a Galilean) and his messianic aspirations (being a son of David and from Judaea). In the absence of any evidence of belief in the Messiah son of Joseph before the Destruction, one must consider the possibility that the Rabbinic figure of Messiah son of Joseph, destined to die, might express an internalization of the figure of Jesus as messiah. He too was the son of Joseph, he too was killed, and he too was a northerner.

The similarity between Messiah son of Joseph and Jesus is evident in another central point: Jesus is not only from the house of David but is also described as a high priest.[14] The figure of Jesus thus united both messiahs of the late Second Temple period: Messiah son of David and Messiah son of Aaron, the king and the priest. But since Jesus was not of priestly lineage, he was offered a new lineage, to Melchizedek. The Rabbinic Messiah son of Joseph, who likewise replaced the priestly messiah of the Second Temple period, was given a similar function. There would seem to be a direct connection between the figure of Jesus and that of Messiah son of Joseph, since both reflect a similar process: a parallel search, among both Christians and Jews, for a new messianic narrative that would fit two difficult and painful historic facts—the death of Jesus, on the one hand, and the Destruction of the Temple, on the other. The former needed to include in its messianic narrative temporary failure, death followed by new life; the latter needed to propose a new messianic figure, one independent of the temple or priesthood, since the substitute for the high priest was to be found in his own person.[15]

The possibility that the Rabbinic Messiah son of Joseph is an internalization of the messianic figure of Jesus is reinforced by several Midrashim in *Pesiqta Rabbati,* in which the Messiah son of Joseph or son of Ephraim is described as anticipating the coming of the Messiah son of David:

14. Heb 4:7.

15. Another solution for this may have engendered the attribution of Elijah's lineage, the herald of deliverance, to the priestly clan, and his identification with Phinehas son of Aaron. For a recent summary of various opinions on this problem, see M. Eyali, "Where Did Elijah Come From? The Lineage and Origin of the Prophet Elijah in Rabbinic Homilies" [in Hebrew], in his *Kirevivim: Hinukh Yehdui ve-heqer ha-meqorot,* ed. A. Shapira (Oranim, 1996), 259–83; originally published in *Tura* 3 (1994).

Iron beams will be brought and loaded upon his neck until the Messiah's body is bent low. Then he will cry and weep, and his voice will rise up to the very height of heaven, and he will say to God: Master of the universe, how much can my strength endure? How much can my spirit endure? How much my breath before it ceases? How much can my limbs suffer? Am I not flesh and blood? It was because of the ordeal of the son of David that David wept, saying "my strength is dried up like a potsherd" [Ps. 22:16]. During the ordeal of the son of David, the Holy One, blessed be He, will say to him: Ephraim, my true Messiah, long ago, even since the six days of creation, thou didst take this ordeal upon thyself.[16]

Note the reference to Psalms 22, which is interpreted in Christian exegesis as a typological description of the Crucifixion of Jesus, among other things because of the second verse "My God, my God, why hast thou forsaken me," Jesus's final words on the Cross (Matt 27:46). Jesus's complaint is reminiscent of that of the Messiah son of Joseph in this Midrash, "How much can my spirit endure?" Alongside the Christian exegesis of this verse, there exists an entire line of exegesis in *Midrash Tehillim* interpreting the entire chapter as referring to Esther.[17] In other words, rather than a Christian exegesis interpreting the chapter in terms of the Crucifixion of Jesus, which occurred at Passover, the Jewish Midrash offers a parallel line of interpretation reading Psalm 22 as referring to another event that occurred at Passover: the hanging of Haman. We shall have more to say about the connection between Haman and Jesus further on; at this point we will merely note that the image of Messiah son of Ephraim bearing iron beams on his neck is rather reminiscent of the description of the Crucifixion (John 19:17).

Mention of the Messiah son of Ephraim's suffering in a potentially Christological context was also known to medieval authors. At the end of the thirteenth century, Raimondus Martini found an allusion to Jesus in those Midrashim.[18] Rabbi Azariah de Rossi also sensed the "Christianness" of those Midrashim, arguing that they "do not have the flavor of [authentic] Rabbinic midrashim," but were added to the Midrash "by some of those who come to discuss the 'new thing,'" that is, Christians.[19] Meir Ish-Shalom

---

16. *Pesiqta Rabbati*, sec. 36, ed. William G. Braude, 680. Fishbane (n. 6, p. 33) considers the descriptions of the suffering of the Messiah son of Joseph as an internal Jewish development, and denies any approach that seeks in them traces of Christian influence.

17. *Midrash Ps.*, 22, ed. Braude, 297–326.

18. See Saul Lieberman, *Shki'in* (Jerusalem, 1970), 58.

19. Azariah de Rossi, *The Light of the Eyes*, trans. J. Weinberg (New Haven, 2001), chap. 19.

(Friedmann), the modern editor of *Pesiqta Rabbati,* correctly stated that the authenticity of these things cannot be denied,[20] but he thought that *Pesiqta Rabbati's* doctrine of Messiah son of Ephraim predated Christianity—an assumption that is difficult to accept. To the contrary, these Midrashim should be considered a Jewish internalization of the figure of the Christian Messiah.

In this context, the legend of the sons of Ephraim leaving Egypt ahead of time assumes a broader significance. Just as there was a duality in the figure of the Messiah—the warrior son of Joseph, who is killed and who heralds the coming of the son of David—so was it imperative to establish a duality in the process of deliverance and to find a typological precedent for that duality in the Exodus from Egypt. Thus was born the legend of the sons of Ephraim who left Egypt ahead of time. This legend implies that the generation of the Destruction (or that of the war of Bar Kokhba) erred in its calculation of the End, and God's vengeance for their death is itself part of the correction involved in the final deliverance.

VINDICTA SALVATORIS (THE VENGEANCE OF THE SAVIOR)

To understand the messianic hopes pinned by the Jews on the destruction of Rome, we must compare these hopes to the significance the Destruction of Jerusalem had for the Christians; we will thereby find a complete system of complex, reciprocal relations. Both the intimacy and the intensity of the dialogue conducted between the two religions may be clearly seen by tracing the metamorphoses of one Christian legend and the Jewish responses to it. I refer to the legend of *Vindicta Salvatoris*—one of the most famous legends of the Middle Ages and the early modern era.[21] In its later transformation, this legend was the subject of a number of dramatizations and was staged as part of the popular repertoire for Easter. Its popularity was the result of its theological importance, since it offers a basis for the affinity between the Crucifixion of Jesus and the Destruction of the Temple and Jerusalem. In Christian eyes, the Destruction of Jerusalem is the

---

20. *Pesiqta Rabbati* 164a–b, in *Pesikta Rabbati: Midrash für den Fest-Cyclus und die ausgezeichneten Sabbathe,* ed. M. Friedmann (Vienna, 1880; repr. Tel-Aviv, 1963), fol. 164a–b.

21. E. V. Dobschütz, *Christusbilder: Untersuchungen zur christlichen Legende* (Leipzig, 1889), 209–17; H. Schreckenberg, *Rezeptionsgeschichtliche und textkritische Untersuchungen zu Flavius Josephus* (Leiden, 1977), 53–68; S. K. Wright, *The Vengeance of Our Lord: Medieval Dramatizations of the Destruction of Jerusalem* (Toronto, 1989).

vengeance of the Savior who has already come; for the Jews, who still await the Redemption, the Destruction of the Temple gives rise to the expectation of future vengeance. Both say "for it is the vengeance of the Lord, the vengeance for His temple" (Jer 51:11).

Jesus already prophesied the Destruction of Jerusalem: "For the days shall come upon you, when your enemies will cast up a bank about you and surround you, and hem you in on every side, and dash you to the ground, you and your children within you, and they will not leave one stone upon another in you; because you did not know the time of your visitation" (Luke 19:43–44).[22] The Destruction is described as the vengeance of God: "For these are days of vengeance, to fulfill all that is written" (Luke 21:22). From the fourth century on and throughout the Middle Ages, these verses were included in the pericope (the weekly reading from the Gospel) read at Mass on the eleventh Sunday after Pentecost, that is, during the week of Tisha b'Av, thereby clearly paralleling the Jewish day of mourning for the Destruction of their Temple.[23] This is a crucial point for understanding the polemical aspect of the Jewish *Kinot* (liturgical poems of lamentation) composed for that day.

The Destruction of Jerusalem assumes a central place in a sermon for Easter Sunday, apparently written in France in the eleventh century. In it the Destruction is represented as an expression of the inferior position of the Jews in God's eyes, a position they are to occupy throughout their Exile. Rather than granting the Jews protection, as in the past, God takes vengeance on them and punishes them: "Therefore, Jerusalem, you have paid the price for your treachery."[24] The preacher links the Crucifixion of Jesus on Passover

---

22. For this idea and its development, see L. Gaston, *No Stone on Another: Studies in the Significance of the Fall of Jerusalem in the Synoptic Gospels* (Leiden, 1970). On the place of the Destruction of Jerusalem in Christianity, see H. J. Schoeps, "Die Tempelzerstörung des Jahres 70 in der jüdischen Religionsgeschichte," *Aus frühchristlicher Zeit: Religionsgeschichtliche Untersuchungen* (Tübingen, 1950), 144–83; S. G. F. Brandon, *The Fall of Jerusalem and the Christian Church* (London, 1951); G. W. H. Lampe, "AD 70 in Christian Reflection," in *Jesus and the Politics of His Day*, ed. E. Bammel and C. F. D. Moule (Cambridge, 1984), 152–71. And cf. H. Nibley, "Christian Envy of the Temple" *JQR* 50 (1959–60): 97–123, 229–40; M. Simon, "Retour du Christ et reconstruction du temple dans la pensée Chrétienne primitive," *Recherches d'histoire Judéo-Chrétienne* (Paris, 1962), 9–19.

23. Ammon Linder, "The Destruction of Jerusalem Sunday," *Sacris Erudiri* 30 (1987–88): 253–92.

24. A. Linder, "Jews and Judaism in the Eyes of Christian Thinkers of the Middle Ages: The Destruction of Jerusalem in Medieval Christian Liturgy," in *From Witness to Witchcraft*, ed. J. Cohen (Wissbaden, 1996), 113–23.

with the commencement of the Roman siege of Jerusalem, which also occurred on Passover.[25] Interestingly, a Hebrew chronicle from Trier about the 1096 pogroms against the Jews sees the pogroms as beginning on Passover of that year, although, in fact, they started later.[26] The destruction of the communities of Ashkenaz is perceived as a reenactment of the Destruction of the Temple, a motif which we will discuss later in detail.

Yet the connection between the Crucifixion and the Destruction of Jerusalem, a central idea in Christianity and its relation to Judaism, is referred to only in the New Testament (Matthew 23) and in no other contemporary source. Josephus knows nothing about it, a fact that perplexed the Church Fathers, Origen and Eusebius.[27] The legend of *Vindicta Salvatoris* came to compensate for that lack. While its earliest recorded versions are from the sixth century, it contains allusions to events in the early fifth century.[28] I shall argue below that its dating ought to be moved up to the second half of the fourth century.

The following is the gist of one version of the legend: during the reign of Emperor Tiberius, Titus ruled over Aquitaine. He was afflicted with an ulcer of the nose that distorted his face. Once an emissary from Judaea named Nathan was traveling to Rome to meet with Tiberius, but headwinds blew his ship off course, and it was wrecked on the shores of Aquitaine. He was brought to Titus and told of Jesus's miraculous ability to cure illnesses, of the evil deeds of the Jews who crucified him, and of Jesus's resurrection from the dead. Titus cursed Tiberius for not preventing the Crucifixion of Jesus and swore vengeance on the Jews. Thanks to this vow, he was cured immediately. He accepted the authority of the King

---

25. This connection was made earlier by Eusebius, *Hist. Ecc.* trans. G. A. Williamson, (London, 1965), bk. 3, chap. 5.

26. A. M. Haberman, *Gezerot Ashkenaz ve-Tzarfat* (Jerusalem, 1971), 52–56. Setting Passover as the beginning of the pogroms in Trier seems like interpretation after the fact. Nothing out of the ordinary took place on that day, apart from the furtive visit to the city of Peter of Amiens. Perhaps marking the day on which Passover began that year (p. 25) indicates an intention to associate the beginning of the pogroms with Passover.

27. Origen, *Contra Celsum*, 1.47, ed. H. Chadwick (Cambridge 1986), 43 n. 2. The view that the Temple was destroyed as punishment for the Crucifixion of Jesus is also found in the writings of the Church Father Hippolytus, who lived about 200; see R. Ruether, *Faith and Fratricide* (New York, 1974), 128. On the development of this idea in the early Church, see Heid, (n. 1, p. 31) and R. L. Wilken, *John Chrysostom and the Jews: Rhetoric and Reality in the Late 4th Century* (Berkeley and Los Angeles, 1983), 132–38.

28. Dobschütz (n. 21, p. 38), 216 n. 1.

of the Jews, whom he had never seen, and prayed for divine guidance in his campaign of vengeance against the Jews. He and Vespasian set out on a campaign of retaliation against Jerusalem. After a lengthy siege, the Jews surrendered and were subjected to harsh punishments. Vespasian and Titus stoned some of them to death, while others were crucified upside down and stabbed with spears. Those who remained alive were sold into slavery.

This legend is similar to that of the *Cloth of Veronica,* which appears in the *Kaiserchronik* of 1150–1160.[29] In this case the sick emperor was Tiberius, who awaited a cure from a wonder-working Jewish physician from Judaea, namely Jesus. But because the Jews had killed him, the emperor made do with an image of Jesus that had been impressed on the cloth of Veronica when she wiped the sweat off the brow of Jesus. After he was cured, the emperor sent Vespasian and Titus to exact vengeance on the Jews for their deeds. The description of the siege and its horrors demonstrates the harsh punishment of the Jews.[30]

In two poems of *Der Wilde Mann,* from 1170–1180, the legend of *Vindicta Salvatoris* is told in a slightly different form.[31] Here it is Vespasian who

29. Schreckenberg (n. 21, p. 38), 58.

30. Another, parallel version is the legend of *Cura Sanitatis Tiberii;* see Dobschütz, (n. 21, p. 38), 209–11: the Emperor Tiberius heard about the wonders of Jesus and decided to send for him so that he could cure him. Tiberius sent a senior official named Volusianus to bring Jesus from Jerusalem. The Jews and Pilate were frightened by the arrival of the official because they had crucified Jesus. Pilate was condemned and imprisoned. Volusianus was told of Veronica, a woman from Tyre, who three years earlier, when Jesus was still alive, had painted his portrait as a mark of esteem for being cured of her illness. At first, Veronica tried to deny it, but ultimately she turned over the picture. On his way back to Rome, Volusianus took the woman and her picture with him, as well as Pilate, who was in fetters. When the emperor saw him, he asked him, Why did you not execute Pilate? Volusianus apologized and said that he had decided to wait for the emperor's judgment. Pilate was exiled. The emperor prayed to the image of Jesus, was healed, and converted to Christianity. This is the end of the legend. As noted by Dobschütz (n, 21, p. 38), 212, Veronica plays a limited role in this legend. Her main function is to relate Pilate's guilt and punishment. That is, this legend can be seen as a parallel development to the *Vindicta Salvatoris,* since both legends describe the punishment of those who crucified Jesus. While the legend of *Cura Sanitatis Tiberii* places the blame on Pilate, the *Vindicta Salvatoris* places the blame, the punishment, and the vengeance on the Jews. Both legends are taken from a string of stories in the Apocrypha, *Acta Pilati,* also known as the *Gospel of Nicodemus.* For current scholarship on the subject, see W. Schneemelcher, *Neutestamentliche Apokryphen* (Tübingen, 1990), 1:395–424, esp. 423–24 (*New Testament Apocrypha,* English translation, ed. R. Mcl. Wilson [Westminster, 1991], 501–36); and J. H. Charlesworth, *The New Testament Apocrypha and Pseudoepigrapha: A Guide to Publications, with Excursuses on Apocalypses* (Metuchen, N.J., 1987).

31. Schreckenberg (n. 21, p. 38), 59.

suffers a serious illness, wasps having nested in his head. His son, Titus, decides to go to Jerusalem to cure him, having learned of Veronica's wondrous cloth. Titus returns to Rome with Veronica and her cloth, and the emperor is cured. The two of them decide to set forth on a campaign to take vengeance on the Jews for killing Jesus, in the course of which they destroy Jerusalem.

Yet another version appears in Landolfus Sagax at the beginning of the eleventh century.[32] When Titus received the news from Rome that his father has been appointed emperor, he was so happy that his right foot swelled up, and he could not put on his shoe. Josephus assisted in his cure by advising him to bring before him a person whom he hated. This story is based on Josephus's claim that he correctly prophesied the appointment of Vespasian as emperor.[33] Yohanan Lewy has noted the similarity between the story of Landolfus Sagax and the Talmudic legend reporting that Rabban Yohanan ben Zakkai foretold to Vespasian his appointment as emperor. Owing to his joy at the news, Vespasian's foot swelled up, and he could not take off his shoe.[34] Lewy assumed that the Talmudic legend was the source of the Christian legend, but Yitzhak Baer concluded that Landolfus's legend was based on Orosius's book *History Against the Pagans*, written about 417. Baer suggests reading the Talmudic story as a Jewish response to the Christian story. In the Jewish story, Rabban Yohanan ben Zakkai takes the place of Josephus as the healer of Vespasian and as the one who prophesied his appointment as emperor.[35] The similarity between Landolfus's story and the legend of *Vindicta Salvatoris* is explicit. In both stories, Titus becomes sick and is cured by a Jew from Judaea. The difference is the illness: in *Vindicta*

32. Schreckenberg (n. 21, p. 38), 56–57.

33. Josephus, *Bellum Jud.*, 3.399–408; Yitzhak Baer, "Jerusalem in the Times of the Great Revolt" [in Hebrew], *Zion* 36 (1971): 171–75, 180–84.

34. *b. Gittin* 56b; H. Lewy, "Josephus the Physician: A Medieval Legend of the Destruction of Jerusalem," *Journal of the Warburg Institute* 1 (1937–38): 221–42. Another article, reaching similar conclusions, was published at the same time: G. Kisch, "A Talmudic Legend as the Source for the Josephus Passage in the Sachsenspiegel," *Historica Judaica* 1 (1938–39): 105–18.

35. Baer (n. 33, above), 181–84. Baer's brief comments on this issue are very important. Our analysis of the legend of Titus and the gnat, below, supports his assumption about the anti-Christian tendency in the legends of the Destruction. Compare, however, the objections of P. Schäfer, H. Temporini and W. Hasse, eds., "Die Flucht Johanan b. Zakkais aus Jerusalem und die Gründung des 'Lehrhauses' in Jabne," *Aufstieg und Niedergang der römischen Welt* 19, pt. 2 (Berlin, 1979), 93–97.

Salvatoris the illness affects the nose, here it is in the foot; there a wasp is nesting (or an ulcer), here he suffers from swelling.[36]

But there is also a clear and explicit parallel to the Christian legend of *Vindicta Salvatoris* in the Jewish legends of the Destruction: namely, the

36. Baer (n. 33, p. 42) thinks that the legend of Abgar (Pangar), Duke of Arabia, found in the legend of the Destruction of the Temple in *Lam. Rab.* 1 (p. 33), is a Jewish answer to the Christian legend of "the black Abgar"; see Dobschütz, (n. 21, p. 38), 102–20; Schneemelcher (n. 30, p. 41), 389–95. According to Eusebius, *His. Ecc.* 1.13, 31, "Abgar the Black" appealed to Jesus, declared his faith in him, and asked that he cure him of his illness. In a Syrian version of the legend of the ascent of Mary, *Transitus beatae Virginis,* Abgar wished to punish the Jews for the Crucifixion of the Deliverer and to destroy Jerusalem; see M. R. James, *The Apocryphal New Testament* (Oxford, 1924), 219; William Cureton, *Ancient Syriac Documents* (London, 1864), 111; presented by S. Lieberman, *Midreshei Teiman* (Jerusalem, 1970), 15 n. 1. This Abgar parallels Vespasian/Titus in the legend of *Vindicta Salvatoris.* In the legends of the Destruction in *Lamentations Rabbah* as well, Abgar is portrayed as equivalent to Titus, and he supports the total destruction of the Temple. When the four dukes divided the walls of the city, the Western Wall fell to Abgar, but he did not destroy it, so that it would remain as a memento of the Temple so that people may have some small inkling of the magnitude of the destruction. He is punished for this and condemned to leap from the rock and die. This legend makes use of the Western Wall for an anti-Christian polemic, to say that Jesus's prophecy "there shall not be left here one stone upon another that will not be thrown down" (Luke 21:6) was not fulfilled in the Destruction of the Temple. In this connection, *Lam. Rab.* quotes the saying of Rabbi Aha, who lived in Caesarea in the second half of the fourth century: "The Western Wall will never be destroyed." The Jewish legend of Abgar, who was ultimately prevented from destroying the Western Wall, is the Jewish obverse of the Christian legend that attributes to him the intention to take revenge on the Jews for the Crucifixion of Jesus by destroying their Temple. The legend of the Destruction of Jerusalem in *Lam. Rab.*, like that in *b. Gittin,* thus offers a Jewish mirror story to the Christian story. Baer saw Rabbi Yohanan ben Zakkai's request—"give me Yavneh and its sages"—in the Babylonian Talmud as a reflection of the political reality of the late fourth century and suggests that the description there of "Yavneh" reflects the political reality of Tiberias, which became the center for Jewish life and leadership in Galilee. He states, "The legend also bears historical witness . . . to its own time, when the gates to the exile of the Middle Ages were truly opened. The leading rabbi of all Israel seeks permission from the Roman Emperor for the continuation of the existence of the central yeshiva of Israel!" ("Jerusalem," 185) Note the formal similarity between the request of Rabban Yohanan ben Zakkai—"give me Yavneh and its sages"—and the Christian legend of the *Donatio Constantini.* Both stories are based on the miraculous healing of the emperor of an illness by a religious leader, and as a reward, the secular, imperial regime grants recognition to the religious authority. *Donatio Constantini* was not known before the eighth century, but the Talmudic story may indicate its much earlier topos. On this cf. Israel J. Yuval, "Jews and Christians in the Middle Ages: Shared Myths, Common Language; Donatio Constantini and Donatio Vespasiani," in *Demonizing the "Other": Antisemitism, Racism, and Xenophobia,* ed. R. S. Wistrich (Amsterdam, 1999), 88–107.

legend of Titus's gnat.[37] Not only is the gnat similar to the wasp, but the entire structure and the ideology of the story indicate both the symmetry between the two stories and the deliberate oppositions: against the Christian *Vindicta Salvatoris* stands a Jewish *Vindicta Dei*. The following is the essence of the Jewish legend, as it appears in the Babylonian Talmud:

> "Where is their God, the rock in whom they trusted?" (Deut. 32:37). This was the wicked Titus who blasphemed and insulted Heaven. What did he do? He took a harlot by the hand and they entered Holy of Holies and spread out a scroll of the Law and committed a sin on it. He then took a sword and slashed the curtain. Miraculously blood spurted out, and he thought that he had slain himself . . . Titus further took the curtain and shaped it like a basket and brought all the vessels of the sanctuary and put them in it, and then put them on board ship to go and triumph with them in his city . . . a gale sprang up at sea which threatened to wreck him. He said: "apparently the power of the God of these people is only over water. When Pharaoh came He drowned him in water, when Sisera came He drowned him in water. He is also trying to drown me in water. If He is really mighty, let him come up on the dry land and fight with me." A voice went forth from heaven saying: sinner, son of sinner, descendant of Esau the sinner, I have a tiny creature in my world called a gnat . . . go up on the dry land and make war with it. When he landed the gnat came and entered his nose, and it knocked against his brain for seven years . . . It has been taught: R. Phineas b. 'Aruba said: "I was in company with the notables of Rome, and when he died they split open his skull and found there something like a sparrow two *selas* in weight."[38]

Both stories tell of an illness suffered by Emperor Titus and of the firm connection between that illness and the Destruction of Jerusalem. Both in-

---

37. *b. Gittin* 57a; *Abot R. Nat.*, version B. 7; and *Lev. Rab.* 22.3 (pp. 499–502). Y. Lewy (n. 34, p. 42), 274 n. 32, sensed the similarity between the wasp in the Christian legend about Vespasian and the gnat in the Jewish legend of Titus, but he thought that in the eleventh century the Talmudic gnat had metamorphosed into the wasp of the Christian legends. He did not perceive the great, albeit inverted, similarity among the other components of the stories or the religious polemic latent in them. He thus overlooked as well the place of the stories in the ancient Jewish-Christian polemic. Another approach to the story, different from that presented here, is G. Stemberger, *Die römische Herrschaft im Urteil der Juden* (Darmstadt, 1983), 67–73.

38. *b. Gittin* 56b. I do not discuss parallel versions of this legend in other sources, since most of the motifs parallel to the Christian legends are preserved specifically in the version of the Babylonian Talmud.

volve a voyage: in the Christian story, Titus goes to Jerusalem to destroy it, while in the Talmudic one he leaves after destroying it. In the former he is cured, while in the latter he dies after great suffering. In the former case the destruction of the city is seen as a meritorious act, while in the latter it is the greatest sacrilege. In the Christian story, Titus is presented from the outset as a great believer in Jesus, even though he does not know him, while in the Jewish story, his first act is to desecrate the Holy Name. In both stories, crossing the sea plays a central role. The Christian story begins with the shipwreck of the emissary from Judaea and continues with Titus's prayer: "My King and my God, Your face I have never seen, and You have cured my disease. Order me to set sail in a ship over the seas to the land of your birth to wreak vengeance on your enemies, and help me, my Lord, to destroy them and to avenge Your death."[39] The motif of the ship, the sea voyage, and its dangers appear in the Talmudic story as well, but in reverse: Titus sails from Jerusalem to Rome and almost drowns in the sea.

In several of the Christian legends, Vespasian is the sick man, while in the Talmudic version it is Titus. In the Christian legend, Vespasian and Titus act in tandem and set off together on a crusade of vengeance against the Jews, while in the legend in *Gittin* there is a sharp separation between the two. Vespasian's figure is a positive one: he receives Rabban Yohanan ben Zakkai and gives him Yavneh, while Titus is the villain in the story. In the Christian legend, divine justice is accomplished through healing; in the Jewish legend, it is effected by illness. Titus blasphemes God and is brought

---

39. Wright (21, p. 38), 30: "Rex meus et deus meus, quia nunquam te vidi et sanum me fecisti, iube me ambulare cum navigo super aquas in terram nativitatis tuae, ut faciam vindictam de inmicis tuis; et adiuva me, domine, ut possim eos delere et mortem tuam vindicare." The motif of Splitting the Sea recurs in several messianic descriptions. According to the Christian historiographer Socrates Scholasticus, in the fifth century a Jew in Crete named Moses (!) promised to lead the Jews to the Land of Israel and to dry the sea. Many people believed him, and on the appointed day they went up onto a cliff, jumped into the sea, and drowned. On this episode, see R. L. Wilken, "The Restoration of Israel in Biblical Prophecy: Christian and Jewish Responses in the Early Byzantine Period," in *To See Ourselves as Others See Us: Christians, Jews, 'Others' in Late Antiquity,* ed. J. Neusner and E. S. Frerichs (Chico, 1985), 445; Irshai (n. 3, p. 32), 1.166. In *Sefer Zerubavel,* ed. Y. Even Shmuel, *Midreshei Ge'ulah* (Jerusalem, 1954), 86, it states that "on the twenty-first day of the first month [the seventh day of Passover] Menahem ben Amiel will come . . . and they will stand on the great sea and will call. And all the corpses of the Children of Israel who threw themselves into the sea because of their captors will come out." Compare the testimony of Hieronymus (n. 63, p. 57), and the later descriptions of the drowning of the Gentiles in the sea at the End of Days (chap. 3, n. 101, p. 125).

down by the smallest of his creatures, the gnat. Galit Hasan-Rokem has noted the similarity between the Hebrew word for "gnat," *yatush,* and "Titus."[40] To which one might add, Titus's gnat is the Jewish legend's answer to Vespasian's *vespa* (Latin for "wasp").

The anti-Christian backdrop to the legend of Titus's wasp may explain the powerful scene at the beginning: Titus's entering the Holy of Holies, his intercourse with the prostitute, and the tearing of the curtain. Hasan-Rokem has noted that intercourse with the prostitute is a personification of the conquest of Jerusalem ("How the faithful city has become a harlot"— Isa 1:21). The forbidden penetration into the Temple by means of the sword both parallels and complements the intercourse with the prostitute: in both cases, a forbidden penetration occurs, one by the penis, the other by the sword.[41]

The scene of tearing the veil of the Holy of Holies alludes to another image, that of the death of Jesus: "And Jesus cried again with a loud voice, and yielded up his spirit. And, behold, the curtain of the temple was torn in two, from top to bottom" (Matt 27:50–51). Why was the Temple veil torn at the moment of Jesus's death? The answer is found in Hebrews 10:19–20: "Therefore, brethren, since we have confidence to enter the sanctuary by the blood of Jesus, by the new and living way which he opened for us through the curtain, that is, through his flesh." According to this, the veil in the Temple is the flesh of Jesus; that is, just as the high priest of the earthly Temple, who enters the Holy of Holies once a year, atones for the sins of the nation, so did Jesus, who in his death was exalted to the Holy of Holies in the heavenly Temple, atone for the original sin. His sacrifice, the sacrifice of Adam, is an eternal atonement, as opposed to the atonement in the earthly Temple, which is temporal and transient, requiring the performance of fresh sacrifices every single day. Tearing the veil symbolizes the Crucifixion

40. Galit Hasan-Rokem, "Within Limits and Beyond: History and Body in Midrashic Texts," *International Folklore Review* 9 (1993): 5–10. According to the formulation in *Lev. Rab.* 22.3, Titus got out of the bath and "they poured him a double measure." Barukh Bokser, "Changing Views of Passover and the Meaning of Redemption according to the Palestinian Talmud," *AJS Review* 10 (1985): 8–9, correctly notes the connection between this description and that brought in *j. Pesahim* 10.1 (37b–c): "From whence do we drink four cups? . . . Our Rabbis said: For the four cups of retribution that the Holy One blessed be He will give to the nations of the world to drink . . . What is 'the portion of their cup'? R. Abun said, A double portion, like the double portion after bathing. And against them the Holy One blessed be He shall give Israel four cups of consolation."

41. Hasan-Rokem, "Within Limits and Beyond," 7.

of Jesus and his ascent to Heaven, for the veil separates the Holy from the Holy of Holies, where only the high priest is allowed to enter. And in Hebrews 6:19–20: "We have this as a sure and steadfast anchor of the soul, a hope that enters into the inner shrine behind the curtain, where Jesus has gone as a forerunner on our behalf, having become a high priest for ever after the order of Melchizedek." When his spirit leaves his flesh, that is, at his death, Jesus enters the Holy of Holies of the Heavenly Temple. Hence, his stabbing and killing led to the rending of the veil from top to bottom also in the earthly Temple, thereby removing the partition separating the Holy from the Holy of Holies.[42]

The Jewish legend about Titus refers directly to that same scene, but in reverse. Titus's entrance into the Holy of Holies and the rending of the veil are a paraphrase of the Crucifixion story. But Titus is also the destroyer of the Temple, and thus "miraculously blood spurted out, and he thought that he had slain him"—that is, the God who dwells in the Holy of Holies. This is a transparent parody of the Christian legend of *Vindicta Salvatoris*. The destroyer of the Temple (Titus) mistakenly thinks, as in Hebrews, that the veil itself is God ("through the curtain, that is, through his flesh").[43] That which in Christian symbolism was considered the most sublime moment of holiness and atonement in the history of humankind—the death of Jesus and the rending of the veil—here becomes the ultimate sacrilege. The Jewish legend thereby adopted the logic of *Vindicta Salvatoris* but reversed its meaning: Titus's appearance in the Holy of Holies is indeed the result of the Crucifixion of Jesus, but it is not a punishment but rather an awesome sin. The Destruction of the Temple thus becomes the sin of Christianity, and the blame for the Destruction is deflected from the historical Roman, pagan Titus to the mythical, "Christian" Titus of *Vindicta Salvatoris*. It is worth noting that a parallel but opposite process also takes place in the Christian legends mentioned above. They absolve the pagan emperor and

---

42. On tearing the veil in the New Testament and in the Apocrypha and related research literature, see M. de Jonge, "Two Interesting Interpretations of the Rending of the Temple-Veil in the Testaments of the Twelve Patriarchs," in *Jewish Eschatology: Early Christian Christology and the Testaments of the Twelve Patriarchs* (Leiden, 1991), 220–31, esp. n. 2.

43. *Abot R. Nat.* (n. 37, p. 44) and *Sifrei Deut.*, sec. 328, ed. Finkelstein, 378–79, tell of "Titus, the son of Vespasian's wife," which may be an allusion to Jesus, that is, the son of his wife but not his own son—in other words, a bastard. Compare Saul Lieberman, *Hellenism in Jewish Palestine* (New York, 1942), 164–65. I am grateful to Adiel Shremer, who drew my attention to this reference in Lieberman. For the blood (of the sacrifices) on the veil, cf. *b. Yoma* 57a.

his deputy Pontius Pilate from blame for the Crucifixion and transfer it exclusively to the Jews. This process clearly reflects the conversion of Rome to Christianity in the fourth century.

Thus, the Talmudic legend about Titus must be read as a veiled and sophisticated polemic with *Vindicta Salvatoris,* or vice versa.[44] The one is a kind of inverted image of the other. It is difficult to determine which came first, and it may well be that these two legends conduct a dialogue of opposing exegeses of the Destruction of Jerusalem. In terms of the literary evidence, the Jewish story comes much earlier, but it is plausible that the Christian legend is based on an oral source that preceded the written one.

In terms of the Christian context, the legend of *Vindicta Salvatoris* fits the fourth century, following the period of Constantine. It was at that time that the Christian liturgy on the Destruction of Jerusalem developed, parallel to the Jewish fast of Tisha b'Av. An important motif in the legend of *Vindicta Salvatoris* is the partial "conversion" to Christianity of Titus, who is shown as believing in Jesus and being cured, a motif consistent with the figure of Constantine. Eusebius was the first to link Jesus's Crucifixion on Passover with the siege of Jerusalem, which also began during Passover. There is considerable emphasis in Origen and Eusebius on the Destruction of Jerusalem as punishment ("measure for measure") for the Cruci-

44. Galit Hasan-Rokem has recently discussed this legend in her "Narratives in Dialogue: A Folk Literary Perspective on Interreligious Contacts in the Holy Land in Rabbinic Literature of Late Antiquity," in *Sharing the Sacred: Religious Contacts and Conflicts in the Holy Land,* ed. A. Kofsky and G. G. Stroumsa (Jerusalem, 1998), 107–29. Hasan-Rokem's literary analysis is both synthetic and analytic. She discovers therein a well-developed and extensive dialogue with paganism but suggests that simultaneously embedded within it is a dialogue with Christianity. The two prostitutes that Titus brings into the Holy of Holies (according to the parallel version in *Lev. Rab.*) are interpreted by Hasan-Rokem as an allusion to Mary, mother of Jesus, and to Mary Magdalene. By contrast, she interprets the scene of the rending of the veil by Titus in a specifically antipagan context. Regarding my own interpretation, which emphasizes the connection between the Jewish story and the Christian legend, she writes that it is "still heavily indebted to strict historical-philological conventions." As far as my work is concerned, the word *still* should have been omitted, because I am interested in understanding the completed literary product and not in discussing its mysterious embryonic existence as a "folk narrative." Therefore, I saw fit to emphasize here, among other meanings (and regarding all the legends of the Destruction), the anti-Christian meaning of the text. Unlike the folklorist, the historian wants to isolate the dominant melody out of a variety of tones, but this does not mean denying the existence of polyphony. Determining which is the main melody, if there is such a thing at all, depends on the historical-cultural context in which the story was shaped, and during the fourth and fifth centuries the quarrel with Christianity had a stronger presence than the quarrel with paganism.

fixion;[45] as mentioned above, they were the first to discuss the perturbing question of why Josephus did not see fit to link the Crucifixion of Jesus with the Destruction. In terms of its ideological components, the legend of *Vindicta Salvatoris* fits the fourth century. It relates to a problem raised by Origen and Eusebius and their contemporaries, but both these Church Fathers found a learned solution to it, attributing to Josephus the opinion that the Destruction was punishment for the Crucifixion of James, Jesus's brother.[46] The solution offered by *Vindicta Salvatoris* is a popular, mythic solution, and there is good reason to date it to the second half of the fourth century, shortly after the episode of Julian, who once again brought to the forefront the Destruction of the Temple and the Jewish-Christian polemic.

This was apparently also when the Jewish legend was created. While some of its motifs are indeed ancient, as may be seen from a comparison with the formulation in *Sifrei*,[47] in its complete form the legend seems to have taken shape in the fourth century. The version in *Leviticus Rabbah* and in *Gittin* reflects a Jewish-Christian dialogue on the Destruction of Jerusalem and the vengeance it entailed. The Christian legend fulfills a central and fundamental purpose, whose necessity for Christianity is obvious—the Crucifixion led to the Destruction and to the Church becoming the new Israel, whereas the Jewish legend appears merely as apologetics. This strengthens our assumption that the Christian legend precedes the Jewish one. Likewise, the exegesis of the words *vespa* = Vespasian seems primary, whereas the play on *yatush* (gnat) and Titus seems forced and may be viewed as a polemical answer to an earlier, more successful wordplay.[48]

LEGENDS OF THE DESTRUCTION—ANTI-CHRISTIAN?

The hypothesis that the legend of the gnat's vengeance on Titus had an anti-Christian aim leads us to a broader examination of the famous collection of legends of the Destruction in the Babylonian Talmud, *Gittin* 55b–57a, which includes the legend of the gnat. I wish to examine here the

45. Wilken (n. 27, p. 40).

46. Z. Baras, "The Testimonium Flavianum and the Martyrdom of James," in *Josephus, Judaism and Christianity,* ed. L. H. Feldman and G. Hata (Detroit, 1987), 338–48.

47. *Sifrei Deut.*, sec. 328, 378–79. The roots of the anti-Christian polemic concerning the Destruction of Jerusalem are clearly inherent in the antipagan polemic mentioned in note 1.

48. For other anti-Christian aspects of this story, see S. Gero, "Jewish Polemic in the Martyrium Pionii and a 'Jesus' Passage from the Talmud," *JJS* 29 (1978): 164–68.

possibility that the editor of this collection sought to invent a Jewish version of the Destruction of the Temple to compete with the Christian interpretation and with parallel Christian legends.

The collection of legends in the Babylonian Talmud possesses a thematic and conceptual coherence, and the various tales are interwoven with one another: beginning with the background to the Destruction (the incident of Qamza and Bar Qamza); continuing with a description of the siege and the severe famine (the story of Martha, daughter of Boethius), the fall of Jerusalem, the establishment of Yavneh (the encounter of Rabban Yohanan ben Zakkai with Vespasian), the punishment of the destroyer of Jerusalem (Titus and the gnat); and concluding with a discussion of Israel's situation in the post-Destruction period (Jesus in the World to Come). The tales are connected by the repetition of certain expressions: "he sent Emperor Nero against them"; "he sent Emperor Vespasian against them"; "he went and sent him to Titus." Abba Sikra is "the son of the sister of Rabban Yohanan ben Zakkai," while, in contrast, Onkelos, the son of Kalonikos, is described as "the son of Titus's sister." The editor wants to connect the end of this series of tales with their beginning by concluding: "See [from this incident] how serious a thing it is to put a man to shame, for the Holy One blessed be He espoused the cause of Bar Qamza and destroyed His House and burnt His Temple"—a sentence referring to the conclusion of the story of Bar Qamza. Such literary threads are also evident in other elements connecting various stories. The calf sent to be sacrificed in Jerusalem is three years old, Vespasian besieges Jerusalem for three years, and three rich men of the city agree to supply provisions to the city during the siege. In the story of Martha, daughter of Boethius, the fast of Rabbi Zadok is mentioned—that same fast that led to Rabban Yohanan ben Zakkai being healed in a different story. The food of Martha, daughter of Boethius, becomes spoiled, turning from fine clean flour to coarse flour, while the remedy of Rabbi Zadok, who stopped his fast, went in the opposite direction: from water with bran to clean fine flour. The same is true of the motif of hunger and food: a series of stories begins with one about a ruined feast, continues with Martha's hunger and Rabbi Zadok's fast, and concludes after Rabban Yohanan ben Zakkai's rescue, when Rabbi Zadok once again eats. The healing of the intestines of Rabbi Zadok, who resumes eating, "until his stomach expanded little by little," is like the "little deliverance" from the emperor enjoyed by Rabban Yohanan ben Zakkai.

The fact that this collection is complete unto itself should lead us to think that its coherence is not only literary but also conceptual and ideological. I do not intend to argue that every one of the legends embedded in this collection was created a priori with an anti-Christian aim, for some of them have earlier parallels in the Palestinian Midrashim, which lack the anti-Christian edge. Yet the possibility that anti-Christian intentions were involved in shaping at least some of these legends should be considered. It is even more surprising that these anti-Christian sentiments were specifically expressed in the Babylonian collection, far from the Land of Israel, indicating that even in Babylonia, Christianity posed a challenge that required confrontation.[49]

A rebuttal of the opponent's version follows the characteristic pattern of Midrashic literature. It is not an explicit rebuttal, but rather an allusive suggestion of an alternative story that negates and opposes the contrary Christian story. The legends of the Destruction, as formulated in the Babylonian Talmud, confronted a well-articulated Christian position linking the Crucifixion of Jesus with the Destruction of the Temple. As noted earlier, such a connection does not appear in Christian literature before the time of Origen; hence, the Babylonian collection could not have been fully shaped before the fourth century c.e. Traces of anti-Christian sentiment may be found in almost every one of these stories.

Qamza and Bar Qamza

This story places the figure of Bar Qamza at the center of the plot. Despite his name (which means "stingy" or "greedy"), he is willing to give away his whole fortune simply to avoid being shamed by "a certain man," an anonymous figure to whose feast he was mistakenly invited. The purpose of the story is double: first, to reduce to the minimum the sin that caused the Destruction. The story is designed to show that Jerusalem was destroyed because of gratuitous hatred and as the result of an utterly peripheral incident—thereby polemicizing with the Christian interpretation ascribing the Destruction to the grave sin of bloodshed, that is, to the Crucifixion.[50] The Talmudic Sages were willing to explain the Destruc-

---

49. These findings confirm the claims of N. Koltun-Fromm, "A Jewish Christian Conversation in Fourth-Century Persian Mesopotamia," *JJS* 47 (1996): 45–63. She pointed out the intense religious polemic between Jews and Christians in fourth-century Babylonia.

50. This interpretation of the story was suggested by my friend Dr. Oded Irshai. See R. Goldenberg, "Early Rabbinic Explanations of the Destruction of Jerusalem," *JJS* 33 (1982): 517–25. Goldenberg caught the trivial nature of the explanations offered by the Talmudic Sages for the Destruction but did not see this as an apologetic stance vis-à-vis Christian criticism. Cf. A. J. Salardini, "Varieties of Rabbinic Response to the Destruction of the Temple," *Society of Biblical Literature, Seminar Paper 21* (Chico, CA, 1982), 437–58.

tion of the First Temple as the result of idolatry, bloodshed, and adultery, but not that of the Second Temple. This is the main goal of the story. The second, more oblique aim, by which the details of the story were shaped, was to describe the motives underlying Bar Qamza's denunciation of the Jews. The plot focuses on a feast given by "a certain man" in the presence of "the Rabbis." We have here a feast given by a particular man in the presence of scholars, during which tension arises between the anonymous host and the future denouncer.

This scene may be meant to suggest the Last Supper of Jesus ("a certain man" = "that son of Man"): he is surrounded by the apostles ("the Rabbis"), and opposite him is Judas Iscariot ("Bar Qamza"), who delivers Jesus to the Romans for pecuniary gain. But the character is inverted by the trait to which his name, Bar Qamza, alludes, namely, "The Greedy One," an allusion refuted by his offer to host the feast—"I will reimburse you for the whole party!"—an offer scornfully rejected by the host. Like Judas Iscariot, Bar Qamza ends up denouncing others to the authorities and causing the Destruction. But in the Talmudic story he is presented as a victim, a man provoked by the unjust embarrassment caused by his host. His denunciation is also reminiscent of the accusation made against Jesus. In the story of Qamza and Bar Qamza, the Jews are accused of rebelling against the emperor, just as Jesus is accused of being the King of the Jews. The Talmudic narrator completely omits the political context of the revolt, not even bothering to mention its outbreak. According to him, the refusal to sacrifice the emperor's offering provided the Romans with the pretext needed to destroy Jerusalem. The connection between the symbolic revolt and the Destruction of Jerusalem seemed sufficient to the editor—a point also compatible with the Christian exegesis, in which the Crucifixion is linked directly with the Destruction and does not require the real political context that led to the outbreak and suppression of the revolt.

Nero in Jerusalem

The response to the "revolt" against the empire was immediate and was attributed to Nero. The Roman emperor came to Jerusalem to capture it from the rebels, but two heavenly signs caused him to change his mind. The second sign was the biblical verse recited to him by a child: "And I will lay my vengeance upon Edom by the hand of my people Israel" (Ezek 25:14). The Talmudic Haggadah substitutes the Jewish story of *Vindicta Dei* for the Christian one of *Vindicta Salvatoris*. The vengeance against Edom, that is, Rome, for the Destruction of the Temple is the Jewish response to the Christian story that sees the Destruction of Jerusalem as God's vengeance for the Crucifixion of Jesus. The verse recited by the child well suits the context of this Jewish answer. In Christian legend the figure of Nero is one of an Antichrist, who in his day was accused by the Christians of burning down Rome and was considered responsible for the martyr's death of Jesus's brother, James. On the other hand, Jewish legend turns Nero into an almost righteous king who understands the heavenly sign and refrains from destroying Jerusalem. The emperor even runs away from his emperorship and converts to Judaism, Rabbi Meir being numbered among his descendants.[51]

Martha, Daughter of Boethius

The Talmudic legend tells how Martha, a wealthy Jerusalem woman, suffered from the severe famine that afflicted the city during the siege. She repeatedly asked her servant to bring her food, but the latter found nothing. In the end, she decided to set out into the street herself, barefoot. Dung stuck to her feet, and she died of disgust; Rabban Yohanan ben Zakkai applied to her this biblical verse: "The most tender and delicately bred woman among you, who would not venture to set the sole of her foot upon the ground because she is so delicate and tender" (Deut 28:56). Scholars have noted the similarity between this Talmudic story and Josephus's story about a woman with a similar name, Mary, daughter of Eliezer, who, owing to the famine, murdered her son and ate his flesh.[52] Naomi Cohen has noted the end of the biblical verse cited in the Talmudic legend, which she sees as the key to understanding the entire legend. The fate of this "delicate woman" will be that she "will begrudge to the husband of her bosom, to her son and to her daughter." These verses are part of the great Rebuke, stating what would happen if Israel did not heed the voice of its God: "All these curses shall come upon you and pursue you and overtake you" (Deut 28:45), the most horrible curse of all being the cannibalism committed by parents who eat the flesh of their children. Josephus's story is designed to

51. According to A. Yisraeli-Taran, *Aggadot ha-Hurban: Mesorot ha-Hurban bassifrut ha-Talmudit* (Tel Aviv, 1997), 27, achieving victory over the enemy by means of his conversion is characteristic of the Babylonian Talmud, as opposed to the Jerusalem Talmud, which prefers the physical destruction of the enemy. See N. Cohen, "Rabbi Meir: A Descendant of Anatolian Proselytes," *JJS* 23 (1972): 51–59.

52. *Bel. Jud.* 6.3.4 sec. 201. A detailed analysis of the story was recently presented by A. Yisraeli-Taran, "Remarks on Josephus Flavius and the Destruction of the Second Temple" [in Hebrew], *Zion* 61 (1996): 148–52.

show that this curse was carried out in the Destruction of Jerusalem. According to Cohen, the Talmudic legend is intended to soften the harsh impression made by Josephus and conducts a tacit polemic with him. In the Talmudic version, this rich woman did not commit cannibalism, but rather died because of her fastidiousness.[53]

This interpretation makes Josephus a target of Rabbinic polemics, raising the question of how well, if at all, the Talmudic Sages knew Josephus—a problem that has preoccupied many scholars. But this Talmudic polemic may be aimed at a target much closer to home: the Church Fathers, who used Josephus's story as propaganda for their cause.[54] Eusebius begins his descriptions, based on Josephus's writings, by stating that it is necessary to mention how the Jews besieged in Jerusalem were suffering from the famine in order to inform the reader that the crimes of the Jews against Jesus brought God's vengeance upon them shortly thereafter.[55]

Eusebius goes on to quote Josephus's story of Mary, daughter of Eliezer, along with other descriptions of the famine in Jerusalem. He sees these events as proof of the fulfillment of Jesus's prophecy about the destruction awaiting Jerusalem. Eusebius thereby continues Origen's position linking the Crucifixion of Jesus with the Destruction. Eusebius explains the long period of forty years between the Crucifixion and the Destruction as a period of grace, during which the Jews were given a final chance to regret their deeds and to ask for forgiveness. The Talmudic Sages likewise ascribed great importance to events that occurred forty years before the Destruction and heralded the impending Destruction—the exile of the Sanhedrin, the abolition of capital law, and so forth.[56] But these events were also intended to deny the connection between the Crucifixion and the Destruction.

If this later Talmudic legend is viewed as a reply to Christian claims, its message becomes transparent. The Jewish claim is that the biblical rebuke was not at all fulfilled during the Destruction. The Talmudic editor adopts

---

53. Naomi Cohen, "The Theological Stratum of the Martha b. Boethus Tradition: An Explication of the Text in *Gittin* 56a," *HTR* 69 (1976): 187–95. Yisraeli-Taran (n. 52, p. 53), n. 56, expressed reservations about Cohen's interpretation, but it seems to me to accord better with the tendency of the editor of the Babylonian Talmud.

54. This passage is quoted extensively in ancient and medieval Christian literature; see H. Schreckenberg, *Die Flavius-Josephus-Tradition in Antike und Mittelalter* (Leiden, 1972), 190.

55. Eusebius, *Hist. Ecc.*, bk. 3, chap. 5.

56. *B. Shabb.* 15a; *b. Yoma* 39b.

Josephus's story, which he knew from Christian propaganda, but neutralizes it, by producing a version that removes the basis for the Christian argument.[57]

Rabban Yohanan ben Zakkai and Vespasian

I have already discussed elsewhere and at length this legend of Rabban Yohanan ben Zakkai and Vespasian, which may be seen as a Jewish counterpart to the fourth-century Christian legend of Sylvester.[58] Following is a short summary. The Christian legend was intended to secure Pope Sylvester's position in Rome by the "donation" granted him by Emperor Constantine. Parallel to this, the Jewish legend was intended to assure the position of the new Jewish leadership—the Nasi (head of the Sanhedrin)—by showing that he had received the recognition of an ancient emperor. The two are similar foundation legends. Just as the pope received the Lateran Church in Rome, so did the Nasi obtain Yavneh. In both stories, the gift is given in reward for healing the emperor of a disease. Constantine is cured of leprosy by Sylvester, while Vespasian is cured of a swollen foot by Rabban Yohanan ben Zakkai. That is why Vespasian, rather than Titus, is presented as the one who besieged Jerusalem. The Jewish legend wished to ascribe the "gift" to an affable emperor, not to the destroyer of Jerusalem.

Titus and the Gnat

As noted earlier, the legend of Titus and the gnat is designed to describe the punishment of the "villain" of the Destruction. This is neither Nero, who, as mentioned earlier, refrained from attacking Jerusalem, nor Vespasian, who graciously granted a "partial salvation" to the Jewish leadership after the Destruction, but Titus, the destroyer of the Temple.

The Conversion of Onkelos

Onkelos wants to convert to Judaism and therefore evokes the shades of three dead men: Titus, Balaam, and Jesus,[59] asking them who is esteemed in the Next World. The first two, Titus and Balaam, testify that Israel alone is esteemed in the Next World, but nevertheless advise Onkelos not to join

---

57. In light of this, the discussion about whether or not the Talmud knew of Josephus assumes a different meaning. The Talmud may have known Josephus indirectly, through its confrontation with the arguments of the Church Fathers.

58. Yuval (n. 36, p. 43).

59. In the Vilna edition, the name Jesus was censored, and in its place the phrase "the criminals of Israel" (posh'ei Yisrael) was substituted.

the nation of Israel. The third figure, Jesus Christ, takes a different position. He also testifies that only Israel is esteemed in the Next World but, unlike his predecessors, he does not defame the Jews but rather advises Onkelos to defend them: "Seek their welfare, seek not their harm. Whoever touches them touches the apple of his eye." This is followed by a sentence that concludes the entire cycle of legends of the Destruction, with mention of the first legend that opened it: "Rabbi Eleazar said: Note how serious a thing it is to put a man to shame, for God espoused the cause of Bar Qamza and destroyed His House and burnt His Temple."

Positioning Jesus's answer at the end of the story and placing this story at the conclusion of the entire cycle of legends of the Destruction indicate the centrality of Jesus's words in connection with the Destruction of Jerusalem. The Jewish legend has Jesus issuing a call to protect the lives of the Jews—a clear echo of Augustine's doctrine, adopted by the Church in the Middle Ages, that forbids doing bodily harm to the Jews. The Destruction of the Temple and the rise of Christianity made it necessary for the Jews to create new frameworks of survival for themselves, and the legend that concludes the cycle is designed to provide a basis for the rights of the Jews through a "command" that came from the mouth of the founder of the new religion, Jesus.

THE PASSOVER OF EGYPT AND THE PASSOVER OF JERUSALEM

The legend of the sons of Ephraim, discussed above, demonstrates the intensive use made of the Exodus from Egypt as a typological model to describe the future Redemption. In twelfth-century Germany and France, it was customary to read the incident of the sons of Ephraim in the Aramaic translation of the Torah portion for the seventh day of Passover and to identify them with the dry bones of Ezekiel's vision.[60] In this way, a connection was drawn between the sons of Ephraim, "the heralds of the deliverance," who had died and were resurrected, on the one hand, and Passover, on the other. This use of Passover as an archetype for the future deliverance transformed the festival into a central focus of tension between Judaism and Christianity. After the Destruction of the Temple, both religions

---

60. *Mahzor Vitry*, 305. On opposition to the identification of the Ephraimites with the dry bones of Ezekiel's vision, see Avigdor Shinan, "An Early Quotation from Targum Pseudo-Jonathan?" [in Hebrew], *Tarbiz* 65 (1996): 331–32.

developed alternative interpretations of this Temple-centered holiday of sacrifice. The history of the seder night, on the one hand, and of Easter, on the other, are both products of this development. Not only do they have a common origin, but there are also many parallels between them, stemming from subsequent relations between the two holidays.

The use of the Exodus as a typological model for the future Redemption explains the spirit and purpose of a number of Passover symbols, which took shape during the first centuries after the Destruction of the Temple. According to Rabbinic tradition, "in Nissan they were redeemed and in Nissan they shall be redeemed in the Time to Come."[61] While the central message of the holiday is the remembrance of the past Redemption,[62] typological exegesis assumes that events of the past are a mirror reflecting the face of the future.[63] Thus, just as the Redemption from Egypt began with

61. *b. R. H.* 11a–b. Cf. *b. Meg.* 6a.

62. *Exod. Rab.* 15.11 also posits a link between Redemption and the Binding of Isaac: "And then [i.e., in Nissan] they shall be redeemed in the future . . . and in this month Isaac was born and in this month he was bound [as a sacrifice]" (cf. *b. R. H.* 11a–b). According to Shalom Spiegel, *The Last Trial*, trans. J. Goldin (New York, 1967), 51–59, the link between Passover and the Binding of Isaac is that the sacrifice and death of the firstborn son has the power to atone and save. Spiegel said of the appearance of the legend that states that Abraham did kill Isaac (or at least shed some of his blood): "It may be that here are the best and faint echoes of some primitive pagan or pre-biblical version of the Akedah story" (57). Spiegel does not explain why these idolatrous "echoes" appeared specifically in tannaitic literature. It may be seen as a response to the Destruction of the Temple and the loss of atonement by means of sacrifice of living creatures, especially in light of the Christian understanding of the Crucifixion. See R. Wilken, "Melito, the Jewish Community at Sardis, and the Sacrifice of Isaac," *Theological Studies* 37 (1976): 53–69; P. R. Davies, "Martyrdom and Redemption: On the Development of Isaac Typology in the Early Church," *Studia Patristica* 17, pt. 2 (1982): 652–58; J. D. Levenson, *The Death and Resurrection of the Beloved Son: The Transformation of Child Sacrifice in Judaism and Christianity* (New Haven, 1993), 173–232.

63. David Berger has recently perceived the centrality of the messianic typological interpretation and its close affinity with the Exodus from Egypt (n. 7, p. 34). He notes four rabbinic calculations of the End, all typological, two of them based on the duration of the Exile in Egypt: the subjugation to Rome will continue for four hundred years, like the Exile in Egypt, and then deliverance will come. These calculations are based on a perception of the Destruction of the Second Temple (in the year 68 C.E. according to Jewish tradition) as the beginning of the exile of Edom; hence the expectation of deliverance in the year 471 C.E. (with the addition of the three years alluded to in the book of Daniel, as Berger explains). Hieronymus, in his commentary to Joel written in the 390s, relates that the Jews in his day believed that, just as the Exile in Egypt lasted 430 years and at its end the Egyptians drowned in the Red Sea, so will the Romans also be destroyed by God's vengeance after 430 years of subjugating Israel; see *Corpus Christianorum, Series Latina* 76, no. 1, *Opera Exegetica* 6 (Turn-

ten plagues, so will the future Redemption begin with the punishment of the Gentile nations. This parallel is formulated very sharply in the Midrash: "All those plagues which the Holy One brought upon the Egyptians, he shall bring upon Edom [i.e., Rome] . . . In Egypt he brought upon them the plague of blood, so too shall it be with Edom [i.e., Rome]."[64] This may be the background for the exegetical passage in the Haggadah that increases the calamities that afflicted Egypt: fifty plagues in Egypt and two hundred and fifty plagues at sea. This multiplication of plagues in Egypt alludes to the magnitude of the calamities that will befall Esau in the future.

This is also the background for the interpretation given in Midrashic literature of the proscription against eating any leavened food on Passover. Whereas in the Bible this law is associated with the memory of the hasty departure from Egypt, in the Rabbinic sources we find a hint of a connection between destroying leaven and eliminating the Gentiles in the future. The second Targum of the Book of Esther has Haman accusing the Jews of believing that, just as they rid their homes of leaven, so will they gain the ruin of the wicked kingdom (Rome) and be rescued from "the foolish king," namely, Ahasuerus.[65] It may, of course, be argued that Haman's claim is a totally unfounded defamation, but it is difficult to assume that the Jews would put completely baseless words into the mouths of Gentiles. And indeed, the Babylonian Talmud (*Pesa.* 5a) states that, by virtue of fulfilling the commandment of removing leaven on Passover, Israel will be worthy of seeing the annihilation of Esau's seed. The symbolic connection between burning leaven and the annihilation of Gentiles at the End of Days is here

---

halt, 1969), 208; Irshai (n. 3, p. 32), 1:165. If we regard the Destruction of the Temple as the beginning of this calculation of the End, then things are directed toward a messianic expectation around the year 500. But it is difficult to assume that during the 390s (at the latest), Hieronymus heard about messianic hopes that were to be realized a hundred years later. This eschatological calculation may have been based on a calculation of the beginning of the exile of Edom with the conquest of Jerusalem by Pompey in 63 B.C.E., an event that put an end to Jewish political independence. If so, this messianic expectation is aimed at the year 367, a date consistent with the expectations evoked by Julian's initiative in 362 to rebuild the Temple. See Wilken (n. 39, p. 45), 453. On the typology in Christianity and Judaism, cf. Amos Funkenstein, "History and Typology: Nahmanides' Reading of the Biblical Narrative," *Perceptions of Jewish History* (Berkeley and Los Angeles, 1993), 98–120.

64. *Tanhuma*, ed. S. Buber, B, 43–44. And see Rabbi Hama bar Hanina in *Pesiqta de-Rav Kahana*, sec. 7, 133 (English translation by W. Braude, p. 121): "He who exacted vengeance from the former [oppressor] will exact vengeance from the latter. Just as in Egypt it was with blood, so with Edom it will be the same."

65. *Targum Sheni to Esth.* 3:8. On the nature of this work, see chap. 3, n. 77.

made explicit. In the Middle Ages, it was repeated by Rabbi Eleazar of Worms, one of the great Jewish sages of Germany in the thirteenth century.[66] But whereas the Talmudic statement was aimed at the destruction of Rome, Rabbi Eleazar's remarks indicate the covert existence of a view that took an obvious step: transfer of the messianic hope from Rome to Christianity.

Not only was the burning of leaven subject to a new interpretation, but so was the Passover sacrifice itself. One Midrash completely reverses the significance of the sacrifice, identifying it with Edom.[67] The biblical verse "Do not eat any not of it raw or boiled with water, but roasted, its head with its legs and its inner parts" (Exod 12:9) is interpreted as referring to Esau and his punishment at the End of Days. Just as the Passover sacrifice is to be roasted whole in fire, and neither to be boiled in water nor eaten raw, so shall be the annihilation of Esau, who will be roasted with his head and his legs and his insides. The negative Jewish identification of the Paschal sacrifice with Esau parallels the positive Christian identification of that same sacrifice with Jesus.

These examples confirm the centrality of Passover as a focus of the religious and emotional tension between the two religions. In medieval Christianity Easter served as a focus of hatred for the Jews. Most of the blood libels and accusations of desecration of the Host took place during Lent or Holy Week. Even though ethically one cannot compare fantasy and action, the historian is duty-bound to depict the language common to the victim and his persecutor and its ideological background.

The introduction of anti-Christian messages into the Jewish holiday of Passover must be explored against the backdrop of the struggle between the two religions over the meaning of the holiday. After the Destruction of the Temple in Jerusalem in 70 C.E., two competing exegeses emerged about Passover, one Jewish and the other Christian. Instead of the ceremony of the Paschal sacrifice, which had vanished, the two religions instituted the ob-

---

66. *Sefer ha-Roqeah* (Jerusalem, 1967), end of sec. 271. Cf. R. Samuel Edel's (Maharsha) commentary ad loc.: "And this is the reason for eliminating leaven on Passover, because the leaven in the dough is the Evil Urge, which is Samael, which is the Prince of Esau, who will be cut off at the time of the Redemption." Cf. Herbert Basser, "Superstitious Interpretations of Jewish Laws," *Journal for the Study of Judaism* 8 (1977): 127–38; M. H. Lerner, "The Leaven Therein" [in Hebrew], *Leshonenu* 53 (1989): 287–90. For more on the subject of eliminating leaven, see chap. 5.

67. *Pesiqta de-Rav Kahana*, sec. 5, ed. Mandelbaum, p. 108 (English translation by W. Braude, p. 121).

ligation to tell the story of an event that took place at Passover. The Jews adhered to the original meaning of the holiday and accordingly instituted the story of the original deliverance from Egypt, a model for future deliverance; the Christians introduced the story of the final deliverance of Jesus in Jerusalem and the expectation of his future, second coming (Parousia).[68] The two stories were intended not only to provide a liturgical substitute for the sacrifice but also to cope with a difficult and painful challenge: how to celebrate a holiday of deliverance at a time of destruction and political subjugation. The new story, which begins with the "disgrace" of slavery in Egypt or the Crucifixion in Jerusalem and ends with the "glory" of deliverance, contains consolation and hope for the future, for Jews and Christians respectively.

The parallel development of two different narratives of the same holiday among two rival groups living in close proximity necessarily engenders great similarity as well as mutual tensions, and they need to be discussed together. The similarity was especially great during the early centuries of the Common Era, when the two religions confronted a common enemy: paganism. In the Western Church, there was a strong tendency to break with Jewish origins and to fix Easter on Sunday. However, the Quartodecimani in the Eastern Churches insisted on celebrating Easter on the fourteenth day of the month of Nissan (hence the name)—that is, on the date of the Jewish Passover.[69] This custom, widespread among the churches in Asia Minor and Syria, originated in the Land of Israel. While the Western tradition emphasized Jesus's resurrection from the dead on Sunday, the Eastern tradition emphasized the story of the Crucifixion on the fifteenth day of the month of Nissan. In the late second century, Pope Victor attempted to force the entire Christian world to celebrate Easter on Sunday and to declare the Quartodecimani heretics, but these extreme steps encountered opposition even among those groups that celebrated Easter on Sunday.[70] Nevertheless, this custom gradually became universal, and the Nicean Coun-

68. J. Jeremias, *The Eucharistic Words of Jesus* (New York, 1955).

69. On the celebration of Passover among the Quartodecimani, see B. Lohse, *Das Passafest der Quartadecimaner* (Guetersloh, 1953); W. Huber, *Passa und Ostern: Untersuchungen zur Osterfeier der alten Kirche* (Berlin, 1969); T. J. Talley, *The Origins of the Liturgical Year* (New York, 1986), 1–37; S. G. Hall, "The Origins of Easter," *Studia Patristica* 15 (1984): 554–67. I have adopted the spelling "Quartodecimani" rather than "Quartadecimani," following Huber, *Passa und Ostern,* 5–6 n. 35; but see Lohse, *Passafest,* 9 n. 1.

70. J. A. Fischer, "Die Synoden im Osterfeststreit des 2. Jahrhunderts," *Annuarium Historiae Concilliorum* 8 (1976): 15–39; T. C. G. Thornton, "Problematical Passovers: Difficulties

cil of 325 fixed the date of Easter on the first Sunday after the middle of the first lunar month following the spring equinox.[71] As a result of this decision, the Quartodecimani tradition became heretical, although it persisted until the fifth century, when it disappeared and was forgotten. In this way the Christian Easter became separate from the Jewish Passover, even though the two holidays still remained quite close to one another, since the middle of the lunar month following the equinox usually corresponds to the middle of the month of Nissan.

The long process of obscuring the Jewish origin of Easter reached its climax with the decision of the Nicean Council. I wish to argue here that a similar tendency of denying the rival is also evident in the most ancient components of the Passover Haggadah. I would suggest that the contents of the Passover Haggadah—as well as the very obligation to tell the story of the Exodus—are not merely an outcome of coping with the vacuum left by the Destruction of the Temple and the resultant cessation of the Paschal sacrifice[72] but are also a response to the challenge posed by the Christian interpretation of the holiday. Several of the earliest components of the Haggadah reflect a conscious struggle to emphasize the validity of the Jewish interpretation of the festival alongside a covert rejection of an alternative Christian interpretation, which developed at the same time and against a similar background.[73] These are two complementary processes: an exter-

---

for Diaspora Jews and Early Christians in Determining Passover Dates During the First Three Centuries A.D.," *Studia Patristica* 20 (1989): 402–8.

71. L. Duchesne, "La question de la Pâque au Concil de Nicée," *Revue des questions historiques* 28 (1880): 5–42. On the contents of the celebration of Easter among the Quartodecimani just prior to the Nicean Council, see G. A. M. Rouwhorst, *Les hymnes Pascales d'Ephrem de Nisibe* (Leiden 1989), 1:128–205.

72. This aspect of the seder's development was correctly emphasized by Barukh Bokser, *The Origins of the Seder* (New York, 1984); cf. his "Ritualizing the Seder," *Journal of the American Academy of Religion* 56 (1988): 443–71.

73. Confrontation with Christianity in general, and with Jewish Christianity in particular, was at the heart of tannaitic concerns, as may be seen in the sources and scholarly literature. I shall mention here only the most prominent studies: T. Herford, *Christianity in Talmud and Midrash* (London, 1903); Lawrence H. Schiffman, "At the Crossroads: Tannaitic Perspectives on the Jewish-Christian Schism," in *Jewish and Christian Self-Definition*, vol. 2, ed. E. P. Sanders, A. I. Baumgarten, and A. Mendelson (Philadelphia, 1981), 115–56; Reuven Kimelman, "Birkat Ha-Minim and the Lack of Evidence for an Anti Christian Jewish Prayer in Late Antiquity," in *Jewish and Christian Self-Definition*, 2:224–26; Marc Hirshman, *A Rivalry of Genius: Jewish and Christian Biblical Interpretation in Late Antiquity* (Albany, 1996). The sages of the Mishnah and the Talmud displayed extensive knowledge of ancient Christian literature. See J. Schwartz, "Ben Stada and Peter in Lydda," *Journal for the Study of Judaism* 21 (1990): 1–18;

nal polemic, on the one hand, and a redefinition of one's identity, on the other. In the Haggadah itself, there is no explicit reference to Christianity. A liturgical text, intended mainly to express what is shared and acceptable to the community of worshipers, may make do with alluding to a rejected, alternative interpretation.

DEVELOPMENT OF THE STORIES

Any discussion of the Jewish and the Christian stories ought to begin by presenting the similarity in the development of the two, and of the accompanying ceremonies. The Passover Haggadah tells of five *tannaim* (Mishnaic Sages) "who were seated [at a banquet] in B'nai-Berak and told of the Exodus from Egypt that entire night," until their students came and reminded them that "it [was] time to recite the morning *Shema.*"[74] The *Tosefta* relates a similar tale of Rabban Gamaliel II and the elders who were seated at Lydda "and engaged in the laws of Passover the entire night until cockcrow."[75] The frame story is similar, but the contents are different. The group in B'nai Berak spent the night telling the story of the Exodus from Egypt, while Rabban Gamaliel's group engaged in studying the laws of the Paschal sacrifice, in remembrance of the Temple. In the Passover Haggadah, this passage is followed by the words of Rabbi Eleazar ben Azariah and Ben Zoma, who thought that the obligation to remember the Exodus applied at night as well as during the day. Also presented is the opinion of the Sages, that remembrance of the Exodus will not be annulled even after the coming of the Messiah.[76] These opinions and their inclusion in the Haggadah, as well as

---

and see also B. Visotzky, "Overturning the Lamp," *JJS* 38 (1987): 72–80, reprinted in his *Fathers of the World: Essays in Rabbinic and Patristic Literatures* (Tübingen, 1995), 75–84.

74. In a series of articles, Rabbi M. Hershkovitz argues that the gathering in B'nai Berak was intended to launch a struggle against the Christian heretics, since in other contexts it is told that each of its participants adopted anti-Christian or anti-Roman positions. See "The Gathering in B'nai Berak" [in Hebrew], *Or ha-Mizrah* 26 (1978): 71–91; Hershkovitz, "The Tannaim Who Waged War Against Christianity" [in Hebrew], *Or ha-Mizrah* 26 (1978): 229–46; 28 (1980): 62–78, 193–205, 332–49; 29 (1981): 404–14; 30 (1982): 75–89.

75. *t. Pes.* 10.12, ed. Lieberman (New York, 1962), 198.

76. Goldschmidt finds it difficult to understand the connection between the story of the Sages who "tell" of the Exodus on the night of Passover and the obligation to "remember" the Exodus every night of the year, not just on Passover. See Daniel Goldschmidt, *Haggadah shel Pesah ve-toldoteha* (Jerusalem, 1969), 21. Below I shall attempt to offer a solution to that problem.

the tales told of the great Sages and their practices on that night, suggest that the practice of telling the story of the Exodus (studying the laws of the festival) on the seder night was an innovation of the generation of Yavneh. Indeed, such a practice was not known during the Temple period.[77]

77. Many scholars have assumed that the Haggadah existed even before the Destruction of the Temple. Finkelstein wished to date its origins even before the Hasmoneans. See Louis Finkelstein, "The Oldest Midrash: Pre-Rabbinic Ideals and Teachings in the Passover Haggadah," *HTR* 31 (1938): 291–317; Finkelstein, "Pre-Maccabean Documents in the Passover Haggadah," *HTR* 35 (1942): 291–332; "Pre-Maccabean Documents in the Passover Haggadah," *HTR* 36 (1943): 1–39. Goldschmidt, *Haggadah*, 31–39, rejects his approach; although he himself believes that the most ancient parts of the Haggadah were written in the period of the Temple (see, e.g., *Haggadah*, 18, 39, 50), he adopts (on page 55 n. 77d) the opinion of G. Alon, who writes that although there is no "convincing evidence" that the Haggadah was used at the time of the Temple, "it is plausible that it did exist." See Gedaliah Alon, *The Jews in their Land in the Talmudic* Age, trans. G. Levi (Jerusalem, 1980), 1:261–65. Zeitlin likewise asserted that the Passover Haggadah was not created before the third century C.E.; see Solomon Zeitlin, "The First Night of Passover," *JQR* 38 (1948): 431–60. Ephraim E. Urbach tried to infer, from Philo's words "to fulfill the custom of the fathers through prayer and song" that the "prayer" refers to the reading of the verses from the passage dealing with firstfruits, Deut 26 (on which the Midrash of the Haggadah is based). Thus, Urbach assumed, without any evidence, that "the ancient custom was to read this Torah portion upon bringing the Passover offering." See Urbach's review of Goldschmidt's Haggadah [in Hebrew], *Kirjath Sepher* 36 (1961): 144–145. And see J. Tabori, "On the Text of the Haggadah in Temple Times" [in Hebrew], *Sinai* 82 (1978): 97–108; Tabori, "The Paschal 'Hagiga': Myth or Reality?" [in Hebrew], *Tarbiz* 64 (1994): 49. Tabori assumes that the obligation to tell of the Exodus was in force also at the time of the Temple. In the Haggadah itself there is nothing to indicate its composition before the Destruction, nor is there any source prior to the Destruction that would indicate the practice of telling the Exodus from Egypt. The only known liturgy for Passover from the time of the Temple is the recitation of the Hallel (*m. Pes.* 5.7; Matt 26:30; Mark 14:26). One of the innovations of Beit Hillel was to add Psalm 114 ("When Israel went out of Egypt") to the Hallel in order to mention the Exodus from Egypt at night (*t. Pes.* 10.9, ed. Lieberman, p. 198). It is plausible that the obligation to tell the Exodus from Egypt developed from this after the Destruction. In illuminating conversations I held on the eve of Passover in 1995 with Dr. Shlomo Cohen of Philadelphia, he raised three further arguments that strengthen the assumption that the Haggadah was not recited during the time of the Temple. First, that *m. Pesahim* 9.3 speaks only of eating the Passover sacrifice and reciting Hallel and does not mention the story of the Exodus from Egypt. Second, the *Tosefta* to *Pesahim* 10 also discusses the recitation of Hallel alone; secs. 12–13 mentions the custom of Rabban Gamaliel and the elders to study the Passover laws, but there is no allusion here either to the obligation to tell the Exodus from Egypt. This text amazed the Gaon, Rabbi Elijah of Vilna, so much that he saw fit to alter it without any manuscript evidence: in place of the phrase "to engage in the laws of Passover," he wrote, "to relate the Exodus from Egypt" (and compare this with the corrected version of Rabbi Jonah of Geronda, cited by Saul Lieberman, *Tosefta ki-feshutah, Pesahim* [New York, 1962], 655). Third, *b. Pes.* 85b says, "[they ate] an olive's-worth of the Passover offering

A similar practice, imparting to the holiday the contents of a redemption story, began to spread about the same time among the early Christian communities, but they recalled and related the story of the Passion of Jesus, not that of Egypt. The first report appears in the apocryphal work *Epistula Apostolorum*, written in the third quarter of the second century C.E.,[78] which states that Jesus revealed himself to his apostles and commanded them to celebrate Passover by commemorating his death. He told them that, while celebrating this festival, one of them would be imprisoned for his faith and would suffer greatly because he would be prevented from celebrating with the other apostles, but Jesus promised to send an angel to rescue him: the doors of the prison would open, the prisoner would go free, and he would be able to "watch" with the rest of the group and to rest. At cockcrow, when the apostles end their remembrance of Jesus's death, the prisoner would return to his cell.

Jesus's words to his apostles allude to the release of Peter from prison on Passover, as related in Acts 12.[79] This story is a Midrash constructed according to the topos of the Exodus from Egypt.[80] Herod, who imprisons Peter, corresponds to Pharaoh; the angel who releases him corresponds to Moses; and Peter is like the enslaved nation of Israel. The angel awakens Peter at night—"and a light shone in the cell" (Acts 12:7)—parallel to the Haggadah's "and He brought us out from darkness to a great light." The angel urges Peter to hurry and flee from the cell, and his words, "Get up quickly . . . Dress yourself and put on your sandals" (Acts 7–8), parallel Exodus 12:11: "In this man-

---

and [said] the Hallel—and the roofs split." This is an ancient maxim describing the celebration of Passover before the Destruction, and there is no mention of the Haggadah.

78. *Epistula Apostolorum*, 15. See J. K. Elliott, *The Apocryphal New Testament* (Oxford, 1993), 565; Schneemelcher (n. 30, p. 30) (English translation, 1: 257–58).

79. W. Strobel, "Passa-Symbolik und Passa-Wunder in Act XII. 3ff," *New Testament Studies* 4 (1957): 210–15. According to Schwartz (n. 73, p. 61), the Talmudic story of Ben-Stada who was killed in Lydda on Passover eve (*b. Sanh.* 67a) is a Jewish version of this episode.

80. W. Rordorf, "Zum Ursprung des Osterfestes am Sonntag," *Theologische Zeitschrift* 18 (1962): 183ff. But note Huber's reservations about this (n. 69, p. 60), 45–46. And cf. J. Manek, "The New Exodus in the Books of Luke," *Novum Testamentum* 2 (1958): 8–23. In *Exod. Rab.* 15.11, a similar exegesis is brought about Nissan as the month of deliverance: "It can be compared to a king who brought his son out of prison and who commanded: 'celebrate for all time as a day of rejoicing the day on which my son went forth from darkness to light, from an iron yoke to life, from servitude to freedom, and from bondage to redemption. Similarly, God brought Israel out of captivity . . . hence did He fix this month as a season of rejoicing for them that He had avenged them of their enemies, as it is said 'therefore will I give men for thee' (Isa 43:4)."

ner you shall eat it: your loins girded, your sandals on your feet." The four jail watchmen recall the symbolism of the four kingdoms and the idea that the deliverance from Egypt may be interpreted as a personal story recalls the Mishnah in *Pesahim* 10.5: "In every generation a person is duty-bound to regard himself as if he personally has gone forth from Egypt."

Luke, the author of Acts, does not state that this episode took place on the night of Passover, but this is how the story is understood in *Epistula Apostolorum*. According to this source, the Christian group celebrated Passover by remembering the death and suffering of Jesus in a celebration that went on all night "until cockcrow." Jesus revealed himself to the apostles and told how he had rescued Peter from prison—revealing a clear affinity to the characteristic of Passover night as a night of vigil.[81] But his deliverance lasted only a short time. Only the night of vigil (i.e., Passover) can facilitate the salvation; at its end, Peter must return to the task appointed him, to suffer as a martyr. Hence, the apostles conclude that Jesus's suffering on the Cross was not enough, and that they must suffer as he did and ask: "How long?" Jesus's answer is that their suffering, along with that of all those killed for their faith in him, will be necessary until his Second Coming. The meaning is clear: Jesus's Parousia will only occur once the measure of suffering in his name and of testifying adherence to him is full.

The external similarity between the Christian source and the Passover Haggadah is striking. The five *tannaim* also sat and spoke of the Exodus "that entire night," while Rabban Gamaliel and the elders were engaged with the laws of Passover "until cockcrow." Cockcrow marks the return to routine: Peter returns to prison, and the time has come for the morning *Shema*.[82] Groups of sages (in the Christian story, the apostles) gather outside their homes to tell the story of deliverance. The nonfamilial nature of the Jewish gathering apparently changed during the second century, no longer continuing all night. These changes occurred as the seder began to take shape and with the emphasis on the father's obligation to "tell" his son:

81. *Tg. Ps.-J.* to Exod 12:42: "It is a night that is watched and set aside for deliverance in the name of the Lord"; R. Le Deaut, *La nuit pascale: Essai sur la signification de la Pâque juive à partir du Targum d'Exode XII 42* (Rome, 1963). The *Epistula Apostolorum* (n. 78, p. 64) says that Jesus is to reappear between Pentecost and the next Passover, sec. 17; but according to Talmudic tradition the Messiah is to appear in the month of Nissan (*b. R. H.* 11a–b; and cf. *b. Meg.* 6a; Le Deaut, *La nuit pascale*, 214–337.)

82. On the cockcrow in ancient Christianity, see "Gallicinium," *Dictionnaire d'archéologie chrétienne et de liturgie* (Paris, 1924), 4:593–96.

perhaps it was then that it became a family celebration and concluded at midnight. The *Quartodecimani,* in contrast, continued celebrating until dawn, and theirs was not a family celebration.[83]

The function of the story about the Sages of B'nai Berak was apparently to establish the new obligation to tell the story of the Exodus at the seder. The passage, along with the opinions of Rabbi Eleazar ben Azariah, Ben Zoma, and the Sages about remembering the Exodus at night and during the days of the Messiah, also seems to have been embedded in the Haggadah for the same purpose.[84] Rabbi Eleazar ben Azariah said: "I am nearly seventy years old and I never merited to recite the Exodus from Egypt in the nighttime until Ben Zoma explained it by expounding [the verse]: 'That all the days of your life you may remember the day when you came out of the land of Egypt' [Deut 16:3]. [The phrase] 'the days of your life' implies the days; 'all the days of your life' implies the nights [as well]." This statement is presented in the Haggadah to establish the commandment to speak of the Exodus at the seder. The event described occurred when Rabbi Eleazar ben Azariah was old, apparently around the year 120 C.E. Previously, it would seem, the custom was to expound the laws of the Paschal sacrifice and pos-

83. Lohse (n. 69, p. 60), 49; Huber (n. 69, p. 60), 9. According to *m. Pes.* 10.9, the celebration of the sacrifice ended at midnight.

84. The words of Rabbi Eleazar are cited in *m. Ber.* 1.10 regarding the time for the recitation of *Shema* or some other recitation, but not concerning the section of *tzitzit* in the recitation of the *Shema,* for this section is not recited at night at all (*m. Ber.* 2.2). Commentators on the Mishnah and the Tosefta state simply that the words of Rabbi Eleazar ben Azariah do not refer to the reading of the Haggadah; see S. Lieberman, *Tosefta Ki-feshutah, Berakhot* (New York, 1955), 12; but the version in the Jerusalem Talmud (evidently influenced by the Haggadah) and in many Haggadah editions reads, "and Rabbi Eleazar ben Azariah said to them," according to which his words were addressed to the Sages gathered in B'nai-Berak. This clearly seems to have been the view of the editor of the Haggadah, for otherwise what point would there be to including this passage, which is not connected with the night of Passover? Hence, we may infer that there was a tradition that saw in the words of Rabbi Eleazar ben Azariah some connection to the beginning of the custom to relate the Exodus story at the seder. This tradition does not necessarily contradict what is stated in *Mishnah Berakhot.* The institution of the commandment to tell of the Exodus on Passover night may have influenced the remembrance of the Exodus from Egypt on other days of the year as well. Lieberman's argument, that Rabbi Eliezer ben Hyrcanus could not have been alive when Rabbi Eleazar ben Azariah was seventy years old, does not overrule explicit textual testimony. Together with this, one should note that the practice of mentioning (although not telling) the Exodus from Egypt at the seder is the essence of the Hallel, which was already customary during the time of the Temple (n. 77, p. 63).

sibly even to eat a roasted lamb, in memory of the sacrifice.[85] The story of the group of *tannaim* who gathered in B'nai Berak—perhaps in opposition to the position of the Nassi, Rabban Gamaliel II—is therefore a kind of "foundation story" of the new requirement to tell the story of the Exodus on the night of Passover as a substitute for the ceremony of the sacrifice; Ben Zoma's homily in turn provides the Midrashic basis for the innovation introduced in B'nai Berak. The words of the Sages, who interpreted the biblical phrase "all the days of your life" to include "messianic times," may be understood in this context as covert criticism of those messianic Jews who wished to obscure the memory of the Exodus from Egypt and to tell a different, contemporary Passover story—that of the Passion of Jesus, based on Jeremiah 23:7–8; 31:30.[86] The Sages, by contrast, insist that the obligation to recite the story of the Exodus from Egypt should be perpetual, like the commandments given at Sinai, which the Christians considered to be annulled. The Sages interpreted this biblical verse as proving that this commandment would not be annulled, even after the coming of the Messiah.[87]

Those two passages are in turn supported by an earlier one: "We were slaves unto Pharaoh in Egypt," which was also evidently designed to establish the new practice of telling the Exodus story: "Had not the Holy One blessed be He brought our fathers out of Egypt, we and our children

---

85. *m. Beitzah* 2.7. It was Rabban Gamaliel, as opposed to the Sages, who instructed them to make a roasted lamb. On this custom, see Bokser (n. 72, p. 61), 101–6, and for more details, see J. Tabori, *Pesah Dorot* (Tel Aviv, 1996), 92–105. This practice of Rabban Gamaliel may have been linked to his custom of expounding on the laws of the Paschal sacrifice at the seder night. Thus, he preserved the connection between the celebration of the seder and the Passover sacrifice, while the sages of B'nai Berak distanced themselves from mentioning the sacrifice, perhaps because of the claims of the heretics, and concentrated on the story of the Exodus from Egypt.

86. Cf. 1 Cor 11:26: "For as often as you eat this bread and drink the cup, you proclaim the Lord's death *until he comes.*" And note Aphrahat's *Demonstration 12,* which discusses Passover. See Jacob Neusner, *Aphrahat and Judaism: The Christian-Jewish Argument in Fourth-Century Iran* (Leiden, 1971), 31–40. Aphrahat was a Christian bishop who lived in Babylonia in the first half of the fourth century. His work bears a considerable resemblance to the Passover Haggadah.

87. S. T. Lachs, "A Polemical Element in Mishnah Berakot," *JQR* 56 (1965): 81–84, was the first to notice this. See also S. H. Levey, "Ben Zoma, the Sages, and Passover," *Journal of Reform Judaism* 28 (1981): 33–40; Levey sensed the polemical sting, but his conjecture that Ben Zoma was a secret Christian-Jew is speculative. The *Tosefta* (*t. Ber.* 1.10–13) presents long and detailed exegeses to prove the biblical source of rabbinic sayings, whose very elaborateness seems to indicate an attempt to refute opposed opinions.

and our children's children would still be enslaved to a Pharaoh in Egypt. And even if we were all wise, and we were all perceptive, and we were all elders, and all versed in the Torah, it would nevertheless be our duty to tell of the Exodus from Egypt." These words could have been directed against those who doubted the relevance of the story of the ancient deliverance from Egypt. Once again, the alternative Christian story is playing in the background, offering a much more contemporary substitute to the Exodus story.

PARALLELS BETWEEN THE JEWISH HAGGADAH AND THE CHRISTIAN "HAGGADAHS"

The new Passover liturgy—the story and the remembering—was created in Judaism and Christianity in parallel fashion. In both religions, the contents of the Passover night were shaped by a story that begins in "disgrace" and ends in "glory," a story intended to offer consolation and hope for Redemption. The stories themselves are quite different from one another, but despite their differences, there are clear textual parallels between them, which have engaged scholars of Christian liturgy and patristics. The scholarly *opinio communis* is that the parallels are the result of the absorption of ancient Jewish ceremonies and texts into the Christian tradition, based on the common notion that the Passover Haggadah reflects an ancient Jewish composition from the Second Temple period. It was therefore natural that these parallels did not elicit much excitement among scholars of Judaica, who were less interested in tracing the late transformations of ancient Jewish traditions within Christianity. Yet more than fifty years ago, two very important Christian texts were discovered that justify a reexamination of our understanding of the relationship between the Talmudic Passover and the Christian Easter, particularly that of the *Quartodecimani*. One is the homily *Peri Pascha* by Melito of Sardis, and the other is a work of the same name by Origen.[88]

Melito was bishop of Sardis and wrote his work in the 170s C.E.[89] In it

---

88. For Melito's work, see Melito of Sardis, *On Pascha and Fragments*, ed. S. G. Hall (Oxford, 1979). This work was identified in 1936 by C. Bonner, "The Homily on the Passion by Melito Bishop of Sardis," *Mélanges F. Cumont*, Annuaire de l'institut de philologie et d'histoire orientale et slave 4 (Brussels, 1936), 107–19; Bonner, "The New Homily of Melito and its Place in Christian Literature," *Actes du Ve congrès international de papyrologie* (Oxford, 1937), 94–97. For Origen's work, see Origen, *Treatise on the Passover*, trans. R. J. Dally (New York, 1992). This work was discovered in Egypt in 1941.

89. Melito of Sardis, *On Pascha*, xii.

he tells of a visit he made to the Land of Israel,[90] and he may have incorporated things that he saw and heard from Jewish-Christians. In 1960 one of the great scholars of the Haggadah, Daniel Goldschmidt, published his edition of the Passover Haggadah without any mention of Melito's name.[91] In 1984 Baruch Bokser's study of the sources of the seder appeared; he briefly mentions conclusions reached by scholars on Melito, but his discussion of all the Christian sources takes up only four pages in his book, and he regards these sources as additional, external, and hostile testimonies on the development of the festival, which he sees as a thoroughly internal Jewish matter. The possibility that the Christian position had any influence on the Jewish one, and was not merely influenced by it, is not even considered.

Indeed, there is no doubt that the notion of Passover as a holiday of sacrifice and redemption has a Jewish biblical origin and that many Christian customs are based on Jewish ones. It may also be assumed that, in the case of a parallel between a later Midrashic text and an earlier Christian text, the later Jewish text does at times reflect an earlier tradition, owing to the oral nature of the Talmudic and Midrashic literature and its late literary formation. But there are no grounds to support the approach that gives automatic chronological primacy to every Midrashic text, even when it is hundreds of years later than the parallel Christian text.[92] The Jewish view, which regards ancient Christianity solely as influenced and not as influencing, is also based on the theological custom of considering Judaism as the mother religion of Christianity. However, as discussed above, the historical criticism ought to lead us to the conclusion that ancient Christianity and Mishnaic Judaism are in a certain sense two sister religions that took shape in the same period and with a common background of subjugation and destruction.[93] Hence, there is no reason not to assume that there was at times a parallel and even common development of the two religions, dur-

90. Melito of Sardis, (n. 88, p. 68), 76.

91. Even in critical reviews of the second edition of Goldschmidt's *Haggadah* (of 1960), there is no mention of parallel Christian literature. See Urbach, (n. 77, p. 63), 143–50; Y. Heinemann, "E. D. Goldschmidt's *Haggada Shel Pesah vetoldoteha*" [in Hebrew], *Tarbiz* 30 (1961): 405–10.

92. Compare Visotzky's correct comments in his book (n. 73, p. 61), 5–10, 62, 113. For a typical example of Christian influence on Jewish Midrashim on the Binding of Isaac and its connection to Passover, see P. R. Davies, "Passover and the Dating of the Aqedah," *JJS* 30 (1979): 59–67.

93. See A. F. Segal, *Rebecca's Children: Judaism and Christianity in the Roman World* (Cambridge, MA, 1986).

ing which Judaism also internalized religious ideas from its sister and rival religion. These two religions did not emerge as two separate entities with clear identities. During the second and third centuries there were all kinds of Jews and all kinds of Christians, all of them engaged in the struggle against pagan Rome, hence their agreement on the centrality of the messianic idea and the centrality of Passover. The mutual flow of ideas between Jews and Christians during this period and in this context should be considered a more plausible possibility.

An illuminating example of the problematic nature of viewing Judaism as the source of every Christian ceremony or text is the parallel between the *Improperia* prayer, recited on Good Friday, and the poem *Dayyenu* in the Passover Haggadah. The similarity between the two texts is striking, and while Eric Werner and Stuart Hall broadened the terms of discussion of this problem,[94] they both accepted Goldschmidt's claim that *Dayyenu* was composed during the last century of the Second Temple period,[95] therefore concluding that the Jewish liturgical poem is the source of the Christian prayer. But this assumption is very tenuous. Goldschmidt himself stated correctly that there is no trace of this liturgical poem in tannaitic or amoraic literature.[96] The earliest evidence of *Dayyenu* is from the tenth century, where it appears in the Haggadah of Rabbi Saadya Gaon among the optional additions to the statutory text of the Haggadah. Yet while the *Improperia* is itself Byzantine, its source, as Werner clarified, came earlier—namely, Melito of Sardis's *Peri Pascha:*

Ungrateful Israel . . .
How much did you value the ten plagues?
How much did you value the nightly pillar and the daily cloud
And the crossing of the Red Sea?

94. E. Werner, "Melito of Sardis, the First Poet of Deicide," *HUCA* 37 (1966): 191–210; Werner, "Zur Textgeschichte der Improperia," in *Festschrift Bruno Stäblein zum 70. Geburtstag,* ed. M. Ruhnke (Kassel, 1967), 274–86; Werner, *The Sacred Bridge* (New York, 1984), 2:127–48; S. G. Hall, "Melito in the Light of the Passover Haggadah," *Journal of Theological Studies* 22 (1971): 29–46.

95. Goldschmidt (n. 76, p. 62), 50. Finkelstein maintained a similar view; see (n. 77, p. 63, his 1943 article, 73). He wished to date *Dayyenu* back to the beginning of the third century B.C.E., but his theory lacks substantive proof.

96. Goldschmidt (n. 76, p. 62), 48. Hoffmann offered convincing arguments that this *piyyut* is later; see L. A. Hoffmann, *Beyond the Text: A Holistic Approach to Liturgy* (Bloomington, 1987), 195–96 n. 46.

How much did you value the giving of manna from heaven
And the supply of water from a rock,
And the law-giving at Horeb
And the inheritance of the land?[97]

Dayyenu was probably created long before the tenth century, when it first appears in our literature. But is it correct to assume that a Jewish text whose earliest known documentation is from the tenth century is the source for a Christian text clearly dating from the second century? Under these circumstances, *Dayyenu* should be seen as part of the Jewish-Christian dialogue and as a response to the Christian accusations of the ingratitude of the Jews. Praise for the kindness of God, who takes his people out of Egypt, leads them through the desert, and brings them to the Promised Land, is found in Psalms 136. A similar thematic pattern appears in the criticism of Israel's ingratitude found in Psalms 78 and 106. Melito used the critical biblical model and, as far as we know, was the first to connect it with Passover.[98]

The literal meaning of the word *Eucharist*—the ceremony of sacrifice in the Christian Mass imitating the Last Supper of Passover—is gratitude and thanks. Thus, it parallels the Jewish Hallel, the earliest component of the seder, which was practiced even during the period of the Temple. Both the Jewish Passover seder and the Christian Eucharist carried into the second century the character of the Greek Agape (Love Feast), to which paupers and widows were invited to eat together and to praise God.[99] This is the

97. Melito of Sardis (n. 88, p. 68), secs. 87–88; cf. secs. 84–86.

98. J. H. Charlesworth, ed., *The Old Testament Pseudephigrapha* (New York, 1983), 525. *V Ezra* also presents an anti-Jewish poem in the same vein; see Werner, in his 1966 article (n. 94, p. 70), 208–9, and also this work is Christian; see David Flusser, "Some Notes on Easter and the Passover Haggadah," *Immanuel* 7 (1977): 52–60. The string of Christian legends, *Actus Pilati*, also includes such accusations (Werner, his 1966 article, 195). The Christian accusation is clearly understood as a reply to the Hallel, which was customarily recited during the Temple period. The Jews, praising God for the first deliverance from Egypt, were seen by the Christians as deserving condemnation for their acts in the Crucifixion. In terms of intellectual development as well, it makes far more sense to assume that the Christian critique, turning the Jewish Hallel on its head, predated the Jewish response of *Dayyenu*. Another Christian liturgical poem parallel to *Dayyenu* is that of Aphrahat; see Rouwhorst (n. 71, p. 61), 2.117.

99. On the similarity between the seder and the Agape, see A. Sulzbach, "Die drei Worte des Seder-Abends," *Jeschurun* 4 (1917): 216–19. On the Christian Agape feast, see Acts 2:42–47; Luke 6:39–44; 1 Cor 11:17–34. In the fourth century, the celebrations of the Agape were abolished. Compare S. Stein, "The Influence of Symposia Literature on the Literary Form of the

context for understanding the dialogue between the *Improperia* and *Dayyenu*. The Christian prayer accuses the Jews of ingratitude, while the Jewish prayer denies the charge. The conclusion of the liturgical poem—"and he built us the Temple to atone for all our sins"—suggests that the end result was immanent in the mind of the writer from the outset. The author wants to emphasize that the sacrifices and the Temple atone for sin, while Christianity attributes atoning power to the Crucifixion of Jesus.[100] The location of this *piyyut* in the middle of the Haggadah and immediately preceding Rabban Gamaliel's words directed against heretics (discussed below) indicates the importance of the Jewish response to these accusations.

This dialogic link between a Jewish text inserted in the Haggadah and a Christian text may also shed new light on the opening statement of the Haggadah: "This is the bread of affliction that our forefathers ate in the land of Egypt." These words clearly seem to be aimed at the Christian liturgical use of Jesus's words concerning the bread at the Last Supper: "This is my body which is given for you: Do this in remembrance of me" (Luke 22:19) or "This is the bread . . . the bread which I shall give . . . is my flesh" (John 6:50–51). The liturgical purpose of Jesus's words is made clear by the words "do this in remembrance of me" and by Paul's formulation "this is my body, which is broken for you; do this in remembrance of me" (1 Cor 11:24). In Matthew 26:26, the formulation also includes an invitation to eat: "Take, eat; this is my body"—an invitation reminiscent of that in the Haggadah: "Let all who are hungry come and eat." The Christian interpretation of the bread of affliction is the deliverance of Jesus, while the Jewish interpretation is the deliverance from Egypt. Here too, one may argue

---

Pesah Haggadah," *JJS* 8 (1957): 13–44. Huber noted the difference between the Eucharist, symbolizing Jesus's sacrifice and salvation in the past, and the Agape feast, which signifies the Parousia and the future salvation. See Huber (n. 69, p. 60), 27. Eating matzah at the beginning of the feast on Passover night is a reminder of the Exodus and past Redemption, while the *afikoman,* consumed at the end of the feast, signifies future deliverance. On the *afikoman,* see n. 112, p. 76. On the similarity between the two celebrations, see S. Cavaletti, "The Jewish Roots of Christian Liturgy," in *The Jewish Roots of Christian Liturgy,* ed. E. J. Fisher (New York, 1990), 26–30. On the extensive literature about the ancient Eucharist, see E. J. Kilmartin, *The Eucharist in the Primitive Church* (Englewood, NJ, 1965), 144–53; C. Jones et al., eds., *A Study of Liturgy,* rev. ed. (New York, 1978), 184–209; D. N. Power, *The Eucharistic Mystery* (New York, 1994).

100. This explanation was suggested to me by Dr. Shlomo Cohen, and indeed, such is the conclusion of Aphrahat's work (n. 86, p. 67): Moses built the Tabernacle for the Jews, while Jesus promised his believers, "Destroy this temple, and in three days I will raise it up" (John 2:19).

an opposite relationship: the statement "this is the bread of affliction" was already customary during the Second Temple period, and Jesus turned this sentence to his own needs.[101] Although this possibility cannot be entirely ruled out, it is hardly plausible. First, it is difficult to assume that such an opening formulation was current even before the Haggadah existed, since an introduction requires a fixed text to accompany it. Second, such an opening is mentioned neither in the Mishnah nor in the *Tosefta*. Once again, we confront the same methodological problem as before: Is it plausible to assume that a Jewish text mentioned only in later sources would serve as a source for a Christian text whose early provenance is well established? The burden of proof lies with the one who questions the primacy of an older text. Whatever the origin of the opening formula of the Haggadah may be, and even if we assume there to be no strict chronological sequence in polemical dialogues, it is difficult to imagine that Jews used the phrase "this is the bread of affliction" without calling to mind the very similar liturgical statement in the Christian ceremony.

A new story requires that new meaning be granted to old symbols. The three symbols of the holiday—the Paschal sacrifice, the matzah (unleavened bread), and the bitter herbs—were given different meanings in both religions. Christianity identified the Paschal Lamb with Jesus, the lamb of God *(Agnus Dei);*[102] it considered the matzah a symbol of the body of the

---

101. Joseph Scaliger, a Renaissance figure, already noted the similarity between these two sayings and thought that Jesus took the sentence from the Haggadah. See A. Grafton, *Joseph Scaliger: A Study in the History of Classical Scholarship* (Oxford, 1993), 316. Hoffman published an important analysis of "This is the bread of affliction," which he dates after the Destruction, together with the transformation of the matzah into a substitute for the Paschal sacrifice. Hoffman also noted the parallelism with the role of the bread in the Last Supper. See L. A. Hoffman, "A Symbol of Salvation in the Passover Haggadah," *Worship* 53 (1979): 517–37.

102. John 1:29: "Behold, the Lamb of God, who takes away the sin of the world"; 1 Cor 5:7: "Cleanse out the old leaven that you may be a new lump, as you really are unleavened. For Christ, our paschal lamb, has been sacrificed for us." For the meaning of Passover in ancient Christianity, see Lohse (n. 69, p. 60), 52–55. The description of the manner of roasting the Passover sacrifice in *m. Pes.* 7.1 suggests that the animal is roasted with its head down, as opposed to the ancient custom (cited in the *beraita* in *j. Pes.* 7.1 [34a]), in which it is roasted with its head up. J. Tabori commented (*pace* Justin Martyr) that the Passover sacrifice roasted on a spit with its head facing up (as in the method of the ancient *beraita*) "is just like a crucified man" ([n. 85, p. 67], 96). In light of that, Tabori assumes that the Mishnaic tradition of roasting the Passover lamb with its head down "reflects a deliberate attempt to reduce the similarity between the Passover sacrifice and the crucifixion of Jesus, but it is not impossible that this is an attempt to mock the crucified Jesus for being hanged upside down" (96).

Savior *(Corpus Christi)*, a reminder of the bread of the Last Supper (which was the seder, according to the three synoptic gospels);[103] while the bitter herbs were read as a symbol of the torment and suffering of the Savior *(Passio Domini)*[104] or of the punishment in store for the people of Israel for what it did to its Messiah.[105] "The Hymn to Virginity" by Ephrem the Syrian (d. 373) says: "By His sacrifice He abolished sacrifices, and liberation by His incense, and the [Passover] lambs by His slaughter, the unleavened [bread] by His bread, and the bitter [herb] by His passion."[106] Rabban Gamaliel's words in the Mishnah *(m. Pes. 10.5)*, which were integrated into the Passover Haggadah, stand in inverted parallelism to that passage:

> Rabban Gamaliel said: Whoever does not mention these three matters on Passover has not fulfilled his obligation; they are: the Passover offering, unleavened bread, and bitter herbs.

> Why did our fathers eat the Passover lamb at the time of the Temple? Because the Holy One blessed be He passed over the houses of our forefathers in Egypt . . .

> Why do we eat this matzah? Because the Supreme King of Kings, the Holy One blessed be He, revealed Himself to our fathers and redeemed them even before their dough had time to ferment . . .

> Why do we eat these bitter herbs? Because the Egyptians embittered the lives of our fathers in Egypt.

Rabban Gamaliel requires all to make a declaration of faith to the Jewish interpretation of the holiday, and by implication to deny the alternative

103. Matt 26:26; Mark 14:22; Luke 22:19. On the quarrel with Judaism about Passover, see Huber (n. 69, p. 60), 135–37.

104. See Ephrem's hymn in Rouwhorst's translation (n. 71, p. 61), 2.116, and the translator's discussion at 1.146.

105. After his exegesis on Exodus 12, Melito of Sardis (n. 88, p. 68), sec. 46, interprets the symbols of the holiday—the Passover sacrifice and the bitter herbs. "What is the Paschal lamb? It took its name and its nature from the word *pathein*, from which there comes the [Greek] work *paschein* (suffering)." On the widespread dissemination of this mistaken etymology in ancient Christian literature, see the editor's note, in that section. In sec. 93, Melito interprets the bitter herbs as a punishment of the people Israel for the crucifixion of Jesus.

106. Ephrem the Syrian, *Hymns*, trans. K. E. McVey (New York, 1989), 298.

Christian interpretation.[107] He even states that one who refrains from doing so fails to fulfill his obligation to observe the festival commandment—clearly because his restraint makes him suspect of heresy. Like Rabban Gamaliel, Melito of Sardis also considered knowledge of the *mysterium* of Easter a prerequisite for Christian salvation and a means of determining who cannot be included among the faithful. According to him, the Egyptians suffered the smiting of their firstborn, not because they failed to sacrifice the Passover lamb, but because they did not know its *mysterium*.[108] Thus, both religions attributed decisive significance to the "correct" interpretation of the symbols of the holiday, each according to its own notion, as a means of affirming religious affiliation. It should be remembered that *Birkat ha-Minim* (the Malediction Against Heretics), in which a liturgical formulation was used to exclude Jewish Christians from the community, was also introduced during Rabban Gamaliel's leadership. The Talmud likewise attributes to Rabban Gamaliel a parody of the Gospel of Matthew and of a Christian judge who adjudicates by it—a parody that indicates a very sophisticated use of the New Testament.[109]

The assumption that one of the purposes of the Haggadah was to refute the Christian position may also explain the figure of the wicked son. In the extant version of the Haggadah, as well as in the *Mekhilta*, the wicked son is presented as asking, "What is this service to you?" He challenges religious law and commandments and thereby "removes himself from the collectivity and denies a fundamental religious principle"—a description that well suits a Jewish-Christian.[110] The answer he gets is likewise suitable to a Christian: "And you should dull his teeth [i.e., refute him] and say to him: If he would have been there he would not have been redeemed." The expression,

---

107. Sulzbach (n. 99, p. 71) and subsequently S. Y. Fisher, "Three Things" [in Hebrew], *Ha-Tzofeh le-hokhmat Yisrael* 10 (1926): 238–40, noted this. Goldschmidt also supported that explanation; see Goldschmidt (n. 76, p. 62), 52.

108. J. Lieu, *Image and Reality: The Jews in the World of the Christians in the Second Century* (Edinburgh, 1996), 210.

109. On *Birkat ha-Minim* (the Malediction against Heretics), see *b. Ber.* 28b; for the parody, see *b. Shabb.* 116a–b. On this story and its sophistication, see Visotzky (n. 73, p. 61), 72–80.

110. Finkelstein already suggested this explanation (n. 77, p. 63, in his 1943 article), 12. Daube suggests a parallel to the four sons of the Haggadah in Matthew 22; see David Daube, *The New Testament and Rabbinic Judaism* (London, 1956), 158–69. Daube thought that Matthew was influenced by the Haggadah, but the opposite possibility ought to be considered also.

"and you should dull his teeth" indicates an answer that contradicts the opposing claim. To the Christian claim that they are "the true Israel," one answers the wicked son: "'To me' and not 'to him'; if he would have been there, he would not have been redeemed," because he is not one of the true children of Israel. The expression "to dull his teeth" is mentioned in *Genesis Rabbah* in two other contexts, both of them explicitly anti-Christian, and in both cases the expression indicates a complete rejection of the Christian claim.[111]

In light of all this, the answer to the wise son (or the foolish son, in the Palestinian Talmud) assumes new meaning, including the quotation from *m. Pes.* 10.5: "One does not add an *afikoman* after the Passover feast." To understand its full significance, we need to examine Melito's use of the word *aphikomenos* (which means coming or arriving) to describe Jesus's incarnation, his appearance on earth, and his Passion: "He who, coming from heaven to the earth" *(Houtos aphikomenos ex ouranōn epi tēn gēn.)*[112] Melito's remarks about Jesus's *afikoman* and his suffering on earth appear immediately after his homily on the Passover sacrifice as a symbol of Jesus, and thus presenting an entire homily on the Christological meaning of the Paschal offering, the matzah, and the bitter herbs—a parallel to Rabban Gamaliel's homily. In light of that the rule that "one does not add an *afikoman* after the Passover feast" was chosen as the answer to the wise son in order to pull out the rug from under the Christian interpretation.[113] The confrontation of the Talmudic Sages with the Christian interpretation of the ceremonies performed at the Passover feast is consistent with another change concerning the order of the meal made in the early amoraic period. During the

111. *Gen. Rab.* 98.8, ed. Theodor-Albeck, p. 1259): "'Until Shiloh comes' [Gen 49:10]— This refers to the King Messiah. 'And to him shall be the obedience *[velo yiqhat]* of the peoples'—for he shall come and set on edge the teeth of [i.e, refute] the nations of the world" (because in their eyes Shiloh is identified with Jesus). And cf. p. 1220: "'And to him shall be ... the peoples"—this refers to Jerusalem, that shall in the future dull the teeth of the peoples of the world, as is said, 'On that day I will make Jerusalem a heavy stone'" (Zech 12:3). The verse from Zechariah seems to have been chosen carefully to refute Jesus's famous prophecy about Jerusalem: "And they will not leave one stone upon another in you" (Luke 19:44).

112. Melito of Sardis (n. 88, p. 68), sec. 66. And see also sec. 32. Werner (n. 94, p. 70, his 1966 article), 205–6, noted Melito's allusion to the *afikoman*. On this meaning of the *afikoman*, see D. Daube, *He That Cometh* (London, 1966), 1–20. On this study, see below.

113. Note that in the Middle Ages, there was a widespread tradition of pronouncing *afikomen*, and not *afikoman*, as today. This follows from the rhyme written by Rabbi Shimon ben Zemah Duran; see *Haggadah shel Pesah Torat Hayyim, 'im perushei ha-rishonim*, ed. M. Katzenellenbogen (Jerusalem, 1998), 12). This pronunciation is very similar to *aphikomenos*.

period of the Mishnah, the meal preceded the Haggadah, while in the amoraic period it became customary to read the Haggadah before the meal; David Daube has already suggested that this change was also intended to oppose the Christian interpretation of the holiday feast and its symbols.[114]

The *amoraim* debated among themselves over the application of the words of the Mishnah: "One begins with disgrace and concludes with glory" (*b. Pes* 116a). According to Rav, this phrase alludes to the passage "In the beginning our forefathers worshipped idols, but now the Omnipresent has brought us to serve Him"—that is, a sentence expressing the idea of the election of the people of Israel. This is immediately followed by biblical verses on the choosing of Abraham, Isaac, and Jacob: "Your fathers lived of old beyond the River" concluding with "and to Isaac I gave Jacob and Esau, and I gave Esau the hill country of Seir to possess, but Jacob and his children went down to Egypt" (Josh 24:2–4). The quotation in the Haggadah ends at this point, even though the biblical passage continues by alluding to the Exodus itself: "I sent Moses and Aaron and I plagued Egypt . . . " and goes on to relate the wondrous deeds of God, who brings His people out of Egypt (Josh 24: 5–7). Truncating the quotation at a verse dealing with the separation between Esau and Jacob may also be interpreted as a rejection of the Christian protest against the election of Israel.[115]

THE "MIDRASH" OF THE HAGGADAH

The main expression of confrontation with an alternative Christian interpretation may be found in the "Midrash"—the heart of the tannaitic Haggadah. The Mishnah (*m. Pes.* 10.4) states the obligation to expound the biblical verses in Deuteronomy 26:5–8: "A wandering Aramaean was my father," and this Midrash appears in the Passover Haggadah. The Midrash in question creates a parallel between the abbreviated account of the Exodus in Deuteronomy and the lengthy and detailed account in the Book of

114. Daube (n. 110, p. 75), 194–95.

115. Finkelstein already noted the truncation of the quotation from Joshua before the description of the Exodus (n. 77, p. 63, his 1942 article), 329. Aphrahat's sermon for Passover, (n. 86, p. 67) also begins with the polemical claim that the People of Israel is no longer the chosen people. In this context, note Rabbi Shimon ben Zemah Duran's Commentary to the Haggadah on the passage: "'And I gave to Esau Mount Seir' . . . For he [Esau] did not want to accept slavery and torture as Jacob did. . . . Therefore it is fitting for us alone to tell of the Exodus from Egypt, for we suffered slavery and torture and we saw the salvation of God and we clung to His service." See *Haggadah shel Pesah Torat Hayyim* (n. 113, p. 76), 74–75.

Exodus. The level of literary sophistication of the Midrash is quite primitive compared to that of the tannaitic halakhic Midrashim. A number of parallel verses cited from Exodus add nothing to the text expounded from Deuteronomy 26. For example, the Midrash explains the verse "And the Egyptians treated us harshly, and afflicted us, and laid upon us hard bondage" (Deut 26:6) as follows:

"And the Egyptian treated us harshly"—as is written, "Come, let us deal shrewdly with them; lest they multiply, and, if war befall us, they join our enemies and fight against us and escape from the land." (Exod 1:10)

"And afflicted us"—as it is written, "Therefore they set taskmasters over them to afflict them with heavy burdens; and they built for Pharaoh store-cities, Pithom and Raamses." (Exod 1:11)

"And laid upon us hard bondage"—as it is written, "So they [the Egyptians] made the people of Israel serve with rigor." (Exod 1:13)

The parallel from Exodus is no more than a confirmation of what is written in Deuteronomy, and the question that obviously arises is why this parallel had to be presented. Moreover, the very choice of the terse and succinct verses from Deuteronomy is surprising. Why did the Sages select these particular verses, recited upon bringing firstfruits to the Temple, as a basis for the Midrash on the Exodus? Why was the detailed and full story from the Book of Exodus not chosen? This is even more surprising in light of the Midrash's tendency to systematically turn the verses in Deuteronomy into a kind of mirror of the story in Exodus. The Midrashic author substitutes the passage beginning "A wandering Aramaean was my father" for the full story in Exodus, thereby seeking to justify his choice of verses from the Book of Deuteronomy.[116] The preference for the short passage from

---

116. Goldschmidt noted this enigma: "The story of the Exodus from Egypt ought to be based upon the Torah's words in the Book of Exodus." His solution is literary: "The chapters dealing with the miracle [in Exodus] are not written in one place; thus the Sages of the Mishnah chose the verses: 'A wandering Aramean was my father' . . . which, since they were included in the 'Confession' recited upon bringing Firstfruits, were familiar to the people, and their language was also easy and simple." See Goldschmidt (n. 76, p. 62), 30. David Weiss-Halivni also supports Goldschmidt's explanation; see his article "Comments on 'The Four Questions'" [in Hebrew], in Studies in Aggadah, Targum, and Jewish Liturgy in Memory of Joseph Heinemann [in Hebrew], ed. E. Fleischer and J. Petuchowski (Jerusalem, 1981), 67ff. It is not clear why verses recited at most once a year when bringing the firstfruits (in the time of the Temple!) should

Deuteronomy could have been explained as a purely literary choice, had we not known from Melito's exegesis that, by the second century, the Christians preferred to expound on Exodus 12 specifically.[117] Melito mentions the children of Israel, who placed the blood of the lamb on the doorpost and the lintels, thereby preventing the angel of destruction that killed the firstborn sons of the Egyptians from harming them. He regarded the Passover sacrifice as a typological model for Jesus and the salvation he brought with his own blood.[118] His exegesis shows that there is reason to wonder why the Jewish Haggadah refrained from telling the story of the Exodus according to the full and detailed story in the book of that name. Melito's contemporary Pseudo-Hippolyte, and Origen, in the third century, likewise placed Exodus 12 at the center of their exegeses.[119]

The explanation for the Jewish exegete's choice of Deuteronomy 26 seems to be rooted in the desire to draw a clear distinction between the Christian and Jewish interpretations of the holiday. This is not merely a choice of an alternative text but also involves the avoidance of two very important motifs in the story in Exodus that are absent in the passage from Deuteronomy 26—namely, mention of the festival sacrifice and Moses's name. This ignoring of Moses is striking, not only in the context of the Midrash, but throughout the Haggadah.[120] In light of this, it is not surprising that our

---

have been more familiar than other verses that could have been chosen for the Midrash. Presumably, the difficulty in remembering was not in the verses interpreted, but in the exegesis appended to them. For another explanation, see S. T. Lachs, "Two Related Arameans: A Difficult Reading in the Haggadah," *Journal for the Study of Judaism* 17 (1980): 65–69.

117. Melito of Sardis (n. 88, p. 68), secs. 1–2.

118. His words, "Understand, therefore, beloved, how it is new and old, eternal and temporary," are reminiscent of Yannai's liturgical poem for Passover: "What was at the beginning will be at the end." See Z. M. Rabinovitch, *Piyyutei Yannai le-Torah ule-mo'adim* (Tel Aviv, 1985), 1:300.

119. Pseudo-Hippolyte in his exegesis *In Sanctum Pascha*. See *Homélies paschales*, vol. 1, *Une homélie inspirée du traité sur la Pâque d'Hippolyte*, ed. P. Nautin (Paris, 1950), 117–23; Origen (n. 88, p. 68). For Easter sermons on Exodus 12, see Huber (n. 69, p. 60), 139–47; Rowhourst (n. 71, p. 61), 2.111.

120. *Cant. Rab.* 3.2 states: "'Upon my bed by night'—this refers to the night of Egypt. 'I sought him whom my soul loves'—this is Moses. 'I sought him, but found him not.'" On the absence of mention of Moses in the Haggadah, see Petuchowski, (n. 138, p. 44), 95–96; Daube (n. 112, p. 76), 12; A. Shinan, "Why Is Moses Not Mentioned in the Passover Haggadah?" [in Hebrew], *Amudim* 39 (1991): 172–74. Shinan suggests four explanations for the omission of Moses's name, one of which is the dispute with Christianity. Apparently the prayer "Moses rejoiced," recited at the Sabbath Morning Service, was intended to refute the Christian position, which abolished the Sabbath and sanctified Sunday in its stead—this, as opposed to Jesus,

Midrash finds it proper to emphasize, in the following exegesis, God's exclusive redemptive acts:

"And the Lord brought us out of Egypt with a mighty hand and an outstretched arm, with great terror, with signs and wonders." (Deut 26:8)

"And the Lord brought us out of Egypt"—Not by an angel, nor by a seraph, nor by a messenger,[121] but the Holy One blessed be He by Himself, as it is written: "For I will pass through the land of Egypt that night, and I will smite all the first-born in the land of Egypt, both man and beast; and on all the gods of Egypt I will execute judgments: I am the Lord." (Exod 12:12)

"For I will pass through the land of Egypt"—I, and not an angel. "And I will smite all the first-born"—I, and not a seraph. "And on all the gods of Egypt I will execute judgments"—I, and not a messenger. "I am the Lord"—I, and no other.

---

who is described as "lord of the sabbath" (Matt 12:8). Moses is "a faithful servant" to whom the Sabbath is given "as his portion" (b. Shabb. 10b). Moses is described in this prayer as "crowned with splendor" (as in Isa 62:3: "a crown of beauty"), reminiscent of the aura around the heads of Christian saints, and perhaps in contrast to Jesus's crown of thorns. For reservations against reciting this prayer in medieval Franco-Germany, see N. Wieder, "The Controversy about the Liturgical Composition *Yismah Moshe:* Opposition and Defence" [in Hebrew], in Fleischer and Petuchowski (n. 116, p. 78), 75–99.

121. Rav Sa'adia Gaon's text of the Haggadah adds, "And not by the Word," that is, the *Logos,* in clear opposition to John 1:1. Cf. *Avot de-Rabbi Natan,* B, 1, ed. Schechter, 2): "Moses received the Torah at Sinai. Not from an angel, nor from a seraph, but from the King of Kings, the Holy One blessed be He." The anti-Christian edge is clear, as noted by F. E. Meyer, "Die Pessach-Haggada und der Kirchenvater Justinus Martyr," in *Treue zur Tora: Festschrift für Günther Harder zum 75. Geburtstag,* ed. P. V. D. Osten-Sacken (Berlin, 1977), 84–87. He maintains that the words "I and not an angel" are aimed against the interpretation of Justin Martyr, *Dialogue with Trypho,* sec. 75. Trypho sought to find an allusion to Jesus in Exodus 23:20: "Behold, I send an Angel before you" as well as from the comparison between Joshua and Jesus. As my friend Professor David Rosenthal pointed out to me, it is possible to understand in this vein Rashi's interpretation of Rav Hillel's saying in b. *Sanh* 91a, "Israel have no Messiah." Rashi explains: "Rather, the Holy One blessed be He will rule by Himself and will deliver them by Himself." For a discussion of Rabban Gamaliel's saying in a different manner, see Judah Goldin, "'Not by Means of an Angel and Not by Means of a Messenger,'" in *Studies in Midrash and Related Literature,* ed. B. L. Eichler and J. H. Tigay (Philadelphia, 1988), 163–73. On the "word" and the *Logos,* see H. Bietenhand, "Logos Theologie im Rabbinat: Ein Beitrag zur Lehre vom Worte Gottes im rabbinischen Schrifttum," *Aufstieg und Niedergang der römischen Welt* 2, no. 19, pt. 2 (1979): 580–618.

This exegesis is unique in comparison with all the others in the Midrash. In the other sections, the author is content to pose a parallel between Exodus and Deuteronomy, every such parallel beginning with the words "as it is written." The essence of this Midrash is in the creation of the parallel per se, not in developing the idea in the biblical verse. But not only does this passage include such a parallel, but to each of the two parallel verses an identical exposition is attached: not an angel, nor a seraph, nor a messenger, but the Holy One blessed be He Himself. This addition creates a strongly emphasized statement, indicative of its literary and conceptual centrality.[122] This is the very essence of the Midrash and of its purpose—to say that the deliverance from Egypt was achieved by God himself. Hence, verses from Deuteronomy, in which Moses is not mentioned, in contrast to his centrality in the Book of Exodus, were chosen. However, the exegete does not completely give up on the detailed story from Exodus but preserves the natural link to that book with a systematic parallelism between Deuteronomy and Exodus. In this way he succeeds in telling the story of the Exodus without mentioning the "messenger," thereby pulling the rug out from under those who regarded Moses as an archetype of Jesus.

If the Midrash did indeed have an ideological goal, it would be reasonable to expect this purpose to be revealed in its ending. The last verse expounded in the Midrash is "And the Lord brought us out of Egypt with a mighty hand and an outstretched arm, with great terror, with signs and wonders." The final unit of the exegesis is "'And wonders'—this refers to the blood, as is said, 'And I will give portents in the heavens and on the earth, blood and fire and columns of smoke' (Joel 3:3)." This quotation from Joel is of great significance, since in its original context the verse speaks of the future deliverance: "In those days I will pour out my spirit. And I will give portents in the heavens and on the earth, blood and fire and columns of smoke. The sun shall be turned to darkness, and the moon to blood, before the great and terrible day of the Lord comes" (Joel 3:2–4).

The Sabbath before Passover is known among Jews as the "Great Sabbath," while in the New Testament the same term is used for the Sabbath after the Crucifixion, that is, the Sabbath that fell on the first day of Pass-

---

122. According to Goldschmidt, this exegesis appears in all versions of the Passover Haggadah, unlike the other exegeses, some of which are missing in different versions. Hence, Goldschmidt concluded that this exegesis was "widely accepted" but did not explain why. See Goldschmidt (n. 76, p. 62), 44.

over.[123] This term alludes to the messianic expectation of Joel's "Great Day of the Lord," which is linked to Passover. The same verse in Joel is interpreted in Acts 2 in connection with the events that occurred seven weeks after the Crucifixion, at Pentecost, when the apostles were gathered, and had a kind of private epiphany:

> [3] And there appeared to them tongues as of fire . . . [4] And they were all filled with the Holy Spirit . . . [14] But Peter, standing with the eleven . . . addressed them . . . [16] . . . But this is what was spoken by the prophet Joel . . . [22] Jesus of Nazareth, a man attested to you by God with mighty works and wonders and signs which God did through him in your midst, as you yourselves know: . . . [33] Being therefore exalted at the right hand of God, and having received from the Father the promise of the Holy Spirit, he has poured out this which you see and hear . . . [43] And fear came upon every soul: and many wonders were done through the apostles in Jerusalem.[124]

In his sermon, Peter claimed that the "signs and wonders" in Joel's prophecy of deliverance were realized in Jesus. The essence of Jesus's proclamation as Messiah—a proclamation known as kerygma—is in verse 22, which makes covert use of Deuteronomy 4:34: "Or has any god ever attempted to go and take a nation for himself from the midst of another nation, by trials, by signs, by wonders, and by war, by a mighty hand and an outstretched arm, and by great terrors, according to all that the Lord your God did for you in Egypt before your eyes?"

The two verses used by Peter, from Joel and from Deuteronomy, are also integrated into the Jewish Haggadah. The verse from Joel concludes the Midrash, and that from Deuteronomy 4 is presented earlier: "'Great awe'— this alludes to the revelation of the *Shekhinah* [divine presence], as is written: 'Or has any god ever attempted to go and take a nation for himself from the midst of another nation.'" If we assume that the Jewish author used sources similar to those used in the Christian exegesis, his interpretation takes on a profound meaning. This is not merely a hermeneutical or technical parallel of biblical verses. His aim is to prove that the "signs

123. On the meaning of the concept the "Great Sabbath," and bibliography on it, see chap. 5.

124. For more on "wonders and signs," cf. Acts 4:30; 5:12; 6:8. For the affinity between Pentecost and the Giving of Torah on Shavu'ot, see H. Conzelmann, *Acts of the Apostles: A Commentary on the Acts of the Apostles* (Philadelphia, 1987), 16.

and wonders"—signs of future deliverance—happened in Egypt alone. The exegesis— "'Great awe'—this alludes to the revelation of the *Shekhinah*"— parallels the Christian Pentecostal revelation described in Acts 2:43— "Everyone was filled with awe"—and the use made there of Deuteronomy 4:34. The Christian position is of a universal revelation of divinity: the apostles are filled with the Holy Spirit, and their prophecy is understood by all present, in all languages. The Jewish author, by contrast, needs Deuteronomy 4:34 to emphasize the election of Israel ("to go and take a nation for himself from the midst of another nation"). What the entire exegesis implies is that the redemption from Egypt is not a model for the Messiah who has already come, but for one who is yet to in the future.

In this vein, we may understand a passage that many have found difficult to comprehend: "'And He saw our affliction' [Deut 26:7]—this refers to their abstinence from sexual relations [literally, the way of the world], as is written: 'And God saw the people of Israel, and God knew [*va-yeida elohim*] [Exod 2:25]." Daube has suggested that this exegesis is based on the biblical usage of the word *knew*, understanding the phrase "and God knew" as sexual intercourse. Even though the Israelites practiced sexual abstinence, they succeeded in having progeny by virtue of miraculous conception.[125] Daube thinks that this exegesis reflects an ancient Jewish source for the story of Mary's pregnancy, one that was not excised from the Haggadah for some unknown reason. I consider the opposite conjecture to be more likely— that this exegesis responds to the Christian story and polemicizes with it, arguing that a miraculous birth from the Holy Spirit did in fact take place, albeit not of Jesus, but of the Israelites born in Egypt. This is in accordance with the general tendency of the Haggadah to portray the Exodus from Egypt as a prototype of deliverance.[126]

125. Daube (n. 112, p. 76), 5–9. Daube's theory was rejected by Urbach (n. 77, p. 63), n. 16, who described his theory as "absurd" and "curious" and was seconded by D. Henshke, "The Midrash of the Passover Haggada" [in Hebrew], *Sidra* 4 (1988): n. 4 ("Urbach has already noted Daube's bizarre words"). But in his commentary on the Passover Haggadah, the medieval commentator Rabbi Yom Tov ben Abraham Ashbili wrote, "There are those who say that he inferred it from the verse, 'and God knew,' that this was like 'and Adam again knew his wife Eve'"; see *Hiddushei ha-Ritba al ha-Shas, Pesahim*, ed. Y. Leibovitch (Jerusalem, 1984), 31. Similar things appear in *Genesis Rabbah* on the verse, "And the Lord visited Sarah" (Gen 21:1): "R. Huna said: there is an angel appointed over desire, but Sarah had no need for such, as He in His glory [made her conceive]" (*Gen. Rab.* 53.6, ed. Theodor-Albeck, 560).

126. Such an idea is not alien to the Midrash. In *Midrash Hagadol* to Exodus, 22–23, a Jewish version of the birth of Jesus is brought (see the discussion of this below, chap. 5,

This explanation of the Midrash's tendency can also explain its beginning: "Come and learn what Laban the Syrian sought to do to our Father Jacob. For Pharaoh decreed only against the newborn males, but Laban tried to uproot all [Israel], as is written, 'A wandering Aramaean was my father . . . and he went down to Egypt'—compelled by the divine word." In its literal sense, the biblical text expounded here refers to Jacob, the Aramaean, who was an exiled "wanderer." The verse is understood thus in the Septuagint and in *Sifrei*,[127] as well as by Melito,[128] who describes Jesus as taking his followers from slavery to freedom, from darkness to light, from death to life, and from subjugation to eternal kingdom. Jesus suffered a great deal: he was present in the murdered Abel, in the bound Isaac, in the exiled Jacob, in the sold Joseph, in the Moses thrust into the river in a basket, in the slaughtered Passover sacrifice, and in the persecuted David. Stuart Hall and Shlomo Pines independently noted the parallel between the beginning of Melito's exegesis and the passage in the Haggadah: "He brought us out of slavery into freedom, from grief into joy, from mourning into festivity, from darkness into great light, and from subjection into redemption."[129] Hence the notion that this is a fragment of a Jewish-Christian Haggadah from the Land of Israel is highly plausible.[130] In any case, Melito adds "the

---

p. 248). In *j. Ber.* 2.4 (5a), there is also a Jewish version of the birth of Jesus. A Jewish farmer is told by a passing Arab about the Destruction of the Temple and the birth of the Messiah in the palace of the king of Bethlehem. The farmer became a salesman of baby clothes so that he could discover the baby-Messiah. The baby's mother wanted to kill her son, since the Temple had been destroyed because of his birth, but the Jew prevented her from doing so. Later the same man returned and asked about the child, and his mother replied that winds and storms had come and snatched him out of her hand. In this version, the manger is turned into the royal palace, and the role of Herod is filled by the mother. Note, too, the parallel between the birth of the Messiah and the Destruction of the Temple. This story is the basis of the Kabbalistic legend of "the baby Gadiel." See Gershom Scholem, "The Sources of 'The Tale of the Baby Gadiel' in Kabbalistic Literature" [in Hebrew], *Devarim bego* (Tel Aviv, 1976), 1.270–83. For this story and its parallel in *Lam. Rab.* (Buber edition, 89), see Galit Hasan-Rokem, "'La voix est la voix de ma soeur': Figures et symboles feminins dans le Midrach 'Lamentations Rabbah,'" *Cahiers de Litterature Orale* 44 (1988): 13–35.

127. This is discussed in detail in Tabori (n. 85, p. 67); Henshke (n. 125, p. 83).

128. Melito of Sardis (n. 88, p. 68), secs. 49, 68.

129. Hall (n. 94, p. 70), 31–32; Shlomo Pines, "From Darkness into Great Light," *Immanuel* 4 (1974): 47–51; cf. Werner (n. 94, p. 70).

130. The structure of Melito's exegesis considerably overlaps with the central kernel of our Haggadah. He opens with a "Midrash"; moves on to an explanation of the symbolic meaning of the Passover sacrifice, the matzah, and the bitter herbs; and concludes with an "anti-Hallel," which includes a sharp attack on the ingratitude of the people of Israel.

exiled Jacob" to the series of typologies of the suffering Jesus, and we may conclude that this is how he understood the phrase "A wandering Aramaean." The identification of Jesus with Jacob is already mentioned in John 4:12, in the Samaritan woman's question to Jesus: "Are you greater than our father Jacob?" [131]

But in the Aramaic translations, as in the Haggadah, the verse in question is seen as referring to Laban: "Laban the Aramaean sought to make my father perish." The Midrash as extant in the Haggadah raises three difficulties. First, how did the exegete know that Laban sought to kill Jacob, since in Genesis 31:24 the angel warns him, "Take heed that you say not a word to Jacob, either good or bad" and there is no indication that Laban sought to kill Jacob's entire family? Second, how did the Midrashic author know that Jacob went down to Egypt "compelled by the divine word"? "Word" *(dibbur)* is tantamount to *logos* and can mean "an angel"—but where is it written in the Bible that Jacob was ordered by God or by an angel to go down to Egypt? Third, how are we to understand the fact that at the heart of the Haggadah we find the view that Laban's intention to kill Jacob, an aim that was not realized, was more serious than the murder of the children of Israel by Pharaoh? Does this not completely diminish the significance of the deliverance from Egypt?

This last question, which transforms Laban into the villain of the Haggadah, led Louis Finkelstein to his bold theory that the Haggadah was composed at the end of the third century B.C.E. and was intended to serve its authors' pro-Egyptian (Ptolemaic) and anti-Syrian (Seleucid) orientation.[132] Finkelstein also noted the similarity between "Syrian" (Hebrew: *arami;* Aramaic: *arma'i*) and "Roman." (Hebrew: *roma'i*).[133] Accordingly, "A wandering Aramaean was my father" may also be read as a Midrash on the situation of the Jewish people under Roman rule. Laban, who wished to extirpate everyone, is the personification of Rome, whose subjugation was harsher than that of Egypt. Jacob exiled from his home symbolizes the fate of the nation as a whole: just as Jacob's exile in Egypt was temporary— he did not go down there to settle—so would the new Exile of Israel be.

131. See J. H. Neyrey, "Jacob Tradition and the Interpretation of John 4:10–26," *Catholic Biblical Quarterly* 41 (1979): 419–37. There is also a similarity between the description of rolling the large rock off Jesus's tomb (Mark 16:4) and rolling the stone off the well by Jacob (Gen 29:10).

132. Finkelstein (n. 77, p. 63, his 1938 article), 300–301 and n. 20.

133. Finkelstein (n. 77, p. 63, his 1938 article), 300–301 and n. 20, and see the important discussion of Berger (n. 7, p. 34), 161–62.

The typological story created by the Midrash is based on the following frame story: an evil man (Laban) wanted to kill a good man (Jacob); an angel commanded the good man to go down to Egypt, and he went there for a limited time. If we change two of the characters in the story, substituting Laban the Aramaean with Herod the Edumean, who rules by the grace of Rome, and Jacob with Jesus, we receive the following story: "An angel of the Lord appeared to Joseph in a dream and said, 'Rise, take the child and his mother, and flee to Egypt, and remain there till I tell you; for Herod is about to search for the child, to destroy him.' And he rose and took the child and his mother by night, and departed to Egypt" (Matt 2:13–14). The two stories are structured according to the same scheme.

The literary topos used by the Gospel—the birth of the Christian Savior, the danger in store for him, his descent to Egypt, and his rescue—also seems to have been used by the Jewish Midrashic author, who shifted it to Jacob.[134] This is yet another reflection of the tendency to apply the Christian story of salvation to the Jewish story of deliverance from Egypt. In times of subjugation and degradation, both stories offer a consolation and hope for salvation.

At this point, we must return to the peculiarity with which we began our discussion: Why, at least in terms of its literary qualities, is the Midrash "primitive," not going much beyond presentation of the parallel between Deuteronomy 26 and Exodus? And, more generally, why did the Talmudic Sages choose to create a textual Midrash in order to fill the obligation of narrating the story of the Exodus? In point of fact, Melito's "Haggadah" is also none other than such a "Midrash," whose aim is to create a source for the new exegesis of Easter on the basis of the story of the historical Exodus in the Old Testament. Without a textual Midrash and without allegorizing the meaning of the sacrifice, there is no basis for the Christian Easter. For Melito, his Midrash is no mere literary embellishment, but an essential means of turning the biblical story of Passover into a prefiguration of Jesus and the Crucifixion story. Hence, his exegesis begins with a declaration that the biblical verses from Exodus are to be read first, and only thereafter the *mysterium,* that is, their allegorization. Thus, the deliverance

---

134. This interpretation was supported by Daube (n. 110, p. 75), 189–92, and subsequently by R. E. Brown, *The Birth of the Messiah* (London, 1977), 545. But both think that the Christian story in Matthew is a Christian Midrash based on the Jewish exegesis on Laban, while I think that the opposite is more tenable, namely, that the Jewish exegesis responds to the story in Matthew and adapts it to its purpose.

of Israel from Egypt acquires a double meaning: temporal and eternal. The historical Passover is that described in the scriptural text, while the eternal Passover is that of Jesus.[135] This duality runs throughout Melito's exegesis, explaining the need for the exegetical genre to construct the allegorical level above the overt text.

Against this backdrop, the liturgical function of the Jewish Midrash can be seen as a pale response to the Christian homily. The Jewish Midrash uses the same literary technique as that used by the Christian one in countering the Christian attempt to appropriate the story of the Exodus from Egypt.

Thus, at least in this case, it may be argued that the hermeneutical genre has a different function in the two religions. From the very outset, Christianity saw exegesis as a vital means of creative interpretation, for only through it could Christianity construct an allegorical "second story" on top of the scriptural "first story." Yet the Jewish exegesis adopts, at least in our case, the Midrashic genre, not to create an additional level, but to show that everything is present in the first story and that there is no second story at all. For the Jewish author, the story in Deuteronomy is interpreted through the story in the Book of Exodus—that is, the written Midrash takes place on the same textual plane as the biblical text itself. This assumption—namely, that the Talmudic Sages adopted the Christian Midrashic genre to build onto or at times in opposition to it, a parallel (or reverse) Jewish Midrash—provides an historical explanation for the great flourishing of the creative Midrash specifically during the second century C.E.

CONCLUSIONS

Based on the suggestions offered here regarding the development of the Passover Haggadah, we may conclude that this work emerged from a close and intimate dialogue with the Christian exegesis of the holiday. The Jewish-Christian dialogue displayed here is very extensive, essentially polemic, but it also includes a great deal of commonality. This dialogue was intended to define the identity of the two religious groups by mutual rejection but at the same time offers a similar panacea to the common problem: how to celebrate a festival of deliverance during a period of subjection or persecution. Melito expresses himself with acerbic style, writing sharply against the Jews. The Jews respond with restraint, circumventing the obstacles set up for them

135. Lieu (n. 108, p. 75), 210.

by the Christian exegesis. Reading the Haggadah becomes a kind of declaration of fidelity to the Jewish religion. The creators of the Haggadah also saw its function as defining friend and foe. It does not explicitly reject the other side, but rather the validity of its historical, eschatological, or theological interpretations.[136] It denies Christianity as a religion but does not see it as a dangerous political enemy. Rome is still the archenemy, and longings for deliverance are pleas for liberation from Rome.

This interpretation of the Haggadah and the Passover seder demands the following hypothetical reconstruction of the development of the holiday:[137] during the Temple period, the celebration of Passover included two essential components: the feast of the Paschal sacrifice and the recitation of Hallel. The initial substitute for the sacrifice during the first two generations after the Destruction was eating a roasted lamb (which may have been the custom in the Diaspora even before the Destruction) and studying the laws of the sacrifice. This is the tradition described in the passage from the *Tosefta* mentioned above: scholars gather and recite the laws of the Passover sacrifice all night. It was at this stage that the Christian Midrash on Exodus 12 and on the Passover sacrifice developed, while the Jewish Haggadah preferred to get away from the sacrifice and instead emphasized the obligation to tell of the Exodus from Egypt, as described in chapter 10 of *Mishnah Pesahim*. This stage first appears in the early second century C.E. The family celebration developed later out of the content of the seder evening, in which a central place is set aside for the education of the children and the fulfillment of the commandment "and you shall tell your son" (and, in Christianity, the baptism of new adherents). At this stage, the controversy between Jews and Christians over the interpretations of the holiday had arisen—the former telling about the Passover in Egypt and the latter of the Passover of Jerusalem.

According to this reconstruction, not only did the Haggadah take into account the interpretations of the Christian/Quartodecimani, but it also served as a primary tool in the effort to eliminate from the community those who wavered between Judaism and Christianity. The Christian holiday de-

136. Similar definitions were suggested by Amos Funkenstein, "History, Counter-History, and Narrative" [in Hebrew], *Alpayim* 4 (1991): 210; and Funkenstein, *Perceptions of Jewish History* (Los Angeles, 1993), 170.

137. I do not refer here to a definite diachronic chronological development. Presumably, after the Destruction there was considerable deliberation over different ways of maintaining the content of the festival, and different customs existed side-by-side at the same time.

veloped from the observance on the fourteenth of Nissan, which emphasized the Crucifixion and the sacrifice, to the celebration on Sunday, which placed more emphasis on the salvation. A similar move took place in tannaitic Judaism—from a celebration that emphasized the sacrifice (Rabban Gamaliel) to one that focused on the story of the Exodus from Egypt and the redemption.

This proposed reconstruction of the circumstances of the creation of the Haggadah derives from the assumption that its liturgical development was not an "immanent," internal process, but reflected a covert dialogue with a rival liturgy. Indeed, there was no ritual practiced in the Temple for which there emerged such a dangerous alternative as the Christian story of the Passover. If those who think that the Gospel According to Mark was written immediately after the Destruction as "a Jewish-Christian Passover Haggadah" are correct,[138] then this Gospel is to be seen not only as a theological-historical work but also as a liturgical one, in the same way that the Torah served as public reading among the Jews.[139] If such is the case, it may be that already during the first generation after the Destruction, Jewish-Christians would "tell" the story of their deliverance by reading the Gospel. Thus, the Passover Haggadah should be read as a Jewish "countergospel"—story against story, Haggadah against Haggadah. This may be the reason for the similarity between the content of the Midrash and Deuteronomy 26, on the one hand, and the Christian story, on the other: the Midrash opens with an alternative story of Jesus's birth ("Laban sought to uproot all"), continues with a description of the suffering of Israel in Egypt (parallel to Jesus's anguish on the Cross), moves on to a description of the deliverance in Egypt ("not by an angel"), and concludes with Joel 3:3, alluding to the status of Pentecost, which concludes the "life" of Jesus.

By reviewing in one glance the various sections of the Haggadah explained here, we find ourselves harnessing some of the central sections of the Pass-

---

138. J. Bowman, *The Gospel of Mark: the New Christian Jewish Passover Haggadah* (Leiden, 1965); K. Hanhart, *The Open Tomb: A New Approach, Mark's Passover Haggadah ([ca.] 72 C.E.)* (Collegeville, 1994). And cf. Jacob Petuchowski, "'Do This in Remembrance of Me' (I Cor 11:24)," *JBL* 76 (1957): 293–98.

139. For a similar theory, see M. D. Goulder, *Midrash and Lection in Matthew* (London, 1974). He thinks that Matthew was intended to be read annually in the synagogue, while Mark was to be read semiannually. The concluding sections of the Gospels—the Crucifixion and the Resurrection—were read on Passover. For a survey and critique of this view in scholarship, see P. F. Bradshaw, *The Search for the Origins of Christian Worship* (New York, 1992), 30–32.

over Haggadah to the chariot of anti-Christian polemic. And indeed, it seems that the time has come to reevaluate the close and difficult struggle between the great religious reformers, both Christian and Jewish, during the generations following the Destruction. Hence, the literature of the Talmudic Sages should be read not only as a source for Christian ideas and ceremonies, but also as a response to the challenge posed by Christianity to Judaism, for the Oral Torah is, in the deepest sense, a Jewish answer to the Christian Torah, the New Testament.[140]

A NOTE ON THE RESEARCH

The fundamental assumptions underlying this interpretation of the Passover Haggadah are quite similar to those made by David Daube, who in turn seems to have followed a path that was already paved by Robert Eisler. In 1925–1926, Eisler published a two-part article named "Das letzte Abendmahl" in the journal *Zeitschrift für die neutestamentliche Wissenschaft und die Kunde der älteren Kirche*, in volumes 24–25, presenting an approach that compared the *afikoman* of the Jewish ceremony with the Host of the Christian one. Eisler was a great scholar of the New Testament, but he knew less about Judaism, and his article suffered from some errors.[141] Yet this fact still does not confute his essential argument, and his article was an important contribution to uncovering the messianic significance of the *afikoman* and the potential for research latent in an understanding of the parallel developments of Passover and Easter.

This approach became a thorn in the flesh of both Jewish and Christian scholars. Immediately after the first part of Eisler's paper was published, the journal's editor, Hans Lietzmann, wanted to rescind his agreement to

---

140. This is the explanation of the following passage from *Midrash Tanhuma* (*Ki Tisa*, sec. 34): "The Holy One blessed be He said to the nations [i.e., the Christians]: 'You say that you are My sons? Know, that only he with whom my *mysterion* is to be found is my son. And what is that? This is the Mishnah, that was given verbally.'" Bergman noted that the term *mysterion* is intended to refute Paul's argument that the Christian gospel is the mystery (Eph 6:19). See M. Bergman, "The Scales are not 'Even'" [in Hebrew], *Tarbiz* 53 (1984): 289–92, esp. 291 n. 14a.

141. On Robert Eisler, the man and the scholar, see G. Scholem, *From Berlin to Jerusalem: Memories of My Youth* (New York, 1980), 127–34; Y. Liebes, "The Kabbalistic Myth of Orpheus," *Mehqarei Yerushalayim be-Mahshevet Yisrael* 7 (1978): 425–27. On Daube's interpretation of the Seder, cf. D. Bleicher Carmichael, "David Daube on the Eucharist and the Passover Seder," *Journal for the Study of the New Testament* 42 (1991): 45–67.

publish the second part. Eisler refused to give in and insisted that Lietzmann honor his commitment to publish the complete article. He even hired
an attorney and threatened a lawsuit. Lietzmann was forced to come around,
and Eisler's attorney even forbade him to append an editor's note stating
that the article was published against his will and under legal duress. Instead, at the beginning of volume 25 (1926), Lietzmann published his own
critique of Eisler's theory, along with a sharp article by Marmorstein.[142]
Eisler demanded the right to reply in volume 26 (1927), but Lietzmann refused. Eisler then suggested that Lietzmann publish his reply in a journal
outside Germany, on condition that Lietzmann report its contents in the
"From Foreign Journals" section, but Lietzmann refused to do even that.
Eisler remained isolated, attacked on all sides, and unable to reply to his
critics.

Forty years later, in 1966, Daube delivered a lecture on the *afikoman* at
Saint Paul's Cathedral in London, vindicating Eisler's interpretation of the
afikoman, with certain necessary corrections and adding his own new findings. Daube told his audience of the bitter fate of his predecessor and expressed doubts whether the time had come for such comparative studies
between Christianity and Judaism. To illustrate his concerns, he pointed
out the fact that in the Goldschmidt edition of the Passover Haggadah there
was no mention of the New Testament, even though it contains valuable
information on the ancient version of Passover customs. Since Daube was
not sure that the time was ripe, he refrained from disseminating his lecture
widely and was satisfied with its publication in a pamphlet available only
through personal request to the secretariat of the Committee for Christian-
Jewish Understanding in London. Unlike Eisler, Daube was not muzzled,
but his interpretation remained on the periphery of scholarship and has
not yet been accorded the scholarly recognition it deserves.[143]

142. Hans Lietzmann, "Erklärung des Herausgebers über sein Verhalten gegen Herrn Dr.
Robert Eisler," *Zeitschrift für die neutestamentliche Wissenschaft und die Kunde der älteren Kirche*
26 (1927): 96; A. Marmorstein, "Miscellen: I. Das letzte Abendmahl und der Sederabend,"
Zeitschrift für die neutestamentliche Wissenschaft und die Kunde der älteren Kirche 26 (1927):
249–53.

143. About the time the Hebrew edition of this book was completed, on the eve of Purim
1999, David Daube passed away at the age of ninety. Blessed be his memory.

THREE

The Vengeance and the Curse

Hostility to Christianity among Ashkenazic Jewry

HOW DID MEDIEVAL JEWISH APOLOGETICS DEAL with Christianity's standing as the dominant and successful religion? What religious formulation enabled the Jews to adhere to their faith in the election of Israel despite the political reality that every day seemed to demonstrate that God had hidden his face from them? These questions must be understood in the broad context of the connections and interrelations between Jews and Christians. Just as the Jewish position toward Christianity was influenced by the Christians' attitude toward the Jews, so must we assume that the corresponding Christian position was influenced by the Jews' attitude toward Christians. Mutual relations necessarily exist even between the persecutor and the persecuted, and these must be considered.

Gerson Cohen, who wrote two studies on the Jewish attitude toward the Christian world,[1] noted the "blatant contrast between the election of Israel

---

1. Gerson D. Cohen, "Esaü as Symbol in Early Medieval Thought," in *Jewish Medieval and Renaissance Studies*, ed. A. Altmann (Cambridge, MA, 1967), 19–48; Cohen, "Messianic Postures of Ashkenazim and Sephardim," in *Studies of the Leo Baeck Institute*, ed. M. Kreutzberger (New York, 1967), 117–58 (this article was also published in a separate pamphlet with different pagination: 3–42). Both articles were reprinted in Cohen, *Studies in the Variety of Rabbinic Cultures* (Philadelphia, 1991), 243–70, 271–98. Elisheva Carlebach disagreed with Cohen's claim that the Ashkenazic world suppressed and even silenced messianic fervor,

in Heaven and their subjection on earth,"[2] a contradiction aggravated in times of religious persecution. To explain this, Jews interpreted the harsh political reality as temporary, postponing its resolution until the messianic era. Hence, the events anticipated in the messianic era serve as the key to understanding Jewish apologetics in the present. How did the Jews portray the long-awaited victory over Christianity? How did they envision the future routing of the Gentiles? These and similar questions will be discussed in this chapter.

VENGEFUL REDEMPTION

This [final] Redemption . . . will involve the ruin, destruction, killing and eradication of all the nations: they, and the angels who watch over them from above, and their gods. . . . The Holy One blessed be He will destroy all nations except Israel.

These words come from *Sefer Nizzahon Vetus,* a book written in thirteenth-century Germany describing the messianic era.[3] The author's use of language, taken from the Book of Esther, where the intentions of Haman, the archoppressor, are described, demonstrates the power of the notion that during the messianic era the tables will turn and that a complete and final annihilation shall be in store for the Gentile nations. At the same time, Rabbi Meir ben Shimon of Narbonne was writing his polemical work *Milhemet Mitzvah* (The Commanded War), in which he expressed an entirely different attitude toward the end of the Gentiles:

At the End there will be great signs and wonders that He will do with us, lifting us up, so that all the nations will turn to our faith and declare that

---

and noted messianic figures and movements in the Ashkenazic world; see *Between History and Hope: Jewish Messianism in Ashkenaz and Sepharad,* (Third Annual Lecture of the Victor J. Selmanowitz Chair of Jewish History (New York, 1998), 1–30. Carlebach's proofs are based on messianic events from the sixteenth century on and do not weaken Cohen's thesis about the Middle Ages, a period that is our main concern here. For more on the position of the Jews in relation to Christianity, see Jacob Katz, *Exclusiveness and Tolerance: Studies in Jewish-Gentile Relations in Medieval and Modern Times* (New York, 1973).

2. Cohen, "Esau as Symbol," 20.

3. David Berger, ed., *The Jewish-Christian Debate in the High Middle Ages. A Critical Edition of the Nizzahon Vetus* (Philadelphia, 1979), 161 n. 242 (English version, 227); Mordechai Breuer, ed., *Sefer Nizzahon Yashan* (Ramat Gan, 1978), sec. 268, 187.

what they inherited from their fathers was a lie. . . . For all the peoples will turn to the faith of the honored God through the many wonders they will see when the Lord will deliver us from this Exile.[4]

This is preceded by a discussion of the biblical verse "for he avenges the blood of his servants, and takes vengeance on his adversaries" (Deut 32:43). Rabbi Meir ben Shimon thought that the messianic vengeance would hurt only "the evil ones and the oppressors" among the Gentiles but not the "peoples." For him, the end of Exile and the beginning of the Redemption involve a mass conversion to Judaism of "all the nations," not their annihilation.

We have here two positions, the former what I shall call "vengeful redemption," and the latter "proselytizing redemption." The former is expressed in an Ashkenazic source, the latter in a Provençal-Spanish one. Does *Sefer Nizzahon Vetus* reflect the predominant position in Franco-Germany? Was the messianic world of Ashkenazic Jewry characterized by anticipation of total vengeance against the Gentiles? I would maintain that this was in fact the case, although here and there we find Ashkenazim speaking more moderately, integrating into their thought the notion of proselytizing redemption.[5] Even those who considered vengeful redemption a central element in the messianic process might also assume the existence of a second stage, more distant and coming later, in which there will occur the proselytizing redemption of those Gentiles who have not been destroyed by God's wrath.[6] The historian nevertheless needs to explain the importance of the main scenario, which was constantly expressed in the prayers, thought, and

---

4. Ms. Parma–Palatine Library 2749 (De-Rossi Catalogue, no. 155), fol. 19b-20a.

5. Such a position appears once in Rabbenu Gershom Meor ha-Golah, who describes the End of Days thus:

All inhabitants of the world shall acknowledge then and know
together all shall answer and say
Behold, there is no God in all the world
but in Israel, and strong is their Redeemer

(A. M. Haberman, ed., *Rabbenu Gershom Meor ha-Golah: Selihot u-pizmonim*, [Jerusalem, 1944], 14). Yet, as we shall see below, this opinion is overshadowed by other expressions, in which vengeful redemption takes center stage.

6. Avraham Grossman, "'Redemption by Conversion' in the Teaching of Early Ashkanazi Sages" [in Hebrew], *Zion* 59 (1994): 325–42. Grossman's article was written in the context of a polemic with me, but in fact we agree about the main point. See my response, Israel J. Yuval, "'The Vengeance of the Lord is the Vengeance of His Sanctuary'—History Without Anger and without Prejudice" [in Hebrew], *Zion* 59 (1994): 412–14.

visions of those generations, one that filled their hearts with hope and consolation. The dominant view in Ashkenaz saw the annihilation of the Gentiles as a principal component of the messianic vision. This is a notion that wishes to correct history retroactively, assigning to vengeance the role of correcting the past before a new world order can be established. What is the background for this view? Under what historical conditions did it emerge?

In a lament for Tisha b'Av composed in wake of the pogroms of 1096, liturgical poet Kalonymus ben Yehudah wrote:

> Drops of my blood are counted one by one
> And spray their life-blood on your *porphyrion* [a royal garment
>   of crimson]
> He will execute judgment among the nations, filling them with
>   corpses.[7]

This is a literal accounting by blood. Every drop of blood of Jews killed by Gentiles is recorded in a divine "ledger" in the form of a scarlet garment. The account will be settled—if one can say such a thing—to the last drop of blood. This metaphor of the crimson divine garment also appears in a Midrash cited in *Yalqut Shim'oni:*

> "He will execute judgment among the nations, filling them with corpses" [Ps 110:7]. Our Rabbis said: For every single soul of Israel that Esau killed, the Holy One blessed be He took from their blood and dipped in it His *porphyrion* until it was the color of blood; and when the Day of Judgment comes and He sits upon the dais to judge him [Esau], He will wear that *porphyrion* and show him the body of every righteous person that is recorded on it, as it is said, "He will execute judgment among the nations, filling them with corpses." At that selfsame time, the Holy One blessed be He executes against him a double vengeance, as Scripture says: "O Lord, thou God of vengeance, thou God of vengeance, shine forth!" [Ps 94:1][8]

A parallel to this Midrash can be found in the *Midrash on Psalms,* where it is presented in the name of Rabbi Eleazar ben Padath, who lived in Palestine during the third century C.E.:

---

7. Daniel Goldschmidt, *Seder Kinot le-Tisha b'Av* (Jerusalem, 1972), 109.
8. *Yalqut Shim'oni,* Tehillim, sec. 869; the origin of this Midrash is in *Midrash Yelamdenu.*

What is meant by, "He does not forget the cry of the afflicted" [Ps 9:12]? He [God] does not forget Israel's blood [shed] by the nations of the earth. And not only the blood of the righteous, but the blood of all those of Israel slain in times of persecution . . . Rabbi Abbahu taught in the name of Rabbi Eleazar: The Holy One blessed be He records the name of every righteous man whom the nations of the earth put to death upon His purple robe, for the Bible says "He will execute judgment among the nations, filling them with corpses." And the Holy One blessed be He says to the nations of the earth: "Why have you put to death My righteous men, such as Rabbi Hanina ben Teradyon and all the others killed for the hallowing of My Name?" And when the nations of the earth feign ignorance and reply: "We did not put them to death," the Holy One blessed be He will at once fetch His royal robe, and will judge them and decree their doom. Hence it is said, "He does not forget the cry of the afflicted."[9]

The idea expressed in both Midrashim, as well as in the lament of Rabbi Kalonymus, is that the drops of blood of the martyrs are counted one by one and are sprayed on the garment of God, known as his *porphyrion,* so that it may serve as the corpus delicti to punish the killers on Judgment Day. The idea that the spilled blood of the martyrs calls for messianic vengeance also appears in Revelation 6:9–11. In his vision, John sees "under the altar the souls of those who had been slain for the word of God, and for the witness they had borne." The martyrs cry out to God, "O Sovereign Lord, holy and true, how long before thou wilt judge and avenge our blood." God gives each one a "white robe" and tells them to wait "until their fellow servants and their brethren should be complete, who were to be killed as they themselves had been."[10] Chapters 9–10 of the pseudepigraphical work *Assumption of Moses* from the first century C.E., mentions a similar idea; it tells of Taxo's address to his sons during a time of pogroms

9. *Midrash Tehillim,* ed. S. Buber, to 9:13; see *Midrash on Psalms,* trans. W. G. Braude (New Haven, n.d.), 144–46); and cf. W. Bacher, *Die Agada der Palästinesischen Amoräer* (Strassburg, 1896), 35.

10. On this passage, see T. Baumeister, *Die Anfänge der Theologie des Martyriums* (Münster, 1980), 219–25; J. W. van Henten, "Das jüdische Selbstverständnis in den ältesten Martyrien," in *Die Entstehung der jüdischen Martyrologie,* ed. J. W. van Henten (Leiden, 1989), 135. On the garment of vengeance dipped in blood, see Rev 19:11–16. The view that the martyrs are considered sacrificed on the altar of heaven also appears in *t. Sanh.* 13.11, ed. M. Zuckermandel (Jerusalem, 1970), 435: "because they exalted me and were sacrificed on account of me."

and decrees against their religion. The father advises his sons to let themselves be killed rather than to violate the commandments of the religion:

> Let us fast for three days, and on the fourth let us go into a cave which is in the field, and let us die rather than transgress the commands of the Lord of Lords, the God of our fathers. For if we do this and die, our blood will be avenged before the Lord. And then His sovereignty will appear before his entire creation.[11]

The idea of urging God to avenge the blood of the martyrs in order to hasten the Redemption is thus a very ancient one.[12] Although it has few resonances in Midrashic literature, it became a central motif in Ashkenazic liturgical poetry *(piyyut)*. For example, the *selihah* (a petition for pardon) of Rabbi Eliezer ben Nathan says:

> "Their blood bubbles upon the garment of *porphyrion*
> Rather than silver one may bring gold
> but for the sublime saints, no ransom has been prescribed
> I have avenged the blood of those left unavenged
> and the Lord dwells in Zion."[13]

The same image is used in his lament "for the saints of Cologne."[14] The *selihah* of Rabbi Ephraim ben Isaac similarly refers to the blood of the martyrs being sprinkled on the divine garment of crimson,[15] as does that of Rabbi David ben R. Meshullam.[16] And in Rabbi Ephraim ben Jacob of Bonn's, we find: "Receive upon your *porphyrion* the blood of those that purify themselves to sanctify You / Plucking it and laying down [the biblical commandment], 'and live by them,' forbearing to abandon You."[17] So too in the famous Mahzor of Worms, in two different liturgical poems, the *por-*

---

11. Jacob Licht, "Taxo, or the Apocalyptic Doctrine of Vengeance," *JJS* 12 (1961): 95–103.

12. Yitzhak Baer, "The Pogroms of 1096" [in Hebrew], *Sefer S. Asaf* (Jerusalem, 1953), 158 n. 49.

13. A. M. Haberman, *Gezerot Ashkenaz ve-Tzarfat* (Jerusalem, 1971), 87.

14. Haberman, *Gezerot Ashkenaz ve-Tzarfat*, 81.

15. A. M. Haberman, "Liturgical Poems of Ephrāyim bar Yitzhak of Regensburg" [in Hebrew], *Yedi'ot ha-Makhon le-heqer ha-shirah ha-'ivrit bi-Yerushalayim* 4 (1938), 156; Daniel Goldschmidt, *Mahzor le-Yamim Noraim: Vol. 2, Yom Kippur* (Jerusalem, 1970), 557.

16. Haberman, "Liturgical Poems," 69; Goldschmidt, *Mahzor*, 538.

17. A. M. Haberman, *Piyyutei R. Ephraim ben R. Yaakov mi-Bonna* (Jerusalem, 1969), 45; see *Yedi'ot ha-Makhon le-heqer ha-shirah ha-'ivrit bi-Yerushalayim* 7 (1958), 261.

phyrion is mentioned as the garment of God who avenges Edom.[18] A liturgical poem mentioned in *Arugat Habosem* also brings up this motif.[19] Thus, the image appears in at least nine Ashkenazic *piyyutim*.[20]

The biblical source for this appears in Isaiah 63:1–6, which describes God's vengeance against Edom. When asked, "Why is thy apparel red, and thy garments like his that treads in the wine press?" God replies: "I have trodden the wine press alone . . . I trod them in my anger and trampled them in my wrath; their lifeblood is sprinkled upon my garments, and I have stained all my raiment." God is compared to one who treads the winepress, trampling the grapes, or the Gentiles;[21] during the treading, their blood is sprayed on the divine garments, which are stained red. Here, the staining of God's apparel will occur during the vengeance against the Gentiles, and the blood to be sprayed on his apparel will be not that of the martyrs, as in the Midrash and the Ashkenazic *piyyutim*, but of the Gentiles whom he punishes.[22]

Thus, the notion that at the End of Days God will avenge the blood of the martyrs is not a Franco-German innovation. Identification of the Midrashic source that the Ashkenazic poets drew on for their ideas indicates its continuity with the Palestinian Haggadic tradition, which saw vengeance

18. Daniel Goldschmidt, *Mehqerei tefillah u-piyyut* (Jerusalem, 1980), 13, 17.

19. E. E. Urbach, ed., *Sefer Arugat HaBossem le-R. Avraham ben Azriel,* (Jerusalem, 1939), 52; and cf. 38–39

20. See A. M. Haberman, "The *Piyuttim* of Rabbenu Barukh bar Shmuel of Magence" [in Hebrew], *Yedi'ot ha-Makhon le-heqer ha-shirah ha-'ivrit bi-Yerushalayim* 6 (1946), 133 (*selihah* composed for the martyrs of Blois): "Fire devoured fire in His red *porphyrion [adam],*" 152) (in the sense of a royal garment). The messianic *porphyry* is also mentioned in the work of Rabbi Eleazar ben Yehuda of Worms, *Kiryat Sefer* (Lemberg, 1905), 12. On the use of this motif in the Zohar, see n. 72.

21. J. Schwarz, "Treading the Grapes of Wrath; The Wine Press in Ancient Jewish and Christian Tradition," *Theologische Zeitschrift* 49 (1993): 215–28, 311–24. For more on Christian and Jewish parallels in the use of the motif of *porphyry,* see chapter 4.

22. For additional uses of this motif in the biblical context, see Zvi M. Rabinovitch, *Piyyutei Rabbi Yannai la-Torah vela-Mo'adim* (Tel Aviv, 1985), 1:303; "Arose your vengeance upon him, when the king is restless at night / trample out the vineyard like a watchman in the night"; and in *Shir ha-Kavod:* "Dazzling He is and ruddy, his clothes red, when from treading Edom's winepress He comes"; Philip Birnbaum, *High Holyday Prayer Book* (New York); and cf. A. M. Haberman, *Piyyutei R. Shimon b. Yitzhak* (Jerusalem, 1938), 170, 182. The slaughter in Bozrah (Isa 34:6) and the harsh descriptions of vengeance against Edom in this chapter form the main part of the haftarah for the Sabbath before Passover, according to one ancient custom; see Ezra Fleischer, "*Piyyut* and Prayer in the Palestinean Mahzor" [in Hebrew], *Kiryat Sefer* 63 (1990): 240 n. 190. This haftarah was clearly intended to express the wish to see the destruction of Christianity in connection with the holiday of deliverance.

for the spilt blood of the martyrs as an inherent part of the redemptive vision. Nevertheless, the frequency of appearance of the *porphyrion* motif in Ashkenazic laments after the persecutions that accompanied the First Crusade (1096) suggests certain new emphases. An idea that was rare and peripheral in the Midrash became a cornerstone of religious thought and action in Ashkenaz. The Ashkenazim not only rescued a muted voice from oblivion but also endowed it with new content. The concept of vengeance expressed in these two Midrashim is one of a legal event: it is to take place on the "Judgment Day," and God, who both avenges and judges, requires solid evidence to convict the murderers. This is the function of the *porphyrion*. The shed blood and its impression on the divine garment are a legal exhibit, by whose means the guilt of the murderers will be proven. Vengeance is no more than a delayed act of justice, to be performed at Judgment Day. But that is not how the idea was understood in Ashkenaz. In Ashkenazic liturgical poems and chronicles, vengeance is transformed from a legal event to a universal occurrence, one at the very heart of the messianic process. The essence of redemption is not the return to Zion, nor the flocking of all nations to the holy mountain of God in Jerusalem, nor even the acceptance of the yoke of the Kingdom of Heaven by all the inhabitants of earth and the vision of universal peace. Rather, the vision of vengeance against the Gentiles takes center stage, because that vengeance alone will facilitate the upheaval of the messianic period, when the kingdom of Edom will be wiped off the face of the earth.

All this is demonstrated clearly when we examine the mentality reflected in the liturgical poems and dirges of the Ashkenazic sages. As we shall see below, every lamentation concludes with a prayer for vengeance against the Gentiles as part of the long-awaited process of redemption. The Ashkenazic *paytanim* (liturgical poets) drew their imagery and beliefs not only from the Midrash, but also from the classical Eretz-Yisrael *piyyut,* in which vengeance and blood reckoning with Edom also lie in the very center of the eschatological description. In his liturgical poems, Yannai calls on God to

uproot from the earth
the kingdom of Dumah
and impose dread
upon every nation.[23]

---

23. Rabinovitch, *Piyyutei Rabbi Yannai,* 110. On Yannai's scathing anti-Christian positions, see Y. Yahalom, *Sefat ha-shir shel ha-piyyut ha-Eretz Yisraeli ha-qadum* (Jerusalem, 1985), 37–40.

In his well-known *kerovah* (a *piyyut* recited in the Amidah prayer), "Vayehi bahazi halaylah," Yannai enumerates one by one the various horrors involved in the smiting of the firstborn in Egypt.[24] Such a detailing of the deliverance from Egypt is intended to serve as a paradigm for the vengeance awaiting the Gentiles at the End of Days, for "what was at the beginning will be at the end."[25] And indeed, immediately following the lines describing the smiting of the firstborn we find a direct transition to the final deliverance, emphasized by the recurring phrase *shoah u-meso'ah* (utter devastation).

That is, just as God punished the Egyptians by smiting the firstborn, so will he smite and annihilate the nations of the world in the final Redemption.[26] This is the view underlying several seder customs and sections of the Haggadah. There is an Ashkenazic custom to spill drops of wine from the glass at mention of each of the ten plagues of Egypt, alluding to messianic vengeance. This is explained in *Sefer Maharil:* "He [God] will save us from all these [plagues] and bring them upon our foes."[27] *Sefer Amarkal* cites a homily in the name of Rabbi Eleazar Rokeah, according to which one spills sixteen drops of wine (ten drops on mention of the plagues; three drops for their mnemonic acronym; and three drops for "blood and fire and pillars of smoke"), corresponding to "the sword of the Holy One blessed be He [that has] sixteen sides."[28] This explanation of Rokeah does not appear in the printed edition of his book but does appear in Manuscript Oxford-Bodleian 1103. From the original wording, it follows that this custom was current in Ashkenaz even before 1096:

> For each word they put their finger in the cup of wine, which they sprinkle outside. Such is the custom of our forefathers, and thus did

---

24. Yahalom, *Sefat ha-shir*, 297–98.

25. Yahalom (n. 23, p. 100), 300. In *Midrash Tanhuma*, ed. Buber, 2.43–44: "Just as He brought afflictions upon the Egyptians, so in the future will He bring them upon the kingdom of Edom. . . . Just as Egypt was stricken with blood, Edom will also be stricken"; see Samuel A. Berman (Hobocken, NJ), 388. And the exegesis of R. Hamma bar Hanina in *Pesiqta de-Rav Kahana*, 1. 133: "May he who took retribution against the former ones take retribution against the later ones. Just as the Egyptians were punished with blood, so shall Edom be." The *piyyut Mitzrayim tamarta le-dam ye'oreihem* was composed on the basis of this homily; see *Mahzor la-Regalim: Pesah*, ed. Y. Frankel (Jerusalem, 1993), 136–38 (and cf. Frankel, 130–32).

26. Interpretation of the editor, Rabinovitch, (n. 22, p. 98), 299. According to Rev 16–17, the seven afflictions of "the wrath of God" at the End of Days are the mark of the beast, blood (twice), heat, darkness, frogs, and hail—a clear allusion to the afflictions of Egypt.

27. *Sefer Maharil: Minhagim*, ed. S. Spitzer (Jerusalem, 1989), 106–7.

28. N. Coronel, *Hamisha Kuntresim* (Vienna, 1864), 27a.

our Rabbi Eleazar Hagadol and all the members of his household, and so did Rabbenu Kalonymus the Elder and all his family. And so did Rabbi Eleazar Hazan and Rabbenu Shmuel the Prophet and the sons of Rabbenu Abraham and Rabbenu Judah he-Hasid, the father of wisdom. And also my father and teacher, Rabbenu Judah b. Kalonymus. And one is not to ridicule the custom of our holy forefathers, for thereby one sprinkles outside of the cup sixteen times, against the sword of the Holy One blessed be He which has sixteen sides.[29]

The tannaitic Midrash cited in the Passover Haggadah, stating that the Egyptians were afflicted with fifty plagues in Egypt and two hundred and fifty at the Sea, is not merely arithmetic acrobatics but an attempt to multiply the punishments that will descend on the Gentiles in the future, just as Yannai's liturgical poem does. We have already seen, in the previous chapter, that the Passover seder is addressed to the future deliverance no less than it is to preserving the memory of the historical Exodus from Egypt.

The desire for vengeance may also be found in Eleazar Ha-Kallir's lamentations for Tisha b'Av. He asks that the evil of the Gentiles be revealed,[30] so that God may take vengeance on Edom.[31] In a recently published *siluq* for Tisha b'Av by Ha-Kallir,[32] the editor noted "a veritable outburst of curse and hatred" against the Christians. In this *piyyut* he describes his vision of Redemption:

For there is a day of vengeance in my heart
the time has come for the Tishbite to be revealed
. . . .
Now will I take vengeance upon those that embittered me.[33]

The height of animosity is reached in the following section in which, as in Yannai, the ten plagues of Egypt serve as a model for future catastrophe, with the recurring rhyme of the word *dam* (blood).

29. Israel Ta-Shma, "The Origin and Place of *Aleinu le-Shabbeah* in the Daily Prayerbook: *Seder ha-Ma'amadot* and Its Relation to the Conclusion of the Daily Service" [in Hebrew], in *Sefer Zikaron le-Efraim Talmage*, ed. D. Walfish (Haifa, 1993), 85–98.

30. Goldschmidt (n. 7, p. 95), 37.

31. Goldschmidt (n. 7, p. 95), 46. And see the end of the lament, 71–72.

32. Ezra Fleischer, "Solving the Qaliri Riddle" [in Hebrew], *Tarbiz* 54 (1985): 383–427, esp. 412–27.

33. Fleischer, "Solving the Qaliri Riddle," 387.

The Ashkenazim developed and enhanced this Palestinian tradition after 1096. However, the expectation of vengeance as a central component in the process of Redemption had already been expressed even earlier. It was not the atrocities of 1096 that spawned the longings for vengeance against the Christians, nor are these aspirations merely the emotional reaction of a grieving poet, motivated by pain and bereavement. Rather, they are part of an entire messianic teaching, as shown by the presence of this motif in Ashkenazic *piyyut* even before 1096. Rabbi Simeon ben Isaac, who lived at the beginning of the tenth century, in the *selihah* entitled *Arkhu ha-yamimm*, asks God to avenge the blood of his servants and to "fill a deep and broad cup with laughter and derision" of their enemies.[34]

In a *kerovah* for the seventh day of Passover, Rabbi Shimon follows in Yannai's path and draws an analogy between the deliverance from Egypt and the future Redemption:

> Let him wreak his vengeance in Edom before our eyes
> because the vapor of Esau will come to Him at the time of His
>   remembrance.
> His seed, and his brethren, and his neighbors are despoiled, and are
>   no more
> they have drunk the cup of bitterness
> . . . .
> For the Lord is our judge, the Lord is our lawgiver
> The Lord is our king—He will deliver us.
> And as Egypt were made to hear, so shall our enemies
> Edom and Ishmael and all our oppressors.[35]

Vengeance against the Christians likewise occupies a central place in the eschatological vision of his younger contemporary, Rabbi Gershom Meor ha-Golah: "Bereaved and widower you destroy with them / pour out their blood that it may be seen on the ground";[36] "Be zealous for the honor of Your Name if not for our sake / great fury unleash on our torturers";[37] "Fight our quarrel and redeem us / recompense our tormenters sevenfold / pursue

---

34. Haberman (n. 22, p. 98), 170.

35. Haberman, (n. 22, p. 98), 83. A similar style appears in his *kerovah* for Passover, *Eimat norotekha*, 195–218. For more on vengeance in his poetry, see esp. 51, 64–65, 77, 165, 167, 182, 202.

36. Haberman (n. 5, p. 94), 8–9.

37. Haberman (n. 5, p. 94), 13.

them with anger and destroy them, You who bore us";[38] "I have beseeched, save us, and a day of revenge unfold";[39] "He who seeks blood, judge our case / return [punishment] sevenfold to the bosom of those that torture us."[40] The *selihah* entitled *Hashem Elohai Rabat Tzeraruni* by Rabbi David ben Samuel ha-Levi, who wrote at the end of the eleventh century in Speyer, also includes an exalted prayer for vengeance: "Judge my case and avenge the blood of Your servants, spilt by wicked men with fury / Put down those who rise against me and send them anger and fury and rage and misfortune."[41]

These views became aggravated after 1096. The chroniclers attribute vengeance as the motive of the Crusaders: "We seek our recompense and to avenge ourselves the vengeance of our Savior from the Ishmaelites, and here are the Jews who killed him and crucified him, let us first take vengeance of them."[42] Vengeance is understood here as punishment intended to set right the balance of justice.[43] It would seem that here the Jew attributes to the Christian his own view: vengeance as the beginning of deliverance.[44]

This is the background that led Rabbi Solomon bar Shimshon, author of the chronicle on the persecutions of 1096, to ascribe such great impor-

---

38. Haberman (n. 5, p. 94), 9.

39. Haberman (n. 5, p. 94), 27.

40. Haberman (n. 5, p. 94), 33.

41. Goldschmidt (n. 15, p. 97), 227; A. M. Haberman, *Be-Ron Yahad: Yalqut shirei tefillah atiqim gam hadashim* (Jerusalem, 1975), 146: "This may have been written shortly after 1096."

42. Haberman (n. 13, p. 97), 24, 72; Moritz Stern and Adolf Neubauer, eds., *Hebräische Berichte über die Judenverfolgung während der Kreuzzüge* (Berlin, 1892), 36–37; Robert Chazan, *European Jewry and the First Crusade* (Berkeley and Los Angeles, 1987), 243–44; J. Riley-Smith, *The First Crusade and the Idea of Crusading* (Philadelphia, 1986), 54–57.

43. Note the use of the concept of "vengeance" in the Ashkenazic sources. In the responsum of Rabbi Hayyim ben Yehiel Hefets Tov in M. A. Bloch, ed., *Shu"t Meir b. Barukh mi-Rotenburg*, Prague ed. (Budapest, 1895), sec. 241, it is told of the bishop of Cologne, who granted the Jews' request to punish those who rioted against them in connection with the ritual murder accusation of Werner the Good in 1287. But right after he began to punish them, the battle of Worringen took place, the bishop was imprisoned, and his mission was not completed. This is how the matter was reported in the responsum: "The Bishop was arrested after he began the vengeance by killing two of them." The vengeance was thus the execution of murderers in the framework of an official, legal judicial procedure. For more on the significance of the concept of vengeance, see M. Frank, *Kehillot Ashkenaz u-vatei dinehen* (Tel Aviv, 1938), 128; Y. Halperin, *Pinkas Va'ad Arba Aratzot* (Jerusalem, 1945), 547; Simon Dubnow, *Pinkas ha-Medina (Pinkas Va'ad ha-Kehillot ha-rashiot bi-medinat Lita* (Berlin, 1925), sec. 11, 5.

44. On the centrality of the motif of vengeance in the Crusader view in general, and toward the Jews in particular, see Chazan (n. 42, above), 75–80. On the importance of the messianic idea in Crusader ideology, see chapter 4, nn. 16 and 17.

tance to the idea of messianic vengeance. The vast destruction of the Jewish community in Mainz—1,100 people killed—is summed up by the author with the cry: "Will you hold back on such as these, O Lord; for Your sake were killed souls without number, and avenge the spilt blood of your servants, in our days and before our eyes, Amen, speedily."[45] It is not by chance that the author concludes his tale—the episode of Mainz—with a long messianic prayer asking for vengeance against the Gentiles:

> May the Lord God give our vengeance into our hands, and make known to the nations before our eyes the vengeance of the spilt blood of His servants, speedily, for Your great name which is called upon us, that all creatures may know and understand the sin and guilt that they did to us, and that their recompense may turn upon their heads as they did to us. Then may they all know and understand and turn over in their hearts, that for naught they cast down these slain ones to the earth.[46]

The event described here is the Christians' admission of the futility of their faith, which will only be realized by means of messianic vengeance. Blood vengeance is an act of sanctifying God's name ("make known to the nations . . . for Your great name"), and it was to this type of messianic Kiddush Hashem to which the martyrs of 1096 aspired.[47]

The calls for revenge found in the liturgical poems of 1096 must be understood in this light. The lament *Haharishu mimeni* concludes with an appeal to God:

> How long will you look and see all their secret deeds?
> Be zealous on behalf of Your Torah which they have affronted
>
> . . . .
>
> Shall the Master of all Creatures be restrained with such as these?
> Avenge the blood spilt like water![48]

---

45. Haberman (n. 13, p. 97), 32; Stern and Neubauer (n. 42, p. 103), 8; Chazan (n. 42, p. 103), 256; and cf. Haberman (n. 13, p. 97), 46; Stern and Neubauer (n. 42, p. 103); Chazan (n. 42, p. 103), 277.

46. Haberman (n. 13, p. 97), 43; Stern and Neubauer (n. 42, p. 103), 17; Chazan (n. 42, p. 103), 272–73. And also, on the same page in these books: "And may their merit and righteousness and piety and innocence and binding be a righteous intercessory on our behalf and defense before the Almighty, and take us out of the exile of the wicked Edom quickly in our days, and may the righteous Messiah come speedily in our days."

47. Compare with chapter 4, sec. 1 ("The Blood").

48. Goldschmidt (n. 7, p. 95), sec. 23, 88.

This motif is also the essence of the lament *Mi yiten roshi mayim*, whose author likens the destruction of the communities to the Destruction of the Temple: "For their massacre is no less weighty, to mourn and wail / than the burning of the house of our God, the palace and the sanctum" and appeals to God: "O thou who art mighty! Who is like thee, O Lord, who bearest all our burdens in silence? Will thou be quiet and restrain thyself and not gird thyself in wrath?"[49] The liturgical poet Rabbi Binyamin bar Hiyya similarly concludes the *selihah* entitled *Berit kerutah* with a prayer for vengeance.[50]

A bold and straightforward expression of the close link between the death of the martyrs and their vengeance—and thus between vengeance and Redemption in general—is to be found at the conclusion of Rabbi Kalonymus ben Judah's lament:

> For how long shall You be like a warrior who knows not how
> to deliver!
> Make known the vengeance from the Gentiles for the blood
> of Your servants before our very eyes
> . . . .
> Hasten the redemption and speed the vision
> For there is a day of vengeance in my heart and the year of my
> redemption comes near.[51]

The word *vengeance (neqama)* is mentioned fifteen times in this poem, in addition to the synonyms *gemul* (retribution) and *tashlum* (payment), and the verbs *to wipe out (lekhalot)* and *to destroy (lehazmit)*.

One of the few Ashkenazic *piyyutim* that does not conclude with this pattern of pleading for vengeance as part of the Redemption is that of Rabbi Menahem ben Makhir of Regensburg.[52] But even in this poem a later hand added the conventional conclusion calling for vengeance. And the works of a more moderate poet and writer, such as Rabbi Eliezer ben Nathan, end with a call for vengeance:

> Turn, O Lord. Pour out Your heart to confound and destroy them
> for Your vengeance, make the arrows drunk with blood

49. Goldschmidt (n. 7, p. 95), sec. 26, 46, 97; Haberman (n. 13, p. 97), 68.
50. Goldschmidt (n. 15, p. 97), 544; S. Bernfeld, *Sefer ha-Dema'ot*, 3 (Berlin, 1926), 310–13.
51. Goldschmidt (n. 7, p. 95), sec. 30, 106–9.
52. Haberman (n. 13, p. 97), 63–64; Goldschmidt (n. 7, p. 95), sec. 34.

the enemies to eat the sword with redding shield
salvation from the foe bring, and vain is the deliverance of man.[53]

    The rhyme ends with *dam* (blood) and, quite predictably, continues with an appeal to God to judge and punish the assailants, to have mercy on his people, and to hasten the Redemption. In another lament, his words are even more forceful:

> For the holy pious ones no ransom can be set
> I have avenged the unavenged blood, and the Lord dwells in Zion
> ·
> May all the evil of my torturers go before you
> Pursue them with angry fury and destroy them beneath the heavens
> Set a day to destroy my neighbors
> The vengeance of your servants shall be made known to the nations
>   before my eyes.[54]

The motif of vengeance reaches poetic heights in the liturgical poem by Rabbi Hakim, *Ayeh Qinatkha,* which is entirely devoted to arousing the zeal of God.[55] After describing Israel's sufferings under Edom and Israel's devotion to its faith, the author concludes his poem with the words: "May the voice of the Lord recompense His enemies / and like the sun rising in strength, shine upon them that love Him."

    We thus find that the motif of vengeance was deeply rooted within Ashkenazic consciousness from the very start, as indicated by the intensity and centrality of this theme even after the atrocities of 1096 had passed. During the two hundred years following 1096, Ashkenazic Jewry did not suffer particularly severe pogroms, yet their hope for vengeance did not subside. Rabbi Ephraim ben Jacob of Bonn repeatedly emphasizes the centrality of vengeance in the messianic consciousness of his generation, a fact that stands out clearly in his liturgical poem *Asiha bemar nafshi,* about the riot of Blois in 1171.[56] The well-known *piyyut* for Hanukkah, *Maoz Tzur* (O Mighty Rock), concludes with the plea:

---

53. Haberman (n. 13, p. 97), 83.
54. Haberman (n. 13, p. 97), 87–88.
55. Haberman (n. 13, p. 97), 90–92.
56. Haberman (n. 17, p. 97), 44–47.

Bare Your holy arm
and hasten the final salvation
Avenge the vengeance of Your servants' blood
from the wicked nation.

The connection between vengeance and salvation is obvious. The motif of vengeance is also central in the works of Rabbi Meir of Rothenburg, who took pains in his lament, *Ahbirah milin,* to incorporate the word *neqama* (vengeance) thirteen times in the ten concluding strophes. I cite here only those biblical verses that include the word *vengeance:*

O Lord, thou God of vengeance, thou God of vengeance, shine forth! [Ps. 94:1]

And I will lay my vengeance upon Edom. [Ezek. 25:14]

Let the avenging of the outpoured blood of thy servants be known among the nations before our eyes. [Ps. 79:10]

The God who gave me vengeance and subdued peoples under me. [Ps. 18:47]

The Lord is avenging and wrathful. [Nahum 1:2]

The Lord is a jealous God and avenging. [ibid.]

The God who gave me vengeance. [II Sam. 22:48]

For he avenges the blood of his servants. [Deut. 32:43]

To execute the Lord's vengeance. [Num. 31:3]

Strong one, in the great vengeance of your hand, Amen.[57]

I shall conclude my discussion of vengeful redemption in Ashkenaz by quoting from *Ma'amar 'al Shenat Ge'ulah* (An Essay on the Year of Deliverance), a work written during the first half of the thirteenth century.[58] The author describes Redemption as an ongoing process that will begin in 1296

---

57. Haberman (n. 13, p. 97), 181–83.
58. Alexander Marx, "On the Year of Redemption" [in Hebrew], *Ha-Tzofeh le-hokhmat Yisrael* 5 (1921): 194–202.

and conclude in 1352, involving two stages: the first is vengeance (twenty-one years), and the second is the Ingathering of the Exiles (thirty-five years). The author refers to both these stages as "the revealed things" *(haniglot),* based on the biblical verse "The secret things belong to the Lord our God; but the things that are revealed belong unto us and to our children " (Deut 29:29), interpreting the word *lanu* (us) in terms of its numerical value, "to fifty-six"—that is, the Hebrew year 5056, or 1296 C.E. Regarding the "secret things"—the redemptive events that will follow these two stages—he says nothing, since they are known only to God:

> And during the sixth millennium [fifty-six of the "small" counting; i.e., 1296 C.E.], there shall begin the redemption and the vengeance that the Holy One blessed be He shall perform among the nations. And that vengeance will continue for 21 years [1296–1317 C.E.], and this is what is said, "I shall be that I shall be" [Exod 3:14]—"I shall be" in the exile of Egypt and Persia, as "I shall be" in the final exile, and I will redeem them. The numerical value *(gematria)* of the word "I shall be" *(ehyeh)* is 21. And after those 21 years, Elijah will come and begin the Ingathering of the Exiles, and he shall cast down the evil nation. And this will occur in the year 77 of the sixth millennium [i.e., 1317 C.E.]. And this is what is said, "The Lord will give strength *['oz]* to his people" [Ps 29:11]. When the Holy One blessed be He will give "strength," then He will bless his people. And from the year [50]77 on there will begin the Ingathering of the Exiles, and there shall occur the ingathering in which all of them will be gathered into the Land of Israel, which will be during the 35 years following this, for during those 35 years [i.e, 1317–1352 C.E.] there will be fulfilled what is said "By the side of princes you shall be lifted, and kings shall be your nursemaids"— that kings of the nations shall see the vengeance that He did with them on behalf of Israel and will see the Ingathering of the Exiles. . . . And during that same year, 35 years after [50]77, which will be the one-hundred-twelfth year of the sixth millennium [1352 C.E.], this nation [Edom, i.e., Christendom] will be completely obliterated and Jerusalem will be rebuilt.

This author saw vengeance as the event ushering in the Redemption, and the destruction of all the nations as its conclusion. It is worthwhile noting the close connection he draws between the Redemption from Egypt and the future Redemption, a connection intended to define the duration of the first stage—that of vengeance. That is, the deliverance from Egypt serves as a model, particularly regarding the future punishment in store for the Gentiles. The specific model in the Exodus from Egypt that served as an example for the future is the plagues that afflicted the Egyptians.

I began this chapter by contrasting the position of the Ashkenazic work *Sefer Nizzahon Vetus* with that of the Provençal book *Milhemet Mitzvah*. In the next section I shall expand the comparison, thereby demonstrating more emphatically the uniqueness of the Ashkenazic view. How were the biblical prophecies concerning vengeance against Edom interpreted outside Franco-Germany?

PROSELYTIZING REDEMPTION

Rabbi Hai Gaon described the messianic process in great detail, claiming that when the Redemption starts "most of the Jews will live in the lands of their Exile, for it will not be clear to them that the End has come." Then "the Messiah son of Joseph will rise, together with the people who have gathered to him from the Galilee, to Jerusalem, and they will kill the officer of the King of Edom and the people who are with him. Concerning that hour it says 'And I will lay my vengeance upon Edom by the hand of my people Israel' [Ezek 25:14]."[59] This is a local event, concerning the remnant in the Land of Israel, not a world event. Afterward Gog, the king of Edom, will attack Jerusalem, together with many other nations, and God will smite the foes of Jerusalem with four kinds of disaster. This is a description of a defeat in battle, without the slightest trace of vengeance. The messianic description then concentrates primarily on the internal situation of Israel, on the repentance of the sinners, on the resurrection of the dead, and on the Ingathering of the Exiles. The reprisal against the Gentiles sounds like a marginal event, lacking resonance. The task of the nations of the world is to join the messianic process: "And all the remaining nations will convert to Judaism," and then the Messiah will command them to stop the wars, and eternal peace will reign. In brief, that which in Rabbi Hai Gaon stays at the periphery of the messianic events is at the center of the Ashkenazic scenario.[60]

59. Urbach (n. 19, p. 98), 1:256–63. Also published by Y. Even-Shmuel, *Midrashei Geulah* (Jerusalem, 1954), 133–41.

60. A similar description appears in Rabbi Saadyah Gaon's *Sefer Emunot ve-De'ot* 8.5–6, ed. J. Kapah (New York, 1970), 245–52 (= *Midreshei Geulah*, 115–28). Its source is in *Sefer Zerubavel*, 55–88. And cf. *Aggadat ha-Mashiah*, in *Beit Midrasch*, ed. A. Jellinek (Leipzig, 1855), 3, 141; *Signs of the Messiah*, 60. R. Joseph ibn Avitor composed his liturgical poem *geulah* in the same vein; see E. Fleischer, *Ha-Yozrot behithavutam uve-hitpathutam* (Jerusalem, 1984), 595. And compare *Hazon Daniel* (*Genizah Studies*, vol. 1 [New York, 1928]), 321–23; and the study of Robert Bonfil, "'The Vision of Daniel as a Historical and Literary Document' [in Hebrew], *Zion* 44 (1979): 111–47. Note two ancient liturgical poems of the moderate sort:

An approach greatly reducing the tension with Edom is self-evident in the Muslim world. While Ashkenazic Jewry continued the Byzantine Palestinian tradition, the Jews of Spain continued the Babylonian tradition, as exemplified by Rabbi Hai Gaon. The outstanding representative of the desire to weaken the connection between the vision of vengeance against Edom and historical reality is Rabbi Abraham ibn Ezra, who states in his exegesis on the Bible that the Edom mentioned in the prophecies of messianic vengeance is the biblical Edom and not Rome.[61] This position persisted even after Spain became Christian. The messianic world of Spanish Jewry was one of conversionary redemption, not redemption through vengeance.

Spanish liturgical poets also concluded their laments for Tisha b'Av with words of consolation and hope for Redemption. Rabbi Solomon ibn Gabirol concludes his lament *Shomron kol titen* with the prayer to God:

Behold their desolation, and the length of their exile
be not exceedingly angry, but see their humiliation
and remember not forever their iniquity and their folly.[62]

The messianic events are between God and his people, and there is no mention of Gentiles. In the collection entitled *Al Neharot Sefarad* (On the Rivers of Spain), containing more than a hundred Sephardic laments for Tisha b'Av, we find barely five laments concluding with the sweet savor of wreaking vengeance on the Gentiles at the End of Days.[63] The harshest description in Spanish literature of the fate of the Gentiles at the End of Days

---

Oto hayom sheyavo Mashiah ben David, published by Y. Yahalom, "On the Validity of Literary Works as Historical Sources" [in Hebrew], *Cathedra* 11 (1979): 130–33; and the *piyyut* of *Haduta, Gavoha ve-nakhon ve-nisa,* published by Ezra Fleischer, "Haduta–Hadutahu–Chedweta: Solving an Old Riddle" [in Hebrew], *Tarbiz* 53 (1984): 71–96. On the eschatological vision of this liturgical poem, see 84–90.

61. In his commentary to Ps 137:6; Obad 1:10; Dan 2:39. And cf. Y. Yahalom, "The Transition of Kingdoms in Eretz Israel (Palestine) As Conceived by Poets and Homilists" [in Hebrew], *Shalem* 6 (1992): 12–13. However, Rabbi Abraham ibn Ezra is not always consistent in this position; see A. Lipshitz, "The Exegetical Approach of Abraham Ibn-Ezra and Isaac Abravanel to Prophecy" [in Hebrew], *Proceedings to Sixth World Congress of Jewish Studies* (Jerusalem, 1976), 1:133–39; M. Orfali, "R. Abraham Ibn Ezra and Jewish-Christian Polemics" [in Hebrew], *Te'uda* 8 (1992): 198–201.

62. D. Goldschmidt (n. 7, p. 95), 28–29.

63. S. Bernstein, *'Al Naharot Sefarad* (Tel Aviv, 1956). And see D. Pagis, "Dirges on the Persecution of 1391 in Spain" [in Hebrew], *Tarbiz* 37 (1978): 355–73.

is that of Rabbi Abraham bar Hiyya, of twelfth-century Barcelona, in his book *Higayon ha-Nefesh ha-'Azuvah:*

> The Holy One blessed be He shall cut off all the wicked nations of the world and there shall not remain of them even a remnant. . . . Most of the nations of the world will be completely destroyed and cut off, and none will remain in the world save for the righteous who fear the Lord, [whether] from among His people or from those who believe in Torah that shall take shelter beneath the wings of the Shekhinah from the other nations.[64]

Here too the author speaks of killing Gentiles, but the purpose of the killing is not vengeance, which by its very nature would involve the imposition of collective, retroactive responsibility on all Gentiles, no matter who they are. For Abraham bar Hiyya killing the Gentiles is part of the uprooting of evil in messianic time; hence, wicked Jews can also expect to die. On the other hand, some Gentiles will be saved—namely, those who convert to Judaism. Similarly in Maimonides' famous description of the messianic epoch there is no mention of vengeance against or annihilation of the Gentiles.[65] Elijah's function is to "bring peace in the world," not to declare war on the Gentiles. His words are well-known: "The Sages and Prophets did not desire the days of the Messiah so that Israel might [rule the entire world or] exercise dominion over the heathens, or be exalted by the nations . . .

---

64. Abraham bar Hiyya, *Hegayon ha-Nefesh ha-'Azuvah*, ed. G. Wigoder (Jerusalem, 1971), 128–29. And cf. bar Hiyya, *Megillat ha-Megalleh*, ed. Z. Poznansky (Berlin, 1924), 76: "The Holy One blessed be He dispersed Israel among the lands to dwell therein until they would multiply and their number would be like the number of all the nations, and the Omnipresent would obliterate all the nations and give their lands and all their inheritance to His people Israel. And at that time there will occur the Resurrection of the Dead, when all Israel shall stand up from their graves, from those who left Egypt to the generation of Messiah, and they shall be as numerous as the seventy nations of the world; and because of this they shall fill all the inhabited places of the earth, where the nations had been dwelling there." The author describes a Jewish "demographic explosion" after the Resurrection, as a result of which the Jews will inhabit all the lands of the earth. There is no hint here of revenge or punishment (in a similar spirit, see 110). The destruction of the nations is also discussed by Rabbi Yehudah ben Barzilai, *Perush Sefer Yezirah*, ed. S. Z. H. Halberstam (Berlin, 1885), 135–37.

65. *Hilkhot Melakhim*, chaps. 11–12; see *The Code of Maimonides; 14. The Book of Judges*, trans. A. M. Hershman (New Haven, 1949). According to Maimonides, the difference between Gentiles and Jews will disappear completely at the End of Days. Cf. Menahem Kellner, *Maimonides on Judaism and the Jewish People*, (Albany, 1991), 33–47.

but so they might be free to devote themselves to the Law and its wisdom." This sounds almost like a polemic against the Askenazic concept of avenging redemption.[66]

The conversion of the Gentiles, rather than their annihilation, is also mentioned as being self-evident in Rabbi Judah Halevi's *The Book of the Kuzari*[67] and in the writings of Nahmanides.[68] The polemical work *Edut Hashem Ne'emenah* of Rabbi Solomon ben Moses de Rossi, who lived in Italy in the second half of the thirteenth century, likewise contains a tranquil description of the end of the Gentiles in the messianic epoch.[69] Here and there in this work, which is in fact a compilation of biblical verses arranged by subject, the author interrupts the flow of verses to disclose his own views. He devotes one section, entitled "God Will Take Recompense Against All Their Foes" to a description of the End of Days, in which he cites biblical verses about the punishment of the Gentiles, who will rise against Israel in the war of Gog and Magog. Prior to this, in a chapter entitled "The Messiah Will Rule Over the Entire World: Who Will Fall and Who Will Rise," he quotes biblical verses describing the divine wrath against the Gentiles, concluding with the sentence "to prove that upon the coming of our Messiah the entire world will turn to one faith, which is the faith of Israel, and wisdom and the knowledge of God will multiply, and the Lord shall be one and His Name one." And further on: "And at that time the entire world will return to one faith, and all will call upon the name of the Lord." He systematically ignores all catastrophic interpretations of the messianic epoch, describing a tranquil and pacifistic world. This is also true of the title of the next chapter: "Proving That When Our Messiah Comes There Will Be Temporal and Eternal General Peace, and Even Wild Animals and Reptiles and Venomous Animals Will Not Cause Harm."[70]

---

66. The polemical tone of Maimonides' words was also noted by Gershom Scholem, "Towards an Understanding of the Messianic Idea in Judaism," in *The Messianic Idea in Judaism and Other Essays on Jewish Spirituality* (New York, 1971), 29. On the polemical tendency in Maimonides, see Isidore Twersky, *Introduction to the Code of Maimonides (Mishneh Torah)* (New Haven, 1980), 451 n. 231.

67. *Kuzari*, 4.23, ed. I. Ibn-Shmuel, Jerusalem, 1973, 178; Yochanan Silman, *Bein filosof lenavi* (Ramat Gan, 1985), 230, suggests examining the plot of the book, whose climax is in the conversion of the Khazar people to Judaism, as a parable illustrative of the end of humanity.

68. *Kitvei Ramban*, ed. C. Chavell 1: (Jerusalem, 1963), 322.

69. J. M. Rosenthal, *Mehqarim umeqorot* (Jerusalem, 1967), 1:388–94.

70. A change in and exacerbation of the attitude toward Christianity took place among the Jews of Spain at the end of the Middle Ages. See Hayyim Beinart, "A Prophesying Move-

Additional support for the ubiquity of the Sephardic concept of conversionary Redemption is found in a manuscript in the Pirkovitz Collection containing about 120 Spanish laments composed between the pogroms of 1391 and the expulsion of the Jews from Spain in 1492—a collection that has recently been studied by Yoseph Yahalom.[71] This compilation demonstrates that the Spanish liturgical poem preserved lofty restraint toward Christians even after the pogroms of 1391—that is, even after Spanish Jewry began to experience persecution by the Christians, and their fate became increasingly similar to that of Ashkenazic Jewry. Many laments conclude with words of solace and anticipation of impending Redemption, in that same place where the motif of vengeance appears among the Ashkenazim. In the Spanish laments, by contrast, there is virtually no mention of the Gentiles, almost as if the pogromists had come from another world. The issue is entirely an internal Jewish one, and the hope for messianic deliverance almost always focuses on the return to Zion as a solution to the suffering of Exile. In these 120 laments, I counted the word *neqama* in all its variants a total of thirteen times—fewer than in a single poem of Rabbi Kalonymus ben Judah!

The war of annihilation against the Gentiles was interpreted in the non-Ashkenazic world as a war against the wicked or against enemies—that is, a selective war that would remove those who delay or oppose the messianic process. The rest will participate in the process as partners in the coronation of the God of Israel as ruler of the world. Keeping the Gentiles alive is thus necessary as proof of the truth of Judaism. What Augustine's doctrine ordered for this world, the non-Ashkenazic messianic doctrine taught regarding the Eschaton: members of the other faith will be kept alive so that they will be able to witness the true faith when the time comes.

The gap between the idea of conversionary redemption, found mostly

ment in Cordova in 1499–1502" [in Hebrew], *Zion* 44 (1980): 199; G. Vajda, "Passages anti-Chrétiens dans Kaf Ha-Qetoret," *Revue des Etudes Juives* 197 (1980): 45–58; Moshe Idel, "The Attitude to Christianity in *Sefer Hameshiv*," *Immanuel* 12 (1981) 77–95; Idel, "Models of Redemptive Activity in the Middle Ages" [in Hebrew], in *Meshihiyut ve-Eskhatologia*, ed. Z. Baras (Jerusalem, 1984), 277–88; Idel, "Minor Writings of the Author of *Kaf ha-Qetoret*" [in Hebrew], *Pe'amim* 53 (1993): 82; Isaiah Tishby, "Geniza Fragments of a Messianic-Mystical Text on the Expulsion from Spain and Portugal" [in Hebrew], *Zion* 48 (1983): 348–54.

71. Y. Yahalom, "The Uniqueness of the Poem as Expressing a Spiritual Reality According to the Late Spanish *Piyyut*" [in Hebrew], in *Galut ahar golah: Mehqarim be-toldot 'Am Yisra'el*, eds. A. Mirski, A. Grossman, Y. Kaplan (Beinart FS; Jerusalem 1988), 337–48. I am grateful to Professor Yoseph Yahalom for allowing me to see his copy of this manuscript.

in the Sephardic world, and that of vengeful redemption, characteristic of Ashkenaz, is consistent with the differences between the views of these two diasporas regarding the identification of the biblical Edom. Gerson Cohen has demonstrated that the Jews of Spain, Babylon, and southern France rejected the Talmudic identification of Edom with Rome. For them, Edom was the Christian faith and not the Roman Empire, unlike the Ashkenazim, who adopted the Talmudic identification of Edom with imperial Rome.[72] To this one must add another development: since the time of Otto the Great (the tenth century), a widespread political ideology in Germany identified Rome with the German Empire; hence, Ashkenazic Jews saw themselves as living under the political rule of Edom, that is, Rome or the German Reich. On this point, Ashkenaz was unique as compared to every other Jew-

---

72. Cohen, "Esau as Symbol" (n. 1, p. 92). Evidently, the differences between the Ashkenazim and the Sephardim gradually decreased at the end of the thirteenth century. The Zohar contains expressions highly reminiscent of the Ashkenazic positions and is the only Sephardic source I know that uses the motif of the *porphyrion* in the sense it was used in Ashkenaz. Zohar I.39a, states: "And then the Messiah puts on his *porphyrion* and thereupon are inscribed and recorded all those who were killed by the pagan nations, on that same *porphyrion*. And the *porphyrion* ascends above and is inscribed upon the supernal *porphyrion* of the king, and the Holy One blessed be He shall in the future wear that same *porphyrion* to judge the nations." Cf. 41a. In several places, the Zohar describes the End of Days in a style reminiscent of the Ashkenazic eschatological vengeance, albeit there too one finds an echo of the Spanish tradition, which seeks the conversion of the nations in the messianic era (II.32a). The entire description is written in the shadow of the liquidation of the Crusader kingdom in the Land of Israel after the fall of Acre in 1291. Cf. R. Kiener, "The Image of Islam in the Zohar" [in Hebrew], in *Sefer ha-Zohar ve-Doro*, ed. J. Dan (= *Mehqerei Yerushalayim be-mahshevet Yisrael*, 8; Jerusalem, 1989), 49–53; Yehudah Liebes, "The Messiah of the Zohar; On R. Simeon Bar Yohai as a Messianic Figure," in his *Studies in the Zohar* (New York, 1993). In several articles, Israel Ta-Shma has noted the influence of the Ashkenazic world on the Zohar: "Miriam's Well: The Devolution of a French Custom at the Third Sabbath Meal" [in Hebrew], in *Mehqerei Yerushalayim be-mahshevet Yisrael* 4 (1985): 269–270 [= his *Minhag Ashkenaz ha-Qadmon* [Jerusalem, 1992] 201–20]; Ta-Shma, "A Note on the *Zohar*" [in Hebrew], *Tarbiz* 60 (1991), 663–65; Ta-Shma, "Ashkenazi Pietism in Spain: Rabbi Jonah of Gerondi, The Man and His Activity" [in Hebrew], in *Galut ahar golah*, 165–94. On the influence of Ashkenazic culture in Spain at the end of the twelfth century, see Avraham Grossman, "The Relation between Spanish and Ashkenazi Jewry in the Middle Ages" [in Hebrew], in *Moreshet Sepharad*, ed. H. Beinart (Jerusalem, 1992), 180–84. The absorption in Spain of the "Ashkenazic" view of vengeance against the Gentiles is also visible in the work of Rabbi Yom Tov ben Abraham Ishbili (Ritba), *Hilkhot Seder ha-Haggadah ubi'urei Haggadah*, ed. Y. Leibowitz (Jerusalem, 1984), 42: "We say at the last cup that the time has come that He should give them to drink of the cup of His wrath, which is also the cup of vengeance, as is written, 'Rejoice and be glad, O daughter of Edom . . . to you also the cup shall pass' (Lam 4:21). Moreover, our main redemption is dependent upon the destruction of the kings."

ish center in Europe. For the Jews of France, England, or Spain, the polit-ical ruler was a king like any other; but for the Jews of Ashkenaz, their ruler was the king of Edom. The vengeful redemption, emphasizing its political dimension, was well suited to the tension between the Jews of Ashkenaz and their Christian milieu. The eschatological vision of the Ashkenazim tended to place much more emphasis on the political destruction of the kingdom of Edom. For the Jews of Spain, conversely, Edom was consid-ered a religious entity, and competition with it was conducted on the reli-gious plane, hence the central importance of conversionary redemption in the Spanish world.

Consequently, the central importance of the idea of vengeance on the Gentiles in Ashkenazic thought is closely connected to an apologetics based on the idea of election. The hope for vengeance is the remedy for the par-adox mentioned at the beginning of this chapter, "the blatant contrast be-tween the election of Israel in Heaven and their subjection on earth." God wreaking vengeance on the Gentiles is the loving father punishing those who torment his chosen son. Messianic vengeance is a new manifestation of the election of Israel and a response to the Christian claim denying that election. This polemical position also stoked expectations of vengeance for the blood of the martyrs, whose death was a desecration of God's name: Where is the honor of a God whose sons are killed? A correction of this will be accomplished through messianic vengeance, when the name of God will be sanctified.

THE CURSE

The central place occupied by vengeance in the messianic process serves to explain a unique ritual widespread in Ashkenaz during the Middle Ages: that of cursing non-Jews. Already in ancient times curses against Christians were inserted within formal prayers, a custom subject to harsh criticism in Jewish-Christian polemics. *Birkat ha-Minim* (Malediction Against the Heretics) was well-known,[73] and its origin may perhaps be traced back to

73. The most recent literature on this issue is Peter Schäfer, "Die sogenannte Synode von Jabne," in *Studien zur Geschichte und Theologie des rabbinischen Judentums* (Leiden, 1978), 45–55; G. Stemberger, "Die sogenannte 'Synode von Jabne' und das frühe Christentum," *Kairos* 19 (1977): 14–21; Reuven Kimelman, "Birkat Ha-Minim and the Lack of Evidence for an Anti-Christian Jewish Prayer in Late Antiquity," in *Jewish and Christian Self-Definition*, ed. E. P. Sanders et al. (London, 1981), 2:226–44, 391–403; W. Horbury, "The Benediction of the Minim

the curses of the Judaean Desert Sect against those who did not abide by the laws of the sect. One fragment of the Qumran scrolls states that in the third month, apparently on the festival of Shavu'ot, the community will gather and curse all those "who veer right or left from the Torah."[74] Shavu'ot was considered the day on which the sect renewed the covenant among its members, when new candidates were accepted for initiation, and when those who had completed two years of training joined the sect. It was only natural that on this day those who had sinned against its laws would be ejected from the sect.[75]

This ceremony of cursing those who deviate from the sect's doctrine might help explain the approach expressed in Galatians 3:10–13. There Paul explains that the observance of the Torah and its laws is based on the power of a curse: "For it is written, 'Cursed be everyone who does not abide by

---

and Early Jewish-Christian Controversy," *The Journal of Theological Studies* 33 (1982): 19–61; T. C. G. Thornton, "Christian Understandings of the Birkath-Ha-Minim in the Eastern Roman Empire," *The Journal of Theological Studies* 38 (1987): 419–31; Ben-Zion Binyamin, "Birkat Ha-Minim and the Ein Gedi Inscription," *Immanuel* 21 (1987): 68–79. These and previous studies discuss the historical and textual question, against whom the *Birkat ha-Minim* was aimed in its various transformations, questions that also occupied Jewish and Christian disputants in the Middle Ages and the early modern era. The expansion of the study of other rituals of cursing, even later ones, should enrich our historical understanding of this issue. These rituals seem to support Schäfer's contention that *Birkat ha-Minim* was originally aimed also against Rome, out of an active messianic position. Horbury's claim that during the second century C.E. the Sages made positive statements about Rome, does not contradict their eschatological view that the destruction of Rome is a preliminary and necessary stage of deliverance. Horbury argued that the conceptual and linguistic affinity of *Birkat ha-Minim* with the biblical eschatological world indicates a messianic-ethical goal of uprooting evildoers within the Jewish camp, not Rome. But it is precisely the biblical affinity that strengthens the assumption that the curse expresses expectations for the destruction of Edom, that is, Rome.

74. *The Dead Sea Scrolls*, ed. Florentino G. Martínez and Eibert J. C. Tigchelaar (Leiden, 1997), 1:596–99.

75. This meaning of the festival of Shavu'ot may plausibly have developed out of an ancient tradition that linked the holiday with the revelation at Sinai and the making of the covenant, even though there is no clear indication of such a connection before the second century B.C.E. The meaning of Shavu'ot in the Judaean Desert sect explains the Lukean interpretation of the holiday, as the occasion when the Christian community gathered and had a kind of "private epiphany" in seventy languages, and at the end three thousand people joined the Christian community (Acts 2). On this connection, see Geza Vermes, "The Impact of the Dead Sea Scrolls on the Study of the New Testament," *JJS* 27 (1976), 108–9. For more on the relationship between Shavu'ot and Pentecost, see Moshe Weinfeld, "The Uniqueness of the Decalogue and Its Place in Jewish Tradition," in *The Ten Commandments in History and Tradition*, ed. B. Z. Segal (Jerusalem, 1990), 42–43.

all things written in the book of the law, and do them' [referring to Deut 27:26]"—which is not the case regarding faith. However, Jesus's death on the Cross exempts all from the obligation to follow the laws of the Torah: "Christ redeemed us from the curse of the law, having become a curse for us—for it is written, 'Cursed be everyone who hangs on a tree' [paraphrase of Deut 21:23]." Jesus, hanging on the Cross, cursed himself, thereby freeing humankind of the burden of the commandments of the Torah.

The inversion of the curse can shed new light on the curse against the heretics in the *Amidah* prayer, for the Jews certainly rejected the Pauline meaning and considered it proper to apply the curse, against those who violate the commandments of the Torah, to Jesus or to his followers, as was done in the sect in the Judaean Desert. One may assume that this is the foundation on which later there developed the medieval texts containing curses against the Christians. Theologically, this ceremony may be seen as a Jewish inversion of Paul's exegesis "for a hanged man is accursed by God." The Jews accepted the Christian exegesis of the hanged Jesus being cursed, but they saw the curse of the one "hanged" as a punishment. This Jewish curse thus had the significance of a repeated crucifixion of Jesus. Note that, in the Middle Ages, Jews were insistent in referring to Jesus as "the hanged one," a fact that may be based on the Jewish exegesis of the biblical verse "for a hanged man is accursed by God"—that is, that one who is "hanged" is also accursed.[76]

Testimony of another ritual of cursing, recited at the end of the daily Morning Prayer, is found in *Yalqut Shim'oni:*

> "It is not for the king's profit to tolerate them" [Est 3:8]. They open their synagogues and read things that do not bear being heard, they say "Hear, O Israel," and then they stand in prayer. And in their prayers they say, "He who humbles the wicked," saying that we are the wicked. And then they say "He who loves righteousness and justice," and hope that the Holy One blessed be He will execute judgment against us; and then they take out the Torah scroll and curse us in a crafty way.[77]

76. For more on bans and excommunication, see W. Horbury, "Extirpation and Excommunication," *Vetus Testamentum* 35 (1985): 13–38.

77. *Yalqut Shim'oni,* Esther, sec. 1054. On this passage, see Samuel Krauss, "Imprecation against the Minim in the Synagogue, *JQR* 9 (1897): 515–17; Krauss, "Zur Literatur der Siddurim: christliche Polemik," *Festschrift für Aron Freimann,* eds. A. Marx and H. Meyer (Berlin, 1935), 128–29. Krauss also mentions *Midrash Tanhuma, Shemini,* sec. 9: "'The craftsmen and the smiths' (Jer 29:2) What is meant by 'the craftsmen' (*ha-heresh;* also "dumb" or

We have here a description of the daily prayer said in proper order. Even before reciting the *Shema* they say "things that do not bear being heard"— that is, that are forbidden to be heard. This may refer to the prayer *Ahavah Rabbah* (Great Love), which includes a messianic plea for the Ingathering of the Exiles. Then comes the acceptance of the yoke of the kingdom of heaven in the *Shema*, which is interpreted as a casting off of the yoke of flesh and blood. This is followed by the *Amidah* prayer, containing two blessings that are interpreted as directed against the Gentiles: the Blessing of Heretics, and the Blessing of Justice. The Blessing of Justice has a significance reminiscent of the vengeance described above. After the *Amidah* prayer a ritual is described in which the Torah scroll is taken out and an imprecation uttered against the Gentiles.[78] This may refer to the recitation of Psalm 83, a chapter that was customarily recited in Ashkenaz at the end of the Morning Prayer: "O God, do not keep silence; . . . For lo, thy enemies are in tumult . . . the tents of Edom and the Ishmaelites . . . O my God, make them like whirling dust, like chaff before the wind . . . so do thou pursue them with thy tempest . . . Let them know that thou alone, whose name is the Lord, are the Most High over all the earth."[79] In Spain, in contrast, it was customary to recite Psalm 86 instead.[80] The Sephardic choice of the latter chapter may have been motivated by verse 9: "All the nations thou hast

---

"silent")? Those who recite the Prayer silently, and overcome by their prayers all the idolators." And perhaps this is also the intention of the Midrash: "'And they read things that it is impossible to hear'? *Targum Sheni* to Esther (at Est 3:8) describes the prayer service on Shabbat and festivals: "They recite from their books, interpret from (the words of) their prophets, and they curse our king and refute our rulers"; see B. Grossfeld, *The Two Targums of Esther, Translated with Apparatus and Notes,* (Minnesota, 1991), 145. According to P. Cassel, "Zweites Targum zum Buche Esther," in *Literatur und Geschichte* (Leipzig, 1885), this work is a polemical work from the time of Justin. The accusations against the Jews of vilifying Christianity are also raised by Agobard. See Chen Merchavia, *Ha-Talmud be-re'i ha-Nazrut* (Jerusalem, 1971), 82–83.

78. Compare the blessing recited (after) reading the Book of Esther: "Blessed are You . . . who avenges our wrong and redeems us and saves us from the hand of all tyrants" (*Sofrim* 14.5–6; Miller ed., xxiv, 191). Krauss ("Zur Literatur der Siddurim") notes that the description of taking out the Torah Scroll does not fit the Sabbath, since the blessings "he who humbles the wicked" and "The King who loves righteousness and justice" are not recited on the Sabbath. Hence, he maintains that the Torah Scroll was taken out for cursing on the occasion of a ceremony of excommunication.

79. S. Horwitz, ed., *Mahzor Vitry le-Rabbenu Simha,* (Nuremberg, 1923; photo ed. Jerusalem, 1963), 74. And cf. Ta-Shma (n. 29, p. 101).

80. *Sefer ha-Manhig le-Rabbi Avraham be-Rabbi Natan ha-Yarhi,* ed. J. Raphael (Jerusalem, 1978), 107–8.

made shall come and bow down before thee, O Lord, and shall glorify thy name," which expresses fully their position, that of championing redemption through conversion, not through vengeance against the Gentiles.

It is also possible that the passages mentioned from *Yalqut Shim'oni* may have been nothing more than a later Ashkenazic Midrash. But if one is in fact dealing with an ancient Palestinian Midrash, it is plausibly the source of the Ashkenazic custom of integrating curses and abuse against the Christians within their prayers.

The anti-Christian status of *Alenu le-shabeah* (It Is Our Duty to Praise), the concluding prayer of all statutory prayer services, will be discussed later. From the twelfth century on, this prayer served as a kind of anti-Christian credo and should not be seen as a ceremony of cursing. Yet some sources show that, during the twelfth and thirteenth centuries, the prayer also included curses. A fragment from *Alenu le-shabeah* found in a prayer book manuscript from England, dated no later than 1190, includes harsh words of abuse against Christians:

> It is our duty to praise the Master of All, to ascribe greatness to the molder of primeval creation, for He has not made us like the nations of the lands, for He has not assigned our portion like theirs nor our lot like theirs, for they bow to vanity and emptiness and pray to a god who cannot save—man, ash, blood, bile, stinking flesh, maggot, defiled men and women, adulterers and adulteresses, dying in their iniquity and rotting in their wickedness, worn out dust, rot of maggot [and worm]— and pray to a god who cannot save.[81]

In addition, two important cursing ceremonies related to special days of the year—Yom Kippur and Passover—may be identified in the medieval liturgy.

THE CURSE ON YOM KIPPUR

In Ashkenaz and Poland it was customary, following the *Kedusha* of the Morning Prayer of Yom Kippur, to recite fifteen liturgical poems based on Jeremiah 10:7: "Therefore, who will not fear thee, O King of the nations,"

---

81. The fragment was published by Moshe Halamish, "An Early Version of 'Alenu le-shabeah'" [in Hebrew], *Sinai* 110 (1992): 262–65. Cf. chap. 4, n. 124, and the text related to this note, p. 193.

and so on; these *piyyutim* are known by the term *rehitim*. Two of them—
Hagoyim efes and *Veha-goyim eimim*—are attributed to Rabbi Kalonymus
the Elder and include sharp condemnations of and curses against the Gentiles and a plea to God to bring destruction upon them.[82] Surprisingly, historical scholarship, which openly discusses all aspects of anti-Jewish hatred,
has passed over these poems in almost total silence.[83] These are texts that
demonstrate the abyss of hostility and hatred felt by medieval Jews toward
Christians. And we have here not only hatred, but an appeal to God to kill
indiscriminately and ruthlessly, alongside a vivid description of the anticipated horrors to be brought down upon the Gentiles. These pleas are formulated in a series of verbs—"swallow them, shoot them, lop them off, make
them bleed, crush them, strike them, curse them, and ban them . . . destroy
them, kill them, smite them . . . crush them, abandon them, parch them"—
and, in the best alphabetical tradition, the string of disasters the poet wishes

82. Daniel Goldschmidt, "Restoration of Missing *Piyyutim* to the Mahzor for the Day of
Atonement (with one Facsimile)" [in Hebrew], *Kiryat Sefer* 31 (1956): 146–51; Goldschmidt
(n. 15, p. 97), 186–87, 196–97.

83. The only one who has dealt extensively with these curses and described their literary
dissemination is C. Merchavia, "The Caustic Poetic Rebuke *(Shamta)* in Medieval Christian
Polemic Literature" [in Hebrew], *Tarbiz* 41 (1972): 95–115. Note also Avraham Grossman,
"Anti-Christian Polemic in the Commentaries of R. Joseph Kara to the Bible and the *Piyyut*"
[in Hebrew], in *Proceedings of the Ninth World Congress of Jewish Sciences*, sec, 2, chap. 1
(Jerusalem, 1986), 75–76; Grossman, "Exile and Redemption in the Thought of R. Joseph
Kara" [in Hebrew], in *Tarbut ve-hevrah be-toldot Yisrael beyemei-habeinayim*, eds. R. Bonfil,
M. Ben-Sasson, J. Hacker (H. H. Ben-Sasson Volume; Jerusalem, 1989), 283. H. M. Kirn, *Das
Bild vom Juden im Deutschland des frühen 16. Jahrhunderts* (Tübingen, 1989), 42–46, deals with
Pfefferkorn's accusations against the Jews and their prayers, in which they express their desire
to rule the world and take vengeance on the Christians. In publications since 1986, Grossman
has repeatedly alluded to the great hatred of German and French Jewry toward Christianity
as it found expression in liturgical poetry and biblical exegesis. See Grossman (n. 6, p. 94),
and earlier literature cited there; Grossman, *Hakhmei Zarfat ha-Rishonim* (Jerusalem, 1995),
142–46. This tendency is also expressed in Jewish desecration of the Cross. See J. Shatzmiller,
"Desecrating the Cross: A Rare Medieval Accusation" [in Hebrew], *Mehqarim betoldot 'Am
Yisrael ve-Eretz Yisrael* 5 (1980): 159–73; F. Lotter, "Hostienfrevelvorwurf und Blutwunderfälschung bei den Judenverfolgungen vom 1298 ('Rintfleisch') und 1336–1338 ('Armleder'),
Fälschungen im Mittelalter, vol. 5 (Monumenta Germaniae Historica, Schriften, 33; Hannover,
1988), 543–48. Lotter clearly emphasized the connection between Christian accusations that
the Jews insult and profane what is holy to Christianity and the desecration of the Host. He
correctly states that these accusations are not to be seen as solely fictitious. Some of them relate to the Jewish custom of burning Haman in effigy on Purim, which was perceived as an
allusion to the Crucifixion of Jesus. For the connection between this custom and the ritual
murder libel, see chapter 4, n. 65. ʼ

for the Gentiles goes on and on. The editor of these liturgical poems, Daniel Goldschmidt, did not deny the amazement he felt on reading them:

> The attacks against the Gentiles are well understood in light of the situation of despair in which the Jews found themselves in the Middle Ages in the Christian countries, and they could not respond to the continuous persecutions by means of an army or power, but turned to their Heavenly Father that he repay their persecutors in kind, and take Israel out of the slavery and darkness. Such harsh expressions as found here are a spontaneous reaction to all the ill they suffered, a reaction based upon broken-heartedness and bitterness of soul, fitting to the deep (if somewhat primitive) piety of their authors. One who expresses surprise at their sharpness and cruelty, must not forget in what period and under what conditions they were written.[84]

Another liturgical poem customarily recited on Yom Kippur was the imprecation *Titnem le-herpah*,[85] first mentioned by Rabbi Nathan ben Yehudah, author of *Sefer Mahkim*.[86] This *piyyut* also contains very harsh abuse of the Gentiles. The following verses, out of a total of forty-four lines, illustrate the scathing abuse of the Gentiles in this work:

> Give them over to shame, to curse and ridicule
> Unleash against them fury, anger and wrath
> Send to them angels of malediction, rebuke and confusion
> Destroy them with bereavement and sword from without, and fear within.

And on and on. Here too we find double alphabetical rhymes. Like Goldschmidt after him, Freimann also saw the liturgical poem as a response of "the leaders of Israel in the past to the persecutions and pogroms of their

---

84. Goldschmidt, *Kiryat Sefer* (n. 82, p. 120), 148. He wrote in the same vein in the introduction to *Seder Ha Selihot ke-Minhag Polin* (Jerusalem, 1965), 12–13.

85. A. H. Freimann, "Put Them to Shame" [in Hebrew], *Tarbiz* 12 (1941): 70–74. Haberman reprinted it in *Gezerot*, 105–6. R. Shlomo Luria attributed this liturgical poem to Rashi, apparently without any clear evidence; see A. M. Haberman, *Piyyutei Rashi* (Jerusalem, 1941), 34.

86. R. Nathan b. Yehudah, *Sefer Mahkim*, ed. J. Freimann (Kraców, 1909), 42. Merchavia, (n. 77, p. 117), 96 nn. 6–7, cites additional sources that mention these liturgical poems: *Seder Troyes le-R. Menahem b. Yosef*, ed. M. Z. Weiss (Frankfurt am Main, 1905), 27; *Siddur Rashi*, ed. S. Buber and J. Freimann (Berlin, 1912), introduction, 48–51. And cf. Ephraim E. Urbach, *Sefer Arugat ha-Bosem le-R. Abraham b. Azriel, 4: Prolegomena* (Jerusalem, 1963), 6–10.

time," that is, to the Crusades. A similar version of the curse, *Titnem le-kelalah*, was published by Chen Merchavia.[87] The invective here is particularly coarse, if only because of the density and variety of the synonyms for annihilation:

> Pour upon them fury, thunder, anger and vehemence
> Break them, make them drunk, give them bitter waters
> Trample them down, crush them, make them disgusting and
>   abominable.

And the conclusion involves the complete opposite of these verses, the anticipation of salvation:

> And bless Israel: Strengthen their arm, save them, soothe them with
>   complete rest.
> Give them added courage, and may they praise Your name, for they
>   have seen the vengeance of their enemies.
> Their king shall pass before them, and at their head shall dwell the
>   uplifted one,
> Zion will be redeemed with justice, and Jerusalem, the name of the
>   city wherein is the Lord.

Two arguments may be adduced to refute the explanation of Goldschmidt and Freimann, who tended to see these curses as a direct response to the distress and suffering of Ashkenazic Jewry. The first is that this is a standard ritual transplanted into the landscape of Ashkenazic prayer. Even if the texts were created against the backdrop of a great disaster, there is far-reaching historical significance to their repetition year after year, even in times of calm and tranquility. We are not concerned here with explaining the exact historical circumstances under which these texts were created—circumstances that will evidently remain obscure—but with their place in the religious and intellectual world of Ashkenazic Jewry after they emerged.[88] Second, these

---

87. C. Merchavia, "The Caustic Poetic 'Rebuke' *(Shamta)* of Abraham b. Jacob" [in Hebrew], *Tarbiz* 39 (1970): 277–284. In another article "The Caustic Poetic Rebuke *(Shamta)* in Medieval Christian Polemic Literature" (n. 83, p. 120), 107, he conjectures that the two liturgical poems were composed by the same Abraham ben Jacob, about whom we have no information.

88. For the use of curses in the chronicles of 1096, see Anna Sapir Abulafia, "Invectives Against Christianity in the Hebrew Chronicles of the First Crusade," in *Crusade and Settlement*, ed. P. Edbury (Cardiff, 1985), 66–72.

cursing formulas are not entirely an Ashkenazic invention. Already in Yannai's time (fifth-century Land of Israel), we find a poem of the *kerovah* genre for the Days of Awe, entitled "Therefore, Pour Out Your Wrath upon Those Who Curse You."[89]

There is a stylistic similarity between this curse and *Titnem le-herpah* published by Freimann, and the Ashkenazic liturgical poem may well be earlier than assumed by Freimann. Another text including a strong curse against a certain person was composed in the tenth century by Rabbi Yosef ibn Avitur, one of the Spanish sages who moved to Egypt and to the Land of Israel,[90] suggesting that these forms of cursing were widespread in much earlier periods.

Rabbi Shimon ben Yitzhak even wrote a poem cursing the "evil impulse" that was stylistically similar to the curse against the Gentiles.[91] This liturgical poem continues alphabetically; the verbs used to curse later on are "sweep him away, hurl him, compel him, banish him, drill him, uproot him, pierce him, purge him, behead him, poison him, sacrifice him." Thus, in terms of content, the Ashkenazic ritual of cursing seems to rely on a similar ritual described in *Yalqut Shim'oni* (rendered into a poetic version by Yannai) and, in terms of form, on the models of curses such as those of Rabbi Joseph ibn Avitur and Rabbi Shimon ben Yitzhak. These and similar liturgical poems were used by those who sought vengeance as having active messianic significance and should not be seen solely as a spontaneous emotional response.[92] We are dealing here with a comprehensive religious ideology that sees vengeance as a central component in its messianic doctrine.

POUR OUT THY WRATH

Another ritual involving cursing the Gentiles is the famous custom of reciting "Pour Out Thy Wrath" *(Shefokh hamatkha)* at the Passover seder. This prayer was not yet known in the period of the Geonim, and all signs indicate that it was compiled in Europe, apparently by Franco-Ashkenazic Jews.[93] Its

89. Zvi M. Rabinovitch, *Piyyutei Rabbi Yannai le-Torah vela-Mo'adim* (Tel Aviv–Jerusalem, 1987), 2:222–23.

90. *Genizah Studies, III* (New York, 1928), 320.

91. Haberman (n. 22, p. 98), 148.

92. See Goldschmidt (n. 15, p. 97), 380–81.

93. Menahem Kasher, *Hagadah Shelemah* (Jerusalem, 1955), 177–80; Daniel Goldschmidt, *Haggadah shel Pesah* (Jerusalem, 1969), 62–64.

earliest mention appears in *Mahzor Vitry*.[94] In some sources, additional biblical verses are added, some twenty in all, containing curses against the Gentiles.[95] This section of the Haggadah is understood by the participants as closely connected with the future Redemption. Opening the door to the prophet Elijah in tandem with the prayer for vengeance signifies a connection between vengeance against the Gentiles and the appearance of the Messiah.[96] It should also be noted that this section of the Haggadah is recited as an introduction to the fourth and last cup of wine, the cup of deliverance.[97]

A detailed description of the ritual of curses in the Haggadah was written (in the first half of the sixteenth century), by the apostate Antonius Margarita[98] who mentions the liturgical poems *Az rov nisim* and *Ometz gevuratekha*, stating that the Jews use them to soundly curse the Christians and to explicitly ask that evils befall the capital city *(Hauptstadt)* of Christendom and its ruler *(Regierer)*. He claims that they hope that on this night Elijah will announce the coming of the Messiah. They have a short prayer called "Pour Out Thy Wrath," immediately after whose recitation they open the door thinking that Elijah will come through it. On this occasion they curse all the nations, especially the Christians, for they hope the Messiah will wreak their vengeance on all the nations. Margarita also relates a custom of making a kind of "Passoverspiel," in which somebody playing the role of Elijah comes through the open door—a custom described in later Jewish sources as well.[99]

The messianic content of "Pour Out Thy Wrath" was illustrated in illuminated Ashkenazic Haggadot through pictures depicting the Messiah rid-

94. Horwitz (n. 79, p. 118), 296.

95. See Y. Gellis, ed., *Sefer Tosafot ha-Shalem: Ozar Perushim Ba'alei ha-Tosafot: Haggadah shel Pesah*, (Jerusalem, 1989), 169–70.

96. This meaning of opening the door is mentioned by Rabbi Moses Isserles (sixteenth century) in the name of Rabbi Israel Bruna (Regensburg, fifteenth century). See *Shulhan Arukh, Orah Hayyim*, end of 480, and cf. *Sefer Yosef Ometz* (Frankfurt, 1928), sec. 788 and Rabbi Jousep Schammes, *Wormser Minhagbuch*, ed. B. S. Hamburger and Erich Zimmer, (Jerusalem, 1988), 1:87.

97. The practice is based on a statement in *j. Pes* 10a (37b): "From whence do we drink four cups? . . . The Rabbis say: Against the four cups of destruction that the Holy One blessed be He shall give to the nations of the world to drink." Cf.: J. M. Rosenthal, "The Cup of Elijah" [in Hebrew], *Mehqarim u-meqorot* 2 (Jerusalem, 1966): 645–51.

98. Antonius Margarita, *Der gantz Juedisch glaub* (Leipzig, 1531).

99. *Sefer Yosef Ometz* (n. 96, above), sec. 788, 172; Schammes (n. 96, above), 1:87.

ing on a donkey with Elijah by his side, proclaiming his coming.[100] Margarita also relates the popular Jewish exegesis of the Messiah's donkey in a brief work devoted to a comparison between the donkey of the Jewish Messiah and the donkey ridden by Jesus into Jerusalem:

> I think that I myself sincerely believed the lies told below. Blessed be God and the Holy Spirit, who saved me from such and other errors. According to the lies of the Jews, when the Messiah comes he will ride upon an ass and seat all the Jews upon the ass, while all the Christians will sit on the ass's tail. Then the Messiah will ride with all his passengers into the sea, and when he comes to the depths of the sea, the donkey will drop its tail and all the Christians will fall into the sea and drown. And indeed, this will have to be a very big ass. But an even bigger ass is a person who believes such things![101]

Once again we find vengeance against the Gentiles at the very heart of the messianic process. This folk belief, which Margarita mocks, is based on the connection between the redemption from Egypt and the final Redemption. The image of the donkey drowning the Gentiles in the sea at the final Redemption is inspired by the splitting of the Red Sea and the drowning of the Egyptians. In the Ashkenazic Washington Haggadah of 1478, people—apparently one family—are depicted sitting on the back of the messianic donkey (Figure 1).[102] Here too, as in Margarita's description, the donkey serves as a way to carry the dispersed of Israel returning to Zion.

---

100. J. Gutmann, "When the Kingdom Comes: Messianic Themes in Medieval Jewish Art," *Art Journal* 27 (1967–68): 173–75; Gutmann, "The Messiah at the Seder: A Fifteenth-Century Motif in Jewish Art," *Raphael Mahler Jubilee Volume* (Tel Aviv, 1974), 29–38.

101. *"Ja mir gedenckt, dass ich die nachvolgende lugen herezlich geglaubet, Belobet sey Got der heyllig geyst, der mich von solchem, und anderm jrthumb erloeset hat Laut aber die lugen also, Wann der Moschiach kombt, werde er auff ainen Esel reyten, un werde alle Juden auf den Esel setzen. Aber alle Christen werden auf des Esels schwantz sitzen, un also werde der Moschiach mit allen durchs Moer reyten, und wann er in die mitten des Moers komen wirt, so werde der Esel den Schwa[n]tz niderlassen, und die Christen werden also in das Moers fallen und ertrincken, Ja das mues ain grosser Esel sein, Aber noch vil mer ein grosserer Esel der solchs glaubt."*

(Antonius Margarita, *Ein kurzer Bericht und Anzaigung* [Wien, 1541], fol. IIv). My friend Jacob Guggenheim called my attention to the existence of this work, which is not mentioned in scholarly literature.

102. F. Landsberger, "The Washington Haggadah and Its Illuminator," *HUCA* 21 (1948): 77–78; M. Metzger, *La Haggada enluminée* (Leiden, 1973), pl. LVI, fig. 320, 1:323–24. Facsimile: B. Narkiss, *Hebrew Illuminated Manuscripts* (Jerusalem, 1992), pl. 50, p. 167: the Christian

Figure 1. The messianic donkey, Jewish version. A family sits on the donkey, while at its rear a non-Jewish servant grasps the donkey's tail. Illustration by Yoel ben Shimon, Florence, 1478. Library of Congress, Washington.

Figure 2. The messianic donkey, non-Jewish version. From Dietrich Schwab's *Detectum velum Mosaicum*, 1666. Historical Museum of Frankfurt am Main.

Margarita's story inspired the Mainz engraving from 1666 (the year of Shab-betai Zevi's conversion to Islam!) in which the Jewish Messiah is seen hold-ing the cup of Redemption—Elijah's cup—and riding on a sow. Beneath the sow, one Jew is licking her teats and the other her anus (Figure 2). The Mes-siah is followed by Elijah, blowing a shofar and proclaiming the Messiah's coming, and by Moses. Behind them trots the Messiah's donkey, crossing the sea, on his back the Jews, and on his tail the Gentiles. Note the corpse of a child lying on the rock (Golgotha), representing Simon of Trent, whom the Jews were accused of murdering in the blood libel of Trent in 1475. This pic-ture reveals the close connection between vengeful redemption and the libel of ritual murder—a connection we shall discuss at length in chapter 4. This engraving also makes it clear that the "Jewish sow" *(Judensau)*—a motif that begins to appear from the thirteenth century on—is none other than the satiric opposite of the messianic donkey.[103] This also explains the presence of the

maid is holding the donkey's tail. On the people sitting on the tail of the messianic ass, see also T. and M. Metzger, *Jewish Life in the Middle Ages* (New York, 1982), 265. This motif also appears in the second Nuremberg Haggadah in the Schocken collection, Jerusalem.

103. I. Shachar, *The Judensau: A Medieval Anti-Jewish Motif and Its History* (London, 1974), pl. 53, and the accompanying explanation on p. 60. Shachar did not give sufficient explana-tion to his interpretation. The cup held in the Messiah's hand symbolizes both "the cup of Elijah" and the cup into which the blood of Simon is collected, and there is no contradiction between the two. On this issue, I have been helped by the suggestion of Galit Nogah-Bannai of the Art History Department of the Hebrew University, and I am grateful to her. On the motif of the Jewish sow, see Claudine Fabre-Vassus, *The Singular Beast: Jews, Christians and the Pig* (New York, 1997).

Figure 3. "The Jewish Sow" of the Brückenturm in Frankfurt. Reconstruction from the eighteenth century.

Judensau specifically in Germany and its environs, that is, in the Ashkenazic cultural orbit. In the drawing found on the old Brückenturm in Frankfurt (destroyed in 1801), these two motifs—the ritual murder libel of Simon of Trent and the Jewish sow (Figure 3)—also appeared side by side. On the back of the sow is a figure of a seated man holding its tail. In the description of this scene, written after the restoration of this drawing in 1678, this figure is portrayed thus: "I am Rav Shiloh, for a long time I have been riding on this bristly sow. . . . You, my brothers, come and gather . . . gather around me . . . for the time has come for us to get up and ascend to the Holy Land without fear, for otherwise our proven crime will be known in public—killing the child of the tanners [= Trent] . . . and the Gentiles will break our bones and kill us." This is undoubtedly the figure of the Messiah.[104]

"Pour Out Thy Wrath" thus joins the custom of dripping wine at the

104. Schachar, *Judensau*, pls. 41–45 and p. 53. In another printing, from 1563, this figure is described as "the great future Messiah of the Jews," surrounded by an entourage and servants

mention of the ten plagues on Egypt in the Haggadah as well as the exegesis multiplying the number of plagues the Egyptians suffered, both mentioned above. These customs base the substance of the seder not on the "historical" memory of the past redemption, but on inspiring hope for the future deliverance. The attention of these medieval sages was directed to the future, to the final Redemption. This messianic significance of Passover is very ancient and is evidently the basis of the Christian tradition identifying the Crucifixion of Jesus and his ascent to heaven with the festival of deliverance.

In an article on messianic doctrines in Ashkenaz and in Spain, Gerson Cohen argues that, unlike among Spanish Jewry, no active messianic doctrine developed among Ashkenazic Jewry.[105] According to Cohen, their passive attitude toward messianism was a function of religious fundamentalism,[106] which made do with fantasies about vengeance against the Gentiles

---

"who spit on Our Lord Christ and curse all Christians and their authorities" (55). This clearly refers to the prayer *Alenu le-shabeah* (during which it was customary to spit) and to the curses of "Pour Out Thy Wrath" or those of Yom Kippur. In Hans Folz's play *The Duke of Burgundy,* written for Fastnacht, there is a scene in which the Jews proclaim the coming of the Messiah. The Duke consults with his knights about how to punish the Jews for this blasphemy. One of them suggests that he bring a sow and put the Jews underneath it so as to suck on her teats, while the Messiah is placed beneath her tail ("Der Messias lig unter dem schwanz"). This scene is the precise opposite of the Ashkenazic ritual of "Pour Out Thy wrath"; see A. von Keller, *Fastnachtspiele aus dem 15. Jahrhundert* (Stuttgart, 1853; repr. 1965), 1:181. And compare the description in E. Wenzel, "Synagoga und Ecclesia: Zum Antijudaismus im deutschsprachigen Spiel des späten Mittelalters," in *Judentum, Antisemitismus und europäische Kultur,* ed. H. O. Horch (Tübingen, 1988), 74; Shachar, *Judensau,* 41. In general, these descriptions draw a direct connection between the curses of the Jews, their messianic hopes, and the ritual murder libel. The interpretation of the ritual murder libel of Trent is that, following the murder of the child Simon, the Jews were supposed to immigrate to the Land of Israel with the coming of deliverance. Hence the use of the "Jewish sow" as an antithesis to the "Messiah's donkey." For mockery of Jewish messianic faith in the late Middle Ages, see B. Z. Degani, "The German Passion Play of the 15th Century as a Method of Establishing a Negative Jewish Stereotype" [in Hebrew], in *Umah ve-toldoteha* ed. M. Stern (Jerusalem, 1983), 1:263–70.

105. Cohen, "Messianic Postures" (n. 1, p. 92). Joseph Dan has noted a possible connection between the doctrine of Redemption of the Ashkenazic Hasidim and their martyrological teachings, on the one hand, and teachings of vengeance against the Gentiles, on the other; see his "The Problem of Kiddush Hashem in the Theoretical Teachings of Ashkenazi Hasidism" [in Hebrew], in *Milhemet Kodesh u-martyrologiyah be-toldot Yisrael uve-toldot ha-Amim* (Jerusalem, 1968), 121–29. Cf. P. Schäfer, "The Ideal of Piety of the Ashkenazi Hasidim and Its Roots in Jewish Tradition," *Jewish History* 4, no. 2 (1990): 15–16.

106. Cohen, "Messianic Postures" (n. 1, p. 92), 29: "Active messianism or quiescence must have derived from sources other than political or economic. If Franco-German Jewry pro-

rather than with active messianism. But representing the Ashkenazim as bereft of any trace of aggressive behavior toward the non-Jewish surroundings is inconsistent with the ritual of cursing and its messianic significance. Cohen reached his conclusion as a result of examining the wrong literature: he searched for messianic thought among the Jews of Ashkenaz in their theoretical religious literature, while their messianic faith was not expressed in this genre, which did not really exist among them, but in ritual, in the concrete religious act—the curse and the *piyyut*. The curse was thought to possess harmful magic potency, thus indicating a stark and aggressive messianic act whose like is not to be found among the Jews of Spain. Cohen is nevertheless correct in his statement about the relative paucity of messianic movements among the Jews of Ashkenaz, which may be explained by the very existence of those cursing rituals, whose magic power made messianic movements superfluous, perhaps even dangerous—as we shall see in chapter 6.

THE IMPRESSION OF THE CURSES ON CHRISTIANS

It is difficult to know how sensitive medieval Jews were to Christian public opinion, and whether the freedom they allowed themselves in expressing those vigorous curses entailed any danger. I demonstrated elsewhere that, while holding fasting rituals in Mainz during the wars of the Hussites in 1421, Jews were very careful not to attract the attention of Christians.[107] What impression, then, did these curses make on the Christians?

---

duced neither a messianic pretender nor a messianic literature, it must be because quiescence and passivity had somehow so permeated the whole mentality of that community as virtually to eliminate such aggressive behaviour."

107. See Israel J. Yuval, "Jews, Hussites and Germans According to the Chronicle *Gilgul B'nai Hushim*" [in Hebrew], *Zion* 54 (1989): 297–98; see "Juden, Hussiten und Deutsche; Nach einer hebräischen Chronik," in *Juden in der christlichen Umwelt während des späten Mittelalters,* A. Haverkamp and F. J. Ziwes, eds. (Zeitschrift für Historische Forschung, 13; Berlin, 1992), 59–102]. Rabbi Israel Isserlin's student Yosef ben Moshe relates of his teacher: "And I remember that I heard from him several times that he told the story of the pogrom in Vienna, may God avenge the blood of the martyrs, to his older students. And this often occurred on Tisha b'Av, and may the wise man understand"; see *Leqet Yosher,* ed. Freimann (Berlin 1903), 1:112. On the eve of Yom Kippur it was customary to go to the cemetery, but Isserlin ordered that "some of the congregation should go to the cemetery, but not all of them, so that the Gentiles not be astonished." In one of Isserlin's Purim sermons, he associated the Bible verse "And the Lord called unto Moses" (Lev 1:1) with the reading of the Scroll of Esther: "'And he called unto Moses'—that is, on Moses. For we find in Scripture that the word *el* ("to") is used to substi-

It would appear that the impression made was significant, and quite negative. Beginning in the twelfth century, particularly in the writings of Petrus Venerabilis, we find a tendency to represent the Jews as enemies of the human race *(odium humani generis)* and as murderers.[108] A chronicle from

---

tute for *'al* ("on"). For we do not find in all the prophets anything that was added to Moses, apart from the reading of the Scroll [of Esther]. Therefore the letter *aleph* is small, for the miracle [i.e., of Purim] was performed by a woman; therefore the word is written as if it were *vayiker*. And I do not wish to elaborate any further, and the wise shall understand" (155). This arcane exegesis is apparently based on a Christian folk homily, which holds that the word *ve-yikra*, which is written with a small *aleph*, as if deleted, is an allusion to Jesus, as the numerical value of the letters of ויקר is the same as that of the letters of ישו ("Jesus"). Thus, the New Testament is alluded to in the verse "And he called to [i.e., on; substituting על for אל] Moses"—that is, that the Torah of Jesus is added to the Torah of Moses. Astonishingly, Isserlin does not reject the exegesis that "to" = "on" (cf. Nahmanides to Num 20:8). He even agrees that this alludes to an addition to the Torah of Moses but interprets this addition as referring to the Book of Esther. Here he may be following the Talmudic statement "They again received it (i.e., the Torah) in the days of Ahasuerus" (*b. Shabbat* 88a). That is, both the Christian and the Jewish sides understand this biblical verse as alluding to an addition to the Torah of Moses: the Christians think this refers to the New Testament; Isserlin reads it as an allusion to the Scroll of Esther.

Thus far, we have here a standard anti-Christian exegesis. But what is the meaning of the disciple's words at the end of the exegesis: "And I do not wish to elaborate any further, and the wise shall understand"? What else is he hiding? It is plausible that in his exegesis Isserlin further develops the idea implicit in his words, according to which the Book of Esther is a kind of answer to "Jesus." Prior to that, he even found an allusion in the biblical verse "And the Lord called unto Moses" to the eradication of Amalek (Deut 25:17–19). In other words, the eradication of Amalek and the hanging of Haman are seen by Isserlin as proof of the destruction of Christianity. He was not afraid to preach this to a closed group, but his pupil refrained from writing down those words.

108. Amos Funkenstein, "Changes in the Patterns of Christian Anti-Jewish Polemics in the 12ᵗʰ Century" [in Hebrew], *Zion* 33 (1968): 141; Funkenstein, "Basic Types of Christian Anti-Jewish Polemics in the Later Middle Ages," *Viator 2* (1971): 380; A. Patschovsky, "Der 'Talmudjude': Vom mittelalterlichen Ursprung eines neuzeitlichen Themas," in *Juden in der christlichen Umwelt während des späten Mittelalters*, ed. A. Haverkamp and F. J. Ziwes (Zeitschrift für Historische Forschung; Beiheft, 13; Berlin, 1992), 25; Anna Sapir Abulafia, *Christians and Jews in the Twelfth-Century Renaissance* (London, 1995). Jeremy Cohen asserts that the Church's revision of its position of tolerance toward Jewish existence did not take place until the thirteenth century. But he also argues that the buds of this change are already visible by the twelfth century, for example, in the rise of the awareness that the Jews who murdered Jesus did so despite their recognition of him as the Messiah, as against the Augustinian position that the Jews who murdered Jesus did not acknowledge his messiahhood; see "The Jews as the Killers of Christ in the Latin Tradition, from Augustine to the Friars," *Traditio* 39 (1983): 1–27. The difference between the two centuries may be described not only quantitatively, but also in terms of the degree of dissemination of anti-Jewish views. From the end of the

1096 already tells of a Jew from Mainz who before his death cursed Christians with the words "and you shall be condemned to hell together with your god and in boiling feces"—alluding to the words of the Talmud about Jesus, who was to be sentenced to boiling feces.[109] Presumably, at least some of what the Jews said reached Christian ears, even before Christian scholars took pains to find the words in the Jewish books themselves. In the following chapters I shall present further examples suggesting fairly intimate acquaintance between Jews and Christians.

This is the background to the accusations made against the Jews in the trial of the Talmud in Paris (1240) based on the Talmudic saying "the best of the Gentiles are to be killed" and on the *Birkat ha-Minim*. Explicit references to the Yom Kippur imprecations are found in Christian literature after the Paris trial, based on Latin translations of these liturgical poems, the earliest of which dates from 1248. These translations were widely circulated in France and Spain; even though they originated in Ashkenaz, they wound up abroad, certainly for propagandistic purposes.[110] Within the boundaries of the Reich, a Christian reaction to the curses was articulated in the debate held in 1399 between the convert Peter and Rabbi Lipmann Mühlhausen. The convert from Judaism argued: "On the Great Fast [Yom Kippur] you say: 'The Gentiles are like Eimim and Zamzumim, Kedar and Adomim, Balaam and Kilaam [a list of ancient, extinct nations].'"[111] The

---

eleventh century and throughout the twelfth century, these views were primarily confined to the masses, and only in the thirteenth century did they become accepted among theologians and the Church.

109. Haberman (n. 13, p. 97), 36; Stern and Neubauer (n. 42, p. 103), 11; Chazan (n. 42, p. 103), 262; *b. Gittin* 57a.

110. Merchavia (n. 83, p. 120). The suspicion that the Jews curse the ruler had been mentioned already in the twelfth century in northern France in another version of the "Persecutions of Blois": "The ruler said to Joseph ha-Cohen: I hear that the Jews are cursing me," and the Jew denied it (Haberman [n. 13, p. 97], 146). It is further told of the accusations at Blois that those who were executed had prayed aloud, in earshot of the Gentiles, the prayer *Alenu le-shabeah* before they were burned at the stake (Haberman [n. 13, p. 97], 43).

111. *Sefer Hanizzahon le-R. Yom-Tov Lipmann Mühlhausen*, with an introduction by E. Talmage (Jerusalem, 1984; facs. ed. of T. Hackspan, Altdorf-Nürnberg, 1644), 193–94. I discussed this debate in my article "Kabbalisten, Ketzer und Polemiker: Das kulturelle Umfeld des Sefer ha-Nizachon von Lipman Mühlhausen, in *Mysticism, Magic and Kabbalah in Ashkenazi Judaism*, ed. K. E. Grözinger (Berlin, 1995), 155–71. There I suggested the theory that this controversy, which began with the imprisonment of Jews and ended with the execution of eighty of them, reflects a trend to impart to Judaism a status similar to that of heresy. In this view, the polemic had the nature of an inquisitorial trial. Reexamination of this episode in

Rabbi of Savoy, Rabbi Shimshon, was arrested in 1417 and interrogated by the Inquisition about the content of the Talmud. According to the Latin protocol of his confession, he said that it was true that the Jews curse the Christians on Yom Kippur.[112] That liturgical prayer was denounced already in the early sixteenth century by the convert Victor von Karben.[113]

During the second half of the fifteenth century, Hans Folz wrote a play for Fastnacht (Carnival) entitled *Emperor Constantine,* in which the Christian advances the following argument against the Jew: "If you had power over us, as we had in our day over you, after a year not a single Christian would remain alive."[114] Expressions such as these may be Christian apolo-

---

light of the present discussion may give it a more limited significance. To do so, we need to reexamine Peter's claims against the Jews: 1) in the prayer *Alenu le-shabeah,* they say "to remove detestable idolatry from the earth and to utterly cut off false gods"; 2) the Jews pray "may all the heretics perish in an instant," referring to the priests; 3) the liturgical poem for Yom Kippur, *Hagoyyim eimim,* includes curses against the Christians; 4) the Jews use the following offensive expressions: *hanged one, impure bread, impure dung, sullied bread;* 5) the separation of challah (a portion of the dough) and its burning, as well as the burning of leaven, are done to insult Christianity. We thus have here two kinds of arguments: the first three relate to accusations that the Jews wish the destruction of Christianity, while the last two reflect the desire of the Jews to desecrate the Host. It is plausible that there is a connection between the two, a connection that will be explained in chapter 5. It would therefore seem that the background to this affair began with an accusation of the desecration of the Host. As was usual in such cases, the Jews were first put in prison until their case was cleared. The Jews presumably argued in their defense that there is nothing in their religion consistent with such an accusation. In contradistinction, the convert sought to establish that Judaism does in fact attribute importance to the desecration of the Host, as part of their larger messianic aspiration to see the destruction of Christianity. It was to this that Lipmann needed to respond. His answers were evidently unconvincing, and after the investigations and inquests were concluded, the Jews were sentenced to death. This incident was very similar in its details to those of the pogroms in Austria in 1420–1421. There too the Jews were imprisoned for about ten months, at the end of which time several hundred were executed. In contemporary sources, two explanations are given for this persecution: accusations of desecration of the Host in the city of Enns, and that of abetting the Hussites. At one time I tended to prefer the second explanation, but it now seems that there is no need to decide between the two, since the accusation of the desecration of the Host is compatible with that of the Jews' desire to join forces with the enemies of Christianity. Both accusations attribute to the Jews the hope of seeing the destruction of Christianity. Cf. the material cited from *Leket Yosher,* n. 107 above.

112. C. Merchavia, "A Spanish Latin MS. Concerning the Opposition to the Talmud at the Beginning of the 15th Century" [in Hebrew], *Kiryat Sepher* 45 (1970): 597, secs. 20–21.

113. Victor von Karben, *Juden Buchlein* (n.p., 1550), pt. 1, chap. 16.

114. "Wann hett ir uns in euerm gewalt, als ir in unser seit gezalt, kein Crist erlebet jares frist" (Von Keller, *Fastnachtspiele,* 804). And cf. D. Kurze, "Häresie und Minderheit im Mittelalter," *Historische Zeitschrift* 229 (1979), 551; E. Wenzel, *"Do worden die Juden alle geschant":*

getics for the terrible lot of the Jews, yet what resonates in these words is that the Christians were not unaware of the Jewish desire to see their destruction.[115]

Jewish aspirations for vengeance profoundly influenced relations between Jews and Christians, particularly in the context of the ritual murder accusations, to be discussed in the next chapter. In the protocols of the blood libel in Trent, the Jews repeatedly admit that on Passover they pray for vengeance against the Gentiles and that they curse them. This is done twice during the seder:[116] once while enumerating the ten plagues, a ritual intended to arouse the hope that, just as Pharaoh was afflicted with ten plagues in the former redemption, so too will the Gentiles be afflicted in the final deliverance. The second time it is done during the recitation of "Pour Out Thy Wrath." This understanding of Passover in its messianic context, in view of the Jewish prayer for blood vengeance against the Christians, hints at the origin of the ritual murder libels—but we are getting ahead of ourselves.

Rolle und Funktion der Juden in spätmittelalterlichen Spielen (München, 1992), 228–29. Similar claims were also uttered by Christian heretics. According to the "Anonymous of Passau," one of the leaders of the heretics said before he was executed: "You are correct in condemning us to death, for if we were not a minority, we would use the same power that you use now to kill us, to kill priests, monks, and lay people" (A. Patschovsky and K. V. Selge, *Quellen zur Geschichte der Waldenser* [Gütersloh, 1973], 72).

115. On the atmosphere in the sixteenth century, see H. A. Oberman, *The Roots of Anti-Semitism in the Age of Renaissance and Reformation* (Philadelphia, 1984), 94–100. For more on Folz's attitude toward the curses against Christians, see Degani (n. 103, p. 127), 277.

116. R. Po-Chia Hsia, *Trent 1475: Stories of a Ritual Murder Trial* (New Haven, 1992), 44–45, 63. This interest in the seder rites proves that the ritual murder libel is not only connected with Easter and the Crucifixion of Jesus, as is commonly thought. See Cecil Roth, "The Mediaeval Conception of the Jew," in *Essays and Studies in Memory of L. R. Miller*, ed. I. Davidson (New York, 1938), 171–90; M. J. Wenninger, "Das gefährliche Fest: Ostern als zeitlicher Kristallisationspunkt antijüdischen Verhaltens," in *Feste und Feiern im Mittelalter*, eds. D. Altenburg et al. (Sigmaringen, 1991), 323–32. But the content of the Jewish festival of Passover and the Jews' aspirations for messianic revenge also fueled the spread of rumors among the Christians.

FOUR

Intersecting Stories

From Martyrdom to Ritual Murder Accusations

THE BLOOD

In the preceding chapter, I noted the messianic function reserved for the blood of those killed: God's mantle, the *porphyrion,* is stained with their blood. Not only will the drops of blood serve as damning testimony against the Gentiles when the time comes for them to pay, but they also have the power to stir up God's wrath and his desire for vengeance. Such an interpretation accompanied the death of the martyrs of 1096, both in the liturgical poems and in the chronicles. This is the sense of the phrase, and of others like it, found in the *piyyut* by David ben Meshullam quoted above: "Before Your eyes may their blood always be boiling."[1] The blood of those killed is ever-present before God as a reminder of the Gentiles' iniquity, to make him punish the foes of the Jews. This idea appears in *Sefer Hasidim:*

> A house in which people were killed for Kiddush Hashem, and the blood is spattered on the wall and on the stones, and the owner wishes to paint the walls of the house with whitewash—the blood may not be removed and he cannot paint over it. . . . For so long as the blood is not covered,

1. A. M. Haberman, *Gezerot Ashkenaz ve-Tzarfat* (Jerusalem, 1971), 70; Daniel Goldschmidt, *Mahzor le-Yamim Noraim II: Yom Kippur* (Jerusalem, 1970), 539.

the Holy One blessed be He takes vengeance, and when it is covered he hastens to exact vengeance."[2]

Thus, in Ashkenaz the biblical verse "O earth, cover not their blood" (Job 16:18) was interpreted literally. *Sefer Hadrat Kodesh,* written in 1400 in Regensburg, contains the author's personal prayer for deliverance: "Be jealous for Your great Name and take vengeance before our eyes for Your Torah and for the blood of Your servants shed for the Sanctification of Your Name."[3] At the End of Days God will avenge the blood of the martyrs, specifically.

Just as the remembrance of Amalek's past deeds is intended to assure vengeance against him in the future, so is the remembrance of the blood shed by the martyrs a means of stirring God to take vengeance (Ex 17:8–13). But while the commandment to "remember" Amalek, along with the vengeance that stems from it, are specifically human concerns, that of the martyrs is God's affair. This is the meaning of the famous two-part prayer *Av ha-Rahamim* (Compassionate Father). In the first part, the worshipers ask God to remember all those killed for the sanctification of his Name. In the second the reason for this remembering is given: God is to remember so that "He will exact retribution before our eyes for the spilled blood of His servants." In the prayer *Avinu Malkenu* (Our Father, Our King) we find the line: "Avenge before our eyes the spilled blood of Your servants." The addition of the phrase "before our eyes" (not found in all versions) derives from the close affinity between blood vengeance and Redemption. The wish is for the Redemption to come "in our days."

The close connection between memory and future vengeance is not restricted to the recollection of past events, but also involves remembrance of the names of specific people killed. This practice—of remembering the dead and of mentioning them for purposes of vengeance—explains the development of the *Memorbuch* (Memory Book) among Ashkenazic Jewry.

---

2. *Sefer Hasidim,* Ms. Parma, ed. J. Wistinezky and Y. Freimann (Frankfurt am Main, 1924), sec. 1533 (quotation from *Sefer ha-Kavod*). Also cf. sec. 1534. This is the background for the custom cited by Rabbi Yaakov Molin: "And it is the usual custom to bury all those killed by robbers and brigands as they are found, in all their clothes, so as to arouse [Divine] wrath and to take vengeance. . . . Those killed by Gentiles, those who killed them shall in the future need to render account." (*Teshuvot Maharil,* ed. Y. Satz [Jerusalem, 1980], sec. 65, 83).

3. Ms. Moscow-Guenzburg 482, fol. 25a. This formulation does not appear in the published edition of the book.

The *Memorbuch* of Nuremberg, begun at the end of the thirteenth century, includes two kinds of lists: 1) names of those killed in the various pogroms from 1096 on; 2) names of those who died natural deaths and the contributions made for the eternal benefit of their souls.[4] The way the second list was created is self-evident: the scribe of the community recorded the names of those who passed away in the community *Memorbuch*. How was the first kind of list compiled? How did people in the community of Nuremberg know the names of the 941 Jews killed in Würzburg during the pogrom of Rindfleisch (1298), or those of the 470 people killed at that time in Rothenburg? It seems plausible that the lists of martyrs appearing in the *Memorbuch* may have been based on the tax rolls of the various communities. After the pogrom, survivors must have gone over this list and marked who had been killed. The list then would have been copied and sent from one community to another, thereby publicizing the names of the martyrs. If the lists of those killed were indeed based on tax rolls, that would explain why they are arranged according to households and why there is no indication of the names of "guests," that is, of foreign residents in the community. It may also explain why the names of children are not mentioned, even though in terms of remembering souls there should have been no difference between children and adults.

The ritual significance of "remembrance of souls" in the *Memorbuch* does not relate to the human beings who remember, but to God who remembers ("May God remember"), as implied by the phrase "the entire House of Israel must mention their names."[5] And since God remembers those who were killed, he will come and avenge their death, as stated explicitly in *Av ha-Rahamim*: "May our God remember them for good with the other righteous of the world. May He, in our day, exact retribution for the spilled blood of His servants." In a moving comment, a man who lost most of his family during the Rindfleisch pogrom wrote in 1299: "And I recorded it as an eternal remembrance before the Lord, and to take vengeance for the Children of Israel."[6]

Such a system of recording the names of those killed demonstrates how

4. Part 1 was published by S. Salfeld, *Das Martyrologium des Nürnberger Memorbuches* (Berlin, 1898). Part 2 was translated into German and published by M. Stern, *Die israelitische Bevölkerung der deutschen Städte, III: Nürnberg im Mittelalter* (Kiel, 1894–1896), 95–172, 190–205.

5. Salfeld, *Martyrologium*, 81.

6. Ms. Vienna, Heb. 16.

deeply the concept of vengeance had penetrated the religious ritual of medieval Ashkenazim. The phrase "the Lord will avenge his blood," applied to one killed by the Gentiles, is also indicative of this. As far as I can tell, the phrase was introduced during the high Middle Ages and was common only among Ashkenazic Jewry. The link between remembrance of the martyrs' souls and the coming of Redemption is also indicated by the closing words of the *Memorbuch* of Koblenz: "By virtue of these saints we shall gain salvation and consolation and He will ingather our exiles with strong arms."[7]

As we observed in the previous chapter, vengeance was conceived as a substantive and vital component of the Redemption, deriving from a theological conception of vengeance as the ultimate realization of divine justice. Vengeance is the suitable punishment for bloodshed—that is, one is not dealing here with mere ordinary vengeance, but with *blood* vengeance. In the Ashkenazic view, therefore, the Day of Judgment will be accompanied by universal bloodshed. Since God is not indifferent to the shedding of Jewish blood, the victims that fall on the altar of faith are not sacrificed in vain, for they may move God to end his passivity and to begin the process of deliverance. Every drop of blood shed by every Jew joins the volume of blood that will stir the Lord to vengeance when the time comes. Concerning two individuals who were martyred, the chronicler records that upon their death, "the two entered together into the treasure house of [his tabernacle], until the day of remembrance of the shed blood of His servants."[8] That is, the souls of those killed as martyrs dwell in the "treasure house," where they await the vengeance that will come at the time of Redemption.

7. Salfeld (n. 4, p. 137), xxxii. As mentioned above, God records the names of those martyred on his *porphyrion* (see chap. 3). It is noteworthy that Rabbi Ephraim of Bonn called his chronicle *Sefer Zekhirah* (The Book of Remembrance), and in the introduction he explained the reason for the name: "Since we have survived to remember it, may He in His mercy avenge swiftly"; that is, the vengeance depends on remembrance.

8. Haberman (n. 1, p. 135), 42; Moritz Stern and Adolf Neubauer, eds., *Hebräische Berichte über die Judenverfolgung während der Kreuzzüge* (Berlin, 1892), 16; R. Chazan, *European Jewry and the First Crusade* (Berkeley and Los Angeles, 1987), 271. And in the *piyyut* of Rabbi Ephraim of Bonn (in A. M. Haberman, *Sefer Zekhirah: Selihot ve-Kinot le-Rabbi Efraim b"r Ya'akov* [Jerusalem, 1970], 98). In a letter written by the Jews of Troyes after the ritual murder libel of Blois (1171), they called on the congregations in Germany to join the public fast that was called in France: "Perhaps the Rock will hear your voice, and do with us according to all His wonders, to make known to all, that because of the blood of His pious ones this has happened. And erase these words from my writing, lest it be seen by apostates and informers" (Haberman [n. 1, p. 135], 146). This also illustrates that the blood of the martyrs works to hasten the deliverance, and they wished to hide this from the Christians.

We have thus reached the complex and intricate link between messianic vengeance and the concept of martyrdom as depicted in the chronicles of 1096. The most developed stories in these chronicles concern those who killed themselves or their loved ones, not those who were killed by Christians.[9] This emphasis on self-sacrifice, or even on the sacrifice of others, lent these acts a ritual character. They were not only acts of killing to avoid apostasy (Kiddush Hashem), but they were carried out within a highly developed symbolic system lending them a ceremonial status. Scholarly literature discusses the great similarity between the acts of Jewish martyrs and those of Christian martyrs, almost as if the Jewish martyrs wished to demonstrate to the Christians: "Our martyrdom is greater than yours!"[10] Without denying this resemblance, one cannot ignore the decisive difference: Christian martyrology did not advocate suicide or the killing of others.[11] Like Jewish religious law, Christian martyrology sees the pinnacle of religious commitment as the believer's willingness to cling to his faith even at the price of being killed by others, but not at the price of killing himself or his loved ones. Nothing in the Christian tradition corresponds to the behavior attributed to the Jewish martyrs of 1096, nor does Jewish halakhah (religious law) recognize that kind of blood ritual.

The religious ideology underlying the sacrificial ritual cannot be understood without noting its relation to the vengeful messianic position. According to this view, the shed blood of the martyrs reaches the very Throne of God and arouses God to set out on his great campaign of retribution, on a messianic holy war. The martyrs are soldiers in the heavenly army who fell in a cosmic war between the heavenly archangel of Edom and that of Jacob. Their death was not in vain because, by virtue of their sacrifice, they arouse the wrath of the avenging God and bring deliverance closer. This position, which sees the martyrs' death as a retrospective opportunity to

9. S. Eidelberg, "The Solomon Bar Simson Chronicle as a Source of the History of the First Crusade," *JQR* 49 (1958–59): 282–87, believes that the reason for this is the wish to strengthen the weak and encourage self-sacrifice during pogroms.

10. See note 55, below.

11. Incidents of voluntary martyrdom, that is, of Christians who sought death at the hands of the Romans, were widespread in certain places, but not suicide, and certainly not the killing of others. On such phenomena and the reservations about them, see R. L. Fox, *Pagans and Christians* (London, 1988), 434–45; W. H. C. Frend, *Martyrdom and Persecution in the Early Church*, (Michigan, 1981), 293; A. J. Droge and J. D. Tabor, *A Noble Death; Suicide and Martyrdom Among Christians and Jews in Antiquity* (San Francisco, 1992); G. W. Bowersock, *Martyrdom and Rome* (Cambridge, 1995).

hasten the Redemption, explains the logic of many of the accounts in the chronicles of 1096.

This notion derives its inspiration not only from the laws of Kiddush Hashem but also from messianic expectations. Avraham Grossman rightly states that the Ashkenazic idea of martyrdom has ancient Italian and Palestinian roots, and that the acts of the martyrs should not be seen merely as "the result of momentary emotions," but as the consequence of a fully developed religious ideology based on ancient traditions.[12] Therefore, it is difficult to accept the later halakhic legitimations as the only explanation for the motive of the 1096 martyrs. The argument heard in the fourteenth century—namely, that the killing of the children was motivated by the calculated fear "lest they dwell among the Gentiles when they grow up; it is better that they die innocent and not die guilty"[13]—certainly had a place in the overall picture of the martyrs' considerations, but this is a justification in retrospect, not necessarily the main cause. It cannot explain the ceremonies of the sacrifice, the blood rite, and the slaughter in some of the descriptions.

Another motive for the suicides found in the sources is self-atonement. To this a later ex post facto layer is added: to "exploit" the deaths in retrospect so as to induce God to take revenge. These two explanations are not necessarily mutually exclusive. Atonement may be seen as a personal and private expression of vengeance. Atonement is an individual redemption, while vengeance is a kind of redemption of the world. When a person seeks to atone for his sins by spilling his own blood or that of his children on the heavenly altar, he assumes that his blood is accepted by God. For what purpose? Here, the generation following 1096 had an answer: for the Redemption of Israel. The heavenly altar is the messianic battlefield between the prince of Edom and the prince of Israel. Before God's garment is reddened with the blood of Christians in the eschatological future, it will be filled with the blood of the Jews in this world. The justification accompanying the acts of killing and suicide must therefore be seen as an attempt to move God to hasten the coming of the Redemption. This view contains a grain of "political" protest against God's conduct of the world. This ex-

12. A. Grossman, "The Cultural and Social Background of Jewish Martyrdom in Germany in 1096" [in Hebrew], in *Kedushat ha-hayyim ve-heruf ha-nefesh; Kovetz ma'amarim le-zikhro shel Amir Yekutiel*, ed. I. Gafni and A. Ravitzky (Jerusalem, 1993), 111.

13. *Sefer ha-Sema"k mi-Zurich*, ed. Y. Y. Har-Shoshanim, I (Jerusalem, 1981), 58; Grossman, "Cultural and Social Background of Jewish Martyrdom," 116.

plains the descriptions that attribute to the martyrs the most extreme and horrific acts—killing children, sprinkling their blood on the Holy Ark, burning the synagogue, and other such acts—all in order to heighten the shock in heaven.

In his description of the "last supper" of the "pious men of Xanten" before their suicide, the chronicler has the "high priest" deliver a farewell address portraying suicide as a pilgrimage ("Let us arise and go up to the House of the Lord") to the heavenly Temple, whose purpose is to offer a sacrifice.[14] The idea of self-sacrifice for Jerusalem lay at the very foundation of the Crusades.[15] But while the Christians sought their altar in Jerusalem, the Jews made do with altars in the valleys of the Rhine and the Moselle. By virtue of their sacrifice, the martyrs would attain "the world which is entirely good in Paradise." The motivation is thus presented in terms of personal deliverance. Moreover, as the ceremony progresses the "priest to Almighty God" recites a blessing, which is filled with motifs of messianic vengeance: "May the Merciful One avenge, in the days of those we leave behind, before their eyes, the blood that has been shed by Your servants and that which is still to be shed." And the chronicler himself concludes the account with a messianic prayer: "And may their merit . . . serve for us as an intercessor before the Most High, to redeem us speedily from the Exile of the wicked Edom, speedily in our days." We thus find here an expression of the double notion: of personal and national redemption.

The centrality of the idea of vengeful redemption in the world of Ashkenazic Jewry and the reflection of this idea in Christianity illustrate more clearly its centrality during the pogroms of the First Crusade. Karl Erdmann has already noted the importance of the eschatological element among the Crusaders.[16] They saw the Crusade to Jerusalem as the realization of the Tiburtine Sibyl's vision about the "last emperor," who was to convert the Jews and the pagans, smite Gog and Magog, come to Jerusalem, and lay down his crown on Golgotha. In so doing he would put an end to the kingdom of flesh and blood and begin the era of the kingdom of heaven—with the appearance of the Antichrist, who would rule until the Second Coming, the Parousia, of Jesus. The conquest of the Holy Sepulcher thus as-

14. Haberman (n. 1, p. 135), 48–50; Stern and Neubauer (n. 8, p. 138), 21–23; Chazan (n. 8, p. 138), 280–83.

15. Karl Erdmann, *The Origin of the Idea of Crusade* (Princeton, 1977), 301, 332–33.

16. Erdmann, "Endkaiserglaube und Kreuzzugsgedanke im 11. Jahrhundert," *Zeitschrift für Kirchengeschichte* 51 (1932): 384–414.

sumed an explicit eschatological significance, and the Crusade to the Holy Land became a chapter in the impending millennial drama.[17]

The legend of the "last emperor" reached Western Europe from Byzantium in the early eleventh century,[18] and it can explain the aspiration of certain groups of Crusaders to convert the Jews to Christianity during the Crusade to Jerusalem, in preparation for the appearance of the "last emperor." The leading pogromist against the Jews in the Rhineland, Graf Emicho of Flonheim, apparently saw himself as the last emperor.[19] The Jews' adamant refusal to convert to Christianity, even at the cost of their lives, could have been interpreted as an attempt to frustrate Christian eschatological expectations. Paul Alexander wondered why Jerusalem, of all places, was chosen as the arena for the destruction of the empire, since Rome or

17. J. Ward, "The First Crusade as Disaster: Apocalypticism and the Genesis of the Crusading Movement," *Medieval Studies in Honor of Avrom Saltman*, ed. B. Albert, Y. Friedman, and S. Schwarzfuchs (Bar Ilan Studies in History, 4; Ramat Gan, 1995), 253–92. On the messianic factor in the First Crusade, see L. Dasberg, *Untersuchungen über die Entwertung des Judenstatus im 11. Jahrhundert* (Paris, 1965), 173–93; N. Cohn, *The Pursuit of the Millennium* (London, 1970), 73–74; J. Riley-Smith, *The First Crusade and the Idea of Crusade* (London, 1986), 50–57; H. Liebeschütz, "The Crusading Movement in its Bearing on the Christian Attitude towards Jewry," *JJS* 10 (1980): 97–111. S. Schein, "The Crusades as Messianic Movement" [in Hebrew], in Z. Baras, ed., *Meshihiyut ve-Eskhatologyah* (Jerusalem, 1984), 177–89. On millenarian expectations during the eleventh century and their connection to the worsening of attitudes toward the Jews, see D. F. Callahan, "Ademar of Chabannes, Millennial Fears and the Development of Western Anti-Judaism," *Journal of Ecclesiastical History* 46 (1995): 19–35. On messianic expectations among Jews during this period, see J. Mann, "The Messianic Movements During the Time of the First Crusades" [in Hebrew], *Ha-Tekufah* 23 (1925): 243–61; 24 (1926), 335–58; S. Emanuel, "A Jewish-Christian Debate—France 1100" [in Hebrew], *Zion* 63 (1998): 143–55.

18. P. J. Alexander, "The Diffusion of Byzantine Apocalypses in the Medieval West and the Beginning of Joachimism," in *Prophecy and Millenarianism. Essays in Honour of Marjorie Reeves,* ed. A. Williams (Harlow, 1980), 53–106.

19. "And he [Emicho] made up [a story] that a messenger of the crucified one came to him and gave his message to make it known, that when he would come to Italy or Greece and he would go by himself and he would be crowned with the royal crown and defeat his enemies"; see Haberman (n. 1, p. 135), 29; Stern and Neubauer (n. 8, p. 138), 5; Chazan (n. 8, p. 138), 250–51. This is also confirmed in the Latin chronicle of Ekkehard von Aura, which states that Graf Emicho received a divine revelation similar to that of Saul/Paul (Acts 9), as a result of which he changed his way of life and became devoted to acts of Christian piety. See F. J. Schmale, ed., *Frutolfi et Ekkehardi Chronica necnon Anonymi Chronica Imperatorum* (Ausgewählte Quellen zur deutschen Geschichte des Mittelalters, 15; Darmstadt, 1972), 146. A more reserved position about the messianic impulses of Graf Emicho is expressed by H. Möhring, "Graf Emicho und die Judenverfolgungen von 1096," *Rheinische Vierteljahrsblätter* 56 (1992): 97–111.

Constantinople would have been much more appropriate. He therefore surmised that this choice indicated a Jewish source for the messianic idea of the last emperor.[20] And, indeed, laying down the crown in Jerusalem does symbolize the destruction of Rome's political power and the divestment of its earthly property in preparation for accepting the yoke of the kingdom of heaven. Here the Christian tradition seems to have preserved the heart of the Jewish messianic tradition, which sees the destruction of Rome as a condition for the establishment of the new Jerusalem. Jews and Christians made similar messianic plans, and each side probably knew of the other's dream, although each interpreted the idea of "vengeful redemption" in its own terms. The "Rome" of one was the "Jerusalem" of the other.

In this context, martyrdom takes on a metaphysical meaning. The acts of the martyrs sanctified God's name, not only by virtue of the protesting and public force of their devotion and their declaration of loyalty to their faith but also by virtue of their acts themselves, which could also hasten the coming of the Redemption. Then when God appears to the nations clad in his garments of vengeance, his name will be sanctified in a final and decisive way before the entire world. Members of that generation, or at least those who attributed those intentions to them, also pinned their hopes on this messianic martyrdom.

The idea of vengeful redemption, which forms the basis of the Ashkenazic martyrs' cult of blood and sacrifice, becomes clearer in light of the intellectual texture of the detailed stories found in the chronicles. There is no way of knowing if these acts took place as written or whether that was merely how they were recounted in the generation after 1096.[21] We are interested here in understanding the ideology of the text, of the narrator, and of the society he was addressing. Therefore, I will discuss in great detail one such story of self-sacrifice, which exemplifies the totality of the symbols of Temple and sacrifice in profound connection with the issues of Exile and deliverance.

20. P. J. Alexander, *The Byzantine Apocalyptic Tradition*, D. Abrahams, ed., (Berkeley, 1985), 151–84 ("the Last Roman Emperor"). And indeed, in some descriptions of the Messiah (J. Even-Shmuel, *Midreshei Ge'ulah* [Jerusalem, 1954], 312), there is a similar picture of the Messiah Son of Joseph, who is to place his garland on the *Even ha-Shetiyah* ("the Foundation Stone")—the Jewish parallel to Golgotha.

21. Ivan Marcus and Robert Chazan have recently argued about this point: Ivan G. Marcus, "History, Story and Collective Memory: Narrativity in Early Ashkenazic Culture," *Prooftexts* 10 (1990): 365–88; Robert Chazan, "The Facticity of Medieval Narrative: A Case Study of the Hebrew First Crusade Narrative," *AJS Review* 16 (1991): 31–56.

The story in question is that of the suicide of Isaac ben David, the *parnas* (Jewish community leader) of Mainz, preceded by his killing his children and mother and setting fire to the synagogue.[22] Most of the Jews of the community were killed while seeking refuge in the courtyard of the bishop; only a few were saved, including Isaac, who agreed to convert. Note the explanation he is supposed to have given, according to the chronicle: "I obeyed the foes only in order to rescue my sons from the hands of the evildoers, so they would not survive [to live] in error, for they are small and cannot distinguish between good and evil." Should a person convert to Christianity in order to save his children from Christianity? The approach described in the sources is the opposite: they are to be killed so that they will not convert. The narrator seems to be aware that forced converts were allowed to return to Judaism, thereby attempting to justify the father's conversion with his desire to save his children. Nevertheless, the narrator identifies completely with the view that Isaac's own deed could be atoned through death alone.

And that is indeed what happened. Two days after the riots in Mainz had subsided, Isaac returned to his father's house and discovered that the family treasure was untouched. The gap between the severe loss of life that had befallen the community, on the one hand, and the sparing of his property, on the other, made him repent of his conversion, and he decided to carry out a ritual of atonement. First he hired workers to repair his parents' damaged home. Next he told his mother of his plan: "I have decided to make a sin offering to God on High, by which I shall find atonement." His mother, who had survived the pogroms without being baptized, lay wounded in the damaged house, and when she heard her son's intention, she pleaded with him for his own life and for hers, but in vain. Frantically, the man shut himself in the house and locked the door. He asked his children—for whose sake he had agreed to be baptized: "Do you want me to slaughter you on the altar of our God?" The children, who had earlier been described as "not knowing the difference between good and evil," reply: "Do with us as you wish"—a clear echo of Abraham's reply to Isaac, "God will provide him-

---

22. Haberman (n. 1, p. 135), 36–38; Stern and Neubauer (n. 8, p. 138), 11–13; Chazan (n. 8, p. 138), 262–65. Jeremy Cohen has suggested a fascinating analysis of the story: "'Persecutions of 1096'—from Martyrdom to Martyrology: the Sociocultural Context of the Hebrew Crusade Chronicles" [in Hebrew], *Zion* 59 (1994): 185–95. He thinks the story should be seen ironically—a point on which I differ from him.

self the lamb for a burnt offering, my son." The man takes his children to the synagogue and there, before the Holy Ark, he slaughters them: "And he sprinkled their blood on the pillars of the Holy Ark . . . and said: 'May this blood be atonement for all my sins.'" He then returns to his father's house and burns it down. It now becomes clear why he carefully repaired its doors beforehand—to prevent those inside from escaping. Thus his mother was burned to death. The man then returns to the synagogue and burns it down as well: "And the pious man went from corner to corner and from side to side, his hands stretched out [in prayer] to his Father in Heaven, and he prayed to God from within the fire with a loud and pleasant voice." Christians who understood what was going on shouted at him: "Wicked man, come out of the light" and even tried to pull him out, but he refused to leave. "And the innocent and honest and pious man was burned there." This is how our chronicler describes a man who killed his mother and his children with his own hands and burned down the synagogue of Mainz, not at the height of the pogroms, but two days later, when the Crusaders were no longer in the city!

The text explains that the synagogue was burned down because our Isaac learned "that the foes and the townsmen were talking about turning it into a house of idolatry or into a mint." It is difficult to believe that two days after the great pogrom in Mainz the townspeople already had a clear plan of what to do with the synagogue, or that Isaac had gotten wind of their intention. This explanation is one offered by Jewish public opinion in retrospect, intended to justify a bizarre and puzzling act. Burning down the synagogue must be seen in conjunction with the other acts performed by this Isaac beforehand. Two main motifs appear in the story: offering sacrifices and burning down the Temple. The synagogue is the place to which Isaac brings his children, and he kills them before the Holy Ark, even performing a ceremony of sprinkling blood. Thus, it is hardly surprising that his acts conclude with burning down the synagogue (= the Temple), punishment for a sin that is too heavy to bear.

To comprehend the ideological underpinnings of this story, we need to examine its literary qualities. The story does not seem to possess complete dramatic logic, because it makes use of an older literary topos. A central motif in the story is the burning of the synagogue and the death of Isaac and his sons inside it (the mother is burned in her own house). At the beginning of his tale, the narrator draws a parallel between the burning of the synagogue in Mainz and the burning of the Temple: "For those I weep and my eye waters, that the Temple of our God was burned, and for the burn-

ing of Isaac bar David the *parnas* who was burned in His [God's] house."
This motif of suicide in the burning Temple/synagogue is remarkably similar to that found in the Talmudic story of the priests' suicide in the burning Temple:

> Our Rabbis taught: When the First Temple was about to be destroyed
> bands upon bands of young priests with the keys of the Temple in their
> hands assembled and mounted the roof of the Temple and exclaimed:
> "Master of the Universe, as we did not have the merit to be faithful treasurers these keys are handed back into thy keeping." They then threw
> the keys up towards heaven, and there emerged the figure of the palm
> of a hand and took the keys from them, whereupon they jumped and
> fell into the fire.[23]

This Talmudic story may almost be read ironically. The Temple is about to be destroyed, and the young priests return the keys to God—but there is nothing to return. Returning the keys symbolizes the idea that, with the Destruction, the earthly Temple has ascended to heavenly Jerusalem. This is the meaning behind the priests' climbing to the roof of the Temple and throwing the keys upward. In its artistic shaping, the legend draws a contrast between "they threw the keys upward" and "they jumped and fell [down] into the fire." While the Temple ascends to heaven, the priests fall down and are consumed in the fire. Yet this descent was for the sake of ascent, for by virtue of their death as martyrs the priests will enjoy life in the Next World. Just as the Temple ascends, so do those who serve in the Holy Place ascend with it, and through their death they are offered as sacrifices on the heavenly altar.

The priests' suicide marks the transition to a new era, that of the Destruction, during which it is no longer possible to expiate sin by animal sacrifices. From now on, only the death of martyrs on the heavenly altar will suffice. "And in *Zevul* [one of the seven heavens] there is an altar built, and Michael the [angelic] prince of Israel is the high priest there. . . . And he offers

---

23. *b. Ta'anit* 29a and parallels. The story of the priests who were burned in the Temple was also presented in Bel. Jud. 6. 280; *Sefer Yosippon*, ed. D. Flusser (Jerusalem, 1978), 1:394. Cf. Yitzhak Baer, "Jerusalem in the Times of the Great Revolt" [in Hebrew], *Zion* 36 (1978): 167. David Goodblatt has shown that these stories reflect a priestly tradition of committing suicide in the burning Temple. See "Suicide in the Sanctuary: Traditions on Priestly Martyrdom," *JJS* 46 (1995): 10–29.

there the souls of the righteous, until the Temple will be rebuilt, and then the Holy One blessed be He will bring the Temple located in *Zevul* down to the earthly Jerusalem."[24] This Midrash relates to two eras: the time of the Destruction and the time of the Redemption.[25] In the era of Destruction the souls of the martyrs are offered on the altar of heaven, until the era of Redemption, when the Temple will once again descend to the earthly Jerusalem.[26] Our Midrash draws a connection between the Destruction and the sacrifice of the martyrs, as if, during the post-Temple era, the world returned to what it had been pre-Temple, when God commanded Abraham to sacrifice his son to him. And indeed, most of the instances of suicide that we know of took place in relation to the Destruction.[27] The Destruction of the Temple is also seemingly the background for the Midrashic exegesis, noted by Spiegel, that Abraham did indeed slaughter his son.[28]

The messianic significance of human sacrifice also underlies the traditions that fix Jesus's Crucifixion at Passover. Jesus's appearance in Jerusalem specifically at Passover may be interpreted as the proper time for messianic revelation. In retrospect, his atoning death also assumed a messianic meaning: he will appear a second time (Parousia) and rebuild (his own) Temple

24. *Midrash Aseret ha-Dibrot,* in Adolf Jellinek, *Bet ha-Midrasch,* I (Leipzig, 1853), 64. And cf. Grossman (n. 12, p. 140), 128.

25. *2 Bar.* 10:18, which was written about the time of the Destruction of the Second Temple in 70 C.E., tells of a call to the priests to throw the keys heavenward and to return them to God, who will guard the House till the coming of Messiah. "Moreover, ye, priests, take ye the keys of the sanctuary, and cast them into the height of heaven, and give them to the Lord and say: "'Guard Thy house Thyself, for lo! we are found false steward.'" Cf. *4 Bar.,* in which Jeremiah takes the keys of the destroyed Temple, goes out of the city, and throws the keys upward as he addresses the sun: "I say to you, sun, take the keys of the Temple of God, and keep them until the days in which the Lord will question you about them" (*Old Testament Apocrypha,* vol. 2., ed. J. H. Charlesworth; trans. S. E. Robinson [Garden City, 1985], 419); and this certainly means until the coming of deliverance.

26. A. Aptowitzer, "The Heavenly Temple in the Agada" [in Hebrew], *Tarbiz* 2 (1931): 137–57, 257–87. On the descent of the Temple from Heaven, see *Sefer Zerubavel* in *Midrashei Ge'ulah* (n. 20, p. 143), 84; *Sefer Eliyahu,* in *Midrashei Ge'ulah* (n. 20, p. 143), 48.

27. Menahem Stern, "The Suicide of Elazar Ben Jair and his men of Masada, and the 'Fourth Philosophy'" [in Hebrew], *Zion* 47 (1982): 383–87 (= *Mehkarim be-toldot Yisrael beyemei ha-Bayit ha-Sheni* [Jerusalem, 1991], 329–33); David Flusser, "The Dead of Massada in the Eyes of their Contemporaries" [in Hebrew], *Yehudim ve-Yahadut beyemei Bayit Sheni, ha-Mishnah veha-Talmud,* ed. I. Gafni, A. Oppenheimer and M. Stern (S. Safrai FS; Jerusalem, 1993), 134–42. Flusser indicated that the suicide of the defenders of Masada was interpreted as an act of atonement. For the preference of human over animal sacrifice, see Hebrews 9–10.

28. See note 53, below.

instead of the one that had been destroyed. In this light, it is worth noting a well-known historical fact that seems, at first glance, completely coincidental: the suicide of the defenders of Masada also took place on Passover night.[29] It may be that this is what Josephus wanted us to believe, or he may have come across a story with an explicitly mythical note. Did the defenders of Masada choose that date deliberately? Is not the speech of Eleazer ben Yair to his fighters on the night of the suicide at Masada reminiscent of Jesus's speech to his disciples at the "Last Supper" in Jerusalem? And are not both of them similar to the speech of the "pious man, the faithful man, the high priest, to the group of guests gathered at his table" in the city of Xanten on the Friday night before their suicide?[30]

The connection between the Destruction of the Temple and the atonement-death in Mainz clearly illuminates the motifs woven into the story of Isaac ben David. The tale opens with a lament over the burning of "the Temple of Our Lord," in which the burning of the synagogue in Mainz is compared to the Destruction of the Temple.[31] The ceremony of sprinkling the blood of the children on the Holy Ark also expresses the notion that the synagogue is a miniature Temple. Isaac himself is not a *kohen,* a member of the honorary hereditary priesthood, but a *parnas,* a communal leader—albeit in an era when the priests no longer served in a sacerdotal role, the *parnas* was the heir to the priests and had to fulfill an ancient priestly obligation: to commit suicide in the burning "Temple." The sin of the *parnas*—his conversion to Christianity—is parallel to that of the priests who did not deserve to be "faithful treasurers." The destruction of the community in Mainz is therefore tantamount to the Destruction of Jerusalem, and the burning of the synagogue is seen as equivalent to the burning of the Temple: "And the pious Isaac came back to burn the synagogue, and he lit fire in all the entrances. And the *hasid* went from corner to corner and from side to side, and his hands were extended [in prayer] to his Father in Heaven, and he prayed to God from within the fire with a loud and pleasant voice."[32] This description is particularly reminiscent of a passage from a parallel version of the priests'

29. Josephus, Bel. Jud. 7. 401.

30. Haberman (n. 1. p. 135), 48; Stern and Neubauer (n. 8, p. 138), 21; Chazan (n. 8, p. 138), 280.

31. This idea was well formulated by Ivan G. Marcus, "From Politics to Martyrdom; Shifting Paradigms in the Hebrew Narratives of 1096 Crusade Riots," *Prooftexts* 2 (1982): 48–51.

32. Haberman (n. 1, p. 135), 37–38; Stern and Neubauer (n. 8, p. 138), 12–13; Chazan (n. 8, p. 138), 264.

suicide: "The enemies sat and took counsel with the elders how to burn the Temple. As they were deliberating, they lifted their eyes and saw four angels descending, with four flaming torches in their hands which they placed at the four corners of the Temple, setting it on fire. When the High Priest saw that the Temple was on fire, he took the keys and cast them heavenward."[33]

This is another small step in understanding the connection, already noted by Yitzhak Baer and Ivan Marcus, between the martyrdom of 1096 and the Destruction of the Temple. Martyrdom is like a burnt offering on the heavenly altar, which can bring Redemption closer and rebuild the earthly altar. The spilt blood of the martyrs boils on the heavenly altar, stirring up the wrath of the vengeful God. While the Crusaders were ascending to the earthly Jerusalem, the martyrs rose to the heavenly Jerusalem.

Another expression of this idea is evidently found in the term the "great light," mentioned in the story of Isaac ben David. He expresses his desire to kill himself and explains his motivation: "I shall reach my companions and come with them to their realm, to the great light." The entire story is

33. *Pesiqta Rabbati*, sec. 26, ed. M. Ish Shalom (Tel Aviv, 1963), 131. [English: trans. W. G. Braude (New Haven,, 1968), 535] And compare 2 *Bar.* 1:6–8: "And I beheld, and lo! four angels standing at the four corners of the city, each of them holding a torch of fire in his hands. And another angel began to descend from heaven . . . and I saw him descend into the Holy of Holies, and take from thence the veil . . . and after these things I heard that angel saying unto those angels who held the lamps: 'Destroy, therefore, and overthrow its wall to its foundations' . . . now the angels did as he had commanded them, and when they had broken up the corners of the walls, a voice was heard from the interior of the temple, after the wall had fallen, saying: 'Enter, ye enemies, and come, ye adversaries, for he who kept the house has forsaken (it).'" This motif of voices emanating from the Temple portending its destruction is also found in the chronicle of Shlomo ben Shimshon: "That night I and my son-in-law Judah heard the souls who were praying that night in the synagogue [i.e., of Mainz] praying with a loud voice, as if weeping. . . . And the door was closed, but we heard the loud voice and the great weeping, but we understand naught of what they were saying . . . and when we heard these things, we fell on our faces and said: You are the Lord God. Shall you allow the remnant of Israel to perish?!" (Haberman [n. 1, p. 135], 28–29; Stern and Neubauer [n. 8, p. 138], 5; Chazan [n. 8, p. 138], 250). Shimshon concludes his story of the burning of the synagogue in Mainz with these words: "And one year before the coming of the great Day of the Lord, before the pogroms came, most of the rabbis of all the communities died, and the important laymen in Israel also died, to fulfill what is said, 'For the righteous man is taken away before calamity' [Isa 57:1]. And our teacher R. Eleazar passed away" (Haberman [n. 1, p. 135], 38). The book of *Josippon* also relates that: "One year before the coming of Vespasian . . . on the festival of Shavu'ot [as in Mainz!], during those days, at night, the priests heard within the ark the sound of people walking, the sound of many human footsteps walking within the ark. And there was an awesome and powerful voice heard saying: Let us go away from this house" (n. 23, p. 146), 413–14. Compare Bel. Jud. 6. 300; Tacitus, *Annals,* 5. 13.

permeated with symbols of light (in Hebrew: אור, *or*), which may also be vocalized as *ur* to mean "fire" and is also present in the name "Mr. Uri":

And he lit fire *[ur]* in all the entrances. . . . And the enemies cried out to him through the windows. "Wicked man, come out of the fire *[ur]*, you may still be saved." And they extended a ladder to him, to pull him out of the fire *[ur]*. . . . And Mr. Uri was also in that same counsel. . . . And Mr. Uri was in a different house, and he also wished to help Mr. Yitzhak to burn the synagogue upon him as well, to sanctify the Name with his friend Mr. Yitzhak, but he was unable to reach him, because the enemies rose from their beds in the middle of the night when they felt the fire *[ur]*, and before they went to it they killed Mr. Uri in the way, before he got to the fire *[ur]*. And Mr. Yitzhak was consumed, and the two of them fell there together before the Lord, with one heart, with a whole heart toward His name. . . . And concerning them and their like it is said, "He who offers a thanksgiving offer honors Me." [Ps 50:23][34]

What is the meaning of this "great light" to which the martyrs are going? And what is the connection between a martyr's death and the burning of the synagogue/Temple? Here too the narrator embellishes his story with explicitly Midrashic motifs. In *Midrash Tanhuma* we find:

The Holy One blessed be He said to Moses: Tell Israel: My sons, in this world you were connected to the light of the Temple and you light lamps within it; but in the World to Come, by the merit of that lamp, I shall bring you the Messianic King who is compared to a lamp, as is said, "There I will make a horn to sprout for David, I have prepared a lamp for my anointed" [Ps 132:17]. "He who brings a thanksgiving sacrifice honors me; to him who orders his way aright I will show the salvation of God" [Ps 50:23]. . . . The Holy One blessed be He said: In this world you need a lamp, but in the World to Come, "And nations shall come to your light, and kings to the brightness of your rising." [Isa 60:3][35]

The similarity between the Ashkenazic story and the Midrash is quite clear. In both cases there is a transition from the motif of "light" to the verse "He who brings a thanksgiving sacrifice honors Me." Our narrator

34. Haberman (n. 1, p. 135), 37–38; Stern and Neubauer (n. 8, p. 138), 12–13; Chazan (n. 8, p. 138), 264–65. My thanks to Jeremy Cohen, who drew my attention to the motif of light.
35. *Tanhuma*, Tezaveh, sec. 8. (S. Buber Recension, trans. John T. Townsend [Hoboken, NJ, 1997], 141).

had before him this or a similar version of the *Tanhuma*. Moreover, David Flusser has demonstrated that the ideas concerning the heavenly Jerusalem found here in *Midrash Tanhuma* also appear in Revelation:

> And I saw no temple in the city, for its temple is the Lord God Almighty and the Lamb. And the city has no need of sun or moon to shine upon it, for the glory of God is its light, and its lamp is the Lamb. By its light shall the nations walk; and the kings of the earth shall bring their glory into it, and its gates shall never be shut by day—and there shall be no night there.[36]

Both the Revelation of John and the Midrash interpret Isaiah 60:1–3: "Arise, shine; for your light has come, and the glory of the Lord has risen upon you. For behold, darkness shall cover the earth, and thick darkness the peoples; but the Lord will arise upon you, and his glory will be seen upon you. And nations shall come to your light, and kings to the brightness of you rising." The light is the light of the Messiah, the light of the Lamb. Our chronicler's use of the term *light* thus serves to emphasize the messianic connection inherent in martyrdom. Martyrs go to the "great light" of the Messiah and to that of the brilliant heavenly Jerusalem. This is the significance of the heavy symbolic weight given to the description of the synagogue's burning and its destruction by fire *(ur)*. This exegesis also sheds new light on the wonderful dialogue between Isaac, who was burned in "fire" *(ur)* and who goes to the "great light" *(or)*, and the Christians who want to save him. They tell him: "Come out of the fire *[ur]*, you can still be saved" and even extend him a pole to "pull him out of the fire *[ur]*." But he does not agree to this, because for him the fire is the same as light. The Christians who want "to pull him out of the fire *[ur]*" only want to distance him and drive him away from "the great light *[or]*."

36. Revelation 21:22–25; David Flusser, *Judaism and the Origins of Christianity* (Jerusalem, 1988), 454–65 ("No Temple in the City"). For more on the mystical meaning of light and its connection with death and human deliverance, see Moshe Idel, "'In the Light of Life': A Study of Kabbalistic Eschatology" [in Hebrew], *Kedushat ha-Hayyim ve-herut ha-nefesh*, 191–211; and cf. E. E. Urbach, *The Sages—Their Concepts and Beliefs*, trans. I. Abrahams (Jerusalem, 1979), 44–46; M. Kister, "'Levi = Light': On the history of an ancient Midrash about the Stones of the Breastplate" [in Hebrew]; *Tarbiz* 45 (1976): 327–30; Itamar Gruenwald, "From Priesthood to Messianism: The Anti-Priestly Polemic and the Messianic Factor," in *Messiah and Christos; Studies in the Jewish Origins of Christianity Presented to David Flusser*, ed. I. Gruenwald, S. Shaked, and G. Stroumsa (Tübingen, 1992), 89.

It may not be accidental that the close connections between the chronicles of 1096 and the ancient Midrashim lead specifically to the Revelation of John, the most Jewish book in the New Testament. The Christian sibyls penetrated Western Christianity from Byzantium during the eleventh century and exercised a great influence on the Crusader's messianic consciousness. The Tiburtine Sibyl, which is known in the West, is based on Jewish sources in general and on the Revelation of John in particular.[37] A similar process befell Ashkenazic messianic martyrology, which also drew on Byzantine and Palestinian Midrashic sources, apparently brought to the West via Italy, several of whose ancient ideas had already been absorbed previously in the Book of Revelation. It is precisely this resemblance between Jewish and Christian messianic visions that explains the fierce tension that erupted over its realization.

Our narrator's ideology reveals his consistent identification with the idea that the blood of the martyrs can rouse God to take messianic vengeance. Isaac harmed the very holiest objects—the Torah scroll, the synagogue, and the lives of his children and his mother. The purpose of these acts and of their telling is to shock and horrify not only the reader, but God himself.

What makes this story unique in comparison with other stories of martyrdom is that death comes by conflagration. In most cases, martyrs kill themselves by the sword or by drowning in a river. The use of fire is especially striking in light of the timing of the deed: on the night of the festival of Shavu'ot! Not only did the *parnas* of Mainz destroy the synagogue and kill his children and his mother, but he also violated the Torah prohibition against lighting a fire on a holiday. Is this what should be told of someone who desires atonement for his acts? And if one wished to argue that it occurred on "the eve of Shavu'ot," as is told there ("and it was on the fifth day of the month of Sivan, on the eve of Shavu'ot"), and that the conflagration may have occurred during the day (especially since at that time of the year the holiday comes late in the evening)—the narrator leaves no room for doubt, and states explicitly: "When the enemies rose in the middle of the night, when they felt the fire"—that is, long after the holiday began.

37. David Flusser, "An Early Jewish-Christian Document in the Tiburtine Sibyl," in *Messiah and Christos,* ed. Gruenwald, Shaked, and Stroumsa, 359–89. Several of his statements there are questioned by B. McGinn, "Teste David cum Sibylla: The Significance of the Sibylline Tradition in the Middle Ages," in *Women in Medieval World,* ed. J. Kirchner and S. F. Wemple (Oxford, 1985), 27–28.

The Midrashic motifs underlying this story, as discussed above, raise the possibility that the choice of fire as a motif may also be the result of a literary decision. The synagogue of Mainz burns down on the night of Shavu'ot, the holiday commemorating the giving of the Torah on Mount Sinai.[38] In Exodus 19:18 we read: "And Mount Sinai was wrapped in smoke, because the Lord descended upon it in fire; and the smoke of it went up like the smoke of a kiln." And in Deuteronomy 4:11–12: "And the mountain burned with fire to the heart of heaven. . . . Then the Lord spoke to you out of the midst of the fire." In *Midrash Tanhuma*, the following description is added:

> You find, that when the Holy One blessed be He gave the Torah, it was entirely of fire, as it is said, "at his right hand a fiery law" [Deut 33:2]. Resh Lakish said: The Torah is of fire, its skins of fire, the writing of fire, it was fashioned from fire, as said "from his right hand a fiery law for them." And the mouth of the intercessor [i.e., Moses] was of fire. . . . And the angels who descended with it were made of fire . . . And the mountain burned with fire . . . and it was given within a fire consuming fire . . . And the Divine Word also emerged from amidst of fire. When they saw the flames and the burning letters, the Holy One blessed be He said to them: Do not imagine that there are separate [Divine] realms. Therefore He began with the words "I am the Lord your God . . . You shall have no other gods before me." [Exod. 20:2][39]

The proximity to Shavu'ot is also tangible in the period that Isaac ben David waited before performing his deed: three days. The community was destroyed on Tuesday, the third of Sivan, while he waited until the fifth of the month, the eve of Shavu'ot. This waiting period corresponds to Exodus 19: 10–11, 15–16: "And [Moses] said to the people, 'Be ready by the third day . . . [And it came to pass] on the morning of the third day there were thunder and lightning, and a thick cloud upon the mountain." Just as the giving of the Torah began "in the morning," so our *parnas* begins preparing for his act during the day. He goes to his father's house and hires workers to repair the doors of the house—an activity that presumably took sev-

---

38. Jeremy Cohen noted the close relation between Shavu'ot and the use of the fire motif in this incident (see n. 22, p. 144), 190–92. On the motif of fire on Shavu'ot, see Moshe Weinfeld, "The Uniqueness of the Decalogue" [in Hebrew], in *Aseret ha-Dibrot bere'i ha-dorot*, ed. B. Z. Segal (Jerusalem, 1986), 31–34.

39. *Tanhuma, Yitro*, sec. 16.

eral hours. At night, after the fire was kindled, the *parnas* is described as one whose "hands are stretched out [in prayer] to his Father in Heaven, and he prayed to God from within the fire"—parallel to God who speaks to his people from within the fire (Deuteronomy 4:33).

The idea expressed in this stratum of the story seems to be to position Isaac ben David's act not only as a parallel to the Destruction of the Temple but also as a kind of inverted Sinaitic revelation. Just as the priests in the Temple return their keys to heaven, so the *parnas* returns the Torah to God. At midnight, at the beginning of the fiftieth day after Passover, the *parnas* offers his children "before the Holy Ark," the place of the Torah, and sprinkles their blood "upon the pillars of the Holy Ark."

As mentioned earlier, these acts described in great detail in the chronicles are not tales of murder at the hands of Christians, but of Jews who killed themselves or their loved ones. We can certainly assume that these cases were rare; however, we have here a literary attempt to shape Jewish public opinion to view self-sacrifice or the sacrifice of others as a desired norm and a model to be emulated. The narrators were full participants in the excitement and atmosphere of 1096. The death of the martyrs was a fact, and it was now possible to invoke it to arouse the divine wrath against the enemies of Israel. The stories selected were those that would most arouse God's wrath and thus were interlaced with repeated pleas for vengeance. Rhetorically, one might sharpen the point by saying more specifically that the chronicles were not intended to shape earthly public opinion, but heavenly public opinion, the World on High.

THE SACRIFICE OF CHILDREN

The cult of blood and its latent potential to arouse horror and turmoil in heaven are most acutely expressed in the liturgical poems describing the death of the children in 1096. These deaths were considered the ultimate in the ideal of self-sacrifice. A child whose blood was shed was like an innocent lamb slaughtered on the altar, with great power to stir up the wrath of the vengeful God. The strong connection between the death of young, innocent children and a pure sacrifice underlies two liturgical poems by Rabbi Isaac ben Shalom:

He [Abraham] with his one [son] made haste
and [punishment] was deferred to his sons on the holiday of holidays
although there were many that slaughtered their children . . .

they prepared to slaughter the children and said the blessing over the
  sacrifice with intent . . .
For the sanctification of His name we were killed
our women and children to fall by the sword . . .
priests were made as burnt-offerings
children were bound with their mothers.[40]

Children appear as a central feature of martyrdom three times in one
sentence. The motif of the Binding of Isaac created a particularly strong
attitude about the sacrifice of children, in emulation of the patriarch who
bound his son as a sacrifice. Thus, in the lament of Kalonymus ben Yehudah, we read:

Fathers slaughter their children and are covered in their blood
. . . .
together fathers and sons, bridegrooms and brides
hurry to the slaughters as to their marriage canopy.[41]

In another dirge of Rabbi Kalonymus, the sacrifice of children is likewise emphasized:

The father overcomes his mercies so as to sacrifice
his children, like one preparing sheep for the slaughter
he prepared his sons for the slaughter.
They declare to their mothers, behold we are slaughtered and killed
like one sanctified for an offering . . .
Women, [weep over] their fruit, their beloved infants:
Who will hear and not shed tears?
The son is slaughtered and the father recites *Shema*.[42]

The lament of Rabbi David ben Meshulam, *Elohim al domi lakh,* is likewise devoted entirely to the slaughter of children:

The holy seed, sons who will not be false
. . . women and children agreed with a whole heart to be bound . . .

40. Haberman (n. 1, p. 135), 112–13.
41. Haberman (n. 1, p. 135), 65.
42. Daniel Goldschmidt, *Seder ha-Kinot le-Tish'ah b'Av* (Jerusalem, 1972), sec. 30 (106–9).
Rabbi Meir of Rothenburg relied on this *piyyut* when giving permission to parents to slaughter their children during the pogroms (see n. 109, below).

Year-old sheep lambs for a pure burnt-offering . . .
Sucklings and babes who are offered entirely as a sacrifice . . .
Righteous women, whose nests had nurtured the delicate ones
. . . . The end of the altar are the children of the study hall
the sacrifice of the people, to atone the student with the scholar
Servants of the priesthood were fit, both women and men
blood of fathers and sons touch and swell up . . .
surely there shall be seen the act of the confident daughters
. . . . The most beautiful women have their innards split apart
between their legs the afterbirth of the child blossom . . .
bringing their sons to the slaughter as to the marriage canopy
Shall God not restrain himself from lifting up his voice in weeping
over these?[43]

In a *selihah* by Rabbi Eliezer ben Nathan, the sacrifice of children by their parents is emphasized as an act of piety:

To their mothers the innocent children said with a sigh
Let us be offered as a perfect sacrifice
For this the daughters of Israel weep
teach your daughters to wail and each woman teach her neighbor
to lament
Sons tall as saplings pleaded with their fathers
hasten quickly to do the will of our Creator
The portion of our cup is the one God
Our days are complete for our end is near
. . . . The mothers rejoiced when they heard the pleasing words . . .
the chant, "God is one," they cried out in comforting
My witness in heaven and testament on High
On their watches they stood and slaughtered with tears
their burnt offering as acceptable as upon the altars of God
the mother fainted and lay upon her sons
For these I do weep.[44]

A similar idea is expressed in Rabbi Joel ben Isaac Halevi's poem *Elohim yireh lo seh:*

43. Haberman (n. 1, p. 135), 70.
44. Haberman (n. 1, p. 135), 86.

Sucklings and infants offered themselves for the slaughter
and filled their hands to draw near to the sacrifice . . .
To their mothers they cried out
Hasten and bind us.[45]

And in a lament by the same author:

And the father weeping and wailing kissed his suckling son
and sanctified his head like the one bound at Moriah
and the mother hid her face so as not to see the death of her child
for her compassion was stirred up for her child
and her tear was upon her cheek.[46]

The killing of children is also of special significance in the chronicles. I
have already discussed the episode in which the *parnas* of Mainz Isaac ben
David killed his mother and children. It is told of the Jews of Worms that,
after they despaired of being saved, "They accepted the judgment / and
trusted in their Creator, and offered a righteous sacrifice, and took their
sons and slaughtered them for the unity of the great Name."[47] As usual,
the narrator dwells on the especially extreme case, whose stylistic affinity
with the account of the Binding of Isaac is particularly striking:

And there was a certain young man named Rabbi Meshullam ben Yitzhak,
who called with a loud voice to all those standing there and to Zipporah
his pure wife: Listen to me, great and small; This son has been given me
by God, and my wife Zipporah bore him in her old age, and his name is
Yitzhak. Now I shall offer him up, as Father Abraham did to Isaac his son.
And Zipporah answered him: My lord, my lord, wait a while, do not yet
thrust your hand against the child whom I raised and brought up and bore
in old age. Slaughter me first, that I may not see the death of my son. And
he answered and said: I will not wait even a moment, He who has given
him to us shall take him as His portion, and place him in the bosom of
Abraham our father. And he bound Yitzhak his son, and he took in his
hand the knife to slaughter this son, and he recited the blessing for slaugh-

45. Daniel Goldschmidt, *Seder ha-Selihot ke-minhag Lita ukehillot ha-Perushim be-Erez
Yisrael* (Jerusalem, 1965), 81.
46. Haberman (n. 1, p. 135), 109.
47. Haberman (n. 1, p. 135), 96.

tering, and the lad answered, "Amen." And so he slaughtered the lad. And he took his screaming wife, and the two of them left the room, and they were killed by the errant ones. [i.e., the Crusaders]

Two women from the city of Moers are said to have killed their children: one killed her ten-year-old daughter, and the other her newborn son.[48] These acts infuriated the townspeople and made them hand the Jews over to the Crusaders.

The most shocking story of all is that of Rachel of Mainz, who asked her friend not to take pity on her four children:

And one of her friends came and took the knife to slaughter her children. And when the mother of the children saw the knife she cried out in a great and bitter cry, and beat her face and her chest and said: Where are Your mercies, O God?! And the woman said to her friend with bitterness of soul: Do not slaughter Yitzhak before Aharon his brother, that he not see the death of his brother. And he fled from her, and the woman took the lad and killed him, and he was small and very pleasant. And the woman spread her hands so as to receive the blood, and she received the blood on her skirts, in place of the sprinkling of the blood [i.e., as was done in the Temple]. And when the child Aharon saw that his brother had been slaughtered, he cried out: Do not kill me! And he hid under one of the cabinets. And she had two daughters, Bella and Madrona, the pride of the house, beautiful, virgins, the daughters of Rabbi Yehudah her husband; and the maidens took the knife and sharpened it so that it not be unfit, and they stretched forth their necks and she offered them to the Lord God of Israel. . . . And when the righteous woman had finished offering her children before their Creator, she raised her voice and called out to her son: Aharon, Aharon, where are you? Upon you too I shall have no pity and no mercy. And she pulled him out by his legs from beneath the cabinet where he was hiding, and offered him before the high and exalted God. And she placed them him with her two hands, two on one side and two on the other, next to her womb, and they were dieing next to her, until the enemies seized the room and found them sitting and mourning for them. . . . And when they saw the children slaughtered, they smote her and killed her upon them.[49]

48. Haberman (n. 1, p. 135), 79.
49. Haberman (n. 1, p. 135), 34, 101; Stern and Neubauer (n. 8, p. 138), 9–10, 53–54; Chazan (n. 8, p. 138), 258–60, 238–39.

This section cannot be concluded without mentioning a well-known source attesting to the strident opposition to killing children within the Jewish community. I refer to a statement explicitly cited in the commentary of the Tosaphists on the Torah:

> And there was an incident involving a certain rabbi who slaughtered many small children during the time of persecution, for he was afraid that they would be converted. And there was another rabbi who was very angry with him and called him a "murderer," but he did not pay any heed [to his words]. And that rabbi said: If things are as I say, let that rabbi die a strange and painful death. And so it was: the Gentiles seized him, and stripped off his skin, and placed sand between his skin and his flesh. And thereafter the edict was nullified, and had he not slaughtered those children they would have been saved.[50]

Note that this attitude involves a double criticism: on the part of the rabbi, and on the part of the narrator, unless we assume that they are one and the same. This unique statement discloses the existence of a strong opposition to the agitation for martyrdom. It is difficult to estimate its scope or force on the basis of the impression it left on the extant literature, for it may have been silenced or may have subsided over time. It is more convenient to glorify and exalt the heroes of the past than to criticize their actions. What matters to us is the existence of an internal Jewish position that saw killing children as murder. If there were those among the Jews who thought this way, how many more must there have been among the Christians?— a question we shall explore in the next section.

THE LIBEL

Yitzhak Baer insisted that "two ancient symbols became a concrete reality during the First Crusade: the Binding of Isaac on Mount Moriah and the sacrificial rite of the Temple. . . . Fathers and mothers bound and slaughtered their children . . . and executed the laws of Temple sacrifices in all their details upon them and themselves."[51] Baer saw the martyrdom of 1096 as another chapter in the long history of Jewish martyrology, and hence he dis-

---

50. *Da'at Zekenim mi-ba'alei ha-Tosafot*, at Gen 9:5; also published in *Sefer Tosafot ha-Shalem*, ed. J. Gellis (Jerusalem, 1982), 262.

51. Baer (n. 23, p. 146), 136–37.

cussed it with great pathos: "The cruel reality of these acts carried within it a noble idea: that the souls of those killed as martyrs are offered as sacrifices in the Heavenly Temple."[52] He saw no contradiction between the "cruel reality" and the "noble idea." This admiration of the martyrs of 1096 was accepted as natural and self-evident by an entire generation of Jewish scholars.

Baer's article was published in 1953. A few years earlier, in 1950, Shalom Spiegel published a brilliant monograph in which he noted the extensive presence of the motif of human sacrifice in the pogroms of 1096.[53] Spiegel was thus the first one to call things by their name. He understood the tremendous exegetical difficulty confronting the Ashkenazic martyrs in their attempt to find justification for their acts. They saw themselves as repeating the acts of the patriarchs, the act of the ancient patriarch Abraham, who bound his son for sacrifice. Yet the ultimate moral of the Binding of Isaac is "Lay not your hand upon the lad or do anything to him." (Gen 22:12). That is, God prefers animal to human sacrifice. The Akedah, the binding of Isaac, could not have been considered a model by those people, since not only did they stand the test and agree to sacrifice their sons, like Abraham, but in the end they in fact did so, with their own hands. Thus their virtue was even greater than that of Abraham. Spiegel showed how the exegesis of the Binding of Isaac changed as a result of this distress and how the isolated, muted voices from the Midrash, stating that Abraham did indeed kill Isaac, found a new lease on life in medieval Ashkenaz.

The articles by Spiegel and Baer were written but a few years after the Holocaust, a fact that doubtless influenced their impression of the suffering and courage of the ancient martyrs on German soil. The mood in those years was not congenial to the idea that there was anything dreadful about such self-sacrifice.

Haym Soloveitchik has recently noted that the martyrological behavior of the generation of 1096 cannot be understood within the halakhic context of the laws of Kiddush Hashem, "Sanctification of the Name."[54] He

---

52. Baer (n. 23, p. 146), 137.

53. Shalom Spiegel, "From the Legends of the Aggadah: A *Piyyut* on the Slaughter of Isaac and His Resurrection by Rabbi Ephraim of Bonn" [in Hebrew], *Alexander Marx Jubilee Volume* (New York, 1950), 471–547; translated into English as *The Last Trial* (New York, 1967).

54. Haym Soloveitchik, "Religious Law and Change: The Medieval Ashkenazic Example," *AJS Review* 12 (1987), 205–21. This has also been noted by H. J. Zimmels, *Ashkenazim and Sephardim* (London, 1958), 263; Jacob Katz, *Exclusiveness and Tolerance* (New York, 1961), 83–84. According to A. Grossman (n. 12, p. 140), 105–19, the martyrs found support in the

maintains that the suicides of 1096 cannot be considered martyrs according to Jewish religious law and that perhaps they even ought to have been buried outside the cemetery fence, as befits suicides. Had the martyrs of 1096 in. fact been guided by Talmudic law, they would not have dared to kill their children or themselves. But that is precisely what they did, or at least what we are told that they did. It is doubtful that we are capable of understanding the motives of those who commit suicide and kill their children. In any event, what is more important is the religious ideology of those who narrated their deeds. The chronicles and the *piyyutim* express views, widespread in the twelfth century, according to which the blood of the martyrs brings the Redemption closer. This is a paean to the heavenly altar of blood, on which human sacrifices are slaughtered, and it is surely based on actual incidents, since preaching cannot be based on outright fiction. Those who shaped public opinion during the twelfth century wished to make normative extreme patterns of behavior, which even in times of persecution could be realized only by a few individuals. Nevertheless, the acts of these individuals left a great impression, and they became a myth expressing the desires of an entire society and its deepest and most authentic religious feelings. This left an impression not only on Jewish public opinion.

THE IMPACT OF THE BLOOD SACRIFICE ON CHRISTIANS

It seems doubtful that Jewish acts of martyrdom were meant to shape Christian public opinion,[55] but they were certainly known to Christians and had a great impact on them. Although there are not many sources indicating the nature of that impact, there are enough to prove that Jewish behavior did make a negative impression on Christian public opinion. Even the Jewish chronicler is aware of the horror aroused by these acts among the Christians. I have already mentioned the response of the burghers of Mainz to the burn-

---

episode of Masada, which they knew through *Sefer Jossippon* and which they considered a compelling ancient tradition. But the story of Masada is not mentioned in the chronicles.

55. According to Katz, "During the Ashkenazic Middle Ages, the act of martyrdom was deliberately and pointedly directed at the Christian world. The Christians were to be made aware of the true faith" (*Exclusiveness and Tolerance*, 79). The source cited by Katz to prove his point is a sentence from the chronicle of Shlomo ben Shimshon: "And may there be known among the Gentiles before our eyes, the vengeance of the spilled blood of His servants, quickly" (Haberman [n. 1, p. 135], 43; Stern and Neubauer [n, 8, p. 138], 17; Chazan [n. 8, p. 138], 273). Hence, it was not the death of the martyrs that was meant to convince the Christians, but the messianic vengeance it would evoke.

ing of the synagogue by Isaac ben David.[56] They tried to save him from the fire and called him a "wicked man"—this according to the Jewish narrator, who himself saw him as an "innocent and honest and pious man." Note likewise the harsh reaction of the Bishop of Mainz, Rothard, to the act of Rabbi Kalonymus, who killed his son: "And when the bishop heard that he had slaughtered his son, he was very angry and said: From now on I certainly do not wish to help them anymore."[57] In the description of the suicide of the Jews of Mainz, the anonymous chronicler emphasizes how "the hands of compassionate women would strangle their sons so as to perform the will of their Creator, and would turn the faces of their tender children towards the Gentiles."[58] To save the Jews of his city, the ruler of the town of Moers took them "and placed them under watch, each one by himself, until the next day, so that they would not thrust their hands against themselves, as they had heard that they had themselves turned their hands against one another."[59]

In the report of the events at Trier—an exceptionally accurate and reliable account—the Christians are described as being concerned from the outset that the Jews would commit suicide and kill their own children: "And three days before they reported to them of this coercion [i.e., forced conversion], the princes who were in the palace [*palais, palatium,* i.e., the local basilica] closed the water cistern in the palace, for they feared lest they throw their children down there to kill them."[60] Hence, the Jews' practice of killing their own children was quickly known among the Christians, since the event in Trier took place shortly after the events in Mainz and Worms. Already then such acts were widely known and had left a deep impression on the Christian milieu. Indeed, the behavior of the Jews was described in the Christian chronicles as well. Albertus Aquensis saw the killing of their children as the most awful act committed by the Jews:

> When the Jews saw that the Christian enemies were attacking them and their children and did not show mercy to anyone, they rose up against

56. Haberman (n. 1, p. 135), 36–38; Stern and Neubauer (n. 8, p. 138), 11–13; Chazan (n. 8, p. 138), 262–65.

57. Haberman (n. 1, p. 135), 41; Stern and Neubauer (n. 8, p. 138); Chazan (n. 8, p. 138), 270.

58. Haberman (n. 1, p. 135), 101; Stern and Neubauer (n. 8, p. 138); 54; Chazan (n. 8, p. 138); 237–38.

59. Haberman (n. 1, p. 135), 79; Stern and Neubauer (n. 8, p. 138), 43.

60. Haberman (n. 1, p. 135), 55–56; Stern and Neubauer (n. 8, p. 138), 27–29; Chazan (n. 8, p. 138), 292–94.

one another, their children, their wives, their mothers and their sisters, and thus each perished at the hand of his comrade. Mothers—it is awful to say this—slit the throats of their own suckling babes and stabbed others, preferring that they die by their hands and not by the weapons of the uncircumcised.[61]

Bernold's chronicle describes the Jews' suicide as a "satanic" act.[62] *Gesta Treverorum* tells of the suicide of the Jews in Trier:

And when they [the Crusaders] in their zealous fervor approached the city of Trier, the Jews of that place said to themselves that they could also expect a similar fate [i.e., to that of the Jews of Worms and Mainz]. [Then] some of them took their children and thrust the blade in their stomach, saying that it was their duty to return them to the bosom of Abraham, lest they become a laughing stock of the Christian madness. And some of their wives went up to the bridge over the river, filled the bodices and sleeves of their garments with stones, and threw themselves into the depths.[63]

This description is identical to that found in the Hebrew chronicle and hence is proof, not only of the reliability of the sources, but also of the deep impression those events made on Christians and Jews alike.

The Cult of Blood and Ritual Murder Libels

The central place of the blood ritual in the consciousness of the generation after 1096, as well as the negative Christian attitude toward that ritual, may

61. *Recueil des historiens des croisades. Historiens occidentaux,* vol. 4, (Paris, 1879), 293: "Judaei vero, videntes Christianos hostes in se suosque parvulos insurgere, et nulli aetati parcere, ipsi quoque in se suosque confratres, natosque, mulieres, matres et sorores irruerunt, et mutua caede se peremerunt. Matres pueris lactentibus, quod dictu nefas est, guttura ferro secabant, alios transforabant, volentes potius sic propriis manibus perire, quam incircumcisorum armis exstingui."

62. *Bernoldi Chronicon,* in *Monumenta Germaniae Historica* (= *MGH*), *Scriptores* (= *SS*), vol. 5 (Hannover, 1844), 465: "diabolo et propria duricia persuadente, se ipsos interfecerunt."

63. *Gesta Treverorum,* in *MGH SS,* vol. 8 (Hannover, 1848), 190: "Cumque eodem fervore civitati Treverorum appropinquassent, Iudaei qui ibi habitabant similia sibi arbitrantes fieri, quidam ex eis accipientes parvulos suos, defixerunt cultros in ventribus eorum, dicentes, ne forte christianorum vesaniae Iudibrio fierent, debere eos in sinum Habrahae transmittere. Quaedam autem ex mulieribus eorum, ascendentes super pontem fluminis et adimpletis sinibus earum et manicis lapidibus, praecipitaverunt se in profondum."

shed new light on the appearance at precisely that time of yet another hostile and distorted Christian interpretation of Jewish martyrology: namely, the accusation of ritual murder. The first medieval ritual murder accusation occurred in the 1140s. The nearly simultaneous appearance of these two historical episodes—Jewish martyrdom and the ritual murder libel—requires comment, since these events may well be interrelated.[64]

I would like to explain, by means of the suggested connection between the incidents of martyrdom and the ritual murder libel, the great proximity between the worldview that characterized the chronicles of 1096 and that of the accusations underlying the ritual murder libel. In both cases, the Jews are described as engaging in a rite involving human sacrifice: in the one, they sacrifice their own children, and it is considered an exemplary act; in the other, they kill a Christian child, and it is considered a loathsome act. The only difference between the ritual murder libel and martyrdom lies in the question of whom the Jews kill: their own children or those of the Christians. Just as the Jews of the twelfth century told one another the heroic stories of the martyrs of the pogroms of 1096, so were rumors and tales of the deeds of the Jews common on the Christian side. The Jewish version, with its positive interpretation, appears in the chronicles of 1096. The ritual murder libel is a distorted echo of the Christian exegesis, which demonstrated awareness of Judaism's battle against Christianity as a universal struggle with a messianic dimension. Its current manifestation—the blood ritual—was inextricably connected to its end—eschatological vengeance.

Historical research has dealt repeatedly with the question of why the Christians began to accuse Jews of the ritual murder libel specifically in the twelfth century. Some saw those accusations as a reincarnation of ritual murder accusations that had been widespread in antiquity. According to this view, Europe's reacquaintance with classical literature in the twelfth century stirred up the ancient, dormant charges. This explanation has recently been rejected by Gavin Langmuir, who has proven that those groups be-

---

64. To the best of my knowledge, the first scholar to suggest examining the connection between the martyrdom of 1096 and the ritual murder libel was Ivan Marcus: "A further avenue that needs to be explored is the relationship between Jews ritually killing Jews as martyrs and the Christian accusation, first attested in Norwich 1144, that Jews ritually kill Christians"; see "Hierarchies, Religious Boundaries and Jewish Spirituality in Medieval Germany," *Jewish History* 1 (1986): n. 27.

lieving in the existence of a blood rite among the Jews had no knowledge of the ancient sources of the accusation of ritual murder.[65]

Another explanation, proposed by Cecil Roth, argues that the Jewish custom of hanging Haman in effigy on Purim was interpreted by Christians as a mockery of Jesus.[66] There developed from this the notion that the Jews

65. Gavin I. Langmuir, "Thomas of Monmouth: Detector of Ritual Murder," *Speculum* 59 (1984): 827. For charges of blood libel against Christian heretics, see A. Patschovsky, "Der Ketzer als Teufelsdiener," in *Papsttum, Kirche und Recht im Mittelalter; Festschrift für Horst Fuhrmann zum 65. Geburtstag,* ed. H. Mordek (Tübingen, 1991), 317–34. Patschovsky notes that such charges were widespread during late antiquity, but the literary sources that tell of such charges were not known during the Middle Ages. He cites two reports about charges against heretics for the murder of children in the Latin world: one in the eleventh century (by a monk named Arefast in 1078), and the second recorded in the autobiography of Guibert de Nogent in 1115. It was only from the first third of the thirteenth century on that these accusations become widespread and conventional with regard to heretics. Even if the ritual murder libel against the Jews is an expansion of the accusation against the heretics, we still need to explain what led to identifying Jews with heretics and why this happened specifically in the middle of the twelfth century. Most important, ritual murder libels against the Jews swept over England, France, and Germany during the second half of the twelfth century, long after such a wave of accusations against heretics had arisen.

66. Cecil Roth, "The Feast of Purim and the Origins of the Blood Accusation," *Speculum* 4 (1933): 520–26. Elliot Horowitz discusses at length the Jewish custom of burning Haman in effigy on Purim as an allusion to the Crucifixion of Jesus: "'And It is Turned Around': Jews Against their Enemies in the Festivities of Purim" [in Hebrew], *Zion* 59 (1994): 129–68; Horowitz, "The Rite to Be Reckless: On the Perpetration and Interpretation of Purim Violence," *Poetics Today* 15 (1994): 9–54. The affinity, suggested by Roth, between the hanging of Haman in effigy on Purim and the ritual murder libel is accepted by G. Mentgen, "The Creation of the Fiction of a Blood Libel" [in Hebrew], *Zion* 59 (1994): 343–49; Mentgen, "Über den Ursprung der Ritualmordfabel," *Aschkenaz* 4 (1994): 405–16. This would also seem to be the context of the following story: in 1066 the bishop of Trier, Eberhard, threatened to expel the Jews of the city if they did not convert to Christianity by the Sabbath before Easter. During Passover the Jews prepared an effigy of the bishop, and bribed a priest to baptize it. When that Sabbath on which the bishop had planned to baptize the Jews arrived, they burned the image, and the bishop became ill and died ([n. 63, p. 163] 182–83). The incident is discussed by A. Haverkamp, "Die Juden im mittelalterlichen Trier," *Kurtrierisches Jahrbuch* 19 (1979): 6. A similar story is presented in the Hebrew Chronicle, *Ma'aseh nora.* In 992 a Jewish convert to Christianity named Shehok accused the Jews of Le Mans, France, of plotting to kill the bishop: "And they fashioned a waxen image of him in the form of a person, so that his soul might melt like wax in the fire. And they placed it inside a wooden box in their synagogue near the idols, where they place the Law of God. And they went to the prince of the land and said to him: Do you know what this people has done? They have made a wax statue in your image, and they place pins within it three times a year, so as to make you disappear from the earth. And thus did their ancestors do to your God. . . . They also wrote letters against

in fact required the blood of a Christian child on Passover, which follows soon after Purim. Roth's starting point was the assumption that Easter on occasion coincides with Purim—as indeed happened in 1932, a year before his article was published. But such a conjunction could only occur after the introduction of the Gregorian calendar in 1582. During the Middle Ages, these two festivals never fell on the same day. At the latest, Purim fell during Lent.

Even though the basic assumption underlying Roth's explanation is wrong, his essential notion is correct. Purim is closely linked with Passover and hence with Easter. Indeed, Jewish law decrees the study of the laws of Passover thirty days before the holiday, that is, on Purim.[67] Purim is a story of deliverance, whose beginning is rooted in Passover, since Haman was hanged in the middle of Passover. According to the Book of Esther, Haman cast the

---

you in which every day they curse your name. Go now with your servant, and I will show you in their box the statue of wax they have made, and if there is not you may put me to death." And so it was: "And the ruler ordered that they should search in the box of the Torah scrolls, and he found the wax image therein within it, and this was its manner: its hands on its hips and nails between its knees, and the palms of the hands cut off," but the writings in which the Jews cursed the ruler of the land were not found; see A. Berliner, *Ozar Tov* (Berlin, 1878), 49–52; Haberman (n. 1, p. 135), 13–14; R. Chazan, "The Persecution of 992, " *REJ* 129 (1970): 217–21. The Jewish custom of crucifying a wax image of Jesus every year is also recounted by Arnold of Lübeck; see H. Schreckenberg, *Die christlichen Adversus-Judaeos-Texte [11.–13. Jh.]* (Frankfurt, 1988), 399. The motif of showing contempt for the Cross was also used by Elijah Capsali to explain why the Ashkenazic Jews were expelled from their country. He recounts the story of a prince who tempted a Christian cobbler by telling him: "Take this image and put it inside the Jew's shoe and sew it up well." As a result, the Jews were accused of disgracing the Cross and were burned to death (*Seder Eliyahu Zuta,* ed. A. Shmuelevitzch, S. Simonsohn, and M. Benayahu [Jerusalem, 1977], 2:230–32). Johann of Winterthur tells of an accusation against an Austrian Jew who put the Host in his shoe. F. Lotter ("Hostienfrevelvorwurf und Blutwunderfälschung bei den Judenverfolgungen von 1298 ['Rintfleisch'] und 1336–1338 ['Armleder']," *Fälschungen im Mittelalter V* [MGH, Schriften, 33; Hannover, 1988] 579), alluded to by Rabbi Meir of Rothenburg in his liturgical poem, *Ahbirah Milin:*

> Their hand became increasingly harsh, and they made an edict concerning their bread
> and they said, 'Behold, they carry our God in their clothing
> in worn and tattered shoes on their feet.'

(Haberman [n. 1, p. 135], 181). And cf. J. Shatzmiller, *La communauté juive de Manosque au moyen âge* (Etudes Juives, 15; Mouton, 1978), 133–34. On the connection between Purim and the destruction of Christianity, cf. chap. 3, n. 107; Christoph Cluse, "Blut ist im Schuh. Ein Exempel zur Judenverfolgung des 'Rex Armleder,'" in *Liber Amicorum necnon et amicarum für Alfred Heid,* ed. F. Burgard, Christoph Cluse and A. Haverkamp (Trier, 1996), 371–92.

67. *b. Pesahim* 6a. But *b. Bekhorot* 58a speaks of only two weeks.

lot on the thirteenth day of the month of Nissan, and the date set aside for the destruction of the Jews was eleven months later, on the thirteenth of Adar. Immediately after the lot was cast, Esther fasted for three days, and on the third day (the fifteenth day of Nissan) invited the king to the first banquet. The next day Haman was invited to the second banquet, on which occasion she asked for his head, and the next day he was hanged. The typological motifs of the deliverance in Shushan also recall the redemption involved in the Passover of Egypt. On that fateful night, the night of the fifteenth of Nissan, "the king could not sleep" (Esther 6:1)—a clear echo of "and it came to pass that at midnight the Lord smote all the firstborn in the land of Egypt" (Exod 12:29) and "it was a night of watching kept to the Lord" (Exod 12:42). The story of the Purim deliverance overlaps in part the ancient topos of the Exodus. Thus, the connection between the hanging of Haman and the Crucifixion of Jesus is clear, a topic that will be discussed at greater length in chapter 5.

Roth was the first to suggest that the accusation of ritual murder against the Jews was connected with a Jewish custom. Even an utterly wild, imaginary fabrication may have an actual, authentic context. Thus, the ritual murder accusation is a distortion of a characteristic quality or behavior of the Jews. I would like to develop this line of thought, suggesting an additional explanation for the appearance of the ritual murder accusation specifically in the twelfth century. By providing an "explanation," I do not intend to offer a single and direct reason, but to point out the circumstances that provoked the invention of the ritual murder libel and to explain how such a falsehood succeeded in capturing the hearts and imaginations of certain circles within Christian society. I am not so much interested in uncovering the reason for the appearance of the first accusation of ritual murder as I am in explaining the "success" of this accusation, that is, its rapid spread from the mid-twelfth century on.

It is conventionally accepted that the first ritual murder libel of the Middle Ages took place in Norwich, England, in 1144.[68] Close to Easter time a Christian boy named William, who was employed in a Jewish home, disappeared, and his family accused the Jews of his murder. The proximity of

68. G. Langmuir (n. 65, p. 165), 820–46; Langmuir, "Historiographic Crucification," in *Les Juifs au regard de l'histoire—Mélanges en l'honneur de Bernard Blumenkranz,* ed. G. Dahan (Paris, 1985), 109–27; F. Lotter, "Innocens Virgo et Martyr: Thomas von Monmouth und die Verbreitung der Ritualmordlegende im Hochmittelalter," in *Die Legende vom Ritualmord— Zur Geschichte der Blutbeschuldigungen gegen Juden,* ed. R. Erb (Berlin, 1993), 25–72.

the event to Easter raised the suspicion that the Jews had murdered him for ritual purposes, as an imitation of the Crucifixion, and the public was willing to accept an accusation of this kind. In 1149 a Benedictine monk named Thomas of Monmouth, who believed that William was indeed a saint who had died as the victim of ritual murder, arrived in Norwich. To prove the child's sainthood, Thomas began writing a book, *The Life and Miracles of St. William of Norwich.*[69] Langmuir believes that Thomas began writing this book in 1150, but John McCulloh believes he did not start before 1155.[70] McCulloh likewise found proof that knowledge of the accusation in Norwich reached continental Europe even before Thomas began writing his book: the list of martyrs written in Bavaria includes an entry from the late 1140s about the crucifixion by Jews of the lad William in England on April 17.

The fact that information about the accusation made in Norwich reached Germany in about 1147 reinforces the argument that the accusation of ritual murder appeared in Bavaria almost at the same time as it appeared in Norwich.[71] In the spring of 1147, a Jew from Würzburg was accused of murdering a Christian. There are two extant sources for this incident, a Hebrew one and a Latin one. The Hebrew source is presented in the memoir of Ephraim ben Jacob of Bonn:

On the 22nd day of the month of Adar evil ones rose up against the community of Würzburg, for all the other communities had already

---

69. A. Jessop and M. R. James, eds., *The Life and Miracles of St. William of Norwich,* (Cambridge, 1896). Note that in Peuckert's list of ritual murder libels, the one at Norwich is listed as occurring in 1148 (E. Peuckert, "Ritualmord," in *Handwörterbuch des deutschen Aberglaubens,* ed. E. Hoffmann-Krayer, VII [Berlin, 1935–36], 728).

70. J. McCulloh, "Jewish Ritual Murder: William of Norwich, Thomas of Monmouth, and the Early Dissemination of the Myth," *Speculum* 72 (1997): 698–740.

71. S. Baron maintained that the first appearance of the ritual murder libel in Germany took place in Fulda in 1235; see *A Social and Religious History of the Jews,* vol. 4 (New York, 1957), 138. Langmuir also maintains that all cases of murder in which Jews were accused in Germany prior to the incident in Fulda in 1235 were cases of "clandestine murder" and not of "blood libel"; see *Toward a Definition of Antisemitism* (Berkeley, 1990), 268. And indeed, if we distinguish between "blood libel" in the literal sense (i.e., the cannibalistic use of human blood) and "ritual murder," the case in Fulda is the first to present the claim that the Jews needed Christian blood (for baking matzot, for healing, and so forth). Yet accusations of ritual murder against the Jews were widespread in Germany back in the twelfth century, as will be proven below. Langmuir criticizes Jewish historians for using the term "blood libel" to describe accusations of ritual murder in which there were no cannibalistic motifs (266–67), but the term "blood libel" in Hebrew has taken root to indicate any false accusation against Jews of shedding blood in a ritual context, even without the cannibalistic use of blood.

taken to the hills and fortresses, and they had planned to live in peace, and it was turned to sorrow. Alas, alas, alas. And they accused them with false words and deceit in order to assault them and fall upon them. And they said: we have found a non-Jew in the river, whom you have killed and thrown into the river, and he was made a saint by them and works miracles. And from this the mistaken ones arose, and all the rifraff who were happy to make much out of nothing arose and slew them . . . about twenty-one people.[72]

Rabbi Ephraim of Bonn's description is confirmed by the *Annals [Annales] of Würzburg*.[73] The two sources even give an identical number of victims killed, and the *Annals* also tell of the rapid spread of the rumor that the body of the slain Christian was working miracles. The Latin source adds that the local bishop took care to bury the Jews in his own garden, which was later bought by the Jews and turned into a cemetery. Three facts support the assumption that the murder in Würzburg was considered a ritual one: the episode took place about a week after Purim, that is, during a period marked by high religious emotion; the corpse of the slain person worked miracles; and many Jews were killed, suggesting a collective accusation.

These events occurred during the anti-Jewish pogroms of the Second Crusade, at a place that was on the Crusaders' route. The relation between the accusation of ritual murder and the Crusade underlies Rabbi Ephraim's story. Ultimately, the pogroms during the Second Crusade were limited in scope because the Crusaders were closely supervised, but at the time the people did not know in advance how things would turn out. They retained the image of the First Crusade and the behavior of the Jews at that time. In Christian memory, there reemerged the image of the Jews killing themselves and their loved ones. These acts were interpreted as proof of the "murderousness" of the Jews and their willingness to do anything to harm the Christian religion. This is the background for understanding the creation of the libel against the Jews of Würzburg.

Because of the condition of the extant sources, it is difficult to determine which libel occurred first, that which definitely took place in Würzburg in

72. Haberman (n. 1. p. 135), 219; *Sefer Zekhirah* (n. 8, p. 138), 22–23. Further details of the incident were presented in the *Memorbuch* of Nürnberg (Salfeld, *Das Martyrologium des Nürnberger Memorbuches*, 120).

73. *Annales Herbipolenses*, in *MGH SS*, XVI (Hannover, 1859), 3, A. 1147; J. Aronius, *Regesten zur Geschichte der Juden* (Berlin, 1902), 113–14, no. 245.

1147 or that related about Norwich allegedly in 1144. McCulloh's study shows that knowledge about what took place in the British Isles reached the continent quite quickly, and it is plausible that channels of communication went both ways. Although it is difficult today to reconstruct how things developed, his argument that the family of the murdered boy in Norwich in fact claimed that the Jews had killed him for ritual purposes in 1144 seems reasonable. This accusation (or something similar) easily caught on in Germany in 1147 against the backdrop of the Second Crusade.

The Dissemination of the Libels

Our interest here is not in meticulous examination of the circumstances behind the appearance of one or another accusation, but in their dissemination. What gave those accusations against the Jews such profound weight in Christian public opinion? The view that the Jew is capable of murder because of his hatred of Christianity was certainly not an innovation of the twelfth century. Its sources are found in the Crucifixion story in the Gospels and in Christian legends that were widespread from the sixth century on, to be discussed below. We nevertheless need to explain why these dormant images suddenly burst forth with such force and over such a wide geographic scope specifically during the 1140s. In my opinion, the martyrological image of the Jews against the background of the pogroms of 1096 contributed decisively to this course of events.

Hence, Thomas of Monmouth's work should be seen as an attempt to harness to local needs rumors of the Jews' being a murderous and dangerous element, which had been widespread in England and on the European continent. What motivated Thomas to disseminate these rumors was England's distance from their focal points, which is why the first medieval tractate on the ritual murder libel was written in England. This may also explain a very surprising fact. Thomas's book is the most detailed source for the ritual murder accusation in the Middle Ages. The "first" ritual murder libel is also, for some reason, the most extensively documented—a fact that demands some explanation, since historic events generally become more thoroughly documented the more they are prolonged and repeated. Here, apparently, the opposite occurred. The explanation lies in the need felt by Thomas and the monks who supported him to persuade the public, which tended not to easily accept the claim that William's death was in fact that of a martyr. Thomas himself refers to this skepticism in his text. Yet it is told of the ritual murder libel at Blois that, whenever the corpse of a Christian was found, Christians tended to accuse Jews of having killed the Christian.[74] In France and Germany there was no need for propaganda in order to win support for the accusation. Rabbi Eleazar ben Judah, author of *Sefer ha-Rokeah,* writes that in 1187 the Jews of Mainz were accused of killing a Gentile. The Jews swore that they were not guilty, and on that occasion they were even forced to swear that "they do not kill any Gentile on the eve of Passover."[75] So we know that in 1187 there was a widespread belief in Germany that Jews kill Christians on the eve of Passover.

The ritual murder libel of 1171 in Blois also took place on Passover. A Christian saw a Jew going down to the Loire in the night with a skin under his arm and then throwing it in the river. The Christian believed that the Jew was drowning a Christian child. As Robert de Torigny explicitly says: "Frequently, as has been said, they do so during the days of Easter, if they have an opportunity."[76] Langmuir thought that the accusation in Blois did not relate to ritual murder, but only to a "regular," and brutal, murder.[77] He argues that Robert fabricated the motif of ritual murder (Crucifixion, at Easter) in retrospect, in wake of the story in Norwich, and attributes to Robert the major responsibility for spreading the accusation of Norwich. However, the Jews of Blois were executed on the twentieth day of Sivan,

---

74. Haberman (n. 1, p. 135), 145. This also happened to the Jews of Speyer in 1195: "There was a Gentile woman who was found murdered about three parasangs from the city of Speyer. And the Gentiles rejoiced for no reason [a pun on the Latin name of the city: Nemetum] to accuse the Jews of killing her" (*Sefer Zekhirah* [n. 8, p. 138], 42–43). In 1197 a Jew of the city of Neuss did indeed murder a Christian girl: "God's wrath touched His people by means of a crazy Jew, who attacked a Gentile maiden in the city of Neuss and slaughtered her in the sight of all" (*Sefer Zekhirah* [n. 8, p. 138], 40; the source gives the year as 1186). As a result, six Jews of the city were executed. And compare also the incident in Boppard (Haberman [n. 1, p. 135], 126). Langmuir noted the difference between the ritual murder libels in Germany, on the one hand, and those in England and France, on the other (L. Langmuir, "L'absence d'accusation de meurtre rituel à l'ouest du Rhône," *Cahiers de Fanjeaux, XII: Juifs et Judaisme de Languedoc* [Toulouse, 1977], 235–49). In Germany these libels were of a popular nature, and the Jews were represented as dangerous to the entire world, not only to Christians (the motif of cannibalism). Yet in France and England the ritual murder libels were instigated by churchmen and had more prominent Christian religious motifs (the motif of the Crucifixion). The explanation proposed here for the origin of the ritual murder libels accords well with this finding. Similarly, they are compatible with the differences described in chapter 3, about the attitude of the Jews of Ashkenaz toward Christians at the End of Days and that of Jews in other countries of Europe.

75. Haberman (n. 1, p. 135), 161.

76. R. Howlett, ed., *Chronicles of the Reigns of Stephen, Henry II, Richard I,* vol. 4 (Rolls Series, 82; London, 1889), 250–51.

77. Langmuir (n. 71, p. 168), 284.

following a trial; hence, it is plausible that the accusation was brought against them about two months earlier, around Easter. This may be confirmed by the description of the date of the accusation found in a letter written by the congregation of Orléans, written shortly after the Jews were burned to death. According to the letter, the accusation took place "on Thursday, the cursed day, in the evening, after dark."[78] Ephraim of Bonn repeats the date: "that evil day, the fifth day after the Sabbath, towards evening."[79] Neither mentions the date, because it is hinted at in the expression "Thursday, the cursed day"—the exact opposite of *jeudi saint,* that is Maundy Thursday, the Thursday before Easter. In 1171 the first two days of Passover fell on Tuesday and Wednesday (March 23–24), and on those days it is certain that no Jew went down to the river with a skin under his arm, as is told there. The incident thus took place on Thursday, when *jeudi saint* fell that year, prior to Good Friday, the day of the Crucifixion. The preciseness of the dating proves that the accusation in Blois involved ritual murder from the outset and that Robert did not fabricate anything. A clear echo of the accusation in Blois and the dating suggested here follows from the writings of the chronicler Rigord, who states that Philipe-Auguste expelled the Jews from France in 1182 because of rumors that he heard in his childhood that the Jews of Paris kill a Christian every year on Maundy Thursday.[80] Thus, the first expulsion of the Jews in Europe was due to the proliferation of rumors regarding Jewish ritual murder.

In the two cases mentioned—Mainz and Blois—there is no talk of cannibalistic use of the blood, nor is there any mention of crucifixion. According to Langmuir, the absence of these two conditions demonstrates that the accusation was one of simple murder, not of ritual murder. Yet the direct connection to Passover and Easter indicates, beyond any doubt, that this was an accusation of ritual murder connected to a season of messianic significance, even if its motifs were still taking shape and developing.

Thus, the accusation that Jews engaged in the ritual murder of Christians was seen as self-evident during the twelfth century—first in Germany, then in England and in France. Yet in the Mediterranean countries in general, and in Spain in particular, the ritual murder libel did not take hold before 1350. This fact is consistent with the Jews' restrained attitude in those places

78. Haberman (n. 1, p. 135), 143.
79. Haberman (n. 1, p. 135), 124.
80. Lotter (n. 68, p. 167), 51.

toward the idea of martyrdom and with their religious—not political—understanding of the eschatological struggle with "Edom."

Ritual Murder Libel and Vengeful Redemption

The presumed connection between the ritual murder libel, on the one hand, and martyrdom and vengeful redemption, on the other, becomes clear on examination of the most important argument evoked by Thomas of Monmouth to prove that the child William of Norwich was indeed killed as a martyr by the Jews. He relied on the confession of the converted Jew Theobold of Canterbury:

> In the ancient writings of his fathers it was written that the Jews, without the shedding of human blood, could neither obtain their freedom, nor could they ever return to their fatherland.[81] Hence it was laid down by them in ancient times that every year they must sacrifice a Christian in some part of the world to the Most High God in scorn and contempt of Christ, that so they might avenge their sufferings on Him; inasmuch as it was because of Christ's death that they had been shut out from their own country, and were in exile as slaves in a foreign land. Wherefore the chief men and Rabbis of the Jews who dwell in Spain assemble together at Narbonne, where the Royal seed [reside], and where they are held in the highest estimation, and they cast lots for all the countries which the Jews inhabit; and whatever country the lot falls upon, its metropolis has to carry out the same method with the other towns and cities, and the place whose lot is drawn has to fulfill the duty imposed by authority. Now in that year in which we know that William, God's glorious martyr, was slain, it happened that the lot fell upon the Norwich Jews, and all the synagogues in England signified, by letter or by message, their consent that the wickedness should be carried out at Norwich.[82]

This passage contains two parts. The first discusses the motivation behind the Jews' crime; the second attempts to explain the choice of Norwich, of all places, for a location. The motive for the crime is described as being of universal dimensions. The convert quoted here does not speak of ordinary vengeance, but of a religious worldview that sees vengeance against the Gentiles as a necessary condition of the messianic process. Through this

81. This may be a confused version of ideas found in *Exod. Rab.* 15.12.
82. Jessop and James (n. 69, p. 168), Book 2: 93–94.

vengeance, the Jews seek to regain their freedom and return to their land. From Theobold's words, one can see the clear connection between the notion of vengeance in Judaism and in Christianity. Whereas Christianity sees God's vengeance as already having been realized in the Destruction of Jerusalem and the Exile of the Jews, Judaism sees divine vengeance as still awaiting its messianic realization. The ritual murder libel is based on a distorted Christian interpretation of the Jewish idea of vengeful redemption, as follows: the Jews crucified Jesus and therefore were cursed and expelled from their land. This was "the vengeance of the Redeemer." But because, in their blindness, they did not lose hope of returning to their land, this hope must obviously depend on an opposite vengeance, namely, the killing of Christians.

This convert did what clever liars always do: he told a half-truth. The Jews indeed believed that the Redemption depended on the annihilation of the Gentiles. During the first half of the twelfth century messianic notions such as these assumed a new meaning, in the eyes of both Christians and Jews, when both camps ascribed enormous importance to the myth of sacrifice and blood.

This interpretation, which attributes universal messianic meaning to the murder of one boy in England, provoked the need to explain why the Jews chose Norwich, specifically, as a suitable arena for realizing their vision of vengeance. Thus, the fiction of the assembly in Narbonne took shape, which removed from the event in Norwich its local meaning and imparted it with a pan-Jewish meaning. This fiction would also nourish the accusation of well poisoning in the fourteenth century. Using the motif of casting lots connects the story with Purim, as a proof of Jewish aggressiveness.[83] The second part of the passage reinforces the impression that, for the "benefit" of Norwich (which thereby acquired its own "saint"), Thomas of Monmouth mobilized rumors that had already been circulating on the continent about the murderousness of the Jews and their blood ritual.

Baptism in River and Water

The connection between the accusation of ritual murder and the idea of vengeance deliverance is expressed quite clearly even in later periods. As mentioned in chapter 3, Christian inquisitors who interrogated the Jews on the occasion of the ritual murder libel in Trent saw fit to extract from the

83. Gerd Mentgen commented on this in both his papers (n. 66, p. 165).

tortured Jews a confession that they were accustomed to reciting "Pour Out Thy Wrath" on Passover. The connection between the ritual murder libel, on the one hand, and Jewish messianism, on the other, is also clear from the various pictures of the "Jewish sow," which appeared on the *Brücken-turm* in Frankfurt. In all of them, the Jewish Messiah appears riding on a sow, and next to him the figure of the crucified child, Simon of Trent (see Figure 3).[84]

The connection between the acts of martyrdom in 1096 and the ritual murder libel has another symbolic expression. In the chronicles of 1096, the main arena for acts of martyrdom is the river. Both Christians and Jews considered the river a potential baptismal font;[85] hence, the Jews were allegedly eager to turn the water into blood and the ceremony of baptism into a ceremony of slaughter. Thus, it is related that the pious Yitzhak ha-Levi of Neuss was unwillingly baptized, under torture. When he recovered, he traveled to Cologne, went into the Rhine, "and drowned himself in the river. And concerning him and those like him, it is said 'I will bring them back from Bashan, I will return my people from the depths of the sea'"— a biblical verse with a long history in the annals of martyrdom (Ps 68:23). Rabbi Yitzhak's body floated "in the water until it came to the town of Neuss, and the water cast it up upon the bank of the river."[86] The water carried him, returning him in purity to the exact place where he had been baptized—a distance of nearly forty miles! Moreover, the river deposited

---

84. I. Shachar, *The Judensau: A Medieval Anti-Jewish Motif and Its History* (London, 1974), 53.

85. Berthold von Regensburg tells of the custom of Christian youths to throw Jews—both children and adults—into the river for amusement, to baptize them against their will (Berthold von Regensburg, *Vollständige Ausgabe seiner Predigten*, ed. F. Pfeiffer and J. Strobl (Vienna, 1862–1880; repr. Berlin, 1965), 1:298; 2:85, 228; Aronius, [n. 73, p. 169], sec. 757, 319–20). On the aversion to water that was used for Christian ritual, even when needed for Jewish rituals of immersion, see *Sefer Hasidim*, (n. 2, p. 136), sec. 1369: "In a certain city there was not enough water to immerse oneself therein . . . and Jews wanted to live therein. The Rabbis said to them: Since there is no water there but the water in which they test their thieves, and the priests call them there in the name of their pagan god, it is inconceivable that women should immerse themselves there to purify themselves, nor even that one might immerse knives and metal and glass vessels to be purified in that water." For a similar motif from the fifteenth century, see Israel Yuval, "Juden, Hussiten und Deutsche; Nach einer hebraischen Chronik *Gilgul B'nei Hushim*," in *Juden in der christlichen Umwelt während des späten Mittelalters*, ed. A. Haverkamp and F. J. Ziwes (Berlin, 1992), 59–93; "Jews, Hussites and Germans: according to the Chronicle *Gilgul b'nai Hushim*" [in Hebrew], *Zion* 54 (1949): 316.

86. Haberman (n. 1, p. 135), 44–45; Stern and Neubauer (n. 8, p. 138), 18–19; Chazan (n. 8, p. 138), 275–77.

his corpse precisely on the burial place of the Hasid Mar Shmuel, who refused to be baptized and was buried "on the banks of the Rhine River." This fantastic story is intended to express the idea that the deeds of the two—the one who did not sin, and the one who was forced to sin and atoned for it—are equivalent. Both the sin and its punishment take place in the river, and the one who was not baptized and died is buried by the river. There is also the literary presence of the symbolic water motif. In this passage, which occupies less than two pages in the Haberman edition, the words *water, river, sea,* and *basin* recur twenty-two times!

The reason for this is alluded to in the text. The chronicle of Rabbi Shlomo ben Shimshon states at the beginning of the passage: "As it was their festival day and they had all gathered there from the villages,"[87] but it does not say which holiday it was. Rabbi Eleazar ben Nathan is a bit more explicit: "And on that day the enemies came, and the others as well, as it was the day of the festival of Yihum (Hebrew: "in heat" or "oestrus"), and they gathered for that reason in the village of Neuss."[88] This was the birthday of John the Baptist (Johannistag), which falls on June 24, summer solstice in the Middle Ages.[89] On that night, it was customary to bless all the sources of water: rivers, basins, and wells. According to folk belief, bathing in that water was thought to have healing power and to bring good luck.[90] For that reason, martyrdom by water on that particular day assumed enormous importance. The Jewish narrators, and perhaps the martyrs themselves, were well aware of the significance of that day to the Christians, hence the images of Jews who suffered martyrdom in the same place where they had been forced to convert to Christianity. This may also be the explanation for the amazing act of the Hasid Rabbi Shmuel, father of Yehiel, who "slaughtered his son with the sword in the water" after the son had already jumped into the Rhine but was not yet dead (see below).

The birthday of John the Baptist was a kind of "Christmas" in midsummer. Just as the winter holiday of Jesus's birth is associated with the

87. Haberman (n. 1, p. 135), 44; Stern and Neubauer (n. 8, p. 138), 18; Chazan (n. 8, p. 138), 275.

88. Haberman (n. 1, p. 135), 77; Stern and Neubauer (n. 8, p. 138), 41.

89. On this holiday and its symbols, see A. Franz, *Die kirchlichen Benediktionen im Mittelalter* (Graz, 1960), 1:294–334; *Handwörterbuch des Deutschen Aberglaubens* (Berlin, 1931–32), 4:704–27. On the fear of water on that day and its dangers, see 726.

90. L. A. Veit, *Volksfrommes Brauchtum und Kirche im deutschen Mittelalter* (Freiburg im Breisgau, 1936), 45–46. I am grateful to my friend Alfred Haberkampf, who called my attention to this work.

winter solstice, when the light of the sun begins to increase, so does the festival of John the Baptist mark the summer solstice, the longest day, when the sunlight begins to wane. Hence the custom, already practiced in ancient times, of lighting bonfires on hilltops on that day (Johannisfeuer),[91] a practice of which the Jewish chroniclers were thoroughly aware. Rabbi Shlomo ben Shimshon concluded his account of the two martyrs who were buried on the riverbank in Neuss with these words: "And they sanctified the Name of Heaven in the sight of the sun,"[92] an expression repeated in the words of Ra'avan: "And Rabbi Shmuel ben Asher sanctified the Name in the sight of the sun."[93]

This is proof of the existence of Jewish hermeneutics relating to the contents and symbols of Christianity. Baptism in the "raging waters" becomes an act of martyrdom. Thus, the powerful scene of the father's slaughtering his son and pouring his blood into the water can be seen as the opposite of the scene of the Crucifixion of Jesus (the son) by his Father (God), in which Jesus is stabbed and "at once there came out blood and water."[94]

The magical power of the river is also expressed in the story of the martyrs of Wevelinghofen, who "gave their souls to sanctify the Name, in the pools of water surrounding the city." A few of the Jewish Pietists climbed onto the tower

and hurled themselves *into the River Rhine* that goes around the city, and drowned themselves *in the river,* and they all died. . . . Only these two young men were not able to die *within the water.* . . . When they decided to throw themselves *into the water,* they kissed one another. . . . And they said . . . It is better that we die here . . . so that the impure, uncircumcised ones will not take us and contaminate us unwillingly in their *wicked waters* . . .

And when the pious Shmuel saw that his son Yehiel had thrown himself into the *river* and had not yet died . . . He cried out: Yehiel my son, my

91. J. G. Frazer, *The Golden Bough* (London, 1941), 622–32.

92. Haberman (n. 1, p. 135), 45; Stern and Neubauer (n. 8, p. 138), 18; Chazan (n. 8, p. 138), 275.

93. Haberman (n. 1, p. 135), 77; Stern and Neubauer (n. 8, p. 138), 41.

94. John 19:34. It should be noted that one of the blessings of the Christian holiday was the turning of water into wine; hence, they would read the passage in the New Testament describing Jesus turning water into wine at the wedding in Cana (John 2:1–11; Franz [n. 89, p. 176], 316).

son, stretch your neck before your father and I shall offer you, the soul of my son, as a sacrifice before the Lord. And I will recite the blessing over the slaughter, and you shall say "Amen." . . . So he slaughtered his son with his sword, *into the water.* And when R. Shmuel [his] son-in-law, son of R. Gedaliah, heard that his friend Yehiel the righteous had agreed to his father slaughtering him *in the water,* he also decided to do so . . . and they died together *in the river . . .* Thus did these pious men sanctify the holy, jealous and vengeful Name *within the water.*[95]

God is thus holy, jealous, and vengeful. Death is intended not only to sanctify his name but also to arouse his jealousy and vengeance. The symbolic importance of water as a baptismal font elicits the thought that there is special significance to the fact that in many ritual murder libels the river served as the locus for acts of murder attributed to the Jews. In Würzburg the Jews were accused of murdering a Christian in the River Main.[96] The 1168 accusation in Gloucester was based on the accusation that the Jews tortured a Christian child to death and threw him into the Severn. The body of the child, who had disappeared four weeks earlier, was pulled out by fishermen.[97] In 1171 the Jews of Blois were accused of killing a Christian child and throwing his body into the Loire.[98] Also noteworthy are the

95. Haberman (n. 1, p. 135), 45; Stern and Neubauer (n. 8, p. 138), 18; Chazan (n. 8, p. 138), 275; emphasis added.

96. This link may be alluded to in the description by Rabbi Ephraim of the event in Würzburg (Haberman, *Sefer Zekhirah* [n. 8, p. 138], 22–23). In the section preceding this description, Rabbi Ephraim tells that: "A certain Jewess was caught in Aschaffenburg, Mrs. Guthella, of blessed memory. And she did not wish to be polluted in the bitter accursed waters, and she sanctified the Holy Name and drowned in the river. May God remember her for good, like Rachel and Leah."

97. *Historia et Cartularium Monasterii Sancti Petri Gloucestriae,* ed. W. H. Hart (Roll Series; London, 1863), 1:20. For a description of the incident, see Z. E. Roke'ah, "The Kingdom, the Church, and the Jews in Medieval England," in *Antisemitism through the Ages,* ed. S. Almog; trans. N. H. Reisner (Oxford et al., 1988), 106–7; Hebrew original: *Sinat Yisrael le-toldoteha* (Jerusalem, 1980), 130–31.

98. As told by Rabbi Ephraim of Bonn (Haberman [n. 1, p. 135], 124). Robert de Torigny also tells in his chronicle that the Jews threw a boy into the Loire; see *Chronica Roberti de Torigneio,* in *Rerum Britannicarum Medii Aevi Scriptores. Chronicles of the Reigns of Stephen, Henry II, and Richard I,* vol. 4, ed. R. Howlett (Rolls Series, 82; London 1889), 250–51. On the incident, see R. Chazan, "The Blois Incident of 1171: A Study in Jewish Intercommunal Organization," *PAAJR* 36 (1968): 13–31; and cf. S. Spiegel, "In Monte Dominus Videbitur: The Martyrs of Blois and Early Accusation of Ritual Murder" [in Hebrew], in *M. Kaplan Jubilee Volume,* ed. M. Davis (New York, 1953), 267–87.

details of the murder accusation in 1199 brought against Jews who sailed on the upper Rhine, south of Cologne, while a ship of Christians sailed behind them. On the riverbank, near Boppard, the porters who were pulling the Christian ship discovered the body of a Christian woman and immediately accused the Jews sailing in front of them of the act, because "some of the Jews from the first ship were walking on the riverbank." The Jewish passengers, including those who had not gotten off the ship and gone to the riverbank, were jailed. They were required to convert, and when they refused they were condemned to death "and were thrown live into the Rhine."[99] We have here a standard frame story: the Jews turn into murderers specifically at the riverbank, hence their punishment also had to take place in the river.

Thus, the Jews could tell about killing and martyrdom that took place specifically on the river. In Christian public opinion, these same facts were given the opposite interpretation: the murderousness of the Jews is connected with rivers, because they desire blood instead of water (i.e., baptism), death rather than salvation. The Jews, it was believed, wanted to turn the water into blood—a clear allusion to the plague of blood in Egypt—for "that which was in the beginning shall be at the end." Moreover, in the accusation that Jews required Christian blood in order to bake matzot—an accusation that became explicit only in later ritual murder libels—we find an implicit assumption that, instead of water, the Jews use blood on Passover.

This motif also follows from a story found in the annals written in the Egmond monastery in the Netherlands between 1173 and 1215.[100] The story relates to events that occurred in 1137 in the city of Regensburg, all of whose Jews converted to Christianity during the Crusade. A Jewish boy, Jacob, who had secretly loved Christianity ever since his childhood, wished to convert. He deposited with the archdeacon a sum of money he had saved and declared his desire to be baptized. But the priest was greedy, and when the boy's father came looking for his son, the priest offered to return his son in exchange for money. The father agreed and decided to punish his son. He drowned him in the Danube, pouring lead on his body to prevent it from

99. Haberman (n. 1, p. 135), 126. Regarding the pogroms against the Jews of Speyer in 1195, it is told that Christians threw holy books and Torah scrolls into the water.

100. M. Minty, "Responses to Medieval Ashkenazi Martyrdom (Kiddush ha-Shem in Late Medieval German Christian Sources)," *Jahrbuch für Antisemitismusforschung* 4 (1995), 13–38 (Hebrew: *Zion* 59 [1994]: 234–37).

floating. Near the place of the crime lived a blind widow. That night, she felt an itch in her eye and went to soothe the pain with water from the river. "She rinsed her eyes with water, and in an instant her sight returned to her, with God's grace, and she saw a brilliant light and a kind of human body sunken in the water in the middle of the river." The woman immediately told this miracle to the head of the monastery and the bishop, and everyone came to the riverbank. "While everyone was awaiting the results of this event and were engaged in prayer from the depths of their hearts, the body of the saint floated up to the bank of the river loaded down with lead and glowing with a shining light." The body was taken into the church, and for the rest of the night all those gathered sang paeans to God. The next day, they learned that the murdered boy was a Jew, and the father confessed to his murder, saying that he had done it because of the deacon, who was burned at the stake, while the father, along with many other Jews, converted to Christianity.

Mary Minty cited this story to demonstrate that Christians exhibited sensitivity to acts of bloodshed performed by Jews for martyrdom. And indeed, from a Christian viewpoint, this story may be considered a case of Jewish martyrdom. The father murders his son to prevent him from converting to Christianity, but the child ultimately becomes a saint in the eyes of both Jews and Christians. The father's act is certainly loathsome and repulsive (his plan to murder his son is called "satanic"), but in the end he converts to Christianity, and his act is forgiven. The main criticism is of the priest, who rejected the son while contracting a shameful deal with his father.

Minty notes that the child's being killed by his father affects a transformation in his status—he is transformed from a Jewish boy into a Christian saint, even though he was not baptized before his death.[101] From a factual viewpoint, this is of course correct, but in terms of the story's symbolism the child was baptized—in the river. The water effects a transformation in the boy's status, just as the water brings about a transformation in the blind old widow whose sight was restored. There is a distinct similarity between the description of the body floating on the water toward the bank of the river and that of the martyr from Neuss who drowned himself in Cologne and whose body was carried by the river to the riverbank near his home. As for the paean to God concluding the miraculous event, we will examine that below.

---

101. Minty, "Responses to Medieval Ashkenazi Martyrdom, 236.

The great importance attributed by both sides to the motif of water is also alluded to in *Ma'aseh ha-gezerot ha-yeshanot* (History of the Olden Pogroms). The author of this chronicle states that the pogroms in Worms began as the result of a fabricated accusation.[102] On May 5 (10 Iyyar), the Christians disinterred the body of a man who had died thirty days earlier— that is, around the time of Passover and Easter. The Jews were accused of boiling the dead man's body in water and then pouring the water into the wells to poison the Christians. As proof of the truth behind the accusation, the Christians held a procession in the city in which they presented the corpse for viewing. Once again, the central motif in this libel is the Jews' attempt to "defile" the water. Boiling the Christian can be seen as a kind of baptismal ceremony. Unlike the Christian baptism, which gives life and allows divine grace to reside in a human being, Jewish baptism kills, and its waters are treacherous. Moritz Stern and Harry Breslau suggest that this story is an interpolation from the second half of the fourteenth century, since, in the pogroms that followed the Black Plague, the Jews were accused of poisoning wells.[103] This is unlikely, since the accusation made during the Black Plague was intended to explain the spread of the plague and its rapid dispersion, a motif completely absent in the present description. Boiling a person's body in water, thereby defiling the water, accords well with the tone of the stories about 1096 (the changing of water to blood). It is also said that the Jews boiled the body of William of Norwich in water, from which it follows that such accusations were widespread at the time that story was told.[104]

A mid-fourteenth-century altarpiece displayed at the Catalonian Museum in Barcelona depicts a Jew desecrating the Host by throwing it into a kettle of boiling water.[105] A similar accusation was made in Paris in 1290.[106] Accusations of putting to death by water involve a kind of demonization

102. Haberman (n. 1, p. 135), 95. Haberman corrected the text there on his own, and instead of "Sunday" wrote "Monday," so as to make the date conform to 10 Iyyar, which on that year fell on a Monday. Cf. Stern and Neubauer (n. 8, p. 138); Chazan (n. 8, p. 138), 228.

103. Stern and Neubauer (n. 8, p. 138): introduction, x (Stern) and xiv–xv (Breslau).

104. Jessop and James (n. 69, p. 168), 22.

105. E. M. Zafran, "The Iconography of Antisemitism" (PhD diss., New York University, 1973) pl. 208. For other cases of desecration of the Host by throwing it into a kettle, see Zafran, secs. 212, 231, 240.

106. See Lotter, "Hostienfrevelvorwurf und Blutwunderfälschung," 537; M. Rubin, "Desecration of the Host: The Birth of an Accusation," in *Christianity and Judaism*, ed. D. Wood (Studies in Church History, 29; Oxford, 1992), 169–85. For another case, in 1306, in which a

of the Jew: they describe the Jew as one who is also supposedly engaged in baptism, but whose act of baptism kills. This explanation involves another facet. The maidservant in Norwich testified that she peeked through a crack in the kitchen door and saw the Jews pouring boiling water on William. What boiling water could a Christian maidservant have observed in a Jewish kitchen on the eve of Passover? The water used for "kashering" (i.e., scalding) the vessels, of course. From here on, the whole event is a product of her imagination, but this distorted imagination has some factual basis: in the eyes of the Christians, the "strange" custom of scalding vessels is bound up with messianic vengeance. In preparation for the holiday of deliverance, the Jews rid their houses of leavened foodstuffs by burning (with fire) or by scalding (with boiling water). As we will see in the next chapter, the eradication of leaven was given the symbolic significance of the messianic destruction of the Gentiles. The convert Peter understood that in a similar way: in his 1399 debate with Yom Tov Lipmann Mühlhausen, he condemned the burning of leaven, to which he attributed an anti-Christian meaning.[107] It is not surprising, then, that a Christian maidservant in a Jewish house could connect the custom of scalding vessels to the murder of William. This Christian interpretation of the scalding of the vessels may also explain the descriptions of the desecration of the Host in a boiling kettle. The visual similarity between the two ceremonies will be discussed in the next chapter. Indeed, the three cases mentioned (in Worms, Norwich, and Paris) all took place on Passover/Easter. Thus, the act of boiling in water possesses a highly charged symbolic meaning.

It may be that the accusation reported from Worms regarding 1096 represents an earlier archetype that portends the later accusations in Norwich and Würzburg. Even if it was not a real event—the incident is not reported in any other chronicle—it is still of great value in revealing the retroactive Christian interpretation of Jewish behavior. The story presents the Jews' murderousness and their desire for vengeance—that is, it attributes to the Jews both a motivation and an opportunity for the crime. These two motifs were not created out of thin air but derive from a distorted explanation of Jewish behavior during the pogroms of 1096 and of the ritual of ven-

---

Jew from Forcalquier was accused of throwing the body of a Christian child into a well in Manosque so as to poison it, see Shatzmiller, *La communauté juive*, 133–34.

107. *Sefer ha-Nizzahon le-R. Yom Tov Lippmann Mühlhausen*, introduction by F. E. Talmage (Jerusalem, 1984; repr. 1644, Altdorf-Nürnberg), 193–94.

geance as part of their notion of deliverance. Those who accused the Jews did not make up everything. The lies had a certain basis in fact, which is why they spread so quickly and took hold so firmly.

The possibility of some sort of connection, in Christian consciousness, between the image of the Jews as murderers—and especially their image as murderers of their own children—and the accusations that they killed Christian children, was already raised by contemporaries and is not merely a hypothetical reconstruction by a modern historian. It is clearly implied by the Jewish author of a letter in Hebrew, written in Orléans a few days after a large group of Jews from Blois were executed, on 20 Sivan 1171, following a trial at which the Jews of that city were found guilty of ritual murder.

The incident in Blois was not the first case of accusation of ritual murder in Europe, but it was the first time that an entire community was placed on trial and found guilty in the murder of a Christian child—on Easter eve, the night when, according to Christian tradition, the Last Supper took place. The letter from Orléans serves a double purpose: to prove the innocence of the Jews, and to explain the appearance of this strange accusation. The author offers two separate explanations: personal and mental. On the personal level, he attributes the accusation to the desire for vengeance on the part of a local Christian who hated a certain wealthy Jewess who was close to the ruler. What interests us here is the second explanation, related to mentality, presented by the author in a passage that seems like an interpolation to his letter. Following a description of the execution of the Jews of Blois, he suddenly turns away from the logical progression of events to describe another incident that had occurred some time earlier in Loches sur Indre, about forty miles south of Blois:

> Before the trouble [in Blois], the community of Loches made it known that they had safely fled, and that the informer alone was caught. I, Baruch b. Meir, will tell you about the incident: a certain young man from Loches wanted to marry a certain maiden, and he asked her father and her relatives [for her hand], and they answered him: "We would sooner drown her in water [before] she would marry you!" The young man secretly went and betrothed [i.e., married] the maiden in the presence of witnesses, and came to her father and said: "We have already married without your permission." And the father answered: the treacherous thing you have done will not help. Until the young man went to the ruler and told on them, and they were caught. And they were released,

thank God, but he has not yet been released. And we do not know whether this trouble has, Heaven forbid, spoiled their reputation or not.[108]

What did the disappointed young man tell the authorities at the end of that case of tragic love? Why was the community of Loches imprisoned? And was the parents' refusal to marry their daughter to her lover a cause for imprisonment? It would seem that the denunciation and the arrest came about as a result of the things that the father and the other relatives said to the young man: "We would sooner drown her in water [before] she would marry you!" The boy saw this as a murder threat, and therefore the local Jews were arrested, since most or all of them were certainly members of the same family.

The author of the letter from Orléans included this incident to raise the conjecture that this may have been what "spoiled" the reputation of the Jews of Blois in Christian eyes. We must therefore assume that the public repercussion of the incident in Loches, at least in the eyes of our Jewish author from Orléans, was sufficiently extensive to explain what happened subsequently in Blois. In other words, the accusation that a Jewish father threatened to kill his daughter was considered an adequate explanation for a collective accusation against the Jews of the ritual murder of a Christian child.

There seems to be another connecting thread between these two images: namely, the act of being put to death in water. The threat of the father in Loches ("We would sooner drown her in water!") is parallel to the accusation against the Jews of Blois ("he stirred up a dead child in the water"). And perhaps an additional aspect, quite common in the Middle Ages, was involved in the incident of the secret marriage in Blois: the disappointed young man and his beloved threatened to convert to Christianity. If this was the case, then the father's threat may have been interpreted as an attempt to prevent his daughter's conversion, even at the cost of her life—a motif we encountered in the event at Regensburg. The father's words, alluding to his willingness to drown his daughter, could have been interpreted by Christians as a Jewish answer to the threat of Christian baptism. In this connection, it is worth noting, the guilt of the Jews of Blois was "proven" by means of the procedure of trial by water: "And they brought the impure one [i.e., the Christian witness] in water, and they found the wicked innocent and the just guilty."

108. Haberman (n. 1, p. 135), 144.

In this incident a great deal remains obscure. It is difficult to know whether what we have here is a random chain of motifs or whether this was a common line of interpretation in Christian public opinion: namely, that the murderousness of the Jews—toward their own children, and all the more so toward Christian children—found expression specifically in water. One way or another, we again confront the centrality of the motif of immersion in water, which is certainly due to the centrality of baptism in Christianity as an act of conversion. The fact that the Jews were suspected of a murder attempt because of an unfortunate expression reminiscent of drowning in water indicates the Christian memory of Jewish martyrdom that was carried out in the presence of water. Or was it the proximity to the season of Passover/Easter that evoked the association "every son that is born you shall cast into the Nile" (Exod 1:22)? Or do these Jewish images reflect a certain level of internalizing the legal procedure of the ordeal in water? These questions remain unanswered, and only the historian's imagination can fill in what is absent in the sources.

Generally speaking, we find three central motifs in the twelfth-century accusations of ritual murder: 1) the presentation of the murder as an act fulfilling a specific ritual need; 2) the exclusive connection of the ritual with Passover and Easter; 3) the murder of a child. These motifs are also deeply embedded in the Jewish martyrology of the First Crusade. The vision of vengeance against the Gentiles, with its messianic context, was interpreted as proof that the Jews had a ritual interest in killing Christians. Seeing the Passover holiday as an omen of the future and as an allusion to future deliverance connects the messianic vision of vengeance with the ritual act of murder/crucifixion on Passover or Easter. The behavior of the Jewish martyrs in 1096, and especially the agitation surrounding those acts, was seen as emphasizing the Jews' alleged great fondness for sacrificing children specifically. In the medieval world of reverse exegeses, this served to strengthen the impression that the Jews were particularly cruel to children. In fact, the Jews were cruel to their own children alone, but in Christian public opinion this behavior was taken as proof that Jewish murderousness had one main target: all children. The accusations of ritual murder were therefore a "symmetrical opposite" of Jewish martyrdom.

This explanation of Jewish behavior on the part of the Christian public, which originated with the generation that came after 1096, continued even into the late Middle Ages, even though there was no event comparable to 1096 in its intense awareness of martyrdom. Ritual murder libels and accusations of desecration of the Host became the daily bread of the Jews throughout the thirteenth to fifteenth centuries, independent of any acts of martyrdom on their part. There are two possible reasons for this. First, once they had emerged, the ritual murder libel and the accusations based on it no longer required any new "confirmation," and their later history can be seen as a self-perpetuating development of this motif cut off from its origin. Second, both Jews and Christians, without knowing the facts firsthand or even being familiar with the texts that professed to describe it, continued to treat 1096 as a paradigm, as a specific case illustrating a general principle.

I tend to support the second possibility. The myth of 1096, which arose in the twelfth century, created the image of Ashkenazic Jewry from then on, both in their own eyes and in the eyes of their Christian neighbors, especially since now and then there were still cases that "confirmed" it.[109] The vitality of this myth in Jewish society is obvious and well-known.[110] I would like to demonstrate its existence in Christian society as well, by means of a story presented by Victor von Karben.[111] Immediately after describing

---

109. A responsum of Rabbi Meir of Rothenburg, appearing in *Sha'arei Teshuvot*, ed. M. A. Bloch (Berlin, 1891), 346–47, tells of an incident that occurred in Koblenz. During the pogroms that took place in the city on April 2, 1265, a father slaughtered his wife and four children and asked Rabbi Meir if he needed to atone for the act. Rabbi Meir replied, "The permission to do so is widespread, for we have heard of many great men who slaughtered their sons and daughters. And R. Kalonymus permitted doing so in the dirge entitled *Amarti sh'eu mimeni*." Rabbi Meir alludes here to 1096; hence the words, "the permission to do so is widespread," should not be understood as indicating the ubiquity of the phenomenon. A similar case, evidently at the turn of the fourteenth century, is told in *Hilkhot u-Minhagei Rabbenu Shalom mi-Neustadt*, ed. S. Y. Spitzer (Jerusalem, 1976), sec. 402, 137. "During a pogrom," a woman from the city of Striegau in Schlesia slaughtered her children, while she herself was saved and fled to Poland. She asked Rabbi Shalom Neustadt for atonement. He replied that she did not need any repentance. It is also told of Rabbi Nathan of Eger that, during the Crusade against the Hussites in 1421, he gathered all the children of the Jewish community in his home and ordered his wife to slaughter them should pogroms take place (Yuval [n. 85, p. 175], 316). In the chronicle of the pogrom of Austria in 1420, a central place was also given to the martyrdom of the children; see A. Goldmann, *Das Judenbuch der Scheffstrasse zu Wien (1389–1420)* (Vienna-Leipzig, 1908), 125–32.

110. J. Hacker, "About the Persecution during the First Crusade" [in Hebrew], *Zion* 31 (1966): 225–26. We must, of course, distinguish between the actual historical outcome of the pogroms of 1096, whose importance has been debated by scholars; see A. Grossman, *Hakhmei Ashkenaz ha-Rishonim* (Jerusalem, 1989), 435–40; Grossman (n. 12, p. 140), 100–105; Chazan (n. 98, p. 178), 63–64; S. Schwarzfuchs, "The Place of the Crusade in Jewish History" [in Hebrew], in *Tarbut ve-hevrah be-toldot Yisrael biyemei-habeinayim*, ed. R. Bonfil et al. [H. H. Ben-Sasson Memorial Volume; Jerusalem, 1989], 251–67), on the one hand; and their impact on the fashioning of the self-consciousness of Ashkenazic Jewry, on the other.

111. Victor von Karben, *Juden Buchlein* (n.p., 1550), pt. 1, chap. 16.

---

the Jews' custom of cursing the Christians on Yom Kippur, he writes that Jewish women are far more evil and crueler than Jewish men. As proof, he tells the following tale:

In a certain town there lived a Jewish family—husband, wife, and their five- or six-year-old son named Menchin. This child used to play with his Christian friends and go to church with them. One day, when he returned home, he said to his mother: "Oh! What a nice shul the Gentiles have." The mother was shocked to hear this and whipped the child. But the next day the boy returned to the church with his friends. The mother told the father, and he also whipped the child, but in vain. The boy's visits to the church did not cease. This made the parents very sad, and the mother told her husband: this child will bring sin and disgrace upon us; it would be better if we killed him secretly, for nothing good will ever come from him. In an attempt to silence her, the father replied that the child was still small and not responsible for his actions and that once he grew up he would surely change his ways. But she did not heed his words and brought forth scriptural proofs to show that the boy deserved death: from Deuteronomy 21:18–21 (the case of the stubborn and rebellious son); from Zechariah 13:3 ("And if anyone again appears as a prophet, his father and his mother who bore him will say to him, 'You shall not live, for you speak lies in the name of the Lord'; and his father and his mother who bore him shall pierce him through when he prophesies"); from Proverbs 2:17–18 ("who forsakes the companion of her youth, and forgets the covenant of her God; for her house sinks down to death, and her paths to the shades"). The woman went on to say that Abraham also took pity on his son, but God told him to heed the voice of his wife and to banish Ishmael. Even though in the Torah Ishmael is called "a lad," and according to Rashi he was twenty years old, he still deserved death. Further, Isaiah 65:20 says: "For the child shall die a hundred years old; but the sinner a hundred years old shall be accursed." Through these words, the woman tried to incite her husband to kill the child, and when the father refused to do so, she decided to kill the child secretly. Here von Karben deviates from his story and tells how strict the Jews are about observing their Sabbath: they do not light a fire on the Sabbath, and they prepare their food in advance, on Friday. If someone becomes sick, they refrain from lighting a lamp, even if he or she is in mortal danger. They refrain from killing a gnat or a fly, even if it stings them, and they will not harm a spider even if it walks over their food and their table. All their male and female servants, their herds and their donkeys, have to cease working (Exod 20:10). They are also commanded to be happy and to sing on that day. Isaiah 63:1 says: "Who is this that comes from Edom, in crimsoned garments from Bozrah?"[112] Yet the poor Menchin did not get to enjoy the Sabbath, but was instead condemned to death. As mentioned, the Jews prepare their Sabbath food on Friday, including a dish made from white flour and eggs called *Grumel* (kugel), which they leave in the oven the entire Sabbath. While our Jew was sitting with his wife to eat joyously and to sing as is commanded, his wife put poison in her son's portion of *Grumel* with her own hands, and as soon as the child ate, he died. Here Victor's story ends.

This story is a metamorphosis of the ancient story about the "Jewish Boy," first mentioned in the sixth century by Gregory of Tours.[113] The older version tells of the son of a Jewish glassblower who was tempted by his friends to attend Mass and to partake of the Host. When the child returned home, he told his father what he had done. The latter threw him into the oven in a fit of rage. Hearing the mother's shouts of horror, the Christian neighbors came and rescued the child from the oven. In wake of this event, the child converted to Christianity, along with many other Jews. The father was thrown into the oven instead of his son, and no trace remained of his body, not even ashes.

In all versions of this story it is the father who tries to murder his son by throwing him into an oven. Not so in Victor's story, in which it is the father who takes pity on his son and the mother who is the murderer. The method of killing is also changed—poisoning instead of burning in the oven—even though the oven still plays a certain vague and unnecessary role in the story. Why did Victor transfer the murderous quality from the father to the mother? Apparently it was because of his belief that Jewish women are extremely orthodox in their faith—far more so than the men—which, according to him, stems from a desire to compensate themselves for their lowly position in the Jewish religion. This is the explanation he offers for the characteristic of Jewish women, who display more courage than the

---

112. This sentence is missing completely in the Latin version of the book (*Opus aureum ac novum . . .* [Cologne, 1509]). As noted, this verse is the main source for eschatological vengeance and forms part of the haftarah for the "Great Sabbath" (see chapter 5). The German version may have sought further proof for the murderousness of the Jews.

113. Twenty-seven of the numerous versions of this story—in Greek, Latin, and French—are presented in E. Wolter, *Der Judenknabe* (Halle, 1879). Cf. T. Pelizaeus, *Beiträge zur Geschichte der Legende vom Judenknaben* (Halle, 1914); B. Blumenkranz, "Juden und Jüdisches in christlichen Wundererzählungen," *Theologische Zeitschrift* 10 (1954): 441–42; S. Thompson, *Motif-Index*, vol. 5 (Copenhagen, 1957), V363; F. C. Tubach, *Index exemplorum. A Handbook of Medieval Religious Tales* (FF Communications, 204; Helsinki, 1969), sec. 2041.

men in their willingness to die as martyrs.[114] Victor's story depicts the same tendency. He reinforces the image of the Jewish woman, who is quick to kill her children to keep them away from Christianity. This image draws on the Jewish chronicles of 1096 in which, as we know, women played a large part in acts of self-sacrifice. Victor's story thus uses the Jewish image of a Jewish woman who kills a Jewish child (martyrdom) and turns it into that of a Jewish woman who murders a "Christian" child (ritual murder libel)— the Jewish child who is killed is drawn to Christianity. This story, intended for Christian readership, may thus be considered a Christian response to the Jewish view that killing children is allowed "lest they become absorbed among the Gentiles when they grow up,"[115] proving that the transition from Jewish martyrdom to murder accusation was very close.

The connection between martyrdom and ritual murder libel may be explained as a process of projection, whereby Christians extrapolated conclusions from Jewish behavior toward Jews to Jewish behavior toward Christians. But there is another link between tales of martyrdom and ritual murder libels, even tighter than the previous one. *Libel* is a subjective term, meant to indicate a baseless accusation. But in the eyes of its foolish admirers, it was not a "ritual murder libel" but a "tale of the saints." Already in the first two accusations, in Würzburg and Norwich, the murdered person was considered a "saint." The purpose of making an accusation of ritual murder is to beatify the martyrs. The interrogation of the Jews and the wringing of confessions from them were an integral part of many ritual murder libels, not only to prove their guilt, but primarily to establish the sainthood of the martyred child. This is also the immediate importance of the miracles performed by the victim, proving that he was a martyr. The affinity between the two types of tales is therefore complete, when examined from within, according to the worldview of their believers. In other words, the difference between the chronicle of Rabbi Shlomo ben Shimshon and of Thomas of Monmouth's *The Life of William* may be boiled down to the fact that the former tells of Jewish saints and the latter of a Christian saint. Both stories are designed to exalt their heroes. Accordingly, we could have given this chapter the heading "From Tales of Jewish Saints to Tales of Christian Saints."[116]

114. von Karben (n. 111, p. 186), pt. 1, chap. 19.

115. *Sefer ha-Sema"k mi-Zurich* (n. 13, p. 140).

116. And this is indeed the name that Shlomo ben Shimshon gave to his chronicle: *Kiddush* (i.e., "Martyrdom"); Haberman (n. 1, p. 135), 48; Stern and Neubauer (n. 8, p. 138), 21; Chazan (n. 8, p. 138), 280.

In order to examine the parallels between these two narratives, we shall now analyze some of the motifs common to both the Jewish and the Christian martyrdom stories. We will study Jewish accounts of the execution of thirty-two Jews from Blois in 1171, on the one hand, and a Christian *fabula* concerning a ritual murder libel that allegedly took place in Bristol, England, during the second half of the twelfth century, on the other.

As mentioned earlier the Jews of Blois were accused of ritual murder on the eve of Easter and the day after Passover.[117] The ceremony of execution was described thus:

> The foe ordered them to take two righteous priests *(kohanim)*, the pious R. Yehiel b. David ha-Cohen and the righteous R. Yekutiel b. Yehudah ha-Cohen, and they tied them at the pyre upon one stake, for the two of them were brave men . . . and they also tied the hands of Rabbi Yehudah ben Aharon, and they lit the fire with bunches of twigs, and the fire caught upon the ropes that were on their hands, and they came apart. And the three of them went out and said to the servants of the foe: Behold, the fire does not prevail over us, why should we not go free.[118]

The scene described here serves a transparent purpose—namely, to show that fire did not prevail over the first three condemned to death. Therefore the three demanded to be released completely from the death sentence imposed on them. In their opinion, the fact that the fire was unable to destroy them proved their innocence. The Christians' answer to this claim came immediately: "And they said to them: by your lives, you will not get out of this. And they pushed to get out, and they were again placed upon the pyre, and they again went out." This sentence reflects the tension be-

117. Haberman (n. 1, p. 135), 124–26; Stern and Neubauer (n. 8, p. 138), 66–69; reprint: Haberman, *Sefer Zekhirah* (n. 8, p. 138), 30–33. The episode described by Rabbi Ephraim of Bonn, of the wounding of Rabbenu Tam in 1146, has recently been reinterpreted by I. G. Marcus, "Jews and Christians Imagining the Other in Medieval Europe," *Prooftexts* 15 (1995): 209–26. His method is quite similar to the interpretation suggested here for the incident of Blois. For a general description of the incident at Blois, see Chazan (n. 98, p. 178), 13–31; Spiegel (n. 98, p. 178) 267–87. On Rabbi Ephraim's work and its literary qualities, see R. Chazan, "Ephraim ben Jacob's Compilation of Twelfth Century Persecutions," *JQR* 84 (1994): 397–416.

118. Haberman (n. 1, p. 135), 142–44; Stern and Neubauer (n. 8, p. 138), 31–35.

tween the fact that the fire repeatedly failed to prevail over the condemned men, on the one hand, and the Christians' persistence in repeated attempts to burn the Jews at the stake, on the other. And indeed, the Christians' scheme did not succeed until the end:

> And they killed them there by the sword, and threw them into the fire, and they were not burned—neither them nor all of them, thirty-one souls, only their souls were consumed but their bodies remained. And the uncircumcised ones saw this and were astonished, and said to one another: These are holy people. And there was one Jew there, Rabbi Barukh ben David ha-Cohen, who saw all these things with his own eyes.

The connection of the story to the biblical incident of Hananiah, Mishael, and Azariah is transparent. In Blois, as in the book of Daniel, three people were condemned to the fire. But in the biblical story, the one who is put to the test, so to speak, is God, who saves the three from the furnace and whose Name is thereby sanctified; while in our case there is no happy ending, and the three are ultimately killed. The scene of escape from the fire thus serves another function, which can be understood if read in conjunction with the preceding scene, that describing the trial against the Jews.

How was their guilt proven? This question was of decisive importance for the narrator, since the physical safety of the Jews throughout the kingdom depended on it. If the slanderous and false accusation that the Jews murder Christian boys on the eve of Easter was not refuted, they faced a horrible danger everywhere. Clearly our author attributed supreme importance to completely refuting the accusations against the Jews of Blois. The execution was carried out on the twentieth of Sivan; if my assumption, that the event itself took place on the eve of Easter, is correct, then there were about two months between the act and the sentence. During these two months a trial was conducted against the Jews of Blois, and the prosecution clearly did all it could to prove the accusation made against the Jews. Keep in mind that in Blois, unlike in other places, the body of the Christian boy was not found. It was thus doubly difficult to prove the guilt of the Jews.

What does our narrator say about this? He claims that the Jews' guilt was proven through trial by water: "For this is the law of the Gentiles, to test according to their law, laws that are not good and statutes by which one shall not live." In this test, the witness is thrown into a barrel of water. If he is telling the truth, his body will float, and if he is lying, it will sink.[119] For the author, not only was this test invalid, an "unrighteous law," but it was also done deceitfully: "And they did as they wished, and they floated the witness and brought him up, and exonerated the wicked and found the guilty innocent." Evidently the execution scene should be read in this context as well. Within the system of trial by ordeal, ordeal by fire was also accepted, alongside ordeal by water. Though the Jews failed the ordeal by water, our author treats their execution as a kind of ordeal by fire proving their innocence. The fire did not catch them, and death was caused only by the sword. The narrator makes use of language taken from the other side to prove the validity of his case. The impression gained is that this is not only an external polemical use of the opponent's charges, but an internalization of the opponent's language and its subordination to internal needs. The fact that after the execution the body was not consumed by the fire is presented as an event at which even the Christian onlookers admitted the holiness of those killed. The opponent is thus enlisted to reinforce the claim made for internal public opinion: that the Jews were innocent and died a martyrs' death. We shall return later to the issue of the sanctity of the martyrs.

We are further told of the execution of the Blois martyrs in 1171 that "when the flames rose up, and they shouted and sang with one voice, they raised their voices pleasantly. And the Gentiles came and told us: What is your song that is so sweet, and we have never heard such sweet music? For first the voice was soft, and in the end they lifted up their voice loudly, and answered together, *Alenu le-shabeah*, and the fire burned."[120]

The central role played by the prayer *Alenu le-shabeah* (It Is Our Duty to Praise) at that dramatic moment is emphasized in two liturgical poems composed on the occasion of that pogrom; not only is its pleasant melody emphasized, but also the joy of those being killed:

And they said to take them out to the pyre
together they rejoiced like a bride going under the wedding canopy

---

119. Rabbi Ephraim's report (based on a letter from the Jewish community of Orléans) was not precise, and the trial by water in fact worked the other way around: if the accused sank in the water, that was a sign that he spoke the truth, for the water had "accepted" him. On the similarity between trial by water and baptism, see Robert Bartlett, *Trial by Fire and Water: A Medieval Judicial Ordeal* (Oxford, 1986), 88.

120. Haberman (n. 1, p. 135), 143, and cf. *Sefer Zekhirah* (n. 8, p. 138), 126.

Alenu le-shabeah, they sang
extolling with rapturous soul.[121]

This poem was written by Rabbi Hillel ben Jacob of Bonn. His brother, Rabbi Ephraim, wrote similarly: "And they sang melodiously, '*Alenu le-shabeah,*' God is one / and this is the Torah of the burnt-offering, that ascends on the pyre."[122] It is therefore clear that the prayer *Alenu le-shabeah* occupied a central place in twelfth-century martyrdom.

The recitation of *Alenu le-shabeah* served a very clear and impressive, anti-Christian polemical function when recited by the martyrs of Blois. This may well be the ideological background for its becoming the concluding prayer of all regular Jewish prayer services. I. Ta-Shma recently conjectured that the absorption of *Alenu le-shabeah* into the standard liturgy accompanied its removal from the nonobligatory framework of the *Ma'amadot,* optional prayers of individuals, customarily said even in ancient times.[123] He also showed that a French prayer book from the second half of the twelfth century included a scathing anti-Christian addendum to *Alenu le-shabeah.* Moshe Halamish published two more versions of *Alenu le-shabeah,* from the same period, also from France, which include a striking addition. After the words "who has not made our portion like theirs, nor our destiny like all their multitude," it continues "for they bow to vanity and emptiness *[va-rik]*: man *[adam]*—ashes, blood, bile; flesh *[basar]*—shame, corruption, worms; impure and the impurity of adulterers and adulteresses who die in their sin and rot in their transgression, worn, dust, rot, maggots and worms."[124] The word *va-rik* (emptiness) has the same numerical value as "Jesus" *(yeshu).*[125] The words *adam* and *basar* (man/flesh) are read as acronyms of the Hebrew words for ashes, blood, bile, disgrace, corruption,

121. Haberman (n. 1, p. 135), 138.

122. Haberman (n. 1, p. 135), 134.

123. I. Ta-Shma, "The Source and Location of the Prayer *Alenu le-shabeah* in the Siddur: The *Ma'amadot* and the Question of the End of the Prayer" [in Hebrew], in *Sefer Zikaron le-Efraim Talmage, I* (Haifa, 1993), 85–98.

124. M. Halamish, "An Early Version of *Alenu le-shabeah*" [in Hebrew], *Sinai* 110 (1992): 262–65.

125. N. Wieder, "Regarding an Anti-Christian and Anti-Muslim *Gematria*" [in Hebrew], *Sinai* 76 (1975): 1–14. Regarding the prayer *Alenu le-shabeah* see A. Grossman, "'Redemption by Conversion' in the Teaching of Early Ashkenazi Sages" [in Hebrew], *Zion* 59 (1994): 328, and the bibliography there, n. 8. Additional sources and studies of *Alenu* are listed by J. Tabory, *Meqorot le-toldot ha-tefillah* (Jerusalem, 1993), 63–68.

and worms (in Hebrew: קוסו סריהו ויאו / אנו גק או). Thus, *va-rik*—that is, Jesus—is man-flesh, and not a man-God.

The significance of the word *marah* (bile) becomes clear in a letter of Obadiah ben Makhir, which also describes the ritual murder libel at Blois:

> "Who says to his father, 'I have not seen him'"—this is one of the two harlots who said she was his mother, "And their sin shall not be erased." Therefore her name was called *Marah* [bile]. And the shame of the daughters of Adam [a man]. And by our sins she placed her dead son in the bosom of the earth, opposite the lower Sanctuary, because of our sins.[126]

The two harlots are Mary, mother of Jesus, and Mary Magdalene. The passage alludes to the trial of two harlots who were brought before King Solomon to determine which was the mother of the living son (1 Kgs 3:16–28). The lying woman is Mary (*Marah*, "bile" and "bitterness"), the mother of Jesus, who stole the other woman's son, and "laid it in her bosom" (1 Kgs 3:20)—that is, "in the bosom of the earth" (based on Ezek 43:14: "And from the base [lit., bosom] on the ground to the lower ledge"). The theological background for this sentence is explained in an anti-Jewish poem in French, dated to the thirteenth century by H. Pflaum, who published it. This poem contains the following sentence:

Touz jors estoit amont, el sain son pere
Toz jors estoit aval, clos el ventre sa mere.

Always above in heaven, in the bosom of his Father
Always enclosed in the earth, in the belly of his mother.[127]

The Jewish author ridicules this notion of the incarnation of Jesus and his transformation to flesh and blood in the womb of Mary.[128] Hence, the

126. Spiegel (n. 98, p. 178), 286. The letter is also printed carelessly by Haberman (n. 1, p. 135), 258–59.

127. H. Pflaum, "Poems of Religious Disputations in the Middle Ages" [in Hebrew], *Tarbiz* 2 (1931): 451, 468.

128. The image of the "bosom," in which the Christian martyrs and the Jewish martyrs dwell, seems to be related to this issue. On the Madonna and child in relation to Jewish motifs, see Evelyn M. Cohen, "The Teacher, the Father and the Virgin Mary in the Leipzig Mahzor," *Proceedings of the Tenth World Congress of Jewish Studies*, div. D, vol. 2 (Jerusalem, 1990), 71–76; Ivan G. Marcus, *Rituals of Childhood* (New Haven, 1996), 90–94.

anti-Christian addendum to *Alenu le-shabeah* includes a passage condemning both Jesus and Mary.[129] We may assume that this was the version
recited by the martyrs of Blois.

These discoveries suggest the possibility that the literary process described
by Ta-Shma also contained an ideological aspect, one well suited to the atmosphere of the twelfth century. *Alenu le-shabeah* became a Jewish, anti-
Christian affirmation, counterpoised to the Christian credo, and was understood as such by the martyrs of Blois. The scathing anti-Christian
addition made to the prayer in France during the second half of the twelfth
century may be seen as another by-product of the liturgical innovations introduced temporarily following the libel at Blois.[130] The introduction of
Alenu le-shabeah into the prayer book does not indicate any universalist
trend of Ashkenazic, French, or English Jewry, but rather the opposite—
the intensification of the struggle against Christianity and the exacerbation
of language among the Jews as well.

The fact that the martyrs of Blois specifically chose *Alenu le-shabeah*,
which includes mockery and insults of Jesus and Mary, should not surprise
us, since at that time the cult of Mary was growing stronger in northern
France. Three times, the author of our account of the Blois incident emphasizes that the prayer was sung to a wondrously beautiful melody. It was
the beauty of the melody that excited the Christian spectators. "We never
heard such sweet music," they say. It is fascinating that the language and
symbols used by the Jews to describe the holiness of the Jewish martyrs is
also used by the Christians to describe the victims of the ritual murder libels. In *The Canterbury Tales,* Geoffrey Chaucer tells of a choirboy who sang
Gaude Maria (Rejoice, O Mary) in the Jewish street, and the Jews, who

129. Mockery of Mary can be interpreted as a Jewish response to the growth of her cult
in the twelfth century in northern France: for example, in relation to her Immaculate Conception (Immaculatus) and the appearance of the collection *Miracula Sanctae Virginis Mariae*
at the beginning of the century, which includes stories of miracles she wrought. Mary appears
there as the savior of those who sing *Ave Maria* in her honor. On the growth of the cult of
Mary in northern France and the inclusion in it of anti-Jewish motifs, see W. Delius, *Geschichte
der Marienverehrung* (München, 1963), 165–66; W. C. Jordan, "Marian Devotion and the Talmud Trial of 1240," in *Religionsgespräche im Mittelalter,* ed. B. Lewis and F. Niewöhner (Wies-
baden, 1992), 61–76. The disappearance of those invectives from Jewish prayer books in the
thirteenth century may have been a result of the accusation made at the Talmud trial of 1240
charging the Jews with cursing Mary, which made a strong impression on Christian public
opinion.

130. See Haberman (n. 1, p. 135), 126, 146.

could not bear the beauty of his singing, slit his throat. Nevertheless, the song continued to be heard issuing forth from his slit throat.[131]

Chaucer certainly did not invent this motif. A Latin work recently published by Christoph Cluse, "Fabula ineptissima," recounts an apparently imaginary incident that took place in Bristol during the reign of King Henry II (1154–1189).[132] A certain Jew named Samuel allegedly crucified a Christian child named Adam, the son of William. The Jew's wife and son helped him to perform the deed, but the body of the murdered child worked miracles, and the mother and the son were frightened, regretted what they had done, and wished to convert to Christianity. To prevent that, Samuel murdered them. The editor dates the story from the second half of the thirteenth century.

As in the *Annales* of Egmond, the Bristol story is also a Christian literary fabrication with elements familiar to us from their Jewish counterparts. The Jewish narrative of martyrs who kill their wives and children to prevent them from converting to Christianity is presented here in a Christian counternarrative of Jews killing their own wives and children, allegedly because they want to convert to Christianity. In this way the Christian story changes the Jewish martyrs who died for Kiddush Hashem into Christian martyrs. Even though they did not manage to convert to Christianity and to be baptized with the holy water, their death *pro Christo* is considered a baptism by blood, conveying on them the status of martyrs.[133]

Examination of this work evokes further points of similarity between the Christian martyr stories and those of Jewish martyrs. According to the Latin text, the Jew hid the body of the murdered Christian child in a latrine—a

---

131. For the sources of this tale, see C. Brown, "The Prioress's Tale," in *Sources and Analogues of Chaucer's Canterbury Tales*, ed. W. F. Bryan and G. Dempster (New York, 1958), 447–85; *A Variorum Edition of the Works of Geoffrey Chaucer. II: The Canterbury Tales*, pt 20: *The Prioress's Tale*, ed. B. Boyd (Oklahoma, 1987), 8–16. And cf. the song *Tzam'ah Nafshi le'Elohim*, composed by Rabbi Abraham Ibn Ezra: "Recognize the true mistress / the handmaid who dares say / No! For your son is the dead one, and my son is the living one!" The fact that no body was found in Blois is also linked with the cult of Mary, who rose to heaven without leaving relics.

132. Christoph Cluse, "'Fabula ineptissima.' Die Ritualmordlegende um Adam von Bristol nach der Handschrift London, British Library, Harley 957," *Aschkenaz—Zeitschrift für Geschichte und Kultur der Juden* 5 (1995): 293–328.

133. Cluse reports more such stories in "'Fabula ineptissima,'" 296–97. The manuscript includes a picture of the slaughter of the son and the woman by the Jew Samuel. See Zafran (n. 105, p. 181), 40, pl. 93.

place favored by Christian narrators, probably because of the Talmudic passage according to which Jesus was condemned to being punished in boiling feces.[134] The Jew tied the child to a long spit from his head to his feet, placed him next to the fire, and turned the spit around so as to roast him in the fire—a motif reminiscent of the roasting of the Passover sacrifice.[135] A priest then enters the house of the Jew, escorted by two other people, and they hear a beautiful sound, like that of thousands upon thousands of children singing *Soli deo honor et gloria in secula seculorum, amen* (To God alone belong the honor and glory forever and ever, amen).[136] One of the laymen asked: From whence comes this singing, and where is the church? But the priest silenced him and said: Do not say anything; sit here until I return, and meanwhile recite the *Paternoster* and the *Ave Maria*. The priest wanted to go into the latrine by himself, but then he heard a voice commanding him to first confess all his sins. He left the house and went to the nearby church. When he returned to the Jew's house, the two laymen told him that in his absence they had had a vision of a woman and a child dressed in *porphyrion*, radiant like the sun. They pointed to the stab wounds in their bodies that had caused their deaths.

As we saw in chapter 3, the *porphyrion*, or crimson robe, is one of the strongest symbols of Jewish martyrdom in Germany, its function being to evoke the wrath of the vengeful God. In the present Christian story, too,

---

134. *b. Gittin* 57a. This source is cited by Nicholas Donin; see C. Merchavia, *Ha-Talmud bere'i ha-Nazrut* (Jerusalem, 1971), 276–77. However, it was already known earlier, as we can see from Pope Innocent III's letter to Philippe Auguste, King of France, from 1205; see Solomon Grayzel, *The Church and the Jews in the XIIIth Century* (New York, 1966; revised edition), 108–9 n. 14. In the pogroms of Mainz in 1096, the *gabbai*, David ben Nathaniel, exhorted a crowd of Christians before his death, with words of vilification of Jesus, who was sentenced to "boiling feces" (Haberman [n. 1, p. 135], 36; Stern and Neubauer [n.8, p. 138]; Chazan [n. 8, p. 138], 262). On the motif of Jewish desecration of Christian holy objects in the latrine, see Christoph Cluse, "Stories of Breaking and Taking the Cross: A Possible Context for the Oxford Incident of 1268," *Revue d'Histoire Ecclésiastique* 15 (1995): 418. On accusations against Jews desecrating Christian holy objects, cf. Cluse (n. 132, p. 196).

135. The Passover offering was roasted by pushing a spit of pomegranate wood through the entire length of the animal's body, from its mouth to its hindquarters or, according to another tannaitic view, from its hindquarters to its mouth (*m. Pesahim* 7.1 and parallels). Justin Martyr claimed that the roasted Passover sacrifice looked like a crucified man (Justin Martyr, *The Dialogue with Trypho*, trans. A. Lukyn Williams [London, 1930], 80). See J. Tabory, *Pesah Dorot; Perakim be-toldot leil ha-Seder* (Tel Aviv, 1996), 95–96. According to the Bristol story, before roasting the Christian child by fire, the Jew thrust a Cross into his mouth to prevent him from speaking. This may allude to Isaiah 57:3.

136. Cluse (n. 132, p. 196), 322.

the *porphyrion* is also specifically the garb of the Jews, not of the slain Christian child, but it also alludes to the garment worn by Jesus before the Crucifixion (Mark 15:17: "And they clothed him in a purple cloak"). In the case of Jesus, the *porphyrion* is suggestive of royal robes,[137] while the *porphyrion* of the Jews appearing in the descriptions of martyrs in the Midrash and in liturgical poems is a white garment dyed red in the blood of the saints. As noted in chapter 3, the biblical source of this image, common to Jews and Christians alike, is Isaiah 63:1–6, describing God's vengeance on Edom. In Christian exegesis, this chapter was read as referring to the crucified Jesus and his bloodstained clothes.[138]

Further on, the story continues to tell how the priest entered the latrine, wrapped the boy's body in linen, and placed it in the coffin. The angels helped him carry the body from Bristol to Ireland, the land of his birth, where the child was buried. During the funeral, the priest for the last time heard the angelic voices singing *Te Deum laudamus* (We Shall Praise You, O God). It is difficult in this context not to think of the climactic moment in the deaths of the Jewish martyrs at Blois, during which they ascend the pyre while singing *Alenu le-shabeah* (It Is Our Duty to Praise). Is this a kind of circuitous dialogue?

The similarity between *Alenu le-shabeah* and the *Te Deum* is surprising in another respect.[139] Both prayers are very ancient. Legend attributes the *Te Deum* to Ambrose, the fourth-century bishop of Milan, but almost all scholars agree that the prayer was composed in the fifth century in Latin and translated into Greek in the ninth century.[140] *Alenu* also has an ancient

137. See also in Jewish Midrashic literature, in those places where there is a description of royal apparel.

138. A. Thomas, *Die Darstellung Christi in der Kelter* (Düsseldorf, 1936; repr. 1982); J. Schwarz, "Treading the Grapes of Wrath. The Wine Press in Ancient Jewish and Christian Tradition," *Theologische Zeitschrift* 49 (1993): 215–28; 311–24; J. H. Marrow, *Passion Iconography in Northern European Art of the Late Middle Ages and Early Renaissance* (Kortrijk, 1979), 50–52; O. Limor, *Die Disputationen zu Ceuta (1197) und Mallorca (1286)* (MGH. Quellen zur Geistesgeschichte des Mittelalters. 15; München, 1994), 155 n. 100.

139. E. Werner has already noted the similarity in the content of the two prayers, without discussing this further, in his *The Sacred Bridge*, vol 1. (London, 1959), 7. His statement that *Alenu le-shabeah* was introduced into the fixed prayer liturgy after the third century is mistaken. On p. 183 he compares the *Te Deum* with *Modim* ("We give thanks"—the penultimate blessing of the *Amidah*), and on p. 184 compares *Alenu* with the *Credo*.

140. s.v. "Te Deum," *The Catholic Encyclopedia* 14 (New York, 1913–1914), 468–71; M. Hoglo, "Te Deum," *The New Catholic Encyclopedia* 13 (Washington, 1967), 954–55.

attribution to Rab, the early-third-century Babylonian amora,[141] but the most ancient extant version is to be found in the Hekhalot literature.[142] Also like *Alenu le-shabeah*, the *Te Deum* was not initially incorporated within the standard prayer liturgy, only gradually receiving the status of a standard prayer that was incorporated into the Sunday service at the end of Matins *(Matutinum)*, the morning prayer, one of the eight prayers known as the Hours *(Horae)*.[143] It was considered an exemplary prayer of thanksgiving and was customarily sung at the end of especially solemn occasions, such as the consecration of a church, the investiture of a pope or bishop, the canonization of a saint, the signing of a peace agreement, a royal coronation, or the conclusion of a religious pageant. That is, even in terms of its liturgical position, the *Te Deum* bears a certain similarity to that of *Alenu le-shabeah*, which concludes the standard prayers. Thus, ending the Bristol story with the *Te Deum* is compatible with the place allotted to it at the end of liturgical ceremonies.

I do not intend to discuss here the source and meaning of *Alenu le-shabeah*, only to focus on the way in which the prayer was understood in the twelfth century, when it entered the standard prayers in the French and Ashkenazic prayer book, as well as on the possibility that the Jews saw this ancient prayer as a decisive response to the parallel Christian declaration.[144]

141. I. Elbogen, *Ha-Tefillah be-Yisrael be-hitpathutah ha-historit*, ed. Y. Heinemann (Tel Aviv, 1972), 108; J. Heinemann, *Prayer in the Talmud* (Berlin, 1977), 269–75 [in Hebrew: Jerusalem, 1966, 173–75]; A. Mirsky, *Ha-Piyyut* (Jerusalem, 1990), 72–73; J. Neusner, *History of the Jews in Babylonia, II* (Leiden, 1966), 163–66. According to Heinemann, the *Alenu* prayer is unique in that it relates to God in the third person. In this respect, it is also strikingly different from the *Te Deum*. For this reason and because of similar stylistic considerations, Heinemann (as well as Mirsky) surmises that the original *Alenu* prayer (without the addition of "Therefore we put our hope in You") was composed during the Temple period, even though we have no information about it in Talmudic literature, and it first appears in Merkabah literature.

142. A. Altmann, "Kedushah Hymns in the Earliest Hekhaloth Literature" [in Hebrew], in *Panim shel Yahadut* (Tel Aviv, 1983), 54 (originally published in *Melilah* 2 (1946), 1–24); G. Scholem, *Jewish Gnosticism, Merkabah Mysticism, and Talmudic Tradition* (New York, 1965), 105; P. Schäfer, ed., *Synopse zur Hekhalot-Literatur* (Tübingen, 1981), no. 551; M. D. Schwartz, "'Alay le-shabbeah': A Liturgical Prayer in Ma'aseh Merkabah," *JQR* 77 (1986–1987): 179–80 (includes a translation of the prayer into English).

143. On the introduction of *Alenu* into the standard prayer liturgy, see Ta-Shma (n. 123, p. 193), 85–98.

144. Yitzhak Baer noted the similarity between *Alenu le-shabeah* and Colossians 1:12 ("giving thanks to the Father ") but he thought, following his approach, that this indicates that

The likelihood that it is a Jewish counterdeclaration is reinforced by the fact that *Alenu le-shabeah* was perceived as an anti-Christian prayer by both Jews and Christians. The Jewish interpretation is testified to by the twelfth-century French version mentioned earlier, which includes a scathing addition against Jesus and Mary.[145] Curses against Mary are also uttered in the Bristol story by the Jew Samuel, and Cluse considers it almost certain that the crucifixion of the child Adam took place on the night of the Annunciation of Mary (August 15).[146] There is no need to elaborate on the Christian interpretation of *Alenu le-shabeah*, a subject discussed extensively in scholarly literature.[147] There is another possible connection of the Bristol story with *Alenu le-shabeah*. The Christian account claims that the Jew spat three times when Jesus's name was mentioned, behavior that looks like a Christian understanding of the Jewish custom of spitting when reciting the words "vanity and emptiness."[148] What follows from all this is that, for the Jews of France and Ashkenaz during the twelfth century, *Alenu le-shabeah* indeed served as a kind of anti-Christian credo in general, and against the cult of Mary in particular, and that this is apparently the meaning of its incorporation into the Prayer Book at the conclusion of all standard prayer services.

A closer examination of the content of these two prayers reveals a genuine similarity. The *Te Deum* is a hymn of triumph that opens with a double act of praise: *Te Deum laudamus, te Dominum confitemur* (We praise You, O God, and acknowledge You as Lord)—that is, a separation or distinction between "God" and "the Lord." This is analogous to the double praise in "It is our duty to praise *the Master of all*, to ascribe greatness to the *Shaper of Creation*," which also includes a distinction between the Master of All

---

Alenu preceded Paul. This seems less plausible to me. See Y. Baer, "The Manual of Discipline; A Jewish-Christian Document of the Second Century CE" [in Hebrew], *Zion* 29 (1964): 54 n. 145.

145. Halamish (n. 124, p. 193).

146. Cluse (n. 132, p. 196), 300–301.

147. *Alenu le-shabeah* is quoted by Bernard Gui in the manual he prepared for the Inquisitors. See Bernardus Guidonis, *Practica Inquisitionis Heretice Pravitatis*, ed. C. Douais (Paris, 1886), 290–92. Worthy of special note among the scholarship on the place of the *Alenu* prayer in Jewish-Christian polemic is Wieder (n. 125, p. 193); J. Elbaum, "Concerning Two Textual Emendations in the 'Alenu' Prayer" [in Hebrew], *Tarbiz* 42 (1973): 204–8; H. M. Kirn, *Das Bild vom Juden im Deutschland des frühen 16. Jahrhunderts* (Tübingen, 1989), 45–46; Ta-Shma (n. 123, p. 193); Halamish (n. 124, p. 193).

148. Cluse (n. 132, p. 196), 303.

and the Shaper of Creation. In the second verse of the Christian prayer, we find the sentence *Tibi omnes Angeli, tibi caeli, et universae Potestates . . . proclamant . . .* (To thee all Angels cry aloud, the Heavens and all the Powers therein . . . proclaim), while the Jewish prayer says: "We bend our knees, prostrate ourselves, and acknowledge the King Who reigns over kings." The Christian prayer emphasizes the hosts of heaven, the Jewish one the unity of God. The Christian prayer continues: *Pleni sunt caeli et terra majestatis gloriae tuae* (Heaven and earth are full of the majesty of Your glory), while the Jewish prayer says: "For He stretches out heaven and establishes the earth." The Christian prayer praises Jesus, *Tu Rex gloriae Christe,* and the act of incarnation that did not profane the womb of the Holy Virgin, while the addendum to the Jewish prayer, which was widespread in French prayer books in the twelfth century, seems to slander Jesus and Mary. The sentence *Tu ad dexteram Dei sedes in gloria Patris* (Thou sittest at the right hand of God, in the glory of the Father), is countered in *Alenu le-shabeah* with: "And His seat of glory is in the heavens above" or, in another early version, "the throne of His homage is in the heavens above."[149] The Christian prayer

149. In the symbolic language of the twelfth century, "the seat of His homage is in the heavens above" could have been interpreted as a polemical statement against the *sedes sapientae* (seat of wisdom)—the bosom of Mary in which Jesus sat. During the eleventh and twelfth centuries in northern France, the practice of making wooden statuettes of the seat of wisdom called Maiestas developed, in which Jesus is portrayed as the divine Logos, who is made incarnate and turned into flesh and blood in the bosom of his earthly mother. The Holy Virgin is presented as the means by which the divine Logos descended to earth, and therefore she is the "seat of wisdom" or the Throne of Solomon, and either she or Jesus is portrayed as holding a book; see I. H. Forsyth, *The Throne of Wisdom, Wood Sculptures of the Madonna in Romanesque France* (Princeton, 1972). In contrast, the Jew prays and declares that God's "seat of homage" is "in heaven," not in the lap of an earthly mother. In this context, it is worth noting the famous *gematria, yeqaro* (His homage) = *yeshu* (Jesus), which lends to "the seat of His homage" the Christological meaning of *sedes sapientae.* See *Sefer Ha-Nizzahon* (n 107, p. 182), 192; Yosef ben Moshe, *Leqet Yosher* ed. Freimann (Berlin, 1903), 1:29. It is worth noting in this connection that the "seat of His Homage" is also the name used for the seat on which the *sandak* (godfather) sits during a circumcision, holding the baby on his lap (*Pirkei de-Rabbi Eliezer,* sec. 29, end), which from the thirteenth century on was called the "seat of Elijah." On this, and on the parallel between the Jewish godfather present at a circumcision and the Christian godfather present at baptism, see L. A. Hoffmann, *Covenant of Blood* (Chicago, 1996), 200–207. The affinity between Jewish and Christian symbolism associated with the chair can also be found in a fragment from a Jewish-Byzantine source published by A. Jellinek, *Beit ha-Midrasch, II* (Jerusalem, 1967; photo ed.), 85 (and V. 34–41), called *Demut kise shel Shlomo ha-Melekh a"h,* in which it states: "And one causes King Solomon to bend down and places him upon the throne. . . . And a golden dove stood between its pillars and they open him

goes on to express hope for the messianic return of Jesus: *Judex crederis esse venturus* (We believe that You, our judge, shall return), from whence stems the hope, *Te ergo quaesumus* (Therefore we beseech you), reminiscent of the second, messianic part of *Alenu le-shabeah:* "And therefore we put our hope in You, Lord our God, that we may soon see Your mighty splendor, to remove detestable idolatry from the earth." The Christian prayer then continues: *Et laudamus nomen tuum in saeculum* (and we shall praise Your Name forever), like the Jewish prayer, "and to the glory of Your name they will render homage."

One could find more parallels between these two prayers, but our concern here is with how the prayer *Alenu le-shabeah* was understood by Jews in the twelfth century, not with the hypothetical possibility that it was originally composed as an anti-Christian declaration, or as a refutation of the *Te Deum*. Both prayers are present in tales of martyrdom, and the similarity between them demands explanation. The impression gained is that Jews made use of the liturgical language of the other side to declare their opposition, both for themselves and as an externally directed protest.

In light of this, it is hardly surprising that the similarity found between the Jewish narrative and the Christian one lies not only in the details, but also in the ritual of commemorating the saints. Our knowledge of what

---

an ark and he takes the Torah scroll and places it upon his knees." The dove is parallel to the Holy Spirit, Solomon parallels Mary, and the Torah Scroll (the Logos) parallels Jesus. On this text and its Byzantine sources, see I. Perles, "Thron und Circus des Königs Salomo," *MGWJ* 21 (1872): 122–39; E. Ville-Patlagean, "Une image de Salomon de Basileus byzantin," *REJ* 121 (1962): 9–33. On the Byzantine royal throne, see A. Grabar, *L'Empereur dans l'art byzantin* (Paris, 1936). On Solomon's throne in the Catholic West, see F. Wormald, "The Throne of Solomon and St. Edward's Chair," *Essays in Honor of Erwin Panofsky* (De Artibus Opuscula, XL; New York, 1961), 532–39. In the consciousness of the Jews of Ashkenaz, there was a link between the "seat of His homage" and the "seat of wisdom." Support for this can be found in R. Eleazar of Worms' interpretation of the *Alenu* prayer. The author presents the above-cited Midrash on the Throne of Solomon à propos his interpretation of "the seat of His homage is in the heavens above" (*Sodei Razya le-Rabbi Eleazar mi-Worms,* ed. Y. Kamelhar [Belgoria, 1936], 23; M. Herschler, *Siddur Rabbenu Shlomo mi-Germaiza* [Jerusalem, 1972], 213). In the mystical teaching of R. Eleazar of Worms a sexual meaning is given to the sitting of the Divine Glory on the throne, as indicating union between the higher, masculine Glory and the lower, feminine Glory. See E. Wolfson, "The Image of Jacob Engraved upon the Throne: Further Reflection on the Esoteric Doctrine of the German Pietists," *Along the Path* (New York, 1995), 54; Hebrew: in *Mehqarim be-sifrut ha-Kabbalah uve-mahshevet Yisrael,* eds. M. Oron and A. Goldreich (E. Gottleib Memorial Volume; Jerusalem, 1994), 179. The feminization of the seat of Homage is also reminiscent of the *sedes sapientae* and the maternal figure of Mary.

happened at Blois is a result of an effort to grant ritual significance to the event. Returning to the passage quoted above in the letter from Orléans, it is important to note not only that the bodies of the victims were not devoured by fire, but also that there was an eyewitness to the fact: "And there was one Jew there, Rabbi Barukh ben David ha-Cohen, who saw all these things with his own eyes." The need to provide testimony of the martyr's death of William of Norwich was, as we know, the main motive for the writing of Thomas of Monmouth's work. He seeks to prove not only the guilt of the Jews but also the sainthood of the slain child. The Jewish story may be seen as having a similar purpose, albeit with an opposite motive. The Jews of Blois were executed as punishment for the alleged murder of a Christian. Although the Jewish narrator denied their guilt, they were killed for their faith and their refusal to convert to Christianity. They thus died martyrs' deaths. Ora Limor correctly noted that the self-image of Jews and Christians was "a kind of mirror-reflection, in which the same elements are found but they have opposite functions: the slaughterer becomes the victim, and the victim becomes the slaughterer."[150]

This mirror imaging also explains the fixing in the liturgical calendar of the twentieth of Sivan—the day of the execution in Blois—as a fast day in France, England, and Germany. Rabbi Jacob Tam even wanted to grant that day a status equivalent to that of Yom Kippur, and eight liturgical poems were composed for it. In this way the one-time act of martyrdom was commemorated and became a fixed ceremony, repeated annually with its own unique liturgy. A similar process of ritualization also took place, as we know, for some of the legends of ritual murder.

These and many other examples illustrate two fundamental tendencies in the relationship between the language of Jewish symbols and the parallel Christian language. The first is to remove from the rival the sanctity he attributes to his symbols and to destroy it. The second tendency is to adopt the Christian language and to "Judaize" it, as if to say "ours is greater than yours," thereby to expropriate and take control of the opponent's symbols. While the former trend is quite well-known, not enough attention is paid to the second. We are prone to see medieval Ashkenazic Judaism as thoroughly opposed to the symbols, ceremonies, and language of Christianity, as if Jews and Christians inhabited two different worlds. This perception is so deeply rooted that it is difficult for people to imagine that Jews had

---

150. Ora Limor, *Bein Yehudim le-Nozrim; 5: Al'ilat ha-Dam* (Tel Aviv, 1998), 49.

any knowledge of Christian ceremonies or that Christians knew anything about the religious language and customs of the Jews. Yet a reading of the Ashkenazic chronicles indicates a close proximity to and profound familiarity with the opponent's language. Study of Jewish-Christian polemics is still too much influenced by polemical literature, whose function it is to place a high wall between the warring camps. But the real polemics took place in small "smugglings" underneath the fence, in everyday dealings, in the close geographical proximity between church and synagogue—a few dozen meters in most cities—in the small dimensions of dense walled cities turned in on themselves, in which life lacked privacy and the sound of Jewish worshipers in the synagogue disturbed the Christian worshipers in the cathedral.[151]

151. Such complaints are repeated often. In 591 the Jews of Terracina were expelled from their synagogue by the bishop because the sound of their prayer disturbed worshipers in the nearby church; see S. Katz, "Pope Gregory the Great and the Jews," *JQR* 24 (1933–34): 12. In 1205 Pope Innocent III complained in a letter to the King of France, Phillipe Auguste, that the Jews of Sens had built a synagogue close to the local church and prayed there aloud "as is the custom of the Jews." See Grayzel (n. 134, p. 197) sec. 14, 106–7. In 1458 Emperor Friedrich III ordered the Jews of Frankfurt to be settled in a new quarter, far from the center of the city, so as to prevent the worshipers in church from becoming disturbed by the shouts of Jews praying in the synagogue ("das geschray der Judischeit in irer synagog"); see F. Backhaus, "Die Einrichtung eines Ghettos für die Frankfurter Juden im Jahre 1462," *Hessisches Jahrbuch für Landesgeschichte* 39 (1989): 64–65. Rabbi Yitzhak of Corbeil also complained of the tumult rising from the Jewish synagogue as opposed to the quiet that prevailed during prayer in the church: "Woe to those who make idle conversation or laugh and behave frivolously in the synagogue during the prayer, and keep their children from the life of the World to Come. For we must draw an inference to ourselves from the idolators, who do not believe, who stand silently in their house of blasphemy. All the more so we, who stand before the King of Kings, the Holy One blessed be He" (*Amudei Golah, Sefer Mizvot Katan* [Satmar, 1935], 18, end of sec. 11).

FIVE

Inverted Ceremonies

The Host, the Matzah, and the Quarrel

WE SHALL NOW LEAVE THE PAIR OF THEMES, blood libel and martyrdom, that concerned us in the last chapter, and return to that of the second chapter: Passover and Easter. While in the previous discussion we focused on the dialogue and conflict between the two holidays in late antiquity, our discussion here shall focus on the Middle Ages. We shall deal with symbols and ceremonies of the respective holidays and less with their texts. We will attempt to see how the language of the Jewish Passover ceremony developed in relation to the language of the Christian ceremony; what Christians understood of that language, which was both familiar and alien to them. This Christian understanding of some of the Passover ceremonies will help us to understand the rationale underlying another medieval libel: the desecration of the Host.

In discussing the meaning of the Passover matzah, we must be aware that it is a symbol rich in meanings, some explicit, others implicit, and some of which are connected with the theme of Redemption, both past and future. In the ancient world, the rising and leavening of the dough represented the power of civilization, human activity, and interference in nature, while the matzah—the unleavened bread—was the symbol of simplicity and primitivism, the bread of the unsettled nomad, the bread of affliction that lasts a long time. Hence, the matzah was considered a pure sacrifice. In most of the sacrifices offered in the Temple in Jerusalem, the priests were forbidden to bring offerings of leavened bread, and only unleavened bread was considered fit to be eaten in the Temple.[1] According to the halakhah, the shewbread placed on the golden table in the Sanctuary also had to be made only of matzah.[2]

The centrality of bread in the Passover holiday is related to spring and the anticipation of the ripening of the first grain, barley.[3] Leaven thus symbolizes the old crop, while matzah represents the new year's harvest. True, the barley is still green and far from ripe in the Land of Israel at Passover time, but that is precisely why it needs a blessing—so that it can ripen.

In the story of the Exodus from Egypt, the matzah carries a double meaning. The bread that did not have time to rise signals the hasty exodus of the children of Israel from Egypt (Exod 13:34), while it simultaneously symbolizes their slavery in Egypt and is therefore called "the bread of affliction" (Deut 16:3). According to the former meaning, matzah is a symbol of Redemption, while according to the latter it is a symbol of slavery and suffering. The two are of course not mutually exclusive, since Redemption is tantamount to the reverse side of slavery and subjugation. There are also those who think that the word *matzah* is derived from the same root as the verb "to quarrel" (in Hebrew: נצה) and thus symbolizes the quarrel between God and death, between the firstborn son who belongs to God and is condemned to death and the one who is redeemed and delivered. Eating matzah, "the bread of affliction," is thus a redemptive and salvific offering.[4] In the Bible, the former meaning, that of the hasty eating of matzah, is the primary one, and even on the one occasion when it is called "bread of affliction," the commandment to eat it on the Passover night is connected with the haste with which the Israelites departed from Egypt. This is also apparently what Josephus meant when he wrote that one must eat matzah "in memory of the scarcity" suffered by the Israelites during the Exodus from Egypt.[5]

1. Exod 23:18; 29:2; Lev 2:11; Amos 4:5, and elsewhere. It may be that the miracle of its rising may underlie the forgotten identification between man and bread (cf. John 6:32–58. In Arabic the word *lehem* is "flesh"); and cf. J. B. Segal, *The Hebrew Passover from the Earliest Times to A.D. 70* (New York, 1963), 167–69.

2. *m. Menahot* 5.1.

3. At Passover the world is judged regarding grain (*m. Rosh Hashana* 1.2), and on every third Passover it was customary to destroy leftover tithes (*m. Ma'aser Sheni* 5.6).

4. A. Cooper and B. R. Goldstein, "Exodus and Massot in History and Tradition," *Maarav* 8 (1992), 27–28. For the etymology of the word *matzah,* see Segal (n. 1, above), 107–13.

5. *Antiquities* 2.316. In this same vein, Holzinger understood matzah as the bread of desert nomads; see H. Holzinger, *Exodus* (Tübingen, 1900), 42.

The first time that matzah was given the central meaning of martyrological suffering is in an interpretation of Jesus's words at the Last Supper, hence the connection in the Gospels between the story of the Crucifixion and the offering of the Passover sacrifice in the Temple, on the one hand, and the laws of leaven and matzah, on the other, as we shall explore below. Relating the significance of matzah to its future messianic meaning also led to a change in the hermeneutics of leaven. Leaven is the evil spirit that delays the Redemption, and its burning is a prerequisite for the bringing of the offering and the eating of the matzah, the symbol of Redemption.[6] In burning leaven one is burning "the other," the rival. Parallel to this, leaven also assumed an ethical meaning, as a symbol of the evil impulse that needs to be destroyed.[7]

Following the Destruction of the Temple, matzah gradually assumed the place of the Passover sacrifice, and its importance as a symbol of future Redemption increased correspondingly. In both Christianity and Judaism, the bread that rises and the matzah that does not each carry a similar symbolic charge, but in Western Christianity, matzah and the deliverance it promises were placed at the very center of its ceremony, as the Host in the daily Eucharist. Judaism, however, continued to place both leaven and the obligation to burn it at the center of the holiday. During Passover, the Jewish home becomes a kind of microcosm, in which all traces of the old food and its related utensils are removed from touch and sight and in their place a new environment, which includes symbols of past Redemption and alludes to that of the future, is created.

Time and place positioned Passover and Easter alongside one another—and in this respect there was no difference between the Middle Ages and late antiquity. But there is considerable difference between the beginning of the first millennium and the beginning of the second with regard to two issues. In the first centuries of the Common Era, Jewish-Christian relations were marked by a mutual give-and-take, but in the Middle Ages these relations became pretty much one-sided. Christianity saw Judaism as an in-

6. In his *Commentary* on John 10:18, sec. 109, Origen distinguishes between three levels of bread: earthly bread, the lowest type, is leavened; above it is matzah, which is eaten after the end of the darkness of the night of the Passover sacrifice; and highest of all is manna, the heavenly bread of the angels, the bread of the eschatological future (according to Exod 16:32–34). See Raniero Cantalamessa, *Easter in the Early Church: An Anthology of Jewish and Early Christian Texts* (Collegeville, IN., 1993), 54; and cf. Hos 7:4.

7. Segal (n. 1, p. 206), 34.

ferior and peripheral religion, albeit a persistent and annoying one—but certainly no longer as a predominant one. During the second and third centuries Christians were persecuted, whereas Judaism enjoyed the legal status of *religio licita;* by the twelfth and thirteenth centuries, the tables had turned. The Church saw itself as "victorious," while the Jews had become *servi camerae,* or subjects of the Apostolic Throne. Hence, in the Middle Ages whenever we find a similarity between the practices of Passover and Easter—if one is not dealing with an ancient tradition—it almost certainly derives from Christian influence on Judaism, and not the other way around.[8]

Moreover, during the Middle Ages the two holidays, Passover and Easter, were often a time for outbursts of hatred and of libels against the Jews. We have already discussed the libels of ritual murder ("blood libels"), and shall discuss their connection with Passover below. But the notable innovation of the thirteenth century was the emergence of the libel concerning the desecration of the Host.[9] In this chapter, I wish to elucidate the ritual background for the appearance of this libel, without denigrating the accepted scholarly explanations connecting the struggle over the principle of transubstantiation (the transformation of the Host to the body of Jesus) and the aspiration to receive Jewish confirmation for the sanctity of the Host. Behind the accusations that the Jews were desecrating the Host was Christianity's need to obtain the infidel's admission of this miraculous occurrence, which many Christians had trouble believing. The libel of the desecration of the Host is an extension of the libel of ritual murder, because the logic of the principle of transubstantiation implies that the Jew did not

---

8. To me the answer to the question about the extent to which Jews in Europe were aware of Christian rituals seems quite clear: for one thing, there is great similarity between the ceremonies, as described below. Therefore, the burden of proof falls on anyone who would argue the opposite point of view. For more expressions of intimate knowledge of Christian ritual see, for example, *Tosafot* to b. Abod. Zar. 2a; Israel Yuval, "An Appeal Against the Proliferation of Divorce in Fifteenth Century Germany" [in Hebrew], *Zion* 48 (1983): 181 n.16; and cf. Ivan G. Marcus, "Jews and Christians Imagining the Other in Medieval Europe," *Prooftexts* 15 (1995): 220–22.

9. P. Browe, "Die Hostienschändungen der Juden im Mittelalter," *Römische Quartalschrift* 34 (1926): 167–97; F. Lotter, "Hostienfrevelvorwurf und Blutwunderfälschungen bei den Judenverfolgungen von 1298 ('Rintfleisch') und 1336–338 ('Armleder')," in *Fälschungen im Mittelalter* (Hannover, 1998), 533–83; M. Rubin, "Desecration of the Host: The Birth of an Accusation," in *Christianity and Judaism,* ed. D. Wood, (Oxford, 1992), 169–85; C. Cluse, "Blut ist im Schuh. Ein Exempel zur Judenverfolgung des 'Rex Armleder,'" in *Liber amicorum necnon et amicarum für Alfred Heid,* ed. F. Burgard, C. Cluse and A. Haverkamp (Trier, 1996), 371–92.

require a flesh-and-blood Christian; all he needed to do was to stab the Host or to dip it in boiling water.

This chapter is not intended to reject these explanations, but rather to augment them with another dimension that demonstrates the principle of mutuality in the relations between Jews and Christians. I assume that the Christians charged Jews with desecrating the Host, among other reasons, because they saw in certain Jewish ceremonies a partial or indirect confirmation of the Christian accusations against them. This is not merely a theological polemic, but a dialogue of ceremonial language, in which the ceremonial act conveys different meanings. The Passover ceremonies are the "body language" of the Jewish-Christian polemic, and exposure of the hidden meanings of that language may help us penetrate the world of shared images in the Middle Ages. This chapter is thus a continuation of the previous one, which attempted to propose a new perspective on the libel of ritual murder. Its purpose is to better understand how both hatred and libels were engendered by a world of shared images. Ultimately, hatred is also a form of dialogue, and similarity can elicit competition and misunderstanding. Our discussion will thus focus first on exposing the similarity between the two holidays to facilitate perception of the polemic messages implicit in some of its ceremonies, whether or not these messages are deliberate or distorted by the other side.

I shall begin with the "Great Sabbath"—a kind of miniholiday preceding Passover, in which we find a certain similarity to a parallel concept in Christianity. The history of the Jewish "Great Sabbath" clearly illustrates the close relations—of both attraction and repulsion—between Passover and Easter.

THE GREAT SABBATH

The term the "Great Sabbath" *(Shabbat ha-Gadol),* indicates different things in Judaism and Christianity, and much ink has been devoted to its source and its meaning.[10] The earliest mention is in John 19:31. The Jews ask Pi-

---

10. On the affinity between the Great Sabbath in Judaism and in Christianity, see L. A. Hoffman, "The Jewish Lectionary, the Great Sabbath, and the Lenten Calendar," in *Time and Community in Honor of Thomas Julian Talley,* ed. J. Neil Alexander (Washington, 1992), 3–20 (and earlier literature listed in the bibliography there); M. Sharon, "The 'Grand Sabbath' in an Epitaph from Ramlah" [in Hebrew], *Shalem* 1 (1974): 1–14 (the inscription published there is undoubtedly Christian). Additional literature is listed in J. Tabory, *Mo'adei Yisrael beteku*

late to break the thighs of the three crucified men so that they may die while it is still daytime and be taken down from the cross before the Sabbath, "(for that Sabbath was a high day)." The designation of that Sabbath as "(a high [or great] day)" only appears in John, and it corresponds to his view that the Crucifixion of Jesus occurred on the eve of the Passover (fourteenth day of Nissan), which was a Friday, so that the first day of Passover fell on the Sabbath. *Great* or *high* are thus synonyms for *festival day*. In the three Synoptic Gospels, by contrast, because the Crucifixion takes place on the fifteenth of Nissan, there is nothing unique about the Sabbath that follows, so they do not use the word *great* in referring to that Sabbath.

John uses the adjective *great* once more to refer to the seventh day of Sukkoth: "On the last day of the feast, the great day, Jesus stood up and proclaimed, 'If any one thirst, let him come to me and drink. He who believes in me, as the scripture has said, "Out of his heart shall flow rivers of living water"' (John 7:37–38)[11]—a declaration that was interpreted as alluding to his messianic nature (John: 7:40–52). The accepted Jewish name for that day is *Hosha'na Rabbah* (the "Great Hosanna"), a name first mentioned in amoraic sources.[12] The fact that the two earliest references to the "great day" are found in John and that both refer to a date with messianic meaning—the first day of Passover and the last day of Sukkoth (according to Zechariah 14, the eschatological Day of the Lord is connected with Sukkoth)—suggests that, even if the term *great* may designate any holiday, John lends it messianic meaning. It is difficult to know exactly whether this interpretation is his own invention or whether he used a common messianic homily and applied it to Jesus.

---

fat ha-Mishnah veha-Talmud (Jerusalem, 1995), 127–28 n. 186. It is told of the martyr Pionius that he was executed in Smyrna on the "Great Sabbath," in late February 250. The Jews of that city also attended his execution, and according to R. Fox the incident must have happened on Purim or on the Sabbath of Remembrance. The martyr Polycarp was executed on exactly the same date in 155: see R. L. Fox, *Pagans and Christians,* (Suffolk, 1986), 486ff. The authors of the *Martyrdom of Polycarp* and the *Acts of Pionius* sought to attribute an eschatological meaning to the deaths of these saints, and the notation of the time as the "Great Sabbath" alludes to the parallel death and resurrection of Jesus. Hence, it seems that mention of the time as the "Great Sabbath" refers to Easter. See R. Cacitti, *Grande Sabato. Il contesto pasquale quartodecimano nella formazione della teologia del martirio* (Milan, 1994).

11. John 7:37. The image of water is thus connected with the fact that on the festival of Sukkoth judgment is passed regarding water (*m. Rosh Hashanah* 1.2).

12. See *Midrash Tehillim* 17.5 (in one MS. only). The common name in the literature of the Talmudic and in Gaonic literature is "the seventh day of the willow branch" or simply "the day of the willow."

This interpretation is conventionally connected to the "great" day in Malachi 3:23: "Behold, I will send you Elijah the prophet before the great and terrible day of the Lord comes."[13] On the eve of Passover, Jews anticipate the coming of Elijah, the herald of deliverance,[14] in whose wake will come the "great" day, the day of Redemption, and the dead will rise from their graves.[15] This typological order of things fits the Exodus from Egypt: on the fourteenth day of Nissan the destroyer passed through and smote the firstborn of Egypt, and the next day they were delivered and departed from Egypt. The importance of the words the "great day" in connection with Passover is also indicated by the "Midrash" in the Passover Haggadah, which concludes with the words "blood and fire and pillars of smoke," to mark the plagues of Egypt (Joel 3:3); that same verse continues: "Before the great and the terrible day of the Lord comes" (Joel 3:4).[16]

Thus, in early Christianity, the "Great Sabbath" was the name for the Saturday before Easter.[17] For the Quartodecimani in the East, who celebrated Easter on the fourteenth day of Nissan, Easter did not fall on a fixed day of the week; according to the custom of the Western Church, the holiday was always celebrated on Sunday, a practice that became obligatory after the Nicean Council. This created a fixed weekly cycle, as a result of which the "Great Sabbath" became *Sabbatum Sanctum,* and the adjective *great* was assigned to the week preceding Easter *(Hebdomada major* or *Septimana major),* beginning with Palm Sunday. First testimonies of this appear in John Chrysostom[18] and in the writings of the traveler Egeria, who arrived in Jerusalem in 383. The latter relates that the week before Easter was called the "great week" in Jerusalem, and that it began with the Saturday of Lazarus, on which they would "proclaim Easter."[19]

Unlike the frequent usages of the term the "Great Sabbath" or the "great

13. And Joel 3:4; Hos 2:3. And cf., Ps 126:2–3.

14. Cf. Matt 27:47–49.

15. The haftarah for the Intermediate Sabbath of Passover is the "vision of the dry bones" (Ezek 37). See below.

16. See chapter 2, the text referring to n. 123.

17. The Sabbath before the resurrection is also called the "Great Sabbath" in *Apostolic Constitution,* B.5.18.

18. Sermon on Psalms 145:2.

19. John Wilkinson, trans., ed., *Egeria's Travels* (London, 1971), 132, para. 30, sec. 1). On the development of Palm Sunday and the "great week," see *Realenzyklopädie für protestantische Theologie und Kirche,* XXI (Leipzig, 1908), 414ff; T. J. Talley, *The Origins of the Liturgical Year* (New York, 1986), 42–47, 176–83.

week" in Christian sources, in Jewish literature there is no mention of the Great Sabbath throughout the first millennium C.E. Yet there may be an indirect refutation of the "great day" of the Christians in a Midrashic homily for the Sabbath before the New Moon of Nissan *(Shabbat ha-Hodesh)*, based on Exodus 12:3, which discusses the taking of a lamb on the tenth day of Nissan, to be "kept" until the fourteenth day of Nissan, when it was to be offered as a sacrifice:

> Who will take your recompense with Edom? *Natruna*[20] [the Supreme Guardian]: "And He shall be unto you a guard [against Esau]" (Exod 12:6). Of Esau, the Holy One said: His father called him great: "Isaac . . . called Esau his great son" (Gen 27:1); and his mother called him great, "Rebekkah took the garments of Esau her son, the great one" (Gen 27:15). Nevertheless, I call him small: "Behold I make thee small among the nations" (Obad 1:2). Still, seeing that his father and mother call Esau great, I shall see to it that the size of the slaughterer is in keeping with the size of the ox: "the Lord hath a sacrifice in Bozrah, and a great slaughter in the land of Edom" (Isa 34:6). That is, according to R. Berechiah, the slaughterer in the land of Edom—Esau will be the Great One. [God Himself][21]

20. "The Watchman," alluding to the Messiah. Lieberman thinks that *Natruna* is "that which is watched," and is a pun on Shahpur I, king of Persia, on whom hope for Redemption was pinned. See "Palestine in the Third and Fourth Centuries," *JQR*, 37 (1946): 34. But see also Isa 21:11–12; Zvi M. Rabinovitz, *Mahzor Piyyutei Rabbi Yannai le-Torah vela-Mo'adim* (Jerusalem, 1985), 1:299: "The guard said, I will watch for the End." It follows from this that Isaiah 21:11 was one of the haftarot read on one of the two Sabbaths before Passover (below). Cf. 303: "Tread out the vineyards as the guard who asks, 'What of the night.' He cried out like a guard and said, 'The morning comes, and also the night,'" referring to the messianic revenge upon Edom by the Messiah. And perhaps the "Guard" is the Jewish answer to the Christian vigil on the night before the celebration of the Resurrection at Easter. This competition is also indicated by the opening homilies of *Pesiqta de Rav Kahana* for the Sabbath of "and it came to pass at midnight," ed. Dov Mandelbaum (New York, 1962), 1.

21. *Pesiqta de Rav Kahana*, end of *Ha-hodesh ha-zeh*, 107–8 (English translation: W. G. Braude and I. J. Kapstein [Philadelphia, 1968], chap. 5, 120–21); and compare parallels in *Pesiqta Rabbati*, ed. M. Ish Shalom (Vienna, 1880), 79a; and cf. *Pesiqta de Rav Kahana*, 103–4 (English: 116): 'Esau who is large reckons by the sun which is large . . . As long as the light of the larger luminary shines in the world, the light of the lesser one is not noticeable; but when the light of the larger one declines, the light of the lesser one becomes noticeable. Even so, as long as the light of Esau shines brightly in the world, the light of Jacob cannot be made out." This Midrashic notion of "measure for measure" concerning the "Great Day" has biblical roots; see Joel 2:20–21.

Since this was a sermon for a Sabbath close to Passover, it may allude to a quarrel with the Christian exegesis of the "great" day.[22] This assumption is supported by the Palestinian custom of reading Isaiah 34:5 ("For my sword has drunk its fill in the heavens; behold, it descends for judgment upon Edom") as haftarah for the Sabbath before Passover.[23] This chapter of Isaiah deals with the eschatological vengeance on Edom ("For the Lord has a day of vengeance, a year of recompense for the cause of Zion"—34:8) and centers on the verse "a great slaughter in the land of Edom" mentioned in this sermon. The sermon counterpoises the "Great Week" against the "great slaughter" in the land of Edom, thereby becoming part of the developing tradition that embellishes the vengeful redemption in the liturgical poems of Passover, as mentioned in chapter 2.

Another Palestinian custom was to read Isaiah 21:11 ("The oracle concerning Dumah"), a passage that likewise opens with a prophecy about Edom, as haftarah for the Sabbath before Passover.[24] Rabbi Meir's Bible manuscript read, instead of the "burden of Dumah," "the burden of Rumah"—an allusion to Rome.[25] This prophecy mentions the watchman: "'Watchman, what of the night? Watchman, what of the night?' The watch-

22. This interpretation of the Midrash is compatible with the conclusions of L. Venetianer, "Ursprung und Bedeutung der Propheten-Lektionen," *Zeitschrift der Deutschen Morgenländischen Gesellschaft* 63 (1909): 103–70. The author raises a series of fascinating conjectures—even though some of them are rather weak—claiming that the haftarot for the special Sabbaths reflect the Jewish-Christian polemic during the first centuries C.E. More than he succeeds in proving this claim, he highlights several exegeses in *Pesiqta de Rav Kahana* (and in *Pesiqta Rabbati*) as alluding to the covert competition with the reading of the Holy Scriptures that was practiced in the Western Church. Many of his facts are erroneous, particularly since his article was written before the discoveries from the Cairo Genizah concerning the practices of Torah reading and haftarot. But contemporary scholarship seems to have ignored this seminal article. For more on the article and its conclusions, see E. Werner, *The Sacred Bridge* (New York, 1959), 1:77–101.

23. This haftarah was first noted by N. Fried, "Alternative Haftarot in Yannai's *Piyyutim* and in Other Ancient *Paytanim*" [in Hebrew], *Sinai* 62 (1968): 131. It was also noted by Ezra Fleischer, "Piyyut and Prayer in *Mahzor Eretz Yisrael*—The Geniza Codex "[in Hebrew], *Kiryat Sefer* 63 (1990): 240 n. 190. Fried was also the one to discover that on the Intermediate Sabbath of Sukkoth it was the custom to read Malachi 3; see his article, "Notes to A. Yaari's Studies on the *Mi sheberakh* Prayers" [in Hebrew], *Kiryat Sefer* 37 (1962): 514 n. 17; and similarly Fleischer, "The Reading of the Portion '*Asser Te'asser*' (Deut. 14:22)" [in Hebrew], *Tarbiz* 36 (1967): 116–55.

24. Fried, "Alternative Haftarot," and subsequently Fleischer, "Piyyut and Prayer," 240–42.

25. *j. Ta'an.* 64a (1.1).

man says: 'Morning comes, and also the night'" (Isa 21:11–12)—an echo of the *Naturna* mentioned in the earlier homily. According to several Palestinian customs, the Torah reading for that Sabbath was the portion that begins "And it came to pass at midnight" (Exod 12:29)—on which the homilies in *Pesiqta de Rab Kahana* and *Pesiqta Rabbati* are based.[26] These homilies involve a clear attempt to create a typological affinity between the plagues that befell the Egyptians and the destruction of Edom at the End of Days.[27] The preacher turns the plagues of Egypt into a metaphor for the apocalyptic war:

> Rabbi Levi ben Zechariah taught in the name of Rabbi Berechiah: [God] set upon the Egyptians with the tactics of warrior kings. First, He shut off their water conduits,[28] then He brought loud voices to confuse them,[29] after that He shot arrows at them,[30] then He brought legions upon them,[31] then He brought confusion upon them,[32] after that He flung burning stuff upon them,[33] then He shot stones at them from catapults,[34] after that He arrayed the scalers of walls against them,[35] after that He placed them in prisons,[36] and finally He led forth each and every one of the most cherished among them [i.e., the eldest among them] and slew him.[37]

What we have here is a schematic description of the normal moves of war. The "great" killing reminds us of the previous sermon—and indeed, immediately thereafter the exegesis continues with an analogy between Egypt and Edom:

> R. Levi said in the name of R. Hama bar Hanina: With the very means by which He punished the former He will punish the latter. As He pun-

---

26. This is another of Fried's discoveries (n. 23, p. 213), which Fleischer repeats (n. 23, p. 213).

27. *Pesiqta de Rav Kahana* (n. 21, p. 212), 132–34 (Eng.: 151).

28. Allusion to blood.

29. Allusion to frogs.

30. Allusion to vermin.

31. Allusion to wild animals.

32. Allusion to cattle disease.

33. Allusion to boils.

34. Allusion to hail.

35. Allusion to locusts.

36. Allusion to darkness.

37. Allusion to death of the firstborn.

ished Egypt with blood, so too He will punish Edom [Rome], for it is written, "I will shew wonders in the heavens and in the earth, blood, and fire, and pillars of smoke [over Edom]" (Joel 3:3). . . . As with Egypt He took each of the chiefest among them and slew them, so too with Edom: "A great slaughter in the land of Edom, among them to come down shall be the Re'emim [wild gazelle]" (Isa 34:6–7). That is, as R. Meir expounded it: among those to come down shall be the Romans. [preeminent among all the people of Edom]

The preacher homiletically interprets the word *re'emim* (wild gazelle) as if it were derived from the word *ramim*—"high," "great." To understand the full structure of his sermon, we must return to the previous verse: "For the Lord has a sacrifice in Bozrah, a great slaughter in the land of Edom" (Isa 34:6). The choice of these verses is not at all accidental, since they constitute the customary haftarah read for that Sabbath.[38] In other words, this sermon, like the previous one, tends to see the plague of the firstborn as a "great" punishment that befalls those who think of themselves as "great," just as the firstborn is great. As we know, Jesus was thought to be "great,"[39] so that the timing of this sermon for the Sabbath before the Christian "great" week begs for interpretation. It follows, that in Midrashic and liturgical literature, the "Great Sabbath" was a notion to be struggled with, since it reflects the arrogance of the heretical kingdom and its most important holiday. The Jewish polemic is based on confrontation with the Christian "Great Sabbath" and its denial, not on its adoption.

The liturgical poems for this Sabbath also provide the first indications of the custom of preaching about the laws of the holiday before its celebration. The recently published *Eretz-Yisrael Mahzor* from the Cairo Genizah[40] contains a *kerovah* by Rabbi Shlomo Suleiman, *Pela'ot sharu*, intended for one of the two Sabbaths preceding Passover.[41] The poet addresses the congregation, inviting them to listen to his sermon ("draw here and listen to the word of the Lord"), but he is concerned not with the laws of the festi-

---

38. The preacher presents these ten verses to prove that the plagues of Egypt will also be the lot of Edom. Four of them are taken from the haftarah in Isaiah 34.

39. Luke 1:32; Heb 1:3–4.

40. Joseph Yahalom, ed., *Mahzor Eretz-Yisrael: Kodex Ha-Genizah* (Jerusalem, 1986), 5.

41. Fleischer (n. 23, p. 213), 235–42. Fleischer assumed that the Sabbath was the "Great Sabbath," whose ancient existence seemed obvious to him. But in n. 185 he raises the possibility that the *kerovah* was said on the "fifth Sabbath," that is, the first one during the month

val, but with the miracles of the Exodus. In another liturgical poem for that Sabbath by Rabbi Chananel ben Amnon,[42] an Italian liturgical poet from the second half of the eleventh century,[43] a broad sweep of the laws of Passover is presented in rhyme, similar to the well-known *kerovah* by Rabbi Joseph Bonfils of France, *Elohim be-tza'adkha*, also of the eleventh century. Rabbi Chananel ben Amnon's *piyyut* (section 5) is concerned with Hosea 1–2 and the three children the prophet sired with a loose woman: Jezreel, Lo-Ruhamah, Lo-Ammi. The poem is intended to show that, even if God chastens his people and punishes them, he will ultimately redeem and save them. The poem opens with the taking of the lamb on the tenth day of Nissan and an allusion to the ten plagues—the model for future Redemption, and it concludes with the same subject: "He smote the taskmasters on the tenth." The poet's main interest in Hosea 1–2 apparently stems from the end of the prophecy, in which Hosea moves from rebuke to solace: "Then the people of Judah and the people of Israel shall be gathered together, and they shall appoint for themselves one head; and they shall go up from the land, for great shall be the day of Jezreel" (Hos 1:11). The poet concludes his treatment of Hosea with this verse and with the punishment of the Gentile nations: "Those who smash my corner shall be punished, to be made disgusting with the venom of my wrath, for Great will be the day of Jezreel." It seems that one of his main objectives was to use the adjective *great* in the liturgical poem for the Sabbath before Passover. If this is so, then we have here the first vague mention of the word *great* in connection with the Sabbath before Passover. Thus, the origin of the term *Shabbat ha-Gadol* (the Great Sabbath) is to be sought in Italy, where many Ashkenazic practices originated.

And, in fact, the earliest evidence of Jewish use of the term *Shabbat ha-Gadol* is from the twelfth century[44]—a thousand years after it entered standard use in Christianity. Leopold Zunz has conjectured that the Jews

of Nissan (following the four special Sabbaths of Adar: *Shekalim, Zakhor, Parah, Ha-Hodesh*), rather than the "sixth Sabbath," which is equivalent to the "Great Sabbath."

42. Israel Davidson, "The 'Seder Hibbur Berakot,'" *JQR* 21 (1931): 256–66. In the title of the liturgical poem, the editor noted "for the Great Sabbath," assuming that name was already in use.

43. Davidson, "The 'Seder Hibbur Berakot,'" 259–60 n. 11.

44. Haim Karlinsky, "The Midrashic Sources for the Name Shabbat Hagadol" [in Hebrew], *Or Ha-Mizrah* 18 (1969): 172–79; A. Hilvitz, *Hikrei Zemanim* (Jerusalem, 1981), 2:27–40.

adopted the term from the Christian milieu.[45] During the course of its Judaization, the "Great Sabbath" became the name of the Sabbath preceding Passover, not that of Passover itself, as in John. The possibility that it was in fact an ancient Jewish tradition that enjoyed a covert existence for a thousand years until it came to light in Ashkenazic literature is fairly slim, especially since as soon as the "Great Sabbath" was incorporated into Ashkenazic literature, it was mentioned frequently in every work concerning the laws and customs of Passover.

Mahzor Vitry, a liturgical work from the circle of Rashi, portrays the circumstances of the appearance of the "Great Sabbath" in the Ashkenazic world: "And the Sabbath before Passover is known among the people as 'the Great Sabbath,' and they do not know why, since it is no greater than any other Sabbath."[46] This is proof that the name "Great Sabbath" was first adopted on the popular level and made its way from there to the world of halakhah. The explanation offered in Ashkenazic halakhic literature of this Sabbath's name connects it with Exodus 12:3–6 and the obligation to set aside the Paschal Lamb on the tenth day of Nissan. According to Talmudic tradition, the Passover observed in Egypt took place on a Thursday (the fifteenth day of Nissan); hence, the tenth day of Nissan was the Sabbath.[47] In the sermon for the Sabbath before Passover, the *Pesiqta* collections bring a legend concerning the fear felt by the firstborn Egyptians, who demanded that their fathers expel the Israelites from Egypt before the plague of the firstborn takes place; but their fathers refused: "Immediately the first-born went out and slew sixty myriads of their fathers."[48] The preacher relates this Haggadah to Psalms 136:10: "'To Him who smote Egypt with their firstborn'—Scripture does not say here 'to Him who smote the first-born of Egypt in Egypt' but rather 'to Him that smote Egypt with *their own* first-born.'" The legend does not state when this deed was done, and ostensibly there is no link between it and the Sabbath preceding Passover. The first time we hear of such a link is in the words of the Tosaphists,

---

45. L. Zunz, *Der Ritus des synagogalen Gottesdienstes* (Berlin, 1919), 10. On the other hand, A. Jellinek and S. Zeitlin thought that the "Great Sabbath" was common among Jews already at the time of Christianity's inception; see the discussion in Hoffman (n. 10, p. 209), 6–8.

46. Simha ben Samuel, *Mahzor Vitry,* ed. S. Hurwitz (Berlin, 1893; repr. Jerusalem, 1963), 222, and in the parallel literature of the school of Rashi cited there.

47. *b. Shab.* 87b.

48. *Pesiqta de Rav Kahana* (n. 21, p. 212), "And it came to pass at midnight," 129 and parallels.

elaborating on the Talmudic statement that the Exodus occurred on a Thursday:[49]

> If so, they must have slaughtered their paschal lambs on Wednesday, and they must have taken their lambs on the prior Sabbath, which would have been the tenth of the month. Therefore it is called "the Great Sabbath," for on it a great miracle occurred, as we learn from the Midrash: When the Israelites took their paschal lambs on that Sabbath, the firstborn of the nations [i.e., the Egyptians] assembled and asked the Israelites why they were doing this. They responded that it was a Passover offering to God, because He was going to kill the firstborn of Egypt. They went to their fathers and to Pharaoh to ask that he send Israel away, and when they refused the firstborn waged war and killed many of them.[50]

Is the connection between the war of the firstborn in Egypt and *Shabbat ha-Gadol* an invention of the Tosaphists? It is difficult to decide. True, there is no hint in the relevant Midrashim that this battle took place on the Sabbath before the Passover, on the day the lamb was taken. Nevertheless, the legend is presented as a homily for the Sabbath whose Torah reading starts with the verse "and it came to pass at midnight" (Ex 12:29), which is before Passover. It is also alluded to in Yannai's liturgical poem *Onai Fitrei*,[51] which is also for that Sabbath. Moreover, in the above-mentioned liturgical poem of Rabbi Shlomo Suleiman—also for that Sabbath—allusion is made to Psalms 131:10 ("To Him that smote Egypt in their firstborn"), which is the prooftext for this legend. It follows from all this that there is some sort of connection between the legend and the Sabbath before Passover.

Another version of the miracle that happened on the "Great Sabbath" is found in *Siddur Rashi*.[52] The Egyptians wished to punish the Israelites because they intended to slaughter the sacrificial lamb "an abomination to

49. For a discussion of these sources, see M. Kasher, *Haggadah Sheleimah* (Jerusalem, 1967), 50–54.

50. *Tosafot* at *b. Shabb.* 87b, s.v. *ve-oto;* and in nearly identical wording in *Sefer Rabyah,* vol. 2, ed. V. Aptowitzer (Jerusalem, 1964; photo ed. New York, 1983) 2:58–59. Rabbi Ephraim of Bonn referred to this in A. M. Haberman, ed., *Sefer Zekhirah—Selihot ve-Kinot* (Jerusalem, 1970), 35, regarding the outbreak of the pogrom in York in 1190 "on the Great Sabbath and at the time of the miracle." The miracle referred to here is not the Exodus from Egypt, as thought by the editor, but the war of the firstborn in Egypt "on the Great Sabbath."

51. Rabinovitz (n. 20, p. 212), 1:297 ("the impure ones you set one against the other").

52. *Siddur Rashi,* ed. S. Buber and J. Freimann (Berlin, 1911), sec. 352; cf. parallel texts from the school of Rashi, from which later Ashkenazic *minhag* literature copied it; see *Sefer*

Egypt": "When the Egyptian saw [that each person had taken his lamb to be slaughtered] they sought to exact vengeance on them, but their intestines became inflamed [an allusion to Psalms 118:12], and faded away with fire, and they were stricken with sufferings and dire and bitter diseases, and could do Israel no harm. And because miracles were done for Israel on the Sabbath before Passover, it is called the Great Sabbath."

Both explanations see the "Great Sabbath" not merely as a name, but also as an occasion with a unique character. Parallel to the acceptance of the name in Franco-Germany and the establishment of the story that determines its uniqueness, one may also discern the shaping of certain ceremonial characteristics intended to endow this Sabbath with the character of a "special" Sabbath heralding the festival. Thus, there developed in Ashkenaz the institution of the rabbi's *Shabbat ha-Gadol* sermon which, along with the sermon on *Shabbat Shuvah* (the Sabbath of Repentance, between Rosh Hashanah and Yom Kippur), was a central component of the Ashkenazic rabbinate's activity during the Middle Ages.[53] Special liturgical poems were also introduced to be recited on that Sabbath, some of which included rhymed presentations of the laws of Passover,[54] and at the afternoon service it was customary to read the Passover Haggadah.[55] The uniqueness of this Sabbath was also expressed by the newly introduced custom of reading as haftarah chapter 3 of Malachi, which concludes with mention of the expectation of the coming of Elijah "before the great and terrible day of the Lord comes"—an expectation that suits the date of that Sabbath. Hence, in Ashkenaz the "Great Sabbath" was granted the same status as the four special Sabbaths of the month of Adar.

Before discussing this haftarah in greater detail, we must first discuss the date of the Jewish "Great Sabbath," which, unlike the tradition in John, is not the Sabbath of Passover but that which precedes it. The *Tosafoth* indicate that in Ashkenaz the "Great Sabbath" was identified with the date of the "taking" of the sacrificial lamb that occurred on the tenth day of Nis-

---

Minhagim of R. Abraham Klausner, ed. Y. Y. Dissin (Jerusalem, 1978), sec. 89, 84); and *Sefer Maharil*, ed. S. J. Spitzer (Jerusalem, 1989), *Hilkhot Shabbat ha-Gadol*, 52–53.

53. *Sefer Maharil*, 8–11 (sermons for *Shabbat ha-Gadol*); and cf. I. J. Yuval, *Hakhamim bedoram* (Jerusalem, 1989), 37–38, 105, 109, 123, 171.

54. *Sefer Maharil* (n. 52, p. 218), 51; *Sefer ha-Minhagim le-Kehillat Kodesh Worms le-Rabbi Yushpa Shamash*, ed. B. S. Hamburger and Y. Zimmer (Jerusalem, 1988), 1:80.

55. *Sefer Rabyah* (n. 50, p. 218): "The children were accustomed to reading the Haggadah in advance, during the daytime of the Great Sabbath"; R. Solomon Luria, *Teshuvot Maharshal* (Lemberg, 1859), sec. 88.

san, in accordance with the Talmudic tradition that the Exodus (on the fifteenth of Nissan) took place on a Thursday. Yet the Talmudic discussion also mentions a different tradition, that of *Seder 'Olam Rabbah*,[56] according to which the Exodus was on Friday; hence, the tenth day of Nissan fell on a Sunday.

Just as the Sages were meticulous about the chronology of the "great" week when the Israelites came out of Egypt, so were the early Christians meticulous about the chronology of the "great" week during which Jesus was crucified. According to the Synoptic Gospels, the Crucifixion occurred on Friday, the fifteenth day of Nissan, whereas the Johannine Gospel places the Crucifixion on a Friday that coincided with the fourteenth of Nissan. John's date grants the Crucifixion a status parallel to that of the offering of the Paschal Lamb on the fourteenth of Nissan, whereas the Synoptic Gospels grant the Last Supper the status of a Passover meal, and hence they postponed the Crucifixion to the fifteenth of Nissan. It follows from their calculation that the Sunday of the week of the Crucifixion was the tenth day of Nissan, the date of the "taking" of the sacrificial Paschal Lamb in Egypt. In line with the Synoptic chronology, during the fourth century Palm Sunday started to be observed, and Jesus's entry into Jerusalem acquired a status corresponding to that of the biblical preparation and setting aside of the Paschal Lamb until its sacrifice (Exod 12:6). Even earlier, in the third century, another custom began to develop: fasting before Easter for six days, beginning on Monday, rather than for only one or two days.[57] The expla-

---

56. *b. Shabb.* 88a; *Seder 'Olam Rabbah*, chap. 5.

57. This is implied by two sources from the third century that specify a six-day fast prior to Easter: Dionysus of Alexandria, *Letter to Basilides*, 1, and *Didascalia Apostolorum*, 21. According to the *Didascalia*, the day of "taking" and watching of the biblical lamb—the tenth day of Nissan—was also the day when Judas Iscariot was given payment for betraying Jesus, which fell on a Monday. This calculation is compatible with the date given by the Johannine Gospel for the Crucifixion. For these two sources, see Cantalamessa (n. 6, p. 207) sec. 49, 61; sec. 86, 82–83. *Didascalia* says that the significance of the tenth of Nissan as the beginning of the fast also stems from the fact that Jesus's name starts with the letter J, the tenth letter, "and it is not a holiday, as in the ancient custom, but is a fast according to the New Testament." See A. Strobel, *Ursprung und Geschichte des frühchristlichen Osterkalenders* (Berlin, 1977), 334–36. Strobel assumed that these words alluded to the ancient practice that was widespread among Jewish Christian to celebrate the "Great Sabbath." Indeed, the Samaritans begin the celebration of Passover by watching over the sacrificial animal, beginning from the tenth of Nissan. However, since we do not know of any such custom among the Jews, we can interpret *Didascalia* as relating to the biblical description of the Exodus from Egypt and the com-

nation given for this expansion of the fast refers to Exodus 12:3. The taking of the sacrificial lamb and its watching from the tenth day of Nissan, four days before its slaughter, is the typological model for fixing Monday of the "great week" as the beginning of the fast. This calculation is compatible with John's chronology, but not with that of the Synoptic Gospels.

In light of all this, the Talmudic tradition stating that the Exodus occurred on a Thursday takes on new meaning. Two of the traditions—that of the Synoptic Gospels, which sets the Crucifixion on Friday, the fifteenth of Nissan, and that of the Talmud, which fixes the Exodus on Thursday, the fifteenth day of Nissan—yield one clear fact: the tenth day of Nissan, the date of the "taking" of the sacrificial lamb in Egypt, falls on Sunday according to the Christian tradition, and on Saturday according to the Jewish tradition. In other words, the Sabbath preceding Passover is a natural candidate to play a role analogous to that of Palm Sunday. Hence, the Midrash quoted above concerning the "great" Esau, who is to be punished with a "great" slaughter is based on Exodus 12:3, which discusses the taking of the lamb on the tenth day of Nissan—the typological date of Palm Sunday (see table).

To summarize, both in the Talmudic tradition and in the Synoptic Gospels—the basis for the liturgy of the "Great Week"—we find a calculation of times that served as the basis for an "expanded" celebration of Passover. This calculation starts with the beginning of the holy week, and the two traditions are divided only on the question of when that week begins, on Saturday or on Sunday. Both traditions contain only a hint of that calculation. The Gospels do not indicate that the day of Jesus's entry into Jerusalem was a Sunday, and in the Talmud there is no mention of the "Great Sabbath."

Thus far, the assumption that the Ashkenazic "Great Sabbath" is a later development under Christian influence is no more than conjecture.[58] The

---

mandment to set aside the sacrificial animal in advance, an occasion that was considered a holiday. Epiphanius also testifies to the six-day fast (Cantalamessa [n. 6, p. 207], sec. 66, 74). See *The Panarion of St. Epiphanius, Bishop of Salamis*, sec. 50, 3, 4; selected passages translated by Philip Amidon (New York, 1990), 176.

58. The Ashkenazic system raises another serious difficulty concerning the date of Shavu'ot. Everyone agrees that the Torah was given on the Sabbath (*b. Shabb.* 86b), but the Sages and Rabbi Jose disagreed whether the date was the sixth day of Sivan, as the Sages thought, or the seventh day of Sivan, as Rabbi Jose thought. According to the calculation that the tenth day of Nissan was a Sabbath, it follows that, since the Torah was given on the Sabbath, it must have been the seventh day of Sivan rather than the sixth of Sivan, as commonly thought. This

The Month of Nissan—The "Great Week"

	Saturday	Sunday	Monday	Tuesday	Wednesday	Thursday	Friday	Saturday	Sunday
John and Didascalia	8	9	10 Beginning of the fast	11	12	13 Sacrifice of Egypt	14 Crucifixion	15 Great Sabbath	16 Resurrection
Synoptic Gospels and Liturgy	9 Sabbath of Lazarus	10 Palm Sunday	11	12	13	14 Last Supper	15 Crucifixion	16 *Sabbatum Sanctum*	17 Resurrection
Seder Olam Rabbah	9	10 Taking of the sacrificial lamb	11	12	13	14 Sacrifice of Egypt	15 Exodus from Egypt		
Babylonian Talmud, *Shabbat 87* and Ashkenazic custom	10 Taking of the sacrificial lamb Great Sabbath	11	12	13	14 Sacrifice of Egypt	15 Exodus from Egypt			

Talmudic source of the "Great Sabbath" is at most a matter of calculation, but the Talmud itself makes no mention of the uniqueness of that Sabbath. Nor is the "Great Sabbath" included in the ancient lists of prophetic readings (haftarot) for the special Sabbaths of the year. The hypothesis that the "Great Sabbath" emerged in Ashkenaz through an act of absorbing Christian chronology clearly explains the problems of introducing a special haftarah for that Sabbath. A full discussion of this problem is quoted in the halakhic work *Or Zaru'a* by Rabbi Isaac of Vienna (in the first half of the thirteenth century), which I cite here in full:

> It is written in the responsa: Why did they not cease [reading as haftarah] *Oloteikhem*[59] and [in its stead] make it customary to read *Ve-Arvah la-Shem*?[60] Might it be because the conclusion of *Ve-Arvah* is the "great and awesome" day of judgment,[61] and hence they did not make it customary to read as haftarah *Ve-Arvah*?

> But I, Menahem,[62] have a different opinion regarding *Ve-Arvah;* and in order to support the custom of our ancestors, which is like Torah, who served the great ones of the generation, and I see their words as correct. And I say, that when the 14th of Nissan falls on the Sabbath, it is impossible to recite the haftarah [containing the words], "For I did not speak to your fathers or command them [concerning burnt offerings and sacrifices]"[63] on the day when they slaughter the Passover sacrifice, about which it is written, "in its proper time."[64] Nor can one recite on the day of slaughtering the Paschal offering "Cut off your hair and cast it away, raise a lamentation on the bare heights"[65] on the Sabbath which is the eve of Passover, and [thereby] distress the hearts of Israel who are making

---

dilemma was noted by Rabbi Yaakov Reisha in his book *Hok Ya'akov,* commenting on *Shulhan 'Arukh, Orah Hayyim* 430.2.

59. Jer. 7:21: "add your burnt-offerings"—the opening words of the haftarah for the Torah portion of *Tzav.*

60. Mal. 3:4: "then the offering will be pleasing"—the beginning of the haftarah customary today for the "Great Sabbath."

61. Based on Mal 3:23, "the great and awesome day of the Lord."

62. According to Hilvitz, this is Rabbi Menaham ben Yaakov, one of the sages of Worms, who died in 1203. See Hilvitz (n. 44, p. 216), 2:29.

63. Jer 7:22. The passage continues: "For in the day that I brought them out of the land of Egypt, I did not speak to your fathers or command them concerning burnt offerings and sacrifices."

64. Num 9:3.

65. Jer 7:29—continuation of the haftarah for the Torah portion of *Tzav.*

the festival pilgrimage. And I found support for my words when I came across the book of Rabbi Moshe ben Meshulam, of blessed memory,[66] that was brought from the Land of Babylonia, which contains in the Prophets markings for the haftarot for the Torah readings of the entire year. And I saw a sign for [the Torah portion] *Tzav et Aharon* [Lev 6:2] regarding *Oloteikhem* and another sign for *Tzav et Aharon* at *Ve-Arvah*. Therefore my suggestion is confirmed when I say that sometimes one recites for *Tzav et Aharon* the haftarah beginning *Oloteikhem* and at times one recites *Ve-Arvah*. And what determines the thing is that, if it is a regular year and *Tzav et Aharon* falls on the Great Sabbath, that is before Passover, they read as haftarah *Ve-Arvah*—and all the more so when the eve of Passover falls on the Sabbath. But if it is a leap year, and *Tzav et Aharon* falls on one of the Sabbaths of the intercalated month of Adar, and the Great Sabbath coincides with the reading of *Aharei Mot* [Lev 16:1: "After the death"], then they read *Oloteikhem* as haftarah for *Tzav et Aharon*, unless this Sabbath coincides with one of the "four portions" [sabbaths on which special readings are added]. And since there is no regularity in this because of the leap year, therefore it was removed from the tradition, and it became customary to read the haftarah *Oloteikhem* always, because it is more frequent one. Thus far the responsum.[67]

What was the actual practice in Ashkenaz as reflected in this responsum? It is clear to the author that there was no special haftarah for *Shabbat ha-Gadol,* and that the entire discussion revolves around the question of what haftarah ought to be read for the Torah portion known as *Tzav* (Lev 6:2ff.) when it falls on the Sabbath before Passover. In the region where he lived it was customary to read the haftarah from Jeremiah 7 ("therefore it was omitted by those that arranged it") for that Torah portion, but he knew from an ancient source about another custom, namely, to read Malachi 3. In his view, Malachi 3 was the more suitable haftarah for the "Great Sabbath." He thus suggests a compromise: to retain both haftarot for *Shabbat Tzav*— one for regular years, when that Sabbath falls before Passover (Malachi 3), and the other for leap years (Jeremiah 7).

What information did our author have about Malachi 3 being used as

---

66. According to Hilvitz, this refers to Rabbi Meshulam ben Moshe of Mainz, a leading rabbi in Germany in the eleventh century (n. 44, p. 216), 2:29 n. 38).

67. Rabbi Isaac ben Moses of Vienna, *Or Zaru'a, II* (Zhitomer, 1862), sec. 393. Hilvitz presents a lengthy and important discussion of this responsum and of the haftarah for the "Great Sabbath, (Hilvitz, n. 44, p. 216), 25–40.

haftarah, if in his region it was not customary to read it either on the Great Sabbath or for the Torah portion *Tzav?* Joseph Ofer has recently proposed a persuasive explanation of this matter, as follows.[68] According to the ancient Palestinian custom of reading the Torah in a triennial cycle, one *seder* was read every Sabbath, unlike the Babylonian custom, accepted among most Jews from medieval times on, whereby the Torah was divided into 54 *parshiyot*, or "lections," enabling the completion of its reading every year—with doubling over where necessary. The Palestinian custom divided the Torah into approximately 150 smaller *seders*, so that it was read over a three-, or three-and-a-half year, cycle. The haftarah for the *seder* beginning with Leviticus 6:12 was Malachi 3:4 because of the parallel use of the word *minha* in the respective opening verses.[69] As a result of the triennial cycle, the reading of this *seder* and of its haftarah did not correspond to any particular point on the calendar, such as Passover or the "Great Sabbath." After the Palestinian practice of the triennial cycle was rejected in favor of the Babylonian annual cycle, most communities read the annual portion with its accompanying haftarah. But there were some communities that adopted the Babylonian Torah portion yet continued to read the haftarah in accordance with the Palestinian custom—that which had been used for the first *seder* of that portion. This happened in the case of *Parshat Tzav* (Lev 6:2ff.), which in nonleap years fell on the Sabbath preceding Passover. In the Babylonian custom the haftarah was Jeremiah 7:21 *(Oloteikhem),* but in the Byzantine (Romanian) custom and the Karaite custom it was rejected in favor of Malachi 3:4ff.—which, as mentioned, was the haftarah for the Palestinian *seder* that begins with Leviticus 6:12 and completely overlaps with *Parshat Tzav.* Thus, both haftarot—Jeremiah 6 and Malachi 3—are reasonable "candidates" for *Parshat Tzav*, and echoes of this "struggle" arise from the words of *Or Zaru'a.*

Our author favored Malachi 3 for the Sabbath before Passover. Why? According to him, Jeremiah 7 is inappropriate for the Sabbath that falls on the day of a sacrifice, that is, on the eve of Passover ("to distress the hearts of Israel who are making the festival pilgrimage"), because of its harsh expressions against the sacrificial cult. But this would not explain why this

---

68. Joseph Ofer, "The Haftarah for Shabbat Hagadol" [in Hebrew], *Ha-Ma'ayan* 36 (1996): 16–20.

69. On the order of the haftarot according to the triennial cycle, see J. Ofer, "The Masoretic Division *(Sedarim)* in the Books of the Prophets and Hagiographa" [in Hebrew], *Tarbiz* 58 (1989): 173–89.

haftarah would be rejected on the "Great Sabbath" that does not fall on the eve of Passover. To understand our author's eagerness to introduce Malachi 3 on the Sabbath before Passover, we must take into account another ancient Palestinian custom: that of reading Malachi 3 on the Intermediate Sabbaths of Passover and of Sukkoth.[70] According to this custom, there is a substantive connection between Malachi 3 and Passover. It is easy to understand the meaning of the custom, because it is consistent with the reading of the Torah on the Sabbaths of the holiday week according to the Palestinian custom. The regular Torah reading for the festivals—the section concerning festivals beginning with Deuteronomy 15:19 ("All the firstling males"), which includes verses referring to Passover and Sukkoth—is supplemented on the Intermediate Sabbath by another section that discusses tithes ("You shall surely tithe"; Deut 14:22ff.), so as to connect the Torah reading with the verse from the haftarah, "Bring all the tithes into the storehouse" (Mal 3:10). At first glance, this was done to allude to the burning of the tithes customary on Passover, but that does not suit the Intermediate Sabbath of Passover week, and certainly not Sukkoth. The connection between the tithes in Deuteronomy 14 and those in Malachi 3 seems essentially technical; the main point was in fact to read the conclusion of Malachi 3, which alludes to the Redemption and the "great and dreadful day of the Lord."

Proof that this is so is found in the *piyyut* of the tenth-century poet Rabbi Joseph ibn Avitor, which preserves both the matter of reading the Torah portion, "You shall surely tithe" (Deut 14:22) and the reading of Malachi 3.[71] The last line of the first stanza and of all the stanzas from the fifth to the eighth one allude to the haftarah from Malachi 3, beginning with the verse "Bring all the tithes into the storehouse," continuing through to "Behold, I will send you Elijah the prophet," at the end of the seventh stanza, and ending with the phrase "before the great and terrible day of the Lord comes" at the end of the eighth, which is the last stanza. The liturgical poet follows the order of the haftarah and also sees the reference to the great day of the Lord as the climax and essence of the haftarah when read on the Intermediate Sabbath of Passover or Sukkoth. In fact, there is nothing unique to Palestine in stirring up messianic hopes on those two Sabbaths, since in Babylonia it was also customary to read the prophecy about Gog and Ma-

70. Fleischer, "The Reading of the Portion" (n. 23, p. 213), 116–55.
71. Reprinted in Fleischer, "The Reading of the Portion" (n. 23, p. 213), 151–53.

gog (Ezek 38:18–39:16)[72] on the Intermediate Sabbath of Sukkoth, and that of the vision of the dry bones (Ezek 37:1–12) on Passover. We may infer that at the end of the tenth century it was still customary in Palestine to read the haftarah concerning the "great and terrible day" on the Sabbath of Passover week, rather than on the Sabbath before Passover—just as in the Gospel According to John, the "Great Sabbath" of the Jews is that of Passover week, not the one preceding the holiday.

Moving the "Great Sabbath" backward one week is thus an Ashkenazic innovation, which brought in its wake the moving of the Palestinian haftarah from its original place on the Intermediate Sabbath of Passover to the Sabbath before Passover. The practice of using the term the "Great Sabbath" for the Sabbath before Passover had previously been widespread in Ashkenaz among the common people, for the process originated "from below"; it is thus plausible that the name predated the custom, and that only after the name had taken root among the people was the appropriate haftarah from Malachi 3 shifted to it. It was during this transitional stage that the above-cited responsum from *Or Zaru'a* was written.

According to this reconstruction, the transfer of the haftarah from Malachi 3 to the "Great Sabbath" was an internal Jewish move.[73] It is plausible that what happened to the name of the "Great Sabbath" also happened to its haftarah: that both were shifted from the Sabbath of Passover to the Sabbath preceding it. Thus, the Ashkenazic-French reading adopted the concepts of time of the Christian "Holy/Great Week."

But another consideration may have been underlying the decision to reject Jeremiah 7 in favor of Malachi 3 as haftarah for the Sabbath before Passover, as implied by our responder in *Or Zaru'a*. To understand this, we must first examine parts of the sermons that were customarily delivered among the Christians, at Easter in general and on Palm Sunday in particular. These sermons referred to the prophecy of Jesus when he descended from the Mount of Olives with palm fronds spread out before him, prophesying the

72. Fleischer, "The Reading of the Portion" (n. 23, p. 213), 142.

73. According to Werner, *The Sacred Bridge*, 1:85–86, Malachi 3 was part of the readings for Palm Sunday in the Gallic Church in the fifth and sixth centuries, based on P. A. Dold, "Das älteste Liturgiebuch der lateinischen Kirche," *Texte und Arbeiten* (Beuron, 1936). But on p. lviii, Dold explicitly states that the *formular* for Palm Sunday is absent in the manuscript. While Malachi 3 is quoted in the manuscript, it is impossible to know when it was read. Dold thinks (lxxx, ciii) that it was read in the fall, at the time of harvesting the crops, because of the verse "bring all the tithes into the storehouse."

destruction of Jerusalem, and thereafter entering the city. The destruction of Jerusalem plays a central role in the liturgy of Easter, thereby emphasizing the link between the Crucifixion and the Destruction of the Temple, between the sin and the punishment for it.[74] In light of such a line of exegesis, it is only natural that a Jew would feel uneasy about reading the following passages from Jeremiah 7 in the haftarah for the Sabbath before Passover: "For in the day that I brought them out of the land of Egypt, I did not speak to your fathers or command them concerning burnt offerings and sacrifices . . . I have persistently sent all my servants the prophets to them, day after day; yet they did not listen to me, or incline their ear. . . . Cut off your hair and cast it away, raise a lamentation on the bare heights, for the Lord has rejected and forsaken the generation of his wrath," and similar reprimands. The author of our responsum himself expresses his discomfort with those verses. Even though he speaks in the name of imaginary "pilgrims," it seems likely that those words express the distress of a person who feels these are not appropriate verses to be recited in a holy time, charged with an intense polemic with Christianity about the religious meaning of the Passover sacrifice, the Destruction of Jerusalem, and Redemption.

All this leads to an important conclusion. Under the influence of the Christian environment, the Jews of Ashkenaz accepted the name "Great Sabbath" as the title for the Sabbath opening the week preceding Passover. It was initially merely a name, but as the process continued there was a growing need to grant this Sabbath a liturgical status, like that given during this period to Palm Sunday in the West. One of the solutions was to fix Malachi 3 as the standard haftarah for the "Great Sabbath" as a kind of counterweight to Palm Sunday, a solution that cleared the way for the adoption of the Babylonian haftarah for the Intermediate Sabbath of Passover: the vision of the dry bones in Ezekiel 37.

It is difficult to ignore the similarity between the haftarah concerning the resurrection of the dead and the meaning attributed by Christians to Easter, the festival of the Resurrection—and indeed, all ancient versions of Christian scriptural readings include the reading of Ezekiel 37 on the Sunday before Easter.[75] Joseph Heinemann saw a connection between the Jewish haftarah

74. A. Linder, "A Homily for Easter on the Destruction of Jerusalem and the Temple" [in Hebrew], in *Tarbut ve-hevrah be-toldot 'Am Yisrael beyemei-habeinayim*, ed. R. Bonfil et al. (H. H. Ben-Sasson Memorial Volume; Jerusalem, 1989), 19–26.

75. Werner (n. 22, p. 213), 1:87; Venetianer (n. 22, p. 213), 128–32.

and the obscure legend about the sons of Ephraim who left Egypt too soon, died in a battle with the Philistines, and whose bones were left scattered along the way to the Land of Israel.[76] This legend was designed to provide a typological story to suit the image of the Messiah son of Joseph who was to precede the Davidic Messiah and die in a war. In chapter 1 I suggested that the image of the Messiah son of Joseph was a Jewish alternative to another Messiah son of Joseph—Jesus—who was also killed. This view is consistent with my hypothesis that the Passover Haggadah reflects an effort to propose an alternative text to the Gospel story of the Crucifixion and Resurrection. The custom of reading Ezekiel 37 on the Sabbath of Passover fits that trend to establish a Jewish version parallel to the Christian story.

The change in the meaning of the "Great Sabbath" in the Ashkenazic world may also be understood in the same vein, as a vague attempt to connect to the liturgical time and symbols of the neighboring society. The Jewish "Great Sabbath" establishes a counterstory to that of Palm Sunday, and in doing so offers a Jewish time and Jewish context for the week of preparation before Passover; and, as in the Christian time, it also fixes the beginning of the week of preparations on the holy day that concludes the previous week.

THE BURNING OF LEAVEN

According to Mishnaic halakhah, the time for destroying or eliminating *hametz* (leavened foodstuff) is at the beginning of the sixth hour of the day on the fourteenth of Nissan; in the Temple, the Passover offering was not sacrificed before the leaven was burned.[77] Consistent with this, John 19:14 relates that Jesus was crucified "about" the sixth hour. The connection between burning the leaven and bringing the Passover offering within the context of messianic symbolism may also be understood from 1 Corinthians 5:7–8: "Cleanse out the old leaven, that you may be a new lump, as you really are unleavened. For Christ, our paschal lamb, has been sacrificed for us. Let us, therefore, celebrate the festival, not with the old leaven, the leaven of malice and evil, but with the unleavened bread of sincerity and truth." Both Jewish and Christian hermeneutics identified leaven with the evil im-

---

76. J. Heinemann, "The Messiah of Ephraim and the Premature Exodus of the Tribe of Ephraim," *HThR* 8 (1975): 1–15.

77. *m. Pesahim* 5.4.

pulse,[78] and there is in turn a connection between this interpretation and the political-messianic one, which sees the destruction of leaven as an allusion to removing the elements that delay the Redemption.

The political-messianic significance of leaven has already been noted in chapter 2, in which we discussed the words placed in Haman's mouth by the second *Targum* of the Book of Esther. Haman, who wants to persuade Ahasuerus to kill all the Jews, slanders the Jews to the king, claiming that they say "just as the leaven is burned so will the wicked kingdom be lost and salvation will come to us from this stupid king." That is, the Jews are represented as enemies of the government, and the burning of leaven as an act of politically meaningful symbolism. Note the fact explicitly stated in the Book of Esther: Haman is not hanged on Purim, as many think, but on Passover.[79] This is very important, since by late antiquity we find testimonies of both Jewish and Christian exegetes associating the hanging of Haman with the Crucifixion of Jesus.[80] Haman's speech, in which the burning of leaven is interpreted as a symbol for the destruction of the "wicked kingdom," that is, Rome, indicates the existence of a Jewish hermeneutics attributing messianic meaning to the burning of leaven. The source for this statement is the Babylonian Talmud (*Pesahim* 5a): "It was taught by the House of Elijah: in reward for the language of 'first' they merited three 'firsts': to cut off the seed of Esau." That is, as a reward for observing the commandment "on the first day you shall put away leaven out of your houses" (Exod 12:15), Israel will annihilate the seed of Esau, who is likewise described as "first": "the first came forth red" (Gen 25:25). As mentioned in chapter 2, this Talmudic concept was accepted by Rabbi Eleazar of Worms in the thirteenth century:

By virtue of burning leaven, Esau will burn, as is written, "on the first day you shall put away leaven." Is this the first day? Is it not the fourteenth of

78. Compare *b. Ber.* 17a; Matt 15:12; cf. M. B. Lerner, "The Leaven Therein" [in Hebrew], *Leshoneneu* 53 (1989): 287–90; Herbert Basser, "Superstitious Interpretations of Jewish Laws," *Journal for the Study of Judaism* 8 (1977): 127–38.

79. The lots were cast on the thirteenth day of Nissan (Esther 3:7, 12), Esther fasted three days (4:16), and on the third day (the fifteenth of Nissan), she invited the king and Haman to a banquet on that day (5:4), and to a second banquet on the following day, the sixteenth of Nissan (5:8). According to this, the king's night of insomnia (= vigil) was the night between the fifteenth and sixteenth of Nissan, and Haman was hanged the next day.

80. James G. Frazer, *The Golden Bough*, rev. ed., (London, 1994), 666–76; E. Wind, "The Crucifixion of Haman," *Journal of the Warburg Institute* 1 (1937): 245–48.

the month?! But rather, that by virtue of this I destroy Esau. "The first came forth red"; "How Esau has been pillaged, his treasures sought out" (Obad 1:6), "the house of Esau shall be stubble; they shall burn them and consume them, and there shall be no survivor to the house of Esau; for the Lord has spoken." (Obad 1:18)[81]

This major halakhic scholar and spokesman of Ashkenazic Pietism draws a clear connection between the act of burning leaven and vengeful redemption. True, the association between burning leaven and the destruction of Esau/Edom may be understood as having no real internal link, as simply stating that in reward for removing leaven Israel will deserve Redemption. Yet it is difficult to ignore the messianic meaning of leaven in the eyes of the Jew, who sees its burning as an act symbolizing the future destruction of Esau. If, in Christian eyes, Jesus and his sacrifice are symbolized by the Host, for the Jew the leavened bread destined to be burned symbolizes "Edom." The meaning of this hermeneutics in the consciousness of medieval Jews should not be lightly dismissed. The punctiliousness with which the Jews observed the laws about leaven on Passover—particularly in Ashkenaz—suggests that this strictness bore a profound religious significance. In the consciousness of the Jews, the removal of leaven was a symbol of the future messianic victory over Edom, over Esau, and over the Christian world. Hence, burning leaven before Passover was interpreted as parallel to the ten plagues that preceded the deliverance from Egypt, according to the typological model in which the past is posited as a sign for the future.

It does not require much imagination to describe Christian reactions on observing that ceremony: on the eve of Passover—that day which, according to Jewish reckoning, corresponded to the day of the Crucifixion—the Jews removed all remaining leaven from their homes and burned it on a fire, an act they interpreted as symbolic of the destruction of Esau—that

81. *Sefer ha-Rokeah* (Jerusalem, 1967), end of sec. 271. Similarly, Maharsha wrote in his commentary on *b. Pesahim* 5a: "The reason for the removal [of *hametz*] on Passover, of which it is said, 'the first,' is because on that day Israel were redeemed from those that enslaved them. And the Holy One blessed be He judged them [i.e., the enslavers] with all kinds of plagues and punished them in the sea, and by virtue of this removal they shall be redeemed in the future from Esau, who is called 'the first,' who enslaves us. And the Holy One blessed be He will judge him and cut off his seed . . . and this is the reason for the removal of leavening on Passover, because the leaven in the dough is the Evil Urge, which is the power of Samael, the prince of Esau, who will be cut off in the time of the Redemption."

is, of Christianity, and of the impending Redemption. Concern about this interpretation found its expression in a question sent to Rabbi Hayyim, the author of *Or Zaru'a* during the second half of the thirteenth century. The questioner notes that, according to the Babylonian Talmud, *Pesahim* 8b, leaven located in a hole in a common wall shared by a Jew and a Gentile need not be examined, lest the Gentile suspect the Jew of engaging in magic. The questioner wished to know whether such an interpretation ought to be applied to his day, when Jews employed Christian maids in their houses. Rabbi Hayyim answered:

> The case at hand is not at all similar to that of a hole [in a wall] between us and the Gentile, for in that case [i.e., in the Talmud] the non-Jew might find reason to complain and to attack the Jew for bewitching him, but in our own homes there is no reason to fear, since the prohibition [against leaven] is well-known to them. Moreover, we even burn the leaven in their presence, and they conceive this as a severe act. . . . And certainly if we had to worry about charges of witchcraft regarding the burning we would refrain from it, the way we refrain in Provence from the ritual cleansing of an oven on account of suspicion of witchcraft.[82]

In contrast to his interlocutor's suspicions, our author thinks that the Christians clearly understand that burning leaven is not a magical act, but a weighty and strict religious commandment the Jews are obligated to fulfill. But he himself testifies that a different atmosphere prevailed in Provence. Rabbi Hayyim wrote his responsum in the period immediately preceding the appearance of the first accusation of ritual desecration of the Host (Paris, 1290), and he evidently did not anticipate or correctly evaluate the dangers inherent in Christian interpretations of Jewish acts.

These dangers are illustrated by the following incident. In 1399 there was a debate between a convert to Christianity, who had been known as Pesah when he was a Jew and assumed the name Peter after his conversion, and Rabbi Yom-Tov Lipmann Mühlhausen, a remarkable halakhic scholar and philosopher. Mühlhausen presented a brief account of this debate in his work *Sefer ha-Nizzahon*—the most important anti-Christian polemic written in Jewish Ashkenaz during the late Middle Ages. The debate ended very

---

82. *Sefer She'elot u-Teshuvot R. Hayyim Or Zaru'a*, ed. J. Rosenberg (Jerusalem, 1972; photo ed.), sec. 144; compare Joshua Trachtenberg, *Jewish Magic and Superstition* (New York, 1975), 2–3.

badly, with the execution of eighty Jews, suggesting that it was not a scholarly debate but a trial, in which Jews were faced with the charge that they despise Christianity and want to annihilate it.

According to Mühlhausen, Peter argued, among other things: "Of any dough you knead, you burn a little bit as an affront to their [i.e., the Christian] god. Also, on the eve of Passover, which is during the time of the fast [Lent] you burn the bread."[83] This debate and its bitter consequences were the immediate incentive for Mühlhausen to write *Sefer ha-Nizzahon*.[84] The remarks cited above referred to two customs: the burning of challah and the burning of leaven. Mühlhausen's reply indicates that the convert criticized the customs of burning challah (throughout the year) and of burning leaven (on the eve of Passover). He saw both customs as attempts on the part of the Jews to exhibit contempt for the Host. However, the convert may have had in mind the practice of immediately burning the challah that was separated from the matzot baked on the eve of the holiday, after the sixth hour of the day. In the case of ordinary dough that had risen, there was no need to burn the challah immediately after separation, and it could be kept for a long time until a suitable opportunity to burn it arose. But not so the challah separated from matzah, which was likely to rise and thereby become forbidden *hametz;* thus challah was separated from the matzot that were baked after midday and immediately burned. In his new book, David Nirenberg reports an incident that occurred in Sogrob, Spain, in 1321 at Easter time. The Jews of the town were accused of preparing an image of Jesus out of dough and burning it in an oven.[85] It seems logical that the background of this accusation too was the Jewish custom of burning *hametz* on Passover eve.

The connection between destroying *hametz* and the messianic victory over Christianity may also help to explain the manner in which Christians apparently understood the ceremony of scalding vessels, as described in chapter 3. A visual expression of this connection appears in an illustration from a fourteenth-century Spanish manuscript depicting a Jew desecrating the

83. Yom Tov Lipmann Mühlhausen, *Sefer ha-Nizzahon*, ed. F. Talmage (Jerusalem, 1984; photo ed. Nürnberg, 1644), 194.

84. Israel J. Yuval, "Kabbalisten, Ketzer und Polemiker. Das kulturelle Umfeld des Sefer ha Nizachon von Lipman Mühlhausen," in *Mysticism, Magic and Kabbalah in Ashkenazi Judaism*, ed. K. E. Grözinger and J. Dan (Berlin,, 1995), 161.

85. D. Nirenberg, *Communities of Violence. Persecution of Minorities in the Middle Ages* (Princeton, 1996), 220.

Figure 4. Depiction of a Jew desecrating the Host by throwing it into a pot of boiling water, fourteenth century. Catalan National Museum, Barcelona.

Figure 5. Ceremony of "searing" the pots in preparation for Passover in Spain, fourteenth century. Manuscript British Museum, Or. 2737.

Figure 6. The martyrdom of Saint Julita, who was thrown
into a boiling pot along with her son, Saint Quirze in Tarsus,
during the Diocletian persecutions of the fourth century.
Altarpiece from the monastery in Durro, near Lérida, Spain,
twelfth century. Catalan National Museum, Barcelona.

Host (Figure 4), which is remarkably similar to another illustration, also
from Spain, of the ceremony of scalding vessels (Figure 5). The two ceremonies are visually similar to the killing of a Christian martyr (Figure 6).
The motif of throwing the Host into a boiling cauldron is very widespread
in accusations of desecration of the Host.[86] The following description appears in the chronicle of Johannes de Thilrode concerning the accusation
of desecration of the Host in Paris in 1290: *Insuper hostia ponebatur in cal-
dario pleno aqua, ut bulliretur et destrueretur: Hostia vero divina gratia in
carnem et sanguinem se mutavit* (moreover, the Host was placed in a caul-

86. Lotter already noted this (n. 9, p. 208), 538.

dron full of water to boil it and destroy it. But with God's grace, the Host was turned into flesh and blood).[87] Alongside the motif of the boiling cauldron, two other motifs may be discerned in the sources relating to this episode: the throwing of the Host into the boiling cauldron took place in the house of a Jew, and he was aided by his maidservant.[88] The identical scene is described in the responsum cited above by Rabbi Hayyim Or Zaru'a. The combination of those three motifs reinforces the conjecture that behind the accusation in Paris lay the Jewish custom of scalding vessels on the eve of Passover.

THE *ERUV* OF COURTYARDS

Jewish religious law prohibits carrying any objects from the private to the public domain on the Sabbath. To get around this prohibition, it was common for Jews to create an *eruv hatzerot*—an "extension" of the courtyards. That is, the people living in one courtyard or neighborhood would create a fictive partnership, whereby the courtyards separating their houses would be considered a common area. This legal fiction was effected by preparing food that will belong to the entire community. To avoid the bother of preparing food for this purpose every Sabbath, it was customary already in ancient times to use matzah, a foodstuff that keeps for a long time, which was stored in the home of one of the neighbors in a tightly closed box—to prevent it from falling prey to the greed of the ubiquitous neighbors of people during the Middle Ages: mice. This custom is mentioned for the first time in a mid-ninth-century Italian work entitled *Hilkhot Ketzuvot:*

> The following is the law of the *eruv* and its making: If they wish to make an *eruv* on the eve of Passover for the entire year, the sage should take a handful of flour from every household, knead it and bake it into one or two cakes, making them very hard so they will not rot and can be stored away—for so long as the cakes are stored the *eruv* is in force and carrying on the Sabbath is permissible. If, however, the cakes are eaten or rot or perish or are burned, it is forbidden to carry anything until another *eruv* is prepared on the Sabbath eve.[89]

---

87. *MGH SS,* 25, ed. J. Heller (Hannover, 1880), 578; and cf. chap. 4, text referring to n. 106.
88. Rubin (n. 9, p. 208), 169–71.
89. *Halakhot Ketzuvot,* ed. M. Margulies (Jerusalem, 1942), 63–64; and cf. *Kol Bo* (Lemberg, 1860), sec. 33; and Israel M. Ta-Shma, *Early Franco-German Ritual and Custom* [in Hebrew] (Jerusalem, 1992), 243.

The reason for using matzah in the preparation of the *eruv* is thus clearly a technical halakhic one: the desire to use food fit for human consumption the entire year, thereby alleviating the need to renew the *eruv* every Friday afternoon. Further on, *Hilkhot Ketzuvot* states that the *eruv* should be placed "in a box or place of safe-keeping . . . and that *eruv* should be placed in the house of one of their number."[90]

Two developments regarding the *eruv hatzerot* came about in fourteenth-century Germany. First, rather than keeping the matzah in a box, it became customary to hang it on the wall. Second, it became customary to place it in the synagogue rather than in a private home.[91] This practice created a number of halakhic problems (not our concern here), which led some rabbis nevertheless to prefer placing the *eruv* in a home. A student of Rabbi Israel Isserlin, a fifteenth-century sage of Austria, described this *eruv* matzah thus: it "was made on the eve of Passover, and was big, and had a hole in the middle, and was hung by a nail in the winter house where he studied, and not in the synagogue."[92] However, the wish to publicly display the matzah of the *eruv* in the synagogue was stronger than the halakhic considerations in favor of leaving it in a private home. Rabbi Yuspa Shamash's *Book of Customs,* from the seventeenth century, attests to this practice: "On the eve of the Great Sabbath we remove the *eruv* that has been hanging in the synagogue all year long and break it into pieces, giving one to each household head. The sexton divides it up, giving each head of household his share."[93] Yuspa Shamash also gives a detailed description of preparing the matzah for the *eruv* and its placing on the western, that is, the back wall, of the synagogue.[94]

There seems to be a certain similarity between the public display of the matzah on the synagogue wall and the introduction—during the identical time period—of the *monstrantia,* the chalice with a glass window in the middle that was used from the thirteenth century onward to display the Host. Prior to the appearance of the *monstrantia,* the Host was kept in a closed vessel, the ciborium, just as the *eruv* matzah was originally kept in

90. *Halakhot Ketzuvot,* 64–65.

91. *She'elot u-teshuvot Maharil he-hadashot,* ed. Y. Satz (Jerusalem, 1977), sec. 38, 37–39, and in the editor's notes.

92. Rabbi Yaakov ben Moshe, *Leket Yosher,* vol. 1, ed. J. Freimann (Berlin, 1903), 67. The "winter house" is the main room, where the oven was located.

93. *Sefer Haminhagim le-Rabbi Yuspa Shamash* (n. 54, p. 219), 79.

94. *Sefer Haminhagim le-Rabbi Yuspa Shamash,* (n. 54, p. 219), 82.

a closed vessel. The change in attitude toward the Eucharist in the thirteenth century was rooted in the transition from the ceremony of eating in fellowship to one of adoring the hidden essence of the Host, seen as the body of Jesus. As a result, rather than *receiving* the Host, which until then had been the main aspect of the ceremony, the trend of *seeing* the Host grew stronger.[95]

These two changes—the hanging of the *eruv* matzah on the wall and its placement in the synagogue—produced a Christian exegesis that ignored the halakhic background and ascribed a distinctively anti-Christian meaning to these acts. We first hear of this in *Sefer ha-Minhagim* of Rabbi Shalom Neustadt at the turn of the fourteenth century. Neustadt was among those sages who refused to place the *eruv* in the synagogue, for two reasons. One was halakhic—he believed that the synagogue was not a place where people sleep and eat. The second was because of a certain incident: "Once a certain apostate leveled an accusation on account of the *eruv*."[96] We can guess what wickedness that convert wrought. He must have claimed that the Jews hung the matzah, the symbol of deliverance, on the wall in order to degrade Jesus and to allude to his Crucifixion on Passover. Thus, the custom of *eruv hatzerot* was interpreted as confirming Christian accusations concerning the desecration of the Host. It was fear of this interpretation that led Rabbi Shalom Neustadt to keep the matzah in his own home. Even if the similarity between the *eruv* and the Host was purely coincidental, the Christians lent this Jewish custom a clearly anti-Christian meaning. Not only do the Jews burn leaven on the eve of Passover, but they also hang the unleavened bread, symbolizing for the Christians the Corpus Christi, on the wall of their synagogue.

A second incident occurred in 1510, when the Jews of Brandenburg were imprisoned for desecration of the Host, along with some Jews from Spandau, adjacent to Berlin.[97] One of the accused was tortured, and confessed under duress that he had hung the Host on the wall of the synagogue— where a piece of matzah was indeed found. A third incident took place in

95. Peter Browe, *Die Verehrung der Eucharistie* (München, 1933); Caroline W. Bynum, *Holy Feast and Holy Fast* (London, 1987), 53–55.

96. *Hilkhot u-Minhagei Rabbenu Shalom mi-Neustadt*, ed. S. Spitzer (Jerusalem, 1977), sec. 363.

97. *Germania Judaica*, pt. 3, vol. 2, ed. A. Maimon, M. Breuer, and Y. Guggenheim (Tübingen, 1995), 1382–384.

Frankfurt in 1515,[98] when a converted Jew gave testimony leading to the discovery of a quarter of the "Host" hanging on the wall of the synagogue. This gave rise to suspicions that the Host had been desecrated, and the city council was ordered to search the Jewish ghetto.

Yet despite the halakhic criticism and the dangers involved, the custom continued to be observed. Was the halakhic need for an "*eruv* matzah" in fact accompanied by a concealed anti-Christian Jewish exegesis? We know nothing of such an explication, but the historian must take note of the symbolic weight likely to be given to a statue of the crucified Jesus standing in a church, on the one hand, and a pierced matzah hanging on a nail in a synagogue, on the other.

THE *AFIKOMAN*

At the beginning of the Passover seder, traditionally the father takes three matzot, breaking the middle one in two. The broken matzah is then wrapped in a cloth and hidden until the end of the meal, at which time it is returned to the table and eaten ceremoniously. After it is eaten, the third glass of wine is drunk, the section of the Haggadah beginning "Pour out thy wrath" is said, the fourth glass of wine is poured, symbolizing the final Redemption, and the door is opened for Elijah. The *afikoman* matzah thus marks the climax of the seder as a symbol of Redemption, and was therefore eaten before midnight, the time when God passed over the land of Egypt, smote the firstborn of the Egyptians, and saved the firstborn of Israel.[99] After the *afikoman* is eaten, nothing else is consumed. Just as this matzah symbolizes future Redemption, so is it seen as a reminder of the Passover sacrificial lamb that was eaten when one was already sated.

The symbolism of the *afikoman* is thus complex. Of its earliest origins we know only the rule, "One does not conclude with an *afikoman* following the Passover sacrifice."[100] Whatever the meaning of the word *afikoman* might be,[101] in Talmudic times the ban against "concluding" with the *afiko-*

---

98. *Germania Judaica*, pt. 3, vol. 1, ed. A. Maimon, M. Breuer, and Y. Guggenheim (Tübingen, 1987), 368.

99. Lawrence A. Hoffmann, "A Symbol of Salvation in the Passover Haggadah," *Worship* 53 (1979): 510–37.

100. *m. Pesahim* 10:8.

101. See more on this below.

man was clearly intended to give the Passover offering the final position in the feast.[102] The *afikoman* is thus something that is not eaten. But in the Middle Ages its meaning was reversed, and from a nonceremony the practice surrounding it was transformed into a solemn ceremony indeed. The matzah eaten at the end of the feast, after which nothing else is to be eaten, itself became the *afikoman,* a substitute for the sacrificial lamb of the Passover. The annals of the *afikoman* are therefore those of a complex ceremony, laden with varied meanings, whose decisive stage was the recognition that the *afikoman* is a substitute for the Paschal sacrifice.[103] From this stage on, the *afikoman* became, phenomenologically, a kind of Jewish Host.

The reason for taking three matzot is not clear.[104] The Talmud mentions only one, explaining that it is broken because it is the custom of the poor man to divide his bread and save part of it for the next meal.[105] In the thirteenth century Rabbi Yitzhak of Vienna wrote: "We have not found it stated in the Talmud that it is necessary to make three matzot of mitzvah but that, on the contrary, it is demonstrated in the Jerusalem Talmud that we need only two."[106] The literature of Ashkenazic halakhah and *minhag* is filled

---

102. One ought to take note of the ceremonial and terminological similarity between the ancient *afikoman,* as the concluding ceremony of the sacrificial meal ("one does not conclude" in the sense of sending away, taking leave), and the ceremony of the *missa,* that during the first centuries C.E. marked the ceremony of "sending away" from church. This ceremony marks the end of the prayer service—the bishop blessed the worshipers, and they kissed his hand. From *missa* in the sense of "sending away," there later developed *missa* in the sense of the Eucharist, that is, the sacrificial meal. This being the case, the similarity between the Christian Eucharist and the *afikoman* is very ancient. This may also be the meaning of the prohibition "one does not conclude an *afikoman* after the Passover"—that is, one does not conduct a ceremony of "sending away" to conclude the sacrificial meal by eating the matzah of the *afikoman.* The reason for the Rabbinic prohibition is to be seen, according to this interpretation, as a negation of the previously existing ceremony, owing to the rival Christian interpretation proposed for it in the Last Supper and the Eucharist. As late as the end of the fourth century the Christian ceremony of "sending away" still took place in the former meaning. See Ora Limor, *Travels in the Holy Land: Christian Pilgrims in Late Antiquity* [in Hebrew] (Jerusalem, 1998), 89 n. 213. On the meaning of the *afikoman* as a ceremony of "sending away," see also Eliezer Ben-Yehudah, *Milon ha-lashon ha-ivrit ha-yeshana veha-hadasha* (Jerusalem, 1980; photo ed.), 10.4900.

103. Ta-Shma (n. 89, p. 236), 239. The first to see the *afikoman* matzah as a substitute for or remembrance of the Passover sacrifice was R. Shmuel ben Meir. See Joseph Tabory, *Pesah Dorot: perakim betoldot Leil ha-Seder* (The Passover Ritual Throughout the Generations: Hebrew; Tel Aviv 1996), 122–30.

104. Ta-Shma (n. 89, p. 236), 260–70; Tabory, *Pesah Dorot,* 287–305.

105. *b. Pesahim* 115b.

106. *Or Zaru'a* (n. 67, p. 224), II. 251.

with explanations of this custom, but here we are concerned only with how these customs were reflected in the environment. Thus, for example, the convert Pfefferkorn found in the three matzot an allusion to the Christian Trinity, the *afikoman* being the middle, the Son.[107] This explanation doubtless sounds bizarre and contrived to Jewish ears, but we ought not to dismiss the possibility that Pfefferkorn arrived at this interpretation because he saw a similarity between the Jewish custom of taking three matzot and the Christian custom of dividing the Host into three parts.[108] The convert Victor von Karben also provides a description of eating the *afikoman* that is reminiscent of communion:

> The father takes the broken middle matzah, which is considered the most holy in the eyes of the Jews, and hides it in a clean cloth napkin in a place known only to him. Those sitting around the table then say a prayer of praise to God who has brought them out of Egypt. They open the door and ask God to quickly send them their Messiah. After all the prayers of the seder are concluded, the father returns the matzah kept in the cloth napkin, breaks it, and gives a piece of it to all those present.[109]

Subsequently, Victor explicitly states that *"gleicher weiss wir Christen dz Sacrament empfangen"* ("in the same way we Christians accept the Sacrament"). The messianic significance and holiness of the *afikoman* is also attested to by Antonius Margarita:

> They eat the hidden piece of the matzah at the end of the meal after completing the reading of the Haggadah, and they consider it most holy. Therefore, they are careful not to let any crumb of it fall on their beards, on the floor, or in any other place. They say that this matzah is instead of the Paschal Lamb, and therefore they hide it, like their Messiah, the time of whose coming is hidden away.[110]

Converts from Judaism have a bad reputation; hence it is important to emphasize that the halakhic facts presented by von Karben and Margarita are fully confirmed in the literature of customs of the period. Rabbi Yuspa

---

107. H. M. Kirn, *Das Bild vom Juden im Deutschland des frühen 16. Jahrhunderts* (Tübingen, 1989), 47.

108. *Realencyklopädie* (above, n. 19), sec. 21, 425.

109. von Karben, *Juden Büchlein* (n.p., 1550), vol. 3, chap. 31.

110. *Der ganze Jüdische Glaube* (Frankfurt, 1689), 54.

Hahn, the rabbi of Frankfurt, wrote in his work *Yosef Ometz:* "When it comes time to eat the *afikoman,* he should place his hand under his chin and mouth, so that should crumbs from the *afikoman* fall from his mouth, they will fall into his hand and he can eat them again—this, out of a sense of the preciousness of the matzah."[111] Hence, among Ashkenazic Jews the eating of the *afikoman* became a sacred ceremony. A similar custom was also widely known among Christians regarding the crumbs that fall from the Host.[112]

Was the parallel drawn by von Karben between the *afikoman* and the communion an attempt by a convert to explain a Jewish ceremony through use of Christian concepts? It seems to me that what we have here is a Jewish internalization of Christian ritual language. The Christians eat matzah all year long, during communion, while the Jews eat it only once a year, at Passover. Margarita's remarks that the *afikoman* symbolizes the Messiah, "the time of whose arrival is hidden away," are consistent with the heading given to this ceremony in the Ashkenazic Haggadah: *tzafun* (hidden).[113] In the apocalyptic literature *hidden* is also the term ascribed to the Messiah in referring to the period before his revelation. In the Book of Zerubabel, the angel shows Zerubabel, the Davidic Messiah, sitting in Rome and tells him: "That is the Messiah of the Lord, who is hidden here until the time of the End."[114] In the literature explaining the rationale behind various customs, we find an explicit reference to the *afikoman* as a symbol of the Messiah. The seventeenth-century Kabbalist Hayyim ben Abraham ha-Cohen writes that eating the *afikoman* "alludes to the meal that the Holy One blessed be He is to make in the future for the righteous," which is also the reason for covering the *afikoman* at the beginning of the feast, like the Redemption that is as yet hidden.[115] Von Karben also mocks the Jews of his day, who believed that the more they ate of the *afikoman,* the greater would be their

111. Yospe Hahn Neurlingen, *Sefer Yosef Ometz* (Frankfurt, 1928), sec. 774, 170.s

112. Miri Rubin, *Corpus Christi: The Eucharist in Late Medieval Culture* (Cambridge, 1991), 43: "Even crumbs of the Host were precious and were saved from falling out of the mouths of communicants."

113. In *Teshuvot Maharshal* (n. 55, p. 219), sec. 88, it says: "He takes out the hidden thing, that is, the *afikoman,* as it is, wrapped in a cloth."

114. Adolf Jellinek, *Beit ha-Midrasch* (Leipzig, 1853), 2:56; and compare J. Even-Shmuel, *Midreshei Ge'ulah* (Jerusalem, 1954), 77: *ganuz berakat* (= hidden in Rakat, i.e., Tiberias). And cf. English translation: David Stern and Mark J. Mirsky, eds., *Rabbinic Fantasies: Imaginative Narratives from Classical Hebrew Literature* (Philadelphia-New York, 1990), 67–90.

115. Hayyim ben Abraham ha-Cohen, *Tur Bareket* (Amsterdam 1653–54), sec. 477, 83b.

share in the eschatological feast of the Leviathan.[116] These criticisms were repeated by his contemporary the Polish Rabbi Jacob Kitzingen, in his work *Hag ha-Pesah:*

> Do not take heed of those fools who say that, according to the portion they eat from the *afikoman,* so shall be their portion in the Leviathan in the future. Hence, even though they have already filled their bellies with food and are satiated, they take big chunks of the *afikoman* and eat it as if under duress, like one who stuffs a camel until he is disgusted and wants to vomit. They do not act correctly and they shall have to render account of themselves, for this is an insult to the mitzvah. Rather, if he is satiated he should eat no more than an olive's worth.[117]

This is further proof that these converts were not speaking empty words. It was apparently one of those "foolish" men, among the Tosaphists, who made the following comment: "I heard that the Passover seder alludes to the feast that we anticipate eating in the future . . . and the *afikoman* that we eat at the end corresponds to the Leviathan."[118]

In light of this, the details of the ceremony assume new meaning: the wrapping of the messianic matzah in a cloth, its hiding in a secret place, its rediscovery toward the end of the feast, its distribution by the seder leader, and its being eaten by all the participants. Perhaps the white robe worn by the one conducting the seder is also intended to allude to a shroud, just as the *afikoman* is hidden in a cloth before it is revealed.[119] One should not

116. von Karben (n. 109, p. 241), bk. 3, chap. 21, 266.

117. *Hag ha-Pesah* (Kraców, 1797?), fol. 21b. On this work, see David Tamar, "Calculations of the End in the Work *Hag ha-Pesah*" [in Hebrew] *Sinai* 100 (1987): 931–35.

118. *Seder Tosafot Hashalem: Otzar Ba'alei ha-Tosafot 'al Haggadah shel Pesah,* ed. J. Gellis (Jerusalem, 1989), 2. It would seem that a similar connection underlies the rather strange comment cited in *Perush Ba'alei ha-Tosafot la-Torah,* ed. J. Gellis (Jerusalem, 1988), *Beshalah,* to Exod 16:32: "'that they may see the bread'—[the Hebrew acrostic] forms the letters of [the name] 'Elijah,' because it is preserved until Elijah comes"—that is, the manna will be preserved to be seen until the End of Days. It is appropriate that such an acrostic occur to an Ashkenazic sage living in an environment that "displays" messianic bread by means of a *monstrantia* (my thanks to Professor Moshe Idel for calling my attention to this source).

119. The same work of Rabbi Yitzhak Kitzingen says: "He [the leader of the Seder] dons clothes of darkness, that is, clothes of the dead who inhabit the dust in the realm of darkness and the shadow of death, known as *kittel* in their language" (*Hag ha-Pesah* [n. 117, above], 15b). The thirteenth-century sage Rabbi Samson bar Zaddok (*Sefer ha-Tashbetz* [Lemberg, 1858], sec. 160), writes: "Concerning the garment called *Sargenes,* that is worn on festive days, when there is excessive joy; therefore he wears it, so that he not be overly proud; and there-

ignore the phenomenological similarity between the various stages of the *afikoman* ceremony and the Crucifixion of Jesus, his being enwrapped in a shroud, his being placed in a closed cave, until at the climax, on Easter Sunday, he is risen from the dead.

It is difficult to imagine, as Pfefferkorn suggests, that the Jewish ceremony represents an attempt to propose a direct alternative narrative to that of the Crucifixion. It is more plausible that it adopted certain components that were considered the standard language of a messianic ceremony performed with bread. The Jewish ceremony adopted the manner, language, and gestures of the Christian ceremony; nevertheless, against that backdrop a parallel messianic narrative emerges. Traces of such a connection are also discernible in the ceremonies of the Host during the Holy Week of Easter. On Maundy Thursday, two Hosts are consecrated, instead of one, as happens on any other day. One Host is distributed by the priest among the participants in the Eucharist, as usual, while the second is led in a procession to a corner or to another chapel, where it is kept within a closed box or chalice until Mass the following day. On Good Friday, no Host is consecrated at all, but the Host prepared on the previous day is taken out, buried in a *sepulchrum,* and covered with a cloth *(sudarium).* This ceremony is called *depositio.* This Host is kept in the *sepulchrum* until Sunday morning, when it is taken out and placed on the altar in a ceremony called *elevatio,* intended to reenact the Resurrection of Jesus. The earliest reports of such a ceremony in the Western Church are from the tenth century.[120] If we assume that these customs influenced the shaping of similar Jewish ceremonies, we may reconstruct the symbolic system of the *afikoman* as it developed in Ashkenaz. Its being wrapped in cloth and concealed in a closed place cannot, of course, be explained through symbolism taken from the story of the Crucifixion itself. Such a comparison requires an intermediary stage—namely, the ceremonies involving the Host on Good Friday, the day of the Crucifixion. Christians see the Host quite simply and directly as the flesh of Jesus, while for Jews there is only an indirect influence of a ceremony stemming from distant common sources.

---

fore it is worn over one's clothes, to remember the day of death." According to J. Freimann, *sargenes* is derived from the word *Sarg,* meaning "coffin." See *Leket Yosher* (n. 92, p. 237), 130 n. 379. And cf. *Hagahot Maimoniot,* to Rambam, *MT, Hilkhot Shabbat,* chap. 30; *Sefer Haminhagim le-Rabbenu Eisik Tirna,* ed. S. Spitzer (Jerusalem, 1979), 45.

120. *Realencyklopädie* (n. 19, p. 211), 21.424; Karl Young, *The Drama of the Medieval Church* (Oxford, 1933), 1:112–48; Rubin (n. 112, p. 242), 294–97.

The resemblance between the status of the *afikoman* in the Jewish ceremony of the Passover seder and that of the Host in the Christian Mass stems from the dramatic element common to both ceremonies. As Karl Young says, the liturgy of the Christian Eucharist "is designed not to represent or portray or merely commemorate the Crucifixion, but actually to repeat it."[121] A similar definition might easily be applied to the ceremonies of the seder. The Passover Haggadah states that: "In every generation it is a person's duty to regard himself as though he had personally come out of Egypt." Indeed, many seder practices were designed to concretize and reproduce the drama of the Exodus from Egypt.

The external similarity between the details of this ceremony and that of eating the Host implies the existence of a covert dialogue, which also brings the overt polemics to the surface, since the inner context of the ceremonies is completely different in each religion. We thus have a common language, whose contents are opposed to one another. Another extant custom also implies a language common to both the Christian ceremony and the Jewish ceremony. During the second half of the seventeenth century, Rabbi Abraham Gombiner, author of the halakhic supercommentary *Magen Avraham*, mentions the custom of "piercing a piece of the *afikoman* and hanging it up."[122] This testimony sheds light on von Karben's description, some two hundred years earlier: "Upon their houses, opposite the door, the Jews place a black spot on a white wall so that it will be visible to all, young and old, and so that they will not forget their God and the Temple, and over this they pray a special prayer. Similarly, on Passover they bake round cakes of unleavened dough, bless it, and nail it over the black spot, in memory of God."[123]

Hanging the matzah on the unplastered wall unites two things whose meanings complement one another. The matzah, the symbol of Redemption, is attached to the empty spot on the wall intended to commemorate the Destruction of the Temple. By using the word *nailed*, von Karben intended to convey the impression that the Jews were reenacting the Crucifixion, "in memory of God." The messianic context alluded to in his de-

---

121. Young, *Drama of the Medieval Church*, 84.

122. *Magen Avraham* at *Shulhan Arukh, Orah Hayyim* 500.7. In his work *Shevut Ya'akov*, 3 (Lvov, 1896), sec. 22, Rabbi Jacob Reicher writes: "And I always saw my teachers and forefathers behaving thus, and there is no insult to the mitzvah here, and a remembrance of the Exodus from Egypt."

123. von Karben (n. 109, p. 241), bk. 3, chap. 14.

scription fits the hanging of the *afikoman* matzah, not that of the *eruv* matzah, which was likewise affixed to the synagogue wall on the eve of Passover in Ashkenaz. Yet the hanging of the *eruv* matzah had no messianic meaning. Hence this ceremony strengthens the conjecture that the status of the *afikoman* in Ashkenazic society at the end of the Middle Ages was influenced by that of the Host in the Christian communion.

In fact, if we trace the history of the *afikoman,* on the one hand, and that of the Host, on the other, we do in fact discover an ancient similarity between the two. In I Corinthians 11:26, Paul addresses the disciples and commands them: "For as often as you eat this bread and drink the cup, you proclaim the Lord's death until he comes." Thus, eating the holy bread and drinking the holy wine in the Eucharist is intended to help participants recall the Crucifixion of Jesus and the expectation of his Parousia, his Second Coming. This is precisely the derivation of the term *afikoman*—not from *epikomon,* as is generally accepted, but from *aphikomenos,* that is, "the One who Comes," as has been explained by Robert Eisler and David Daube (see chapter 2).[124] The eating of the *afikoman* thus signifies the anticipation of the coming of the Messiah, according to the well-known rule: "In Nissan we were redeemed, and in Nissan we shall be redeemed in the future." In accordance with this rule, we may propose a new interpretation of the ancient halakhic prohibition "One does not conclude with an *afikoman* following the Passover sacrifice." Assuming the messianic symbolism of eating the matzah, as suggested by Jesus's speech at the Last Supper, this Rabbinic prohibition may have been intended to prevent a separation between eating the *afikoman* matzah (symbolizing the anticipation of future Redemption) and eating the Passover offering (symbolizing the Exodus from Egypt). Therefore, this rule may relate to the anti-Christian polemic of the second century c.e.

If such is, in fact, the case, the renewed messianic function of the *afikoman,* on the one hand, and that of the Host, on the other, have a common, very ancient origin, against which background the development of the Jewish ceremony in the Middle Ages needs to be understood. Our earliest information regarding the sacral importance that the *afikoman* matzah acquired

---

124. R. Eisler, "Das letzte Abendmahl," in *Zeitschrift für die neutestamentliche Wissenschaft* vol. 24. (1925), 61–192 and vol. 25 (1926), 5–37; David Daube, *He That Cometh* (London, 1966), 1–20. An edifying summary of Daube's approach appears in the article by D. Carmichael, "David Daube on the Eucharist and the Passover Seder," *Journal for the Study of the New Testament* 42 (1991): 45–67. See also the end of chapter 2.

dates from the beginning of the twelfth century.[125] This may reflect a covert penetration into Judaism of the dispute over the Eucharist that was taking place in the Church at that time, one that was resolved in the early thirteenth century when the dogma of transubstantiation was accepted as binding Church belief. Note in this context the alternative versions in the Passover Haggadah that read "Behold, like this bread of affliction," rather than "Behold this bread of affliction."[126] Can these formulations be seen as a remnant of an analogous Jewish polemic about the status of the bread of affliction: Is the matzah itself the bread of affliction that our forebears ate in the land of Egypt, or is it only a symbol of it—"like this bread of affliction"—that is, is it only similar to that bread?

In any event, the fact remains that during the twelfth century the curtain once again rose on an ancient messianic symbol that had seemingly disappeared a thousand years earlier. Is this a rebirth under the influence of the Christian symbol of the Host? Or had the Jewish symbol perhaps continued to exist underground all those long centuries? Is the later Talmudic interpretation of the *afikoman*—that is, the ban on holding a celebration of *epikomon* and moving from one group to another—the result of forgetting, or a deliberate consigning of the ancient messianic *afikoman* to oblivion? These questions still await their answers.

Deciphering the meaning of the *afikoman* ceremony within a Christian ceremonial milieu helps us to understand the tension latent within it. Only the smallest hint of this mutual exegetical dialogue is revealed in the written halakhic sources. The language of ceremony is closed and coherent, possessing its own internal syntax and patterns of development, ostensibly understood only from within, which does not explicitly declare its contents or its intentions. According to Young, religious symbols serve as an expression of the collective unconscious; hence, a ceremony is a very sophisticated and complex polemical instrument, difficult to decipher. Yet not every

---

125. See *Ma'aseh he-Geonim*, ed. E. Epstein (Berlin, 1910), 22. It follows from this work that during the eleventh century the *afikoman* was not seen as being of central importance. It is related there that Rabbi Kalonymus the Elder once forgot to eat the *afikoman;* remembering only after he had recited the Grace After Meals, he decided not to eat it. In the literature of the school of Rashi, this same incident is attributed to a "Rabbi," without any specific identification; see *Mahzor Vitry* (n. 46, p. 217), 286 and parallels.

126. On this version, see Kasher, (n. 49, p. 218), 5. According to Yosef Hayyim Yerushalmi, *Zakhor* (Seattle, 1982), 118 n. 28: "The addition of the particle *ke* ('like') was apparently the work of a pedestrian mentality that could not tolerate the thorough equation implied in the original reading."

ceremony, even if it exists in a polemical environment, is necessarily polemical. Its function may be specifically to internalize the language of the opponent, as in the case of the *afikoman,* by "Judaizing" the Host. In a similar vein, Ivan Marcus has recently noted a similar phenomenon in his book about the ceremony of bringing a child to school, which included eating cookies in the shapes of the letters of the alphabet, smeared with honey.[127] Marcus notes parallels in terms of the visual and thematic similarity between eating the letters of the Torah, the Corpus Dei in Jewish eyes, and eating the Host, the Corpus Christi for Christians.

HAROSET

Another Passover seder ritual is eating *haroset,* a mixture of ground nuts and fruits. To grasp the symbolic meanings of *haroset* in the Middle Ages, we must first examine a group of Midrashim about the enslavement of the Israelites in Egypt and their Redemption. In a late Midrashic collection, the birth of Moses is described as follows:

> When Moses' mother [Jochebed] became pregnant, the evil Pharaoh
> had a dream in which he saw a ewe in childbirth bearing a lamb. And
> he also saw a set of scales suspended between heaven and earth, and the
> lamb was brought and placed on the scales. Then they brought all the
> silver and gold of Egypt to add to that weight, but the lamb outweighed
> the lot. The next morning, Pharaoh sent for all his court magicians and
> told them his dream. They explained: This childbearing ewe that you saw
> giving birth is the people dwelling in Egypt, and the lamb she bore is a
> son that will issue forth from it. He will destroy Egypt and conquer lands
> for this people.[128]

The similarity between this legend and the story of the birth of Jesus is obvious. Jochebed is parallel to Mary; the recumbent ewe recalls the manger where Jesus was born; the lamb alludes to Agnus Dei, as Jesus was called, here designating Moses, the child who is to be born and deliver his people, while Pharaoh is similar to Herod. Here Pharaoh commands the throwing

---

127. Ivan G. Marcus, *Rituals of Childhood: Jewish Acculturation in Medieval Europe* (New Haven, 1996).

128. *Midrash ha-Gadol, Exodus,* ed. M. Margulies (Jerusalem, 1967), 22–23.

of the children into the Nile, not to prevent the proliferation of the Israelites, as in the biblical text, but to kill Moses, the deliverer of Israel,[129] in the same way as Herod orders the killing of all the children in Bethlehem.[130]

The affinity between the Jewish story and the Christian one is also recognizable in the following Midrash:

> "The King of Egypt died" [Exod 2:23]—He was stricken with leprosy, and a leper is considered as if dead.
> "And the people of Israel groaned . . . " [Exod 2:23]. Why did they groan? Because the magicians of Egypt said: There can be no cure if we do not kill one hundred twenty Israelite children every morning and evening, and wash in their blood twice daily. Once Israel heard this terrible decree, they began moaning and crying out . . . and a miracle occurred: Pharaoh was cured of his leprosy.[131]

This legend may be seen as a Jewish version of the well-known legend of Sylvester, which probably dates from the end of the fourth century.[132]

---

129. This explanation of Pharaoh's motives is found in Josephus, *Jewish Antiquities*, vol. 2, 205–9, a tradition on which the story told in Matthew is certainly based. See W. D. Davies, *Commentary on Matthew* (Edinburgh, 1988), 192–93, where a bibliography of research on the Jewish sources of that story is to be found.

130. *Targum Pseudo-Jonathan* (Exod 1:15) presents an almost identical version, with the addition of one small detail. The names of the magicians of Egypt are stated explicitly: Jannes and Jambres, a pair of magicians mentioned a great deal in Christian and Jewish sources (cf. 2 Timothy 3:8).

131. *Exod. Rab.* 1.34, ed. A. Shinan (Jerusalem, 1984), 99–100.

132. The legend is printed by Boninus Mombritius, *Sanctuarium seu Vitae Sanctorum* (1478; repr. Paris, 1910), 508–31. The legend of Sylvester is the early part of the *Donation of Constantine*. The principal scholarly studies are W. Levison, "Konstantinische Schenkung und Silvester-Legende," *Miscellanea Francesco Ehrle: Scritti di storia e paleografia* (Roma, 1924), 159–247 [= Levison, *Aus rheinischer und fränkischer Frühzeit: Ausgewählte Aufsätze* (Düsseldorf, 1948), 390–465. For an English translation of the legend, see: Henry Bettenson, *Documents of the Christian Church* (Oxford, 1989; repr.), 98–101. For further research on this legend, see Wolfgang Gericke, "Wie entstand die Konstantinische Schenkung?," *Zeitschrift der Savigny-Stiftung für Rechtsgeschichte: Kanonische Abteilung* 43 (1957): 75–88; Horst Fuhrmann, "Konstantinische Schenkung und Silvesterlegende in neuer Sicht," *Deutsches Archiv* 15 (1959): 523–40; W. Schäfer, "The Oldest Text of the 'Constitutum Constantini,'" *Traditio* 20 (1964): 448–61; Nicholas Huyghebaert, "La Donation de Constantin ramenée à ses véritable dimensions," *Revue d'histoire ecclésiastique* 71 (1976): 45–69; Wolfgang Gericke, "Das Constitutum Constantini und die Silvester Legende," *Zeitschrift der Savigny-Stiftung für Rechtsgeschichte;*

The following is the gist of this Christian legend: as a punishment for persecuting Christians, Constantine was afflicted with leprosy. Many physicians tried in vain to cure him, until the priests of the Capitol came and told him to set up a basin and fill it with the blood of three thousand pure children, and that when he bathed in the warm blood he would be cured. Accordingly, many children were collected, but when the pagan priests wanted to slaughter them and fill the basin with their blood, the emperor heard their mothers' pleas and took pity on them. He halted the slaughter, returned the children to their mothers, and sent them happily home in chariots bearing gifts. That night Peter and Paul appeared to him in a dream and told him that because he had refused to shed innocent blood, they had been sent by Jesus to show him how he could be healed. He was to call Sylvester, the bishop of the city (i.e., Rome), who, owing to Constantine's persecution, was hiding with his priests in a cave (of Mt. Seraftim). Sylvester would baptize the emperor, and the leprosy would be removed. Thereafter Constantine was to order the reestablishment of the churches that had been destroyed during the persecutions and to abandon idolatry. The emperor followed their advice and summoned Sylvester to appear before him. Sylvester baptized him, and as soon as Constantine emerged from the water he was cured. Sylvester taught him the essentials of Christianity, and in gratitude for his cure, Constantine introduced laws favoring Christians generally and the Roman Church in particular. He laid the cornerstone of the Cathedral of Saint Peter in honor of the apostles and began building the basilicum in the Lateran Palace (the papal residence in Rome).

The Constantine of the Christian legend is an improved version of another child-murdering king, Herod. The Jewish story presents yet a third king, Pharaoh. In his wickedness Pharaoh is similar to Herod, but like Constantine, he is saved and cured, and the children are also saved. In Constantine's case, it was the pleas of the mothers on behalf of their children being led to slaughter that changed his evil intentions, thereby leading to his cure by the miracle of baptism, while in the case of Pharaoh it was the groans of the Israelites in Egypt that led to his miraculous cure. Constan-

Kanonische Abteilung 44 (1958): 343–50; R. J. Lorentz, "Actus Sylvestri. Genèse d'une légende," Revue d'histoire ecclesiastique 70 (1975): 426–39; Garth Fowden, "The Last Days of Constantine: Oppositional Versions and Their Influence," Journal of Roman Studies 84 (1994): 146–70; Wilhelm Pohlkamp, "Textfassungen, literarische Formen und geschichtliche Funktionen der römischen Silvester-Akten," Francia 19 (1992): 115–196.

tine repented and became a good Christian, while Pharaoh remained a negative figure, like Herod. The Jewish legend seems to carry on a close and intimate dialogue with the Christian one, adopting it to its own needs. In another version, Pharaoh's story is told in slightly different form:

> Pharaoh had three advisors when he contracted leprosy. He asked the doctors what would cure him. Balaam advised him to take the Jews, slaughter them, to bathe in their blood, and thereby be cured. Job kept silent at that advice, as if he agreed. Jethro heard and fled. The one who made the suggestion was killed. The one who kept silent was stricken. The one who fled merited having a letter added to his name. At first, he was called Yeter, and thereafter he was called Yitro [the letter *vav* was added to his name in Hebrew].[133]

Balaam's advice was similar to that of the priests in the Capitol, but instead of murdering children, here he speaks of murdering the Jews. Jethro, leader of the Midianite priests, may have been introduced into the legend instead of Sylvester, the chief priest of Rome. Thus, rather than contradicting the counterstory, a Jewish alternative to it is offered. It follows from both these legends that, like Constantine, Pharaoh also wanted to murder, but did not do so.

However, another group of legends exists that relates to the accusation of murder of the Hebrew children in Egypt, in an attempt to connect Ezekiel 16:6 ("I saw you weltering in your own blood") with the enslavement in Egypt:

> Rabbi Akiba said: Pharaoh's taskmasters would beat Israel so that they might make the straw into bricks, as is written "But the number of bricks which they made heretofore you shall lay upon them" [Exod 5:8]. But the Egyptians would no longer give the Israelites straw [with which to do so]. . . . The Israelites collected stubble in the wilderness, and their donkeys, women and sons and daughters trampled it into straw. And the stubble from the wilderness pierced their heels, until the blood flowed and became mixed with the mortar.[134]

133. *Midrash ha-Gadol* (n. 128, p. 248), 37–38.
134. *Pirkei de-Rabbi Eliezer,* chap. 48; cf. Jellinek (n. 114, p. 242) 1:45: "When an Israelite would open [i.e., break] one of the bricks, they would seal him in the wall against what he had broken"; *Sefer ha-Yashar,* ed. J. Dan (Jerusalem, 1986), 289, 305.

This depiction suggests that the bricks used for construction in Egypt were mixed with the blood of the Israelites, but here we do not have an accusation of murder of children, unlike in the following legend:

> Rachel, the granddaughter of Shuthelah, was pregnant, and was trampling the mortar with her husband, and she gave birth prematurely so that the foetus became mixed within the brick [she was trampling]. And her cry ascended to the Throne of Glory. The angel Michael descended and brought the brick with its mortar, and carried it up before the Throne of Glory. That night the Holy One blessed be He appeared and smote all the Egyptian firstborn.[135]

Here, the connection between the shed blood of a child and the Redemption is explicit. Keeping in mind the passage from *Midrash ha-Gadol* cited above concerning the Pharaoh dream, in which he saw "a ewe in childbirth bearing a lamb," we gain the impression that in this Midrash too, "Rachel granddaughter of Shuthelah" (in Hebrew Rachel means "ewe") is an image reminiscent of Mary, mother of Jesus. As in the Christian story, here too the child dies, his death bringing deliverance in its wake. The language shared by the Midrash and the Christian legend is in this case extremely close. The Jewish exegesis differs in only one point: its claim that the myth of the dead child and the Redemption was realized, not in Jesus, but in Egypt.

The myth that a human sacrifice is needed for constructing and reinforcing buildings is widespread. A ballad from the Balkans, called "The Bridge of Arta," tells of a bridge builder's wife who was buried within a bridge to prevent it from falling. The same happened to her two sisters: one was buried in a bridge over the Danube, and the other beneath the wall of the city of Avlona. A Romanian legend tells of a builder named Master Manole who was asked by the prince, along with nine other builders, to build a monastery. Everything they built during the day fell down at night, until it was revealed to Manole in a dream that the builders needed to place within the wall the first woman to appear the next morning. The woman who appeared was Manole's wife, who was buried alive within the wall. Similar stories are known throughout Europe.[136] Mircea Eliade interpreted this

---

135. *Pirkei de-Rabbi Eliezer*, chap. 48.

136. A similar ballad was popular among the Jews of Kurdistan. See Donna Shai, "A Kurdish Jewish Variant of the Ballad of 'The Bridge of Arta,'" *AJS Review* 1 (1976): 303–19.

myth as follows: "All these forms depend upon a common ideology, which could be summarized as follows: to last, a construction (house, technical accomplishment, but also a spiritual undertaking) must be animated, that is, must receive both life and a soul. The 'transference' of the soul is possible only by means of sacrifice."[137]

This interpretation, however, does not fit the Midrash. It would seem that the legend of the infant child of Rachel, daughter of Shuthelah, is not part of that universal ideology—if indeed there was such a thing—but has a much more limited function: to offer an alternative Jewish version to the story told in the New Testament. The fact that the Jewish preacher found it necessary to do so indicates the existence of a dialogue between the basic myths of the two religions as they took shape in their formative period, which continued to feed their similarity throughout the Middle Ages.

These myths also penetrated the world of religious custom. The Jerusalem Talmud (*j. Pesahim* 10.3 [37c]) says of the *haroset* eaten at the seder: "It must be soft. And the reason is—in memory of the blood." The Jerusalem Talmud does not explain what blood is being referred to,[138] but the Midrashim presented above clearly suggest that the blood of the babies was mixed into the mortar. Things were understood thus by Rabbi Joseph Tov Elem, a French liturgical poet and halakhic scholar of the eleventh century. In the liturgical poem *Ein arokh eilekha* (None Can Be Compared to You), he wrote: "And why the dipping in *haroset?* In memory of the mortar that the woman and her husband trampled."[139]

The tradition of mixing wine into the *haroset* to recall the mortar kneaded with the blood of babies is mentioned in Ashkenazic halakhic collections of the Middle Ages. For example, in the customs of Maharil (Jacob ben Moses Moellin; fifteenth century), he writes: *"Haroset* is first made very thick, but just before being used for dipping it is diluted, in remembrance of the blood."[140] The Ashkenazic custom followed the Jerusalem

137. Mircea Eliade, *Zalmoxis: The Vanishing God* (Chicago, 1972), 182–83.

138. According to Solomon Zeitlin, the Jerusalem Talmud here refers to the blood of the Passover sacrifice and that of circumcision. See "The Liturgy of the First Night of Passover," *JQR* 38 (1948): 434–40.

139. *Siddur Otzar ha-Tefillot,* II (New York, 1946), 250.

140. *Sefer Maharil* (n. 52, p. 218), 91. Cf. Isaac ben Moses of Vienna, *Or Zaru'a* (n. 67, p. 224), II, Pesahim, fol. 117b, who states: "Red wine—in remembrance that Pharaoh would slaughter the infants when he became leprous. And also, in memory of the blood of the Passover offering and the blood of circumcision."

Talmud, which saw *haroset* as a symbol of the mortar and the wine that went into the *haroset* as a symbol of blood. Also of note is the great similarity displayed here between the Christian symbols of the wine transmuted into the blood of Jesus and the Jewish symbols of the wine in the *haroset* that reflects the blood of the Hebrew children in Egypt.

These Ashkenazic legends and customs existed within a milieu that accused the Jews of blood libels.[141] The Jews were accused of the ritual murder of Christian children as part of the Passover ceremonies, and of preparing matzah with the blood of Christian children. This accusation, which seems to us both terrifying and bizarre, here acquires a coherent context. The Jews—like the Christians—attributed a mythic meaning, in their religious rites, to red wine and to the human blood that it symbolizes.[142] When the Christians accused Jews of using blood to bake matzot, they were perhaps thinking of the *haroset,* in which wine (i.e., blood) is of great importance and which, along with the nuts (i.e., bricks), symbolizes the mortar. Such a thought must not have been alien to the Christian imagination, in which wine also symbolizes (or is tantamount to) the blood of the Savior, while the bread is his body.

These suggestions and interpretations were given a factual basis by Ram Ben Shalom, who discovered a Hebrew manuscript relating an accusation against Jews, in southern France during the fifteenth century, who allegedly murdered a Christian to use his blood in making *haroset.*[143] A similar accusation was leveled against the Jews of Savoy in 1329.[144] Accusations positing a connection between *haroset* and the ritual use of Christian blood were also raised by the Frankists.[145]

---

141. D. Malkiel, "Infanticide in Passover Iconography," *Journal of the Warburg and Courtlaud Institutes* 56 (1993): 85–99. And cf. H. Shmeruk, "*Sefer Divrei ha-Adon* by Jacob Frank" [in Hebrew], *Gal'ed* 14 (1995): 34–35.

142. Cf. *Torrei Zahav,* glosses to *Shulhan Arukh, Orah Hayyim* (Hilkhot Pesah) 472, sec. ix: "It is a mitzvah to seek red wine . . . in memory of the blood, that Pharaoh would slaughter the Israelites. And today we avoid taking red wine, because of false lies told about us, in our great sins."

143. Ram Ben-Shalom, "The Blood Libel in Arles and the Franciscan Mission in Avignon in 1453: Paris Manuscript, Heb. 631" [in Hebrew], *Zion* 63 (1998): 397–99.

144. Ben-Zion Dinur, *Yisrael ba-Golah* (Israel in the Diaspora: Hebrew; Jerusalem, 1967), pt. 2, vol. 2, 556–57; Ben-Shalom, "The Blood Libel in Arles."

145. A. Y. Brawer, Studies in Galician Jewry [in Hebrew] (Jerusalem, 1965), 239–40.

SUMMARY

This chapter has suggested a new perspective on the circumstances under which accusations of desecrating the Host appeared and proliferated. Here we are concerned with the history of fabrications and distorted interpretations. The historian needs to examine the history of misunderstandings, errors, and imagined events as much as that of rational and concrete realities.

In 1263 a German pilgrim on his way to Rome is said to have stopped in the Italian city of Bolsena. He participated in the local Mass and, while gazing at the Host, began to experience doubts about whether or not the bread did in fact become the flesh of Christ. At that point a stunning spectacle was revealed before his eyes: drops of blood appeared on the bread and then flowed down onto the altar. Shaken and thrilled, he hurried to see Pope Urban IV, who was at the time staying in the nearby town of Orvieto. It is said that the testimony of this pilgrim hastened the pope's decision to declare the holiday of Corpus Christi to mark that miracle.

This story might be perceived by the modern reader as but one more proof of the wild imagination of medieval people, particularly since similar incidents underlie accusations lodged against Jews for stabbing the Host and making it bleed. However, it turns out that our pilgrim did not make up anything but was simply mistaken in his interpretation of what he saw. The Host he observed did indeed turn red, but this was not because it turned into the body of Christ, but because of reddish bacteria that sometimes appear on foods of high starch content and low acidity under hot and humid conditions. These bacteria are known by two names in scientific literature. In 1848 the German microbiologist Christian Ehrenberg called it *Monas prodigiosa,* because of its seemingly miraculous appearance on Holy Bread, while in 1879 the Italian Bartolomeo Bizio called it *Serratia marcescens,* the scientific name in use today.[146]

146. For a full summary of the history of the research, see J. C. Cullen, "The Miracle of Bolsena," *ASM News* 60 (1994): 187–91. I thank Dr. Leopold Reiner, who kindly brought this information to my attention. An inexact description of the phenomenon is brought forth by Cecil Roth, "Host, Desecration of," *Encyclopaedia Judaica* (Jerusalem, 1972), 8.1043. In a reply to Cullen's article, published in the same volume of *ASM News,* 403, a certain experiment is described. The writer managed to get a holy wafer from a Catholic priest and another host from a Protestant minister and then purchased Jewish matzah manufactured by Manischewitz in a local shop. He exposed these three types of bread to the above-mentioned organism under damp and warm conditions. Two days later, red fungi appeared on all three breads. In-

This episode exemplifies the need to relate to such misunderstandings with utmost seriousness, as a vital part of the historical understanding of the status of the Host and the accusation that the Jews desecrated it. Similarly, we can assume that some of the motifs appearing in the accusations against the Jews resulted from erroneous interpretations of real events. Ceremonies that Jews in fact performed were misinterpreted—with or without malice of forethought—by naïve Christians or by those pretending to be.

But beyond the question of the origin of the Jews' negative image in Christian eyes, interpretation of Jewish Passover ceremonies indicates partial adoption by the Jews of the ritual language accepted in the Christian milieu. True, the Jews, unlike the Christians, did not "eat" God; certainly, the Jew did not see in his "substitute" Host—the *afikoman* or the *eruv*— a foodstuff constituting an embodiment of the divine substance. Nevertheless, the Jews did express certain motifs in their ceremonies that seemed parallel to those of Christian rites. One could say that the grammar of ceremonial language was the same, even if its literal contents were different. Despite the external similarity of the ritual expression, the overt ideological distance between the two celebrations remained great. Just as the term "Great Sabbath" indicates that the liturgical time of the surrounding environment was adopted, the ceremony of the *afikoman* expresses an adoption of the symbol and its ceremonial shaping. In both cases, the adoption does not obscure the different contents attributed by each side to its timeframe, and to its ceremony. On the contrary, it was this very proximity that supported misunderstandings, suspicion, and hostility. The gap between the overt, public articulation—which proclaims a sharp dispute—and their covert and silent articulation—which reflect a similarities in the language of the ceremony—was one that aggravated and deepened the tension between the two groups and their ceremonies.

---

terestingly enough, the redness closest in appearance to blood was that on the Protestant host, to the chagrin of the writer. Clearly he was not a Jew.

SIX

The End of the Millennium (1240)
Jewish Hopes, Christian Fears

JACOB AND ESAU, THE TYPOLOGICAL PAIR with which this book opened, return at its end in medieval garb, starring in the conflict they represent between Exile and Redemption, between slavery and freedom. The Jewish interpretation of the phrase "the elder shall serve the younger" (Gen 25:23) foresaw the overturning of the world order and the transformation of Christianity from a dominant religion to a defeated one. There is no reason to assume that Christianity remained indifferent to these covert hopes of Jewry. In the same way that we found a Christian reaction to Jewish behavior on the ceremonial and ritualistic plane, so too in this chapter we shall take note of the impact of Jewish messianic imagination and calculations of redemption on the Christian world.

Producing calculations of the End is an ancient Jewish pastime. True, the Talmud says: "May the spirits of those who calculate the End depart [i.e., may they die],"[1] but it seems that those who made such calculations did not always take them very seriously. In Mühlhausen's anti-Christian *Sefer ha-Nizzahon* of 1400, the author warns against calculating the End, but immediately thereafter states that the Messiah will come in 1410.[2] But

---

1. *b. Sanhedrin* 97b.
2. Yom-Tov Lipmann Mühlhausen, *Sefer ha-Nizzahon*, ed. F. Talmage (Jerusalem, 1984; repr. Altdorf-Nürnberg, 1644), sec. 335, 187.

then, to be on the safe side, he goes on to caution against disappointment should this expectation be proven wrong. A few years after 1410, the book was recopied.[3] The scribe left the original calculation but changed the result and, instead of 1410, wrote 1426, even adding a calculation of his own to support the new date. The copyist then stated that if the Messiah did not come even in 1426, it would be because of the people's transgressions.

Calculations of the End of this sort are not much different from the horoscopes of our day, and they should be seen as a kind of arithmetic diversion to uplift the spirits of people awaiting Redemption. Hence, not every messianic calculation should be seen as reflecting an active messianic movement. Nevertheless, the opposite extreme, which downplays the significance of the messianic factor as a moving force in medieval Jewish history, should also be avoided. A historian viewing the past retrospectively is likely to underestimate the importance of the messianic issue because, generally speaking, there is more extant documentation reflecting the period of disappointment in Messiahs who failed to come than there is of the period of tense hopefulness before his coming.

In this chapter I wish to discuss one rather important calculation of the End that evoked wide response and intense excitement and that was of profound importance both within the framework of internal Jewish life and in shaping relations between Jews and Christians. I am referring to the Jewish messianic expectation before the year 1240, an episode that clearly illustrates the sensitivity of Christians to the appearance of an acute Jewish messianic expectation.

CALCULATIONS OF THE END AT THE
TURN OF THE JEWISH MILLENNIUM

Four unique qualities distinguish the expectation of deliverance before 1240 from other calculations of the End. First, it was not merely an arbitrary, technical calculation based on interpretations of biblical verses and numerology (*gematriya*). Rather, the messianic expectation of 1240 was related to the end of a millennium on the Jewish calendar and the beginning of a new one, since on the Hebrew calendar the year 1240 corresponded to the

3. Ms. Oxford–Bodleian, Opp. 592, sec. 335; see A. Neubauer, *Catalogue of the Hebrew Manuscripts in the Bodleian Library* (Oxford, 1886), no. 2162.

year 5000 of Creation. Second, reports of the expectation of deliverance come to us from almost every corner of the Jewish Diaspora, from the southern and northern parts of the Mediterranean basin and the European continent. Third, this messianic expectation evoked an unprecedented wave of preparations and responses, as we shall see shortly. Fourth, unlike the usual calculations of the End, which foresee messianic events at a definite time, the expectation of 1240 marked off a rather extended time period during which the messianic process was to take place. Let us begin by examining the main documents.[4]

The most widespread calculation assumed quite simply that the messianic age was connected with the end of the fifth millennium. The Provençal work *Bereshit Rabbati* says: "The entire enslavement was in the fifth millennium, and in it shall be the morning for Israel, that they shall be redeemed."[5] A similar calculation is presented in Rabbi Judah al-Bargeloni's *Commentary to Sefer Yezirah:*

> And that we shall be redeemed quickly and in our own days, at the
> end of the fifth millennium, this is [a tradition] that has been conveyed
> at all times throughout Israel. And even the Christians, who [believe]
> due to their error, because they heard that the Messiah will come at the
> end of the fifth millennium, and they found that this was the time of
> the hangings of the Evil One, which was itself at the end of the fourth
> millennium. And even though that event was more than two hundred
> years before the completion of that millennium, and was only in the
> thirty-seventh century, they fixed their error at the end of the fifth mil-
> lennium, and they calculated one thousand years from Adam to Noah,
> and made several erroneous calculations and deceptions.[6]

4. These sources for messianic expectations are partially collected and discussed by Julius Aronius, *Regesten zur Geschichte der Juden* (Berlin, 1902), 227–30; A. Z. Aescoly, *Ha-Tenu'ah ha-meshihit be-Yisrael* (Jerusalem, 1956), 188–92; Ben-Zion Dinur, *Yisrael ba-Golah* (Jerusalem, 1968), pt. 2, vol. 3, 436–41. For additional sources, see below.

5. *Bereshit Rabbati*, ed. H. Albeck (Jerusalem, 1940), 16–17, and additional sources listed there by the redactor.

6. *Perush Sefer Yezirah leha-Rav ha-Nasi Yehudah bar Barzilai ha-Bartzeloni*, ed. S. Z. H. Halberstamm (Berlin, 1895), 239. A similar calculation is cited in *Megillat ha-Megalleh* by Rabbi Avraham bar Hiyya ha-Nasi (Berlin, 1924), chap. 5, 36, 147. The book was apparently written during the 1120s and enumerates four possible dates for the Eschaton: 1136, 1230, 1358, and 1448. Concerning the second date, 1230, he writes: "And this calculation is the closest of all and is to be relied on more than the first."

What the author means to say is that the Christians also know that the Messiah would come at the end of the fifth millennium, but that this calculation is incompatible with the Jewish one that Jesus lived around the Hebrew year 3700, long before the end of the fourth millennium. Hence, the Christian chronology, according to him, added a thousand years or more to the period between Adam and Noah, putting Jesus's birth at the end of the fifth millennium. Al-Bargeloni's words are not entirely clear, for already in the year 221 Julius Africanus had fixed Jesus's birth as the year 5500 from the Creation of the world—that is, precisely in the middle of the sixth millennium, a calculation accepted by many Christian authors.[7] Moreover, Christian eschatology regularly speaks of the end of the sixth millennium, not the fifth, as the end of history and the date of the Final Judgment.[8]

Al-Bargeloni concludes by stating "and that which has been conveyed to us concerning the coming of the Redeemer at the end of the fifth millennium, has also been passed down and arranged in several *aggadot* that our Sages expounded." It seems likely that he was referring here to the homily from the late Midrashic collection *Bereshit Rabbati* mentioned above. As we shall see, the Jewish notion of anticipating Redemption at the end of the fifth millennium first appears in sources from the twelfth century, based on the "prophecy of Elijah" in the Talmud.[9] Another calculation of Al-Bargeloni fixes the End during the final jubilee before the year 5000 (that is, 1190–1240 C.E). This calculation is based on a perception of the biblical jubilee as a typological number, representing eschatological time:

And in the fiftieth century, quickly in our time, Israel will enjoy complete freedom, and we shall return to our heritage and to our inheritance. . . . And these forty-nine years of seven sabbaths of years, the Omnipresent blessed be He has commanded us concerning that mitzvah, and it is a hint of the Redemption. And by its virtue as well the Redemption shall take place; calculate 49 years as 49 centuries, one century per year, making

---

7. Martin Haeusler, *Das Ende der Geschichte in der mittelalterlichen Weltchronistik* (Cologne, 1980), 6, 7, 10, 15, 22–24.

8. Robert Lerner, "The Medieval Return to the Thousand-Year Sabbath," in *The Apocalypse in the Middle Ages,* ed. R. K. Emmerson and B. McGinn (Ithaca, 1992), 51–71.

9. Haeusler (n. 7, above), 105, claims that, prior to the Reformation, the "prophecy of Elijah" was only known to a few Christians. In the twelfth century it was known to Alanus ab Insulis (Amos Funkenstein, *Heilsplan und natürliche Entwicklung* [München, 1965], 14 n. 28), and at the end of the thirteenth century the southern French Franciscan Peter Olivi knew about it; see Lerner, *Medieval Return to the Thousand-Year Sabbath,* 62 n. 38). For parallel Christian sources from the East, see note 107, p. 294.

four thousand and nine hundred, and the fiftieth century shall be similar to the jubilee year, which is entirely liberty and freedom; for in the fiftieth century we shall perhaps be redeemed speedily in our days, at the beginning of the fiftieth century or its middle or at its end.[10]

The attempt to anchor the millenarian calculation for the year 5000 in a scriptural exegesis leads the anonymous author of a biblical commentary who lived in Montpellier, France, to offer the following exegesis of Balaam's words:

> "'Come, I will let you know what this people will do to your people at the End of Days' (Num 24:14): "I heard that from this we may infer an allusion to the End that will come at the end of five thousand [years]; namely, *be-aharit ha-yamim* ['at the End of Days'] is *be-aharit h' yamim* ['at the end of five days']—that is, of the days of the Holy One blessed be He, that is, a thousand years, as we learn from the verse, 'For a thousand years in thy sight are but as yesterday when it is past' (Psalms 90:4)—we find that five thousand years equals five days."[11]

A remarkably similar calculation appears in another Ashkenazic source, this one from the circle of the Tosaphists, based on Jacob's call to his sons before his death" "Gather yourselves together, that I may tell you what shall befall you at the End of Days" (Gen 49:1). Our exegete explains the following: "'At the End of Days'—*h' yamim* (five days)—five years less than five thousand."[12] According to this, the messianic expectation was about the year 1235. Indeed, a source attributed to Rabbi Judah he-Hasid also states that the end is anticipated in 1235.[13] In the same Tosaphist collection, the editor cites another tradition, attributed to Rabbenu Hananel, according to which "The [zodiac] sign of the goat shall not pass and King Messiah will come, and his is the tenth sign [starting from Nissan], and each sign rules for five hundred years."[14]

10. *Perush Sefer Yezirah* (n. 6, p. 259), 238.

11. Staatsbibliothek München, Heb. 66, fol. 306r. This work is discussed by E. Talmage, "The Anti-Christian Polemic in *Leket Katzar*" [in Hebrew], *Michael* 4 (1976): 63.

12. On Gen 49:1, in *Sefer Tosafot ha-Shalem*, vol. 5, ed. J. Gellis (Jerusalem, 1986), 34.

13. Alexander Marx, "A Treatise on the Year of Redemption" [in Hebrew] *ha-Tzofeh le-hokhmat Yisrael* 5 (1921): 195.

14. Gen 49:1, in *Sefer Tosafot ha-Shalem*. It is worth noting the connection between the zodiac sign of Aries and Agnus Dei as Christian messianic symbols. Alongside Capricorn (the

Thus we have here two very similar calculations, one French and the other German-Ashkenazic. The French one is based on an interpretation of the phrase *aharit ha-yamim* in Balaam's words to Balak, whereas the Ashkenazic one is based on the identical phrase in Jacob's words to his sons. Yet the French calculation results in the year 1240, while the Ashkenazic one yields 1235. The French calculation is mentioned once again in another, far more important source, also of French provenance. In a closing note made by the first copyist about the arguments raised by the Jews during the trial of the Talmud that took place in Paris in 1240, the trial is described as occurring in "the year *aharit,* the 5th day of the month of Tammuz, the 2nd day of the week of *Parashat Balak,* and the 3rd day following."[15] Even at first glance it is apparent that the copyist wishes to state that the trial in Paris occurred in the year *aharit,* that is, he finds a connection between the trial and the messianic expectation. Upon a second reading, his wordplay is also evident. The sentence "the year *aharit,* the 5th day of the month of Tammuz" clearly alludes to the messianic calculation regarding *aharit ha-yamim*. This allusion is to the French calculation, since our author states that the debate took place during the week of *Parashat Balak,* in which appears Balaam's prophecy, which served the French homilist in expounding the messianic prophecy to the year 1240. It follows that the trial of the Talmud in Paris in 1240 was interpreted by the copyist of the protocol against the background of the Jewish messianic expectations—a point we will return to below.

The fact that messianic expectations toward the millennial year of 1240 were widespread is proven by the various and repeated calculations of the End in Ashkenazic sources, where it is reinforced by allusions and numerological calculations *(gematriyot)* from biblical verses, in the best Ashkenazic exegetic tradition. In the commentary *Da'at Zekenim al ha-Torah,* we read:

> "And a man found him wandering" (תעה; Gen 37:15). Here Gabriel alluded to him the three exiles: *tav* = the 400 years of Egypt; *'ayin* = the 70 years of Babylonia; *heh* = the 5 of the exile of Edom. That is, at the

---

sign of the goat), that of the lamb also serves as a messianic symbol in the messianic calculation of Rabbi Petahiah of Regensburg: "You should know that the sign of the lamb cries every day until the End shall come. . . . For Israel are only redeemed on Passover, and therefore the sign of the lamb weeps." See Avraham David, "A New Version of R. Petahya of Regensburg's *Sivuv"* [in Hebrew], *Kovetz 'al Yad* 13 (1996): 257. And cf. Gershom Scholem, "The Sources of 'The Story of Rabbi Gadiel the Infant' in Kabbalistic Literature" [in Hebrew], *Devarim Bego* 1 (Tel-Aviv, 1990): 270–83.

15. *Vikuah Rabbenu Yehiel mi-Paris,* ed. R. Margulies (Jerusalem, 1975), 27.

end of five thousand years it will be completed, speedily in our day—from the mouth of my teacher and father, of blessed memory. And I heard a similar thing from R. Binyamin Gozal, expounding, "and stayed until now" (עתה; Gen 32:4) written about Jacob, meaning, a delay of the three exiles, as I have explained [the word 'atah, "now," is spelled with the same letters as to'eh, "wandering," albeit in different order]."[16]

As for Isaac's words to Esau, "What then can I do for you, my son" (Gen 27:37), uttered after he had already blessed Jacob, the author of *Da'at Zekenim* notes: "'For you' *[lekhah]* it is written in *plenum*, with the letter *heh*. Isaac said to Esau, 'After five thousand years shall pass, then he [Jacob] shall reign. What can I do for you, that then the Holy One blessed be He shall vent his vengeance upon Edom.'"[17]

That this calculation was also known in Spain is indicated by the remarks of the Kabbalist Isaac ibn Latif of Toledo, who in 1238 composed a messianic composition entitled *Sha'ar ha-Shamayim*. This work related to his expectation of the beginning of the messianic era two years later, at the beginning of the sixth millennium.[18] As we shall see below, this was almost certainly the impulse that also moved Rabbi Moses of Coucy to conduct a revival campaign in Spain and thereafter to write his well-known *Sefer Mitzvot Gadol*.

It is with this background in mind that we need to examine a letter written in Arabic, apparently from North Africa, to the Jewish community of Alexandria, found in the Cairo Genizah and published by Simhah Assaf.[19] The letter tells of a prophet who appeared in the city of Saintes in France, who prophesied that the Ingathering of Exiles would occur in the year 1226 and that in 1233 the Messiah, son of David, would come. According to Assaf, this text should be completed as follows: "And in the year 5000 Redemption shall come"—that is, seven years after the coming of the Messiah.[20] The author of this letter tells of a dispatch he received from Marseilles, from Rabbi Joseph ben Abraham, containing messianic tidings. News

16. On Gen 37:15, in *Sefer Tosafot ha-Shalem* (n. 12, p. 261), 4 (1985): 29. Also quoted in *Likkutei Midrash Tanhuma* (Buber) 1: introduction, 128.

17. *Sefer Tosafot ha-Shalem* (n. 12, p. 261), 3; (1984): 76–77.

18. Sarah Heller-Wilensky, "Messianism, Eschatology and Utopia in 13th Century Philosophical-Mystical Kabbalah" [in Hebrew], in *Meshihiyut ve-Eskhatologia: Kovetz Ma'amarim* (Messianism and Eschatology: Hebrew), ed. Z. Baras (Jerusalem, 1984), 221–37.

19. Simhah Assaf, *Mekorot u-Mehkarim be-Toldot Yisrael* (Jerusalem, 1946), 151–54.

20. This letter was evidently written shortly after 1211, since it contains the sentence "he and his brother moved to the Land of Israel," which may allude to the immigration to Israel

of the French prophet's words also reached Rabbi Eleazar of Worms, who investigated the truth of his prophecies and found them correct.

The immediate impulse behind these rumors may have been the Fourth Lateran Council, held in 1215, at which the launching of another crusade to the Holy Land was declared. During the next two years the Fourth Crusade was organized, and eschatological expectations intensified among Christians as well. Perhaps this was alluded to in the following passage from the letter about the prophecies of the French prophet: "That he called out, 'the earth upon . . .' and his words were fulfilled." According to Assaf, this passage alludes to the biblical verse "He stretches out the north over the void, and hangs the earth upon nothing" (Job 26:6), citing the Talmudic homily based on this verse: "The world is only sustained by virtue of he who halts himself in a time of dispute, as is said, 'He hangs the earth upon nothing' [*belimah:* also means, "halting, braking, holding back."]"[21] Such an exegesis sounds suitable for Jewish messianic expectations at a time of Christian efforts to take the Land of Israel from the Muslims, as in the well-known Rabbinic dictum: "If you see the kingdoms provoking one another, anticipate the footsteps of the King Messiah."[22]

In any event, this letter was clearly written a few years before 1226—the first date forecast in it. While it does not explicitly express millenarian expectations, it does reflect the messianic atmosphere that gathered strength during the second decade of the thirteenth century—that is, in the last generation before 1240. This fact will play a decisive role later, when we discuss the immigration from France to the Land of Israel of that decade and its messianic motivations.

At this point we should note another document of extraordinary contents. In a text published by Alexander Marx in 1921, a messianic calculation is presented, which somehow never received the attention it deserved.[23]

---

of Rabbi Yosef Clisson and his brother Rabbi Meir. They are mentioned twice in a similar manner. In Alexandria they were met by Rabbi Abraham son of Maimonides: "And we had heard of Rabbi R. Yosef *z"l* and of his brother Meir *z"l*," and in Jerusalem they were met by R. Judah al-Harizi: "And at their head the pious rabbi R. Yosef b. R. Barukh . . . and his brother the sage R. Meir." See E. E. Urbach, *Ba'alei ha-Tosafot: toldoteihem, hibureihem, shitatam* (Jerusalem, 1980), 318–19.

21. *b. Hullin* 89a.

22. *Genesis Rabbah* 41.4, ed. Theodor-Albeck, 409.

23. Marx (n. 13, p. 261), 194–202. I have discussed this briefly in "The Silence of the Historian and the Imagination of the Writer: R. Amnon of Magence and Esther-Mina of Worms" [in Hebrew], *Alpayim* 15 (1995): 138–39.

This is a thirteenth-century French commentary on Tractate *Avot;* at the end of the fourth chapter, a fourteenth-century Ashkenazic copyist added various messianic calculations. One of these is based on a perception of all of history as built on cycles of 532 years each—a figure derived from multiplying the twenty-eight-year cycle of the sun by the nineteen-year cycle of the moon (astronomical cycles used in Jewish calendrical-liturgical calculations). The end of each such cycle is considered a time of divine grace. If we multiply 532 by 7, which is, as we know, a typological number, we arrive at 3,724 years from the Creation of the world, corresponding to the year 36 B.C.E. That year was thus a year of special grace. And what happened in that year? According to the author, it was the year in which Jesus was crucified. Our text even recounts a conversation between an angel from heaven and Jesus at the time of his Crucifixion:

> And when they took Jesus out to be hanged and stoned, he was knowledgeable [in this] and knew that it was then the year 532. He said: I bear it for the Unity of the Name and for the Yoke of Heaven. And he gave his body over to the fear of his Creator [and said]: May it be the will of my Creator that I be accepted before God. A voice came forth [and said]: For the sake of this hour, the hour of grace of 532, [which is] a time of Divine favor, your prayer has been heard. But your prayer will not [be heard] in your days or in your lifetime, but only a long time after your death. And thus it was, and he answered and said: Since my words are acceptable before You, may it be Your will that my Divinity be sustained like the Torah of Moses our Teacher until now.

In other words, Jesus's wish to be considered God will be fulfilled, since he prayed at the end of the 532-year cycle, a time of grace. But the voice added that this wish could only be realized a "long time" from now—apparently a reference to the time that passed up till the conversion of Rome to Christianity. Jesus also asked that his divinity be sustained "like the Torah of Moses our Teacher until now," meaning that the nations of the world recognize his doctrine for the same period of time that Israel had recognized the Mosaic Torah until that point. Between Moses and Jesus 1,276 years passed, so Jesus would also enjoy 1,276 years during which his doctrine would be accepted by the nations of the world. Given that our author thought, for reasons of his own, that Jesus was crucified in 36 B.C.E., the period allotted to Jesus's doctrine would come to an end in the year 1240. Hence, the author of this calculation also believed in the coming of Redemption in 1240.

The document as a whole contains a variety of different calculations of the End, stretching over a rather long period, ranging from 1236 through 1352. The fact that they were all gathered in one place indicates that the editor of the collection did not find any contradiction among the various dates. One may assume that the editor presumably lived before the earliest of these dates. Indeed, most of the sages whom he mentions with honorifics used for the dead are from the second half of the twelfth century: Rabbi Samuel Hasid, Rabbi Moses ben Maimon, Rabbi Isaac of Dampierre.[24]

Two other reports of a rather unusual type show something of the disappointment felt after the year 1240 had passed. In Oxford manuscript Oppenheim it states: "And by rights he ought to have been eradicated and the faith in Jesus concluded upon the end of the fifth millennium, but because of our sins there came out of them what came out of them. And I, this author, stand today in the year five thousand and [?] by the 'small calculation,' and they still adhere to their false doctrine." Our author mentions the pogrom of Frankfurt in 1241 and the burning of the Talmud in Paris in 1242; hence, it must have been written shortly after 1240.[25] Another source from the circle of Ashkenazic Hasidim presents a messianic calculation for 1257, likewise based on treating the beginning of the sixth millennium as a suitable date for the onset of Redemption. This source was definitely written after 1240 and should be seen as a retroactive effort to "save" the year 5000 as a year of deliverance through a slight "adjustment": the author thinks that seventeen years need to be added to it. His calculation is based on the argument that, just as 2,500 years passed before the first deliverance (the date the Israelites entered the Land of Israel after the Exodus), so another 2,500 years will pass until the final Redemption.[26]

In addition to these Jewish sources, we also find several non-Jewish sources about the Jewish messianic expectation regarding 1240, to be discussed below. At this stage, we can already point to France and, to a lesser extent, to Germany as the center of messianic ferment in 1240. And the letter to Alexandria indicates the spreading of this messianic expectation through the Mediterranean basin.

24. For further discussion of this document, see the end of this chapter.

25. Neubauer, *Catalogue* (n. 3, p. 258), no. 2256, fol. 63. Published by A. Neubauer, *Seder ha-Hakhamim ve-Korot ha-Yamim* (Oxford, 1888), 1:193.

26. A. Kupfer, ed., *Teshuvot u-pesakim me'et Hakhmei Ashkenaz ve-Tzarfat* (Jerusalem, 1973), sec. 183, 308–12.

The central role played by France in this messianic anticipation is indicated by another Hebrew document, still in manuscript in the municipal library of Darmstadt. The author of this anonymous work, entitled "Homilies of King Messiah and Gog and Magog" *(Derashot Melekh ha-Mashiah ve-Gog u-Magog),*[27] identifies himself as a student of Rabbi Yitzhak ben Abraham (Ritzba), one of the important French Tosaphists of the early thirteenth century.

The immediate impetus for writing this composition was the belief that the Messiah was to be revealed by the year 5000 of the Creation, that is, before 1240 C.E. This calculation was based on the "prophecy of Elijah" in the Talmud, which states that the world will exist for six thousand years: two thousand years of "chaos," two thousand years of "Torah," and two thousand years of "Messiah."[28] The messianic era was supposed to have begun in 4000, but, at any rate, cannot tarry beyond the year 4999 (that is, before 1240); otherwise, the Talmud would not have said that the last two millennia are the era of the "Messiah." Our author attributes this calculation to his teacher, Rabbi Yitzhak ben Abraham: "That the fifth millennium will not pass until King Messiah shall come. . . . Thus I received from

27. Ms. Darmstadt, Codex Or. 25. I intend to publish this work in the future. On this work see Urbach (n. 20, p. 263), 270. This work is followed in the manuscript by the anonymous chronicle about the pogroms of 1096. A small section from this treatise has been cited by later authors and published a few times in *Hibbur Totz'ot Eretz Yisrael* in A. Yaari, *Mas'ot Eretz Yisrael shel 'Olim Yehudim* (Tel Aviv, 1946), 98; *Sefer ha-Manhig,* ed. Y. Rafael (Jerusalem, 1978), 81–82; S. Assaf, *Mekorot u-Mehkarim (Texts and Studies in Jewish History:* English; Jerusalem 1946), 90: "We have seen the words of our ancient rabbis who spoke of the prophecy of the King Messiah, may it be His will that he come speedily in our days, and this is their language." The section copied further on is taken from this work, from which we may conclude that *Midrash Melekh ha-Mashiah ve-Gog u-Magog* in Ms. Darmstadt is the source for "the words of our ancient rabbis" in *Totz'ot Eretz Yisrael.* For further discussion of this text see Elchanan Reiner, "Pilgrims and Pilgrimage to Eretz Yisrael, 1099–1517" [in Hebrew] (PhD diss., Hebrew University of Jerusalem, 1988) 114–18, 153–55. The original text in the Darmstadt manuscript was discussed long ago by scholars such as Moritz Stern, ("Analekten zur Geschichte der Juden," *Magazin für die Wissenschaft des Judenthums* 15 (1888) and Harry Breslau, "Juden und Mongolen," *Zeitschrift für die Geschichte der Juden in Deutschland* 1 (1887): 102; Breslau, "Ein Nachtrag," *Zeitschrift für die Geschichte der Juden in Deutschland.* 2 (1888): 382–83.

28. *b. Sanhedrin* 97a.

our teacher Yitzhak to teach." Since Ritzba died in 1210, the messianic expectation for the end of the fifth millennium was palpable already in the generation before 1240; as the years passed, that expectation intensified. But the importance of the work in question for our discussion does not lie in its calculation of the End, but in its description of the preparations necessary for the coming of the Messiah:

> And no person should think, that the King Messiah will reveal himself on an impure land. . . . Nor should any person err, saying that he will be revealed in the Land of Israel among the Gentiles. . . . But it is clear that there will [already] be students of Torah in the Land of Israel, and pious ones and men of great deeds from all four corners of the world, one from a city and two from a family, everyone whose heart inspired him and into whom there has shined a spirit of purity, making him fit for love of the holy. And thereafter King Messiah will be revealed among them.

This fragment was familiar to scholars from a later citation quoted in works from the end of the thirteenth century,[29] but we can now state with certainty that it reflects views that were prevalent in France before 1240. The idea expressed in this fragment is a total innovation. In the past, Jews immigrated to the Land of Israel to prostrate themselves on the graves of their forefathers or to fulfill the commandments concerning the Land of Israel—immigration with no messianic expectations whatsoever. In contrast, according to the traditional view, the Messiah will ingather the dispersed of Israel wherever they are in Exile and return them to Zion, just as he delivered Israel from Egypt while they were still dwelling in an alien land. The Exodus from Egypt thus serves as a typological model for the future Redemption, from which it follows that the redemption will precede the return to Zion.

An active messianic approach was common among the Karaites in Jerusalem in the tenth century. Daniel al-Kumisi issued a call to send a chosen group of people from each place to settle in Jerusalem:[30] "Now you, my brethren of Israel. . . . Rise up and come to Jerusalem . . . and if you

---

29. Reiner (n. 27, p. 267), 114–18, 151–55.

30. The Karaites' attitude toward Jewish settling in Eretz Israel during the tenth century is the only exception. Daniel al-Kumisi's letter was first published by Jacob Mann, "A Tract by an Early Karaite Settler in Jerusalem," *JQR* 12 (1922): 257–98, esp. 283–85; and a second time by A. Yaari, *Iggerot Eretz Yisrael* (Tel Aviv, 1943), 56–59. Cf. Naphtali Wieder, *The Judean Scrolls and Karaism* (London, 1962), 99–103; M. Gil, *Eretz Yisrael ba-tekufah he-Muslemit*

do not come because you are busy with buying and selling your merchandise, then send five people from each city with their livelihood, so that we may form a unique group, to beseech our God constantly upon the hills of Jerusalem."[31] This seeking is reminiscent of the words in *Midrash Melekh ha-Mashiah ve-Gog u-Magog,* regarding the request to bring up to the Land of Israel "one from a city and two from a family" (Jer 3:14). This verse is also a favorite of the Karaite Sahl ben Mazzli'ah: "The servants of the Lord gathered together to her [Jerusalem], one from a city and two from a family."[32]

But such activist views were not generally held within Rabbinic circles. This is still the view of Maimonides in *The Epistle to Yemen:* "After his manifestation in Palestine, Israel will be gathered in Jerusalem."[33] Our anonymous author takes issue with this traditional view, thereby adopting, presumably unintentionally, the Karaite position. He and his teacher think that the presence of a Jewish community in the Land of Israel is a precondition for the appearance of the Messiah:

And when the community in the Land of Israel shall be numerous, and they shall worship on the holy mountain, and their cry shall ascend to Heaven, then the King Messiah will be revealed among them, and he will ingather the other dispersed exiles, for Israel will hear that the King Messiah has been revealed. . . . Then the mighty ones of Israel will gather to him from the four corners of the earth, and they will make a mighty army, and will smite the rulers of Ishmael and Edom in Jerusalem, and expel the uncircumcised ones from it.

The expression "and their cry shall ascend to Heaven," is taken from Exodus 2:23. Just as in Egypt God first heard Israel's cry and delivered Israel, so too in the latter Redemption God will hear the prayer of the Jews pray-

---

ha-rishonah (Tel Aviv, 1983), 1:506–8; Y. Erder, "The Centrality of Palestine Among Early Karaite Circles" [in Hebrew], *Zion* 60 (1995): 37–67.

31. Mann, "Tract by an Early Karaite Settler," 285.

32. Gil (n. 30, p. 268), 507. The Karaite immigrants are referred to as *Maskilim* ("enlightened"), an expression parallel to "those who possess Torah, and pious ones and men of good deeds" mentioned in the present document. On the messianic context in Karaite literature of the *Maskilim* as teachers of Torah, see Wieder (n. 30, p. 268), 104–12.

33. *Iggerot ha-Rambam,* ed. Y. Shilat (Jerusalem, 1987), 1:153; English: *Crisis and Leadership: Epistles of Maimonides,* trans. and notes by A. Halkin, discussion by D. Hartman (Philadelphia, 1985), 125.

ing at the site of the Temple, and only then will he deliver them. The immigration of a select few to the Land of Israel is therefore an essential stage in any messianic scenario, and from that point onward it will progress naturally. After the appearance of a Jewish king in the Land of Israel becomes known, the Jews still in Exile will immigrate to the Land of Israel of their own free will. From among the immigrants, a Jewish army will arise, which will smite the Crusader and Muslim troops, and the Christians will be banished from Jerusalem. The text continues with a description of the counterorganization of a Christian crusade ("the king of Edom will gather all his forces to wage war"), and the Jewish King will likewise mobilize "the heroes of Ephraim" for the decisive war. When it is over, the Christians will be expelled from the Land of Israel, Rome will be destroyed, "and then all the seed of Esau will be cut off."

This scenario, as would be expected, takes into account the political reality of the Crusades. The King Messiah is portrayed in the image of a Crusader king. The idea that the Messiah will be revealed only on condition that the Land of Israel is settled by Jews seems like an adoption of the Crusader ideal of the Christianization of the Holy Land. The Jewish messianic expectation during the Crusades was opposed to the reality of a land that served as an arena of struggle between only two religions, Christianity and Islam. This messianic work reflects a Jewish attempt to bring about a change in that reality and to restore things to their former glory, to the days when the struggle for the holiness of the Land was conducted between the Jews and the Christians.

This call to prepare for the coming of the Messiah by immigrating to the Land of Israel even before 1240 coincides with reports of the immigration of elitist groups of Talmudic scholars from France, which took place beginning from 1211, known in the sources as the immigration "of the Three Hundred Rabbis."[34] Scholars have expressed varying opinions regarding the motivations of this group. Leopold Zunz, Elkan N. Adler, Abba Hillel Silver, and Ephraim E. Urbach suggested a messianic factor, but their opinion was rejected by later scholars: Gerson Cohen, Ephraim Kanarfogel, and most

34. Ephraim Kanarfogel, "The Aliyah of 'Three Hundred Rabbis' in 1211: Tosafist Attitude Toward Settling in the Land of Israel," *JQR* 76 (1986): 191–215; Reiner (n. 29, p. 268), 39–40, 55–69; S. D. Goitein, "A New Source Concerning the Aliyah of the French Rabbis and Their Entourage" [in Hebrew], in *Ha-Yishuv be-Eretz Yisrael be-reshit ha-Islam uve-tekufat ha-Tzalbanim le'or kitvei ha-Genizah* (Jerusalem, 1980), 338–43.

recently Elchanan Reiner.[35] In light of the data presented here, the messianic explanation receives an added weight.

The outstanding figure among the French immigrants was Rabbi Samson of Sens, the younger brother of Ritzba, mentioned earlier. Ritzba, who died a year before his brother immigrated to the Land of Israel, was unable to realize his own messianic teaching, but he did manage to correspond with Rabbi Jonathan of Lunel before the latter's immigration to the Land of Israel, in 1209. He also wrote a halakhic work on the commandments applicable in the Land. Hence, Ritzba was clearly connected to the circle of immigrants bound for the Land of Israel, and it seems likely that it was only his death in 1210 that prevented him from joining them.

His student, the author of the work discussed above, belonged to that same circle of French Tosaphists, from whom the group known as "the three hundred rabbis" emerged. In light of this fact, I suggest that this work be understood as the ideological manifesto underlying the immigration of the rabbis from France.

The author noted with satisfaction: "For a spirit from on High descends on those that are fit to ascend to Zion," signifying the immigration taking place in his day, whose aims were identical to those with expectations of Redemption in 1240. Linguistically, this sentence shows considerable resemblance to the main source relating the immigration of the three hundred rabbis—the chronicle entitled *Malkhei Edom* (The Kings of Edom) that was appended to Solomon ibn Verga's *Shevet Yehudah*, which states that in the year 1211 "God inspired the rabbis of France and the rabbis of Angleterre [i.e., England] to go to Jerusalem."[36] The two sentences are parallel: the expression "God inspired" parallels "a spirit from on High descends on"; "the rabbis of France and the rabbis of Angleterre" parallels "those that are fit"; and the expression "to go to Jerusalem" parallels "to ascend to Zion." Thus, the description in Ibn Verga seems to be based on the present work, which attributes messianic significance to the immigration to Zion. The

35. Leopold Zunz, *Gesammelte Schriften*, vol. 3 (Berlin, 1876), 227; E. N. Adler, "Notes sur l'émigration en Palestine de 1211," *Révue des Etudes Juives* 85 (1918): 71; Abba Hillel Silver, *A History of Messianic Speculation in Israel* (New York, 1924), 75–76; Urbach (n. 20, p. 268), 334 (but see his explanation on 125–26). Against them, see Gerson Cohen, "Messianic Postures of Ashkenazim and Sefardim," *Studies of the Leo Baeck Institute* (New York, 1967), 124; Kanarfogel (n. 34, p. 270), 196; Reiner (n. 29, p. 268), 115–17, 153–54.

36. Shlomo ibn Verga, *Shevet Yehudah*, ed. Y. Baer and A. Schochat (Jerusalem, 1947), 147.

description of the immigrants as "wise, pious, and proper" men is also consistent with the pietistic-messianic trend of the French immigration to the Land of Israel in the first quarter of the thirteenth century.

The assumption that the immigration of the three hundred rabbis from France stemmed from a messianic program may shed new light on another messianic reckoning. In his *Epistle to Yemen*, written about 1172, Maimonides proposed his own calculation for the renewal of prophecy among Jewry, which for him was "one of the signs betokening the approach of the messianic era."[37] According to the original Arabic version, prophecy will be renewed in the year 4970 (1209–1210), while according to Samuel ibn Tibbon's translation, in 4972 (1211–1212). The former date is consistent with the immigration to the Land of Israel of Rabbi Jonathan of Lunel,[38] one of Maimonides' Provençal admirers, while the latter date corresponds to the date of the immigration of the three hundred rabbis, who initially settled in Jerusalem and established close connections with Rabbi Abraham, son of Maimonides. Thus, it is not altogether impossible that, even if Maimonides' messianic calculations are not based on a millenarian understanding of the end of the fifth millennium, such as was widespread among the French immigrants, they were nevertheless an additional element among the factors making up the messianic motivations of this group to settle in Jerusalem. This possibility sheds new light on the intensive activity of renewing the Jewish colony in Jerusalem during the Ayyubid period, activity that was initiated and guided by Rabbi Abraham, son of Maimonides. Reiner has noted that the Jewish colony in Jerusalem was only renewed when Rabbi Jonathan of Lunel settled there in 1210, and that it lasted nine years, until the walls of Jerusalem were destroyed in 1219 by the Ayyubid ruler Al-Malik al-Mu'atam, shortly before the Fifth Crusade arrived at the shores of Egypt.[39]

We may infer something of the later developments of the messianic excitement in France and its relation to the immigration to the Land of Israel

37. *Iggerot ha-Rambam* (n. 32, p. 269), 153; English: 122.
38. Reiner (n. 29, p. 268), 39–40.
39. Reiner (n. 29, p. 268), 43. In 1229 the city passed into the hands of the Christians, as a result of the Jaffa Agreement between the German emperor Friedrich II and Al-Malik al-Mu'atem, and the Jews were strictly forbidden from entering the city. But in 1236 negotiations were conducted with the Crusader rulers of the city, who finally allowed the Jews to come as pilgrims and to settle there permanently. During those years, the messianic fervor of 1240 peaked, and it may be that the effort to renew the Jewish hold on Jerusalem may also have been fueled by it.

from a letter sent to the Egyptian sage Rabbi Hananel the Dayan, Maimonides' disciple and son-in-law. The letter was written in May 1235 by a Jewish merchant from Alexandria, who mentions that some people who had just arrived from Marseilles spoke about a large number of French Jews who planned to come shortly, "may the Lord protect us from the trouble they will make."[40] S. D. Goitein conjectures that this letter refers to a new group of immigrants from France who were planning to go to the Holy Land via Egypt. He finds the background to this wave of immigration in the edicts introduced by King Saint Louis of France against usury. However, it seems more likely that what we have here is an additional organization (whose ultimate fate we do not know) that sprang up in the midst of the messianic ferment in France toward the end of the Hebrew millennium.

Messianic expectation toward 1240 assumed other manifestations. In 1236 Rabbi Moses of Coucy organized a campaign of religious revival among the Jewish communities of Spain; the sermons he preached there were incorporated in his book *Sefer Mitzvot Gadol*, one of the most important halakhic codifications of the Middle Ages. In this respect Rabbi Moses of Coucy acted like the preaching monks, Franciscans and Dominicans, who wandered around with the aim of urging people to repent. In his words, "There was a reason from Heaven that I should go about in [different] lands to chastise the dispersed of Israel."[41] "A reason from Heaven" is somewhat reminiscent of the phrase "a spirit from on High descends on" mentioned above, and may be seen as an allusion to a messianic plan.[42] Rabbi Moses's main teacher, Rabbi Judah ben Isaac Sir Leon of Paris, belonged to the groups in France and Germany who anticipated the coming of the Messiah in 1236.[43] Israel

40. S. D. Goitein, "'R. Hananel ha-Dayyan Ha-Gadol,' Shmuel ha-Nadiv,. Maimonides' Son-in-Law" [in Hebrew], *Tarbiz* 50 (1981): 383

41. *Sefer Mitzvot Gadol* (Venice, 1547), pt. 2: *Mitzvot Aseh*, sec. 3. In his introduction to part 1 of the book, *Mitzvot lo-ta'aseh*, he uses the identical expression: "there was a reason from Heaven, that I should go about in the lands to chastise the exiles of Israel."

42. According to this concept, repentance must precede the messianic age, perhaps on the basis of *b. Yevamot* 24b: "One does not accept proselytes in the days of Messiah." A similar stance was expressed by Maharil, *Minhagim*, ed. S. J. Spitzer (Jerusalem, 1989), 305: "In the days of Messiah repentance is not accepted. And this is analogous to the fact that one does not accept proselytes at that time, for one who converts then does not do so out of love of God, may He be blessed, but only to rejoice in the joy of Israel. And since we anticipate redemption every day, one who does not repent—may Messiah come quickly in our days—shall no longer be able to repent, and will remain in his sins, Heaven forbid."

43. Marx (n. 23, p. 264), 198.

Ta-Shma recently published a sermon of Rabbi Moses of Coucy steeped in messianic expectations, expressing the fear that his generation's fate will be like that of the generation of the desert, which was redeemed and left Egypt but died in the desert because of its sins and never reached the Promised Land.[44] The moral is clear: the approaching messianic scenario required, in his view, mass repentance. The two Jewish responses to the messianic expectation of 1240 reviewed so far clearly reflect two predominant phenomena in Christian religious life in France at the beginning of the thirteenth century: the Crusades, on the one hand, and the birth of the mendicant orders, on the other.[45]

FULDA 1235, PARIS 1240: CHRISTIAN REACTIONS?

How did Christians react to the messianic excitement that gripped the Jews? I would like to argue that the Christian world did not remain indifferent to it. The messianic scenario was designed to restore the political and religious position of the Jews and to elevate them from a humiliated nation into a triumphant one. Messianic expectations included a harsh vision of a universal Day of Judgment, when God would judge and punish the nations that subjugate Israel. The divine messianic justice would be accomplished through the downfall of Edom—the Roman Church—the mythic heir of Rome, destroyer of Jerusalem. Christians could not possibly be indifferent to such a scenario.

And indeed, Christians did not hide their concern that, in some obscure, unknown corner of the world, "beyond the dark mountains," there existed the ancient Jewish kingdom of the ten tribes. The legend of Alexander is an outstanding example of this fear.[46] Andrew Gow discusses the legend of the "red Jew," widespread in Germany from the thirteenth century on, in

44. I. M. Ta-Shma, "An Epistle and a Sermon: Words of Inspiration by One of Our Early Rabbis" [in Hebrew], *Moriah* 19, nos. 5–6 (1994): 7–12; I. Gilat, "Two *Baqqashot* of Moses of Coucy" [in Hebrew] *Tarbiz* 28 (1959): 54–58; Jacob Katz, *Exclusiveness and Tolerance* (New York, 1962), 80. R. Moses expected the conversion of the Christians at the End of Days.

45. See: C. T. Maier, *Preaching the Crusades: Mendicant Friars and the Cross in the Thirteenth Century* (Cambridge, 1994). On itinerant preachers, see Herbert Grundmann, *Religiöse Bewegungen im Mittelalter* (Hildesheim, 1961), 442–52, 503–13.

46. Adolf Neubauer, "Where Are the Ten Tribes?" *JQR* 1 (1889): 14–28, 95–114, 184–201; B. McGinn, *Visions of the End* (New York, 1998); C. F. Beckingham and B. Hamilton, eds., *Prester John, the Mongols and the Ten Lost Tribes,* (n.p., 1996).

which the Jews are presented as evil schemers who want to bring catastrophe to Europe.[47] A number of explanations have been offered as to why the Jews are presented as red. This phenomenon may stem from a reversal of the messianic role assigned by the Jews to the Christians. The Christians were considered by the Jews as "Edom," a word derived in the Bible from the color red (*adom* in Hebrew). According to biblical prophecies, Edom is destined at the End of Days for total destruction. The Christian legend of the "red Jew" attributes to the Jews the same messianic fate that the Jews had assigned to the Christians for the future.

The disaster awaiting the Christians, according to Jewish eschatology, may explain the revelation of relatively restrained acts of Ashkenazic messianism, a restraint deriving from the fear of the Jews in Germany of the Christian response. Ashkenazic Jewry existed under the protection of the Holy Roman Empire—the main candidate for annihilation in the messianic era—and it was only natural that the Jews there would be doubly cautious. This context may also help us to understand the surprising fact, already noted by Kanarfogel, that Ashkenazic Jews were totally absent among the immigrants to the Land of Israel in the thirteenth century.[48] At the very moment that the Jews of France were beginning to take active steps to hasten the Redemption, a pietistic strain was growing among the Jews of Germany, who were firmly opposed to any political or personal act that dared to actively influence the hastening of the advent of the King Messiah.[49] The Ashkenazic Pietists articulated a position resolutely opposed to immigrating to the Land of Israel and to hastening the messianic end, issuing a grave warning: "Not to hasten the End and not to go up to the Land of Israel before the time. . . . Whoever hastens to go up to the Land of Israel shall surely die."[50] This declaration may be seen as a direct and explicit polemic with the French messianic scenario described above.[51] Its sharp-

47. A. C. Gow, *The Red Jews: Antisemitism in an Apocalyptic Age, 1200–1600* (Leiden–New York,, 1995).

48. See n. 34 above.

49. The difference between the passive messianic Ashkenazic teaching and the active Sephardic one has been noted by Cohen (n. 35, p. 271). Cf. Peter Schäfer, "The Idea of Piety of the Ashkenazi Hasidim and Its Roots in Jewish Tradition," *Jewish History* 4 (1990): 15–16.

50. Israel M. Ta-Shma, "The Attitude to Aliya to Eretz Israel (Palestine) in Medieval German Jewry" [in Hebrew], *Shalem* 6 (1992): 315–18.

51. Avraham Grossman, "The Attitude of R. Meir of Rothenburg to the Land of Israel" [in Hebrew] *Cathedra* 9, no. 84 (1997): 82.

ness creates the impression that the Ashkenazic author saw a real danger in the French style of making practical messianic plans.

This is evidently the historical context within which one ought to read the warnings that emanated from the circles of Ashkenazic Pietists concerning the need to conceal the date of the End. One source, *Sefer Hasidim,* states that one who prophesies the End must be doing so by magic, for it is only demons who wish to mislead a person into teaching a false reckoning, and thus he will be an object of mockery and scorn once his prophecy is confuted.[52] Further on (in the Parma edition alone), a miracle is presented that took place in the Slavic countries ("the Land of Canaan"), in which women and simple people could suddenly quote by heart whole chapters of consolation from the Book of Isaiah. Joseph Dan has noted the full source of this story in a German Hasidic work that is still only in manuscript (Oxford 1567):

> And it happened once that a certain person said that Messiah would come [imminently], and this was the sign: the entire city, the ignorant people and the women, would on the next day recite the text of all the chapters of consolation in Isaiah. The next day, all those who did not know the alphabet along with the women, recited all the verses of consolation in Isaiah according to the text. And this was, "and there will be a lying spirit in the mouth of all his prophets." [1 Kgs 22:22][53]

Thus, in Eastern Europe a prophet prophesied the coming of the Messiah and gave a sign to prove his words: that all the women and simple people would know the chapters of consolation in the Book of Isaiah. Even though it was fulfilled, the Hasid reporting it thought it was a false prophecy. Dan notes the similarity between this prophecy and another one from France mentioned above, likewise connected with the messianic expectations toward 1240.[54] The prophecy from France also relates that Rabbi Eleazar of Worms authorized (or perhaps he himself wished to clarify) the authenticity of the prophet: "And there is no deceit in his mouth . . . every time they examined him [they found him] to be speaking the truth," and it also

---

52. *Sefer Hasidim,* Bologna version, ed. R. Margulies (Jerusalem, 1970), sec. 206; Parma version, ed. Vistinetsky and Freimann (Frankfurt, 1924), sec. 212.

53. Joseph Dan, *Torat ha-Sod shel Hasidut Ashkenaz* (The Mystical Doctrine of Ashkenazic Pietism: English; Jerusalem, 1968), 241–45.

54. See n. 19 above.

included some verses of consolation from Isaiah. Thus, the incident discussed in *Sefer Hasidim* is evidently connected with the expectations of 1240.

These sources indicate an internal conflict among the Ashkenazic Hasidim regarding the reliability of prophecies based on eschatological calculations. Dan claims that Hasidei Ashkenaz wanted to keep the End a secret among themselves and opposed its public circulation; that is, they did not completely reject the reliability of the messianic calculations but were afraid of making them known publicly. Dan found proof of that in the following Hasidic homily:[55]

> "For there is a day of vengeance in my heart" [Isa 63:4]. My heart has not told my mouth, nor does my mouth speak or tell the people, lest if they knew they would go raise him with a necromancer and tell them.[56] And those individuals in the world who know the time of Messiah, if they were to tell when they wished to make it known and to tell or to write, they could not exist, for the Holy One blessed be He has concealed the End from Jacob when he wished to tell his sons.[57]

According to Dan, this passage indicates that the leaders of Ashkenazic Hasidim believed in the proximity of the End and knew it, but kept it a deep secret. Why? The explanation I would suggest is that they feared the harsh consequences of imprudent talk about messianic vengeance against the Gentiles and overheated expectation of the Messiah's coming. It is no coincidence that the author of this Hasidic homily chose the biblical verse "For there is a day of vengeance in my heart," which describes the vengeance against Edom at the End of Days, to emphasize that the proper place to hold the hope of eschatological vengeance is in the heart and not the mouth.

And, indeed, the German chronicle *Gesta Treverorum* relates explicitly to the danger awaiting the Jews of Germany as a result of messianic awakening: "Many of the Jews began to rejoice, believing that their messiah

---

55. Joseph Dan, "The Problem of Martyrdom in the Theoretical Doctrine Teaching of Ashkenazic Hasidism" [in Hebrew], in *Milḥemet kodesh u-Martyrologiyah be-toldot Yisrael uve-toldot ha-amim* (Jerusalem, 1968), 125.

56. That is, God does not reveal the End to human beings, even immediately preceding their deaths, lest they be necromanced by magic after their deaths and reveal their secret.

57. This motif is also mentioned in the messianic calculation heard in the 1170s by Rabbi Petahiah of Regensburg from an astrologer in Nineveh named Rabbi Shlomo, who knew the time of the End but concealed it: "Behold, in the Heavens it has been decreed, [but] when I wish to reveal it, immediately it goes away from my heart and disappears, as if I had never seen this in the stars." See David (n. 14, p. 261), 257.

would come that year and lead them to freedom. This was in the year 1241. Some of the Christians suspected that the Jews wanted to do something bad to the Christians; therefore the Jews lost their favor among them, but still received imperial protection."[58]

Moritz Stern tends to think that this chronicle from Trier alludes to the attack on the Jews of Frankfurt in 1240.[59] This event, to which we shall return later, may also relate to the messianic expectations of 1240, but it is hard to believe that the text above alludes to that. Rather, it specifically refers to imperial protection given to the Jews, which may refer to the privilege given by Frederick II in 1236 to all the Jews of the Empire, defining their status for the first time as "servants of the treasury."[60] This turning point in the legal status of the Jews was an imperial response to the blood libel accusation in Fulda, which occurred on Christmas Eve 1235.[61] Three more blood libel accusations—that is, concentrated outbursts of accusations against the Jews—occurred that year in Germany: in Lauda, Tauberbischofsheim, and Wolfhagen.

Immediately upon hearing of the blood libel accusation in Fulda, the emperor ordered an investigation of the charges against the Jews. He summoned church dignitaries and princes from throughout the Empire to his court in Haguenau, but the participants could not reach an agreed decision. Frederick then convened another assembly, this time in Augsburg, to which converted Jews from outside Germany—from England, Spain, and France—were summoned. This assembly, in July 1236, concluded that the blood libels were a complete lie.

Along with taking a firm stand against the blood libel accusation, Frederick also declared that the Jews were to be considered "servants of the imperial treasury" (servi camerae), so as to defend them against similar plots in the future.[62] In my opinion, the chronicle from Trier alludes to these

58. *Gestorum Treverorum Continuatio IV,* in *MGH SS,* XXIV (Hannover, 1879), 404; Aronius (n. 4, p. 259), 228.

59. M. Stern, "Analekten zur Geschichte der Juden," *Magazin für die Wissenschaft des Judenthums* 15 (1888): 113–14.

60. *MGH Constitutiones,* vol. 2, ed. L. Weiland (Hannover, 1896), 274ff., no. 204; R. Hoeniger, "Zur Geschichte der Juden Deutschlands im Mittelalter," *Zeitschrift für die Geschichte der Juden in Deutschland* (1887), 1:136–51.

61. G. I. Langmuir, "Ritual Cannibalism," *Toward a Definition of Antisemitism* (Berkeley and Los Angeles, 1990), 263–81.

62. S. W. Baron, "'Plenitude of Apostolic Powers' and Medieval 'Jewish Serfdom'" [in Hebrew], in *Sefer Yovel le-Yitzhak Baer,* ed. S. W. Baron et al, (Baer FS.; Jerusalem, 1960), 102–24;

events. The sentence "some of the Christians suspected that the Jews wanted to do something bad against the Christians," may relate to events that preceded the enactment of the imperial protection—namely, the blood libel accusation in Fulda. This blood libel accusation expressed the Christians' suspicion that "the Jews want to do something bad against the Christians," in view of the Jewish belief that their Messiah was about to come. Nearly a century earlier, in 1149, the convert Theobold of Canterbury told of the Jewish belief that the Messiah could not come unless Christian blood were shed.[63] Theobold thus drew a connection between the Jews' avenging messianic faith and the accusation of ritual murder. In the apocalyptic text *The Prayer of Rashbi,* composed in the thirteenth century, we find a reflection of this same accusation in a Jewish source.[64] The author, who sees the wars of the Crusaders in the Land of Israel as the beginning of deliverance, levels the accusation that the Christians "remove the brains of little children, and every day they slaughter infants to Jesus." The motifs of Messiah and of ritual murder thus appear conflated in this Jewish source as well, which may be seen as a reaction to similar Christian accusations.

It therefore seems likely that the Jewish messianic expectation toward 1240 was connected in one way or another with larger political events, which may have set the stage for the eruption of the four blood libel accusations in 1235. As we have seen, the Jews of Germany made a messianic calculation that figured the Redemption at 1235, as opposed to the parallel French reckoning, which gave the year as 1240. The imperial proclamation of the Jews as *servi camerae* contradicted the political dimension of the Jewish messianic expectations: that the Jews were about to come out from slavery into freedom. His decree was thus a very clever political step on the part of Frederick II. Bernhard Diestelkamp has recently shown the close involvement of the Dominicans—supporters and allies of the pope—in inflaming the blood libel in Fulda and in its investigation.[65] He demonstrated that the

A. Patschovsky, "Das Rechtsverhältnis der Juden zum deutschen König (9.14. Jahrhundert). Ein europäischer Vergleich," *Zeitschrift der Savitny-Stiftung für Rechtsgeschichte: Germanistische Abteilung* 110 (1993): 331–71.

63. See chapter 4, n. 82.

64. J. Even Shmuel, *Chapters of the Jewish Apocalyptic* [in Hebrew] (Jerusalem, 1954), 281–82.

65. B. Diestelkamp, "Der Vorwurf des Ritualmordes gegen Juden vor dem Hofgericht Kaiser Friedrichs II. im Jahr 1236," in *Religiöse Devianz; Untersuchungen zu sozialen, rechtlichen und theologischen Reaktionen auf religiöse Abweichungen im westlichen und östlichen Mittelalter,* ed. D. Simon (Frankfurt, 1990), 19–39.

investigation in Fulda resembled an inquisitorial trial and was held against the backdrop of a wave of persecutions against heretical movements in Germany at that time. The assemblies convened by Frederick II in Haguenau and Augsburg were a direct response to Dominican intervention in the internal affairs of his kingdom. Frederick understood that Dominican intervention concerned not only the Jews of Fulda but also the Jews of the entire empire. He therefore used the same methods as the Dominicans—an inquisition—to prove the innocence of the Jews. His summoning of witnesses to Haguenau and Augsburg to investigate possible future charges against the Jews exemplified that sort of judicial investigation. Hence we find a close connection between proclaiming the innocence of the Jews, on the one hand, and placing them under "servitude of the imperial treasury," on the other. Both acts served the emperor's purpose of protecting his interests against the pope and his allies.[66] Frederick defended the Jews not only out of decency and broad-mindedness, but also because he was a clever politician who knew that what was good for the pope was bad for the emperor.

The identity of the converts who participated in the second assembly in Augsburg is not known, apart from that of one man, Nicolaus Donin, who later became famous for his accusations against the Talmud, leading to the 1240 trial in Paris. The source for this is a letter by Rabbi Jacob ben Elijah of Venice:

> Have you not heard what befell Donin the apostate, who rejected the laws of God and His Torah, and also did not believe in the religion of Rome . . . and he lost all faith. And became an evil root sprouting wormwood. This apostate went before the king, who was superior to all kings in name and honor, and spoke lies and made false accusations that on Passover nights we slaughter young boys still accustomed to their mothers' breasts, and that the Jews had accepted this upon themselves, and that the hands of merciful women cooked the children and we eat their flesh and drink their blood. And those who believed this slander, the hand of the Lord was upon them to confound them until they were destroyed. This wicked man sought to destroy us, and gave a sword into the hand of the king to kill us. He lied to him. But God returned to him double his iniquity, and cut him off and destroyed him. . . . And the honored king, in his piety

---

66. This tendency is compatible with Baron's interpretation, according to which Friedrich's claim of "ownership" of the Jews was part of the struggle of the empire against the papacy (see n. 62 above).

and cleanness of hands, did not believe his words, and paid no heed to him, knowing that they are folly and nonsense and vanity. And the kings of the earth and all those that dwell therein, did not believe it, apart from a wild donkey trained in the wilderness. Filled with deceit and evil, whose soul desired evil, flattery and wickedness.[67]

Solomon Grayzel and Joseph Shatzmiller suggested linking the events related here with the blood libel accusation in Fulda.[68] And indeed, the description "the king, who was superior to all kings in name and honor," could only fit the German emperor Frederick II. As we have seen, Jewish converts from France were also summoned to the assembly in Augsburg. Donin must have been among them, but he failed in his attempts to persuade the king of the Jews' treachery. Frederick rejected his accusations and adopted the opinion of the other converts, who firmly denied that the Jews need human blood to perform their rituals. Frederick's declaration explicitly mentions the "Jewish laws called the Talmud" that forbid Jews to use animal, not to mention human, blood. There must have been those who argued that the Talmud justifies or even requires ritual murder, and it was against them that Frederick's declaration was issued. This slander of the Talmud fits Donin, as proven by his actions in Paris three years later.[69] Donin's failure in Augsburg led him to seek his fortune precisely where someone who

67. J. Kobak, *Jeschurun* 6 (1868): 29; S. Grayzel, *The Church and the Jews in the XIIIth Century* (New York, 1966), 339–40; R. Chazan, "The Condemnation of the Talmud Reconsidered (1239–1248)," *Proceedings of the American Academy for Jewish Research* 55 (1988): 15.

68. Grayzel, *The Church and the Jews*; J. Shatzmiller, "Did Nicholas Donin Promulgate the Blood Libel?" [in Hebrew], in *Mehkarim be-toldot 'Am Yisrael ve-Eretz Yisrael* 4 (Haifa, 1978), 173–82. For another view, see C. Merchavia, "Did Nicholas Donin Instigate the Blood Libel?" [in Hebrew], *Tarbiz* 49 (1980): 111–21.

69. A close reading of Donin's accusations against the Jews made during the Paris trial against the Talmud reveals that they are based on fact and not a figment of imagination. It is doubtful that Donin would have risked telling outright lies about his former religion, claiming that they needed human blood for their rituals, certainly not before the emperor of Germany. It seems more reasonable to assume that his allegations in Augsburg were far more general: that he stated, for instance, that Jewish law contains expressions justifying the killing of Christians ("the best of the Gentiles are to be killed"), a claim that he also made in Paris. An assertion of this kind in an environment charged with anti-Jewish suspicions, complete with accusations of ritual murder, would have been understood by Jewish public opinion as a dangerous confirmation of the Christian accusations. This may explain the charges made by Rabbi Yaakov of Venice. The assumption that Donin himself did not go so far as to accuse the Jews of ritual murder is confirmed by the fact that, in the end, Friedrich II dismissed all charges against the Jews.

had failed with the emperor of Germany would go: in that same year, he set out for Rome and appealed to Pope Gregory IX.

Pope Gregory IX was not a sworn enemy of the Jews. In late summer of 1236, he in fact defended the Jews of Anjou, Poitou, and Brittany against the Crusader mobs, who had already killed twenty-five hundred of them.[70] Baron thinks that the pope's behavior may also be explained in the context of his struggle with the emperor: it was a reaction to the imperial privilege. Thus, the pope and the emperor competed with one another over who had the authority and ability to protect the Jews.

It took three years for Donin to recruit Gregory to his side. In June 1239— shortly after the pope's second and final excommunication of Frederick— Gregory appealed to the major monarchs of Europe (apart from Frederick, of course) for help in his plan. He ordered the bishops of the various countries to search the homes of the Jews and to confiscate their books on the

---

70. Grayzel (n. 67, p. 281), 226–29. A laconic and limited mention of this same incident is reported in *Chronicon Brittanie* (Grayzel [n. 67, p. 281], 345 n. 31), according to which immediately after Passover in 1236 Crusaders killed many Jews throughout Brittany, Anjou, and Poitu. About the same time (20 Adar 1236), the Jews of Narbonne also confronted the threat of a harsh pogrom. A Hebrew source for this event was published by A. Neubauer (n. 25, p. 266), 251. Cf. D. Kaufmann, "Le Pourim de Narbonne," *Révue des Etudes Juives* 32 (1896): 129–30; J. Régné, *Etudes sur la condition des Juifs de Narbonne* (Narbonne, 1912), 68–71. In 1239 the Jews of Brittany were expelled (Grayzel [n. 67, p. 281], 344–45). The Hebrew protocol of the Paris trial mentions pogroms in Brittany, in which "tens of thousands of Jews" were killed (*Vikuah* [n. 15, p. 262], 22). R. Hillel of Verona reports the killing of 3000 Jews in France after the burning of Maimonides' books; see *Hemdah Genuzah* (Königsberg, 1856), 19. On events in France, see G. Mentgen, "Kreuzzugsmentalität bei antijüdischen Aktionen nach 1190," in *Juden und Christen zur Zeit der Kreuzzüge*, ed. A. Haverkamp (Vorträge und Forschungen herausgegeben vom Konstanzer Arbeitskreis für mittelalterliche Geschichte, 47; Sigmaringen, 1999), 294–301. Across the channel, the anti-Jewish atmosphere was also becoming heated. In 1236 the Jews of Oxford were accused of having circumcised a Christian child and then crucifying him (on Easter). See Z. A. Rokéah, "The Jewish Church-Robbers and Host Desecrators of Norwich (ca. 1285)," *REJ* 141 (1982): 340 n. 26. In 1236 similar ritual murder accusations were brought against the Jews in Norwich (340–46) and in Hampshire; see Rokéah, "Crime and Jews in Late Thirteenth-Century England," *Hebrew Union College Annual* 55 (1984), 101 n. 13. In none of these cases was any attempt made to connect these accusations against the Jews with their messianic expectations; it is therefore plausible that the background to each one of those cases was unique and local. Nevertheless, we cannot rule out the possibility that the 1230s were marked by growing tension and suspicion toward the Jews in wake of their messianic expectations. The Jews themselves may have behaved more freely (hence they dared to convert Christian children—in Norwich the child was presumably the son of a converted Jew who wished to circumcise his son in secret), or Christian public opinion may have displayed increasing sensitivity toward them.

Sabbath, March 3, 1240, while they were at prayers in the synagogue.[71] Whether by chance or not, this day was Shabbat Zakhor, the "Sabbath of Remembrance" immediately preceding Purim, a date marking the destruction of the foes of Israel. Purim held profound symbolic meaning for the Jews in the Middle Ages as a holiday of vengeance preceding the holiday of deliverance on Passover.[72]

Accusations similar to those articulated against the Jews in Fulda were on the agenda of the Paris trial.[73] Having failed in Augsburg to persuade the investigators that the Talmud advocates ritual murder of Christians, Donin used in support of his accusations the Talmudic dictum "the best of the Gentiles is to be killed" *(optimum Chirstianorum occide)*. Much has been written about this dictum and its meaning, but its original literary context needs to be clarified again: it speaks of the Egyptians who pursued the Israelites as they were fleeing Egypt.[74] The Midrash expresses the idea that the Exodus from Egypt proves that one cannot rely on even the best of the Gentiles, for they too joined Pharaoh's troops in pursuit of the Israelites. In light of the typological model of the deliverance from Egypt, this sentence has messianic meaning: namely, that at the time of the Redemption it will be forbidden to show pity even to the good Gentiles. Donin did not mean to say that the Jews were likely to murder Christians for no reason, but that they had a messianic intention to kill even the best among the Christians. Thus, the Judaism placed on trial in Paris was presented as the sworn enemy of Christianity. As mentioned, the copyist of the trial protocol presented the messianic element as relevant to the date of the trial, and we have also seen that in France, unlike Germany, the Jewish millenarian calculation focused on 1240 as the year of the End. Thus, even though the messianic element is not mentioned explicitly in the Paris trial and certainly is not to be considered as the only explanation for the attack on Jewry, the claim that the messianic element played a role in making Donin's accusa-

71. Grayzel (n. 67, p. 281), 240–41.

72. Elimelech Horowitz, "'And It Was Reversed': Jews and Their Enemies in the Festivities of Purim" [in Hebrew], *Zion* 59 (1994): 129–68; G. Mentgen, "Über den Ursprung der Ritualmordfabel," *Aschkenas* 4 (1994): 405–16.

73. C. Merchavia, *Ha-Talmud bir'ei ha-Nazrut* (The Church versus Talmudic and Midrashic Literature [500–1248]: Hebrew; Jerusalem, 1970), 227–360; Jeremy Cohen, *The Friars and the Jews: The Evolution of Medieval Anti-Judaism* (Ithaca,, 1982), 60–76; Chazan (n. 67, p. 281), 15.

74. *Mekhilta de-Rabbi Yishma'el*, 89.

tions both contemporary and relevant should be weighed seriously. The issue of Jewish reliability was placed on the agenda against a background of messianic expectations and the manner in which they were received and interpreted in Christian society.

THE MONGOLIAN THREAT:

THE TEN TRIBES? GOG AND MAGOG?

And indeed, in 1240 Christian tension was aggravated by the appearance of a new arrival in the European arena: the Mongols.[75] At the same time as the trial of the Talmud was being conducted in Paris, the Mongols were at the gates of Eastern Europe. It is difficult to know when news of their rapid conquests first reached Europe, but by the 1230s there was already serious concern that they might storm the heart of Europe.[76] Many considered the Mongols as the descendants of the Ten Lost Tribes.[77] According to Marbach's chronicle, in 1222 the Jews considered the Mongolian leader, Genghis Khan, to be Messiah, son of David.[78] A contemporary, the English chronicler Mathaeus Paris, wrote that both the Jews and the Germans considered the Mongols to be the Ten Tribes, who sought to liberate their brothers from their subjection to the Christians and to attain Jewish rule over the entire world.[79] In 1241 a Hungarian bishop relates in a letter to his colleague in Paris that the Mongols are "Gog and Magog" and that they

75. For a detailed survey of the relevant sources, see S. Menache, "Tartars, Jews, Saracens and the Jewish-Mongol 'Plot' of 1241," *History: The Journal of the Historical Association* 81 (1996), 319–42. The author was not aware of my article, "Towards 1240: Jewish Hopes, Christian Fears" [in Hebrew], in *Proceedings of the Eleventh World Congress of Jewish Studies, Division B, Vol. I* (Jerusalem, 1993), 113–20, in which I suggested for the first time that the messianic aspirations of the Jews toward 1240 exacerbated Christian suspicions of the Jews.

76. Breslau (n. 27, p. 267); Aronius (n. 4, p. 259), sec. 531, 227–30; G. A. Bezzola, *Die Mongolen in abendländischer Sicht (1220–1270): Ein Beitrag zur Frage der Völkerbegegnun* (Bern–München, 1974), 34–36, 44; J. Fried, "Auf der Suche nach der Wirklichkeit. Die Mongolen und die abendländische Erfahrungswissenchaft im 13. Jahrhundert," *Historische Zeitschrift* 243 (1986): 287–332; F. Schmieder, *Europa und die Fremden: Die Mongolen im Urteil des Abendlandes vom 13. bis in das 15. Jahrhundert* (Sigmaringen, 1994), 24–30, 258–61, esp. 259 n. 327.

77. R. Lerner, *The Powers of Prophecy: The Cedar of Lebanon Vision from the Mongol Onslaught to the Dawn of the Enlightenment* (Berkeley and Los Angeles,, 1983), 21–22.

78. *Annales Marbacenses,* ed. G. H. Perts, *MGH SS, XVII* (Hannover, 1861), 174–75; Breslau (n. 27, p. 267), 100–101; Schmieder (n. 76, above), 24.

79. Matthaeus Parisiensis, *Chronica majora,* ed. H. R. Luard (= *Rerum Britannicarum medii aevi scriptores,* vol. 4; London, 1977), 131–33; Haeusler (n. 7, p. 260), 59.

use Hebrew writing.[80] As for the Jews, they are accused of supplying weaponry and food to the Mongols.[81] This was also the background for another report, from 1235, that "the Jews of Prague left the city, sold their belongings, and armed themselves after they received letters in Hebrew telling them of the impending and certain coming of their Messiah."[82]

The impression of cooperation between the Mongols and the Jews deepened, as indicated by a Christian messianic text entitled *The Prophecy of Tripoli,* an earlier version of which is known as *The Cedar of Lebanon,* on the basis of its opening sentence: *Cedrus alta lybani succidetur* (the mighty cedar of Lebanon shall fall). This prophecy has a long history, beginning in 1239 when the Mongols reached Russia, filling Western Christianity with fear. The point of the prophecy was to present the Mongolian threat as the beginning of the End of Days. One passage in this prophecy must have drawn special attention: *Filii Israel liberabuntur a captivitate. Quedam gens sine capite dicta vel reputata vagans veniet.* (The children of Israel will be freed from their captivity. A certain nation known as 'without a head' and known as wanderers shall come.) Who were those "children of Israel"? Robert Lerner thinks that this term alludes to the Mongolians, since they were identified with the Ten Lost Tribes.[83] In his view, these same "children of Israel" are those who are "without a head"—that is, the Mongols, who in sweeping across Asia and Eastern Europe seemed to the Europeans a nation without a leader.[84] Yet there is a problem with this explanation. The text distinguishes between two different groups—the children of Israel, on

---

80. Richter, *Gesta Senonensis Ecclesiae,* ed. G. Waitz, *MGS SS,* XXV (Hannover, 1880), 310; Breslau (n. 27, p. 267), 101.

81. Menache (n. 75, p. 284), 339.

82. Aronius (n. 4, p. 259), sec. 477, 211. The source for this information is the chronicle of Hagek, which, according to Stern (n. 59, p. 278), is to be suspected of forgery. This information was also published by J. Schudt, *Jüdische Merkwürdigkeiten,* vol. 4 (Frankfurt, 1714), 154. A similar accusation of supplying ammunition was also leveled against the Jews of Austria during preparations for the Second Crusade against the Hussites in 1420. This accusation was the pretext for the "Austrian persecution," during which many Jews were expelled from the duchy, many were forced to convert, and several hundred were martyred in Vienna in the spring of 1421. See I. Yuval, "Jews, Hussites and Germans According to the Chronicle *Gilgul B'nei Hushim*" [in Hebrew], *Zion* 54 (1989): 281; German: "Juden, Hussiten und Deutsche; Nach einer hebräischen Chronik," *Juden in der christlichen Umwelt während des späten Mittelalters,* ed. A. Haverkampf and F. J. Ziwes (Berlin, 1992), 65.

83. Lerner (n. 77, p. 284), 21–22.

84. A similar image—"the locusts have no king" (*regem locusta non habet;* Prov 30:27)— is used by both Guibert de Nogent and Shlomo ben Shimshon to describe the participants in

the one hand, and the nomadic nation without a leader, on the other; how then is it possible to speak of them as a single entity? Moreover, it is difficult to square the description of the children of Israel, to be liberated from their enslavement and captivity, to the nomadic, menacing Mongols. Hence, this text must be understood in its literal sense: it is a Christian prophecy of the Redemption of the "children of Israel," that is, of the Ten Tribes, in 1239.[85] The Latin text absorbed something of the Jews' messianic hopes regarding 1240, hopes that clearly intensified with the appearance of the Mongols at the gates of Europe, evoking fear among the Christians.

Testimony to the place of the Mongols in Jewish consciousness may be found in a rather obscure Hebrew document from Sicily that tells of "the king who was hidden"—that is, the king of the Ten Tribes—who sent twelve emissaries to all the kings of Europe ordering them to allow the Jews to leave their countries and to immigrate to the Land of Israel.[86] If they do not do so, he warned, he would wage war against them. According to this document, the kings of Spain, France, Germany, and Hungary were greatly frightened and attempted to appease the "hidden ones" with money. The identification of the "hidden ones" with the Mongols seems self-evident,[87] but it is not so clear when this document was written—a point that is still being debated.[88] The earliest conjectured date is the eleventh century, and the latest is the sixteenth. But the various opinions articulated thus far are based on the assumption that this is a historical document describing actual events. I wish to suggest an alternative reading, which I shall exemplify with one passage from the document.

---

the First Crusade, the former in a positive sense and the latter negatively. See Yitzhak Baer, "The Pogroms of 1096" [in Hebrew], *Sefer Simhah Assaf* (Jerusalem?, 1953), 128 (reprinted in his *Mehkarim u-Masot be-toldot 'Am Yisrael* [Jerusalem, 1986], 2:149).

85. Exegeses of this prophecy from the fourteenth and sixteenth centuries refer explicitly to liberation of the "Jews" (rather than of the "Israelites") from their subjugation. See Lerner (n. 77, p. 284), 146, 162 n. 12.

86. Published for the first time by J. Mann, *Texts and Studies*, vol. 1 (Cincinnati, 1931), 38ff., and more recently by N. Zeldes, "A Magical Event in Sicily: Notes and Clarifications on the Messianic Movement in Sicily" [in Hebrew], *Zion* 58 (1993): 347–63.

87. J. N. Epstein, "On the Messianic Movement in Sicily" [in Hebrew] *Tarbiz* 11 (1940): 218–19. Matthaeus Parisiensis (above, n. 79) uses the word *inclusi* to designate the Mongols: "quos dominus in montibus Caspiis precibus Magni Alexandri quondam inclusit."

88. For a full account of the different opinions regarding the dating of this document see Zeldes (n. 86, above).

According to the document, rumors of the appearance of the Jewish King Messiah caused great danger:

The children of Allemania [i.e., Germany] were about to kill all the Jews. The shaved ones [priests] stood up and said to them: Take care not to do them any harm, for[89] he who does them harm and whoever touches them touches the pupil of his eyes. And he does not cause harm to himself alone, but to the entire world, for if they [the hidden ones] come and hear that they killed Jews, they shall kill you in their stead.

Did such an event take place? The priests' warning consists of two arguments. First, that "whoever touches them touches the pupil of his eyes"; the second, that the "hidden ones" are likely to punish anyone who harms the Jews of Germany. The first argument is a direct quote from the Babylonian Talmud (*Gittin* 57a), which places Augustine's doctrine of tolerance in Jesus's mouth, as if Jesus had commanded his followers to keep the Jews alive. But the formulation of the argument here does not reflect the language of the Church and its priests, but rather that of Jewish propaganda.[90] The same holds true for the warning about the punishment that will befall those who harm the Jews, since it is difficult to imagine that priests in Germany ever uttered such arguments. This is Jewish propaganda, suitable for every generation, that can be adjusted to changing circumstances. I think that those who date the document to the fifteenth century are correct, but the passage discussing the "hidden ones" undoubtedly reflects the atmosphere of the Jewish camp during the thirteenth century when the Mongols appeared. It clearly indicates the messianic hopes among the Jews, the hostility stirred against them among the lower classes in Germany, and the need on the part of the authorities to defend the Jews.

Another event that may have some indirect relevance to this complex of issues is the pogrom against the Jews of Frankfurt in 1241.[91] On April 9, 1241, immediately after Passover, the armies fighting the Mongols were de-

---

89. Should be "whoever" (Heb.: *kol*).

90. In his letter to Rabbenu Tam immediately following the Blois affair of 1171, Nathan ben Meshullam informs him that King Louis VII of France granted protection to the Jews. This author places that same Talmudic expression in the king's mouth; see A. M. Haberman, *Gezerot Ashkenaz ve-Tzarfat* (Jerusalem, 1971), 145.

91. F. Backhaus, ed., *"Und gross war bei der Tochter Jehudas Jammer und Klage"... Die Ermordung der Frankfurter Juden im Jahre 1241* (Sigmaringen, 1995).

feated in Liegnitz, Poland, thereby turning the Mongols into a real threat to the German Empire.[92] Thereafter, relations between Jews and Christians in Frankfurt deteriorated. The Jews tried to prevent the baptism of a Jewish boy who wished to convert to Christianity, and on May 24 street fights broke out between Jews and Christians, in which several Christians were injured. This event stirred up the wrath of the Christians, who slaughtered about 180 Jews of the city. The chronological proximity between the defeat in Liegnitz in April and the pogrom against the Jews in May, as well as the assertive behavior of the Jews, reinforces the assumption that tension increased upon news of the defeat in Liegnitz. It is easy to imagine the excitement aroused by the Mongol victory, if not in the Jewish street, then certainly in their hearts.

A SYNCHRONIC OVERVIEW

In this chapter we have presented a synchronic survey of a variety of seemingly unconnected events: the French immigration to the Land of Israel, Rabbi Moses of Coucy's campaign in Spain, the blood libel accusations in Germany in 1235, the privilege granted to the Jews by Frederich in 1236, the trial against the Talmud in Paris, the Mongol invasion, and the pogrom in Frankfurt—all in context of the messianic expectation of 1240. I did not wish to present the messianic context as the causal explanation for all these events, but to point to it as an organizing factor that gives broader meaning to a series of events, which are each self-contained. Andrew Gow states the issue clearly: "Antisemitism and apocalypticism are so inextricably intertwined in medieval Europe that they must be studied together if a coherent and accurate picture of both phenomena is to emerge."[93] Thus, a discussion of the manifestations of Jewish messianism must take into account not only the internal Jewish process but also the responses of the Christians.

A comparative examination of Jewish messianic expectations, on the one hand, and of Christian responses, on the other, illuminates one of the fundamental assumptions of research on medieval anti-Semitism—namely, that this hatred is the product of irrational fantasies—in a more complex light. Blood libels, accusations of desecration of the Host, the belief that Jewish

92. Schmieder (n. 76, p. 284), 28. Panic spread from Hungary to Germany, reaching France and Spain as well.
93. Gow (n. 47, p. 275), 3.

men menstruate or have a tail—all those are, of course, irrational fantasies. But we must ask where these fantasies came from and what purpose they fulfilled; in short, we need to study rationally the history of irrationality.

Jewish messianism plays an important role in understanding the mechanisms that triggered Christian fantasies about the Jews. There is a tragic asymmetry between the messianic expectations of Christians and of Jews. The Christians awaited the conversion to Christianity of the Jews, while the Jews anticipated the destruction of Christianity. On the eschatological level, Judaism is far more aggressive than Christianity—an understandable reaction on the part of a group that, in reality, is a victim of aggression. This eschatological asymmetry influenced the relations between these two religions, since the eschatological narrative of both is structured on mutual denial and inversion. The Jewish Messiah is the Christian Antichrist, and vice versa. The messianic scenario of each side allots a very active, but dangerous, role to the other side. Not only were Jewish messianic visions esoteric fantasies, but they also influenced the concept of reality on the Christian side. Thus, the Jewish messianic fantasy played a major role in shaping Christian anti-Semitic fantasies.

The year 1240 was very important in the annals of German Jewry. Friedrich Lotter noted that, contrary to the conventional image, the Jews of Germany enjoyed relative quiet during the two centuries between 1096 and 1298;[94] things took a turn for the worse, in his view, in the 1260s. I would propose moving the turning point back twenty years, to 1240, against the background of the Jewish messianic expectations and the parallel eschatological awakening in Christian society. The sense that the Jews' status had taken a great turn for the worse in 1240 was expressed by a Jewish liturgical poet, Rabbi Moshe ben Eleazar, who contemplated the history of his period shortly after the Rindfleisch persecutions of 1298. He describes the great disappointment of the generation after 1240 and the recognition that the world was turning bad:

> Woe unto me for the sixth millennium, for I did not find therein
> grace.
> At its beginning [1240–1241] there rose against me an enemy to
> oppose me;

---

94. F. Lotter, "Hostienfrevelvorwurf und Blutwunderfälschungen bei den Judenverfolgungen von 1298 ('Rintfleisch') und 1336–1138 ('Armleder'), *Fälschungen im Mittelalter* (Hannover, 1988), 533–83.

In the thirteenth year [1253] we are a byword and a laughing stock;
In the seventeenth year our enemies overtook us with honed sword;
And in the years forty-seven and forty-eight [1287–1288] they greatly
    increased against me stench [tried to impose a forced conversion]. [95]

This liturgical poem expresses disappointment at the deteriorating situation of the Jews after 1240, perhaps because of confuted messianic expectations. A similar *post factum* disappointment was expressed by Rabbi Moses Nahmanides in his *Commentary to the Torah*, written in his old age, a full generation after 1240: "At the beginning of the sixth millennium there shall be renewed the rule of a nation that is dominant and frightening and very aggressive and that approaches the truth more than the former ones."[96] Hopes for a better future were exchanged for anticipation of a great change for the worse.

A whole gamut of factors influenced the complex processes leading to a change in the Jews' image in the eyes of Europeans in the twelfth and thirteenth centuries, and I do not intend to list them all here. The main concern of this discussion is to emphasize one motif, which I think has not yet been sufficiently appreciated: messianism and its place in shaping the mutual perceptions of Jews and Christians.

Acknowledgment of the importance of messianism may prompt a reevaluation of everything relating to the massacres of 1096, which may be considered a tragic turning point in the history of relations between Christians and Jews. At that time, as in 1240, the ancient messianic tension latent in the attitude of Jews toward the Christian Edom was revealed. The Crusaders' military struggle against Islam brought to the surface a dormant tradition of harsh messianic competition between Judaism and Christianity. Islam became the political enemy, while Judaism became the eschatological enemy. Such relationships are always mutual, making it so every Jewish messianic expectation must necessarily involve a threatening statement aimed at Christianity: Edom's hour of reckoning would come. Shifting the competition to the eschatological plane transformed Judaism into a dangerous, unreliable element in Christian eyes, giving new meaning to Pharaoh's ancient fear, "Come, let us deal shrewdly with them, lest they

95. Haberman, *Gezerot*, 225–26.
96. *Perush ha-Ramban 'al ha-Torah*, I, ed. H. D. Chavell (Jerusalem, 1972), at Gen 2:3, 32). This apparently refers to the conquest of the Land of Israel by the Mamelukes in 1260.

multiply, and, if war befall us, they join our enemies and fight against us" (Exod 1:10). The significance of the events close to the end of the Jewish millennium can also be understood in light of this very ancient paradigm. In Christian eyes, these events demonstrated that Judaism was preparing to throw off the Christian yoke, just waiting for the suitable messianic moment. Hence, there is room to conjecture that the exacerbated maltreatment of the Jews during the thirteenth century may have expressed, among other things, the tense response of Christians to the messianic expectations of the Jews.

A JEWISH END AND A CHRISTIAN END

The tense messianic expectations at the end of the sixth Jewish millennium also involved an entirely different aspect, bereft of mutual grudges and hostilities. The significance of the end of the Jewish millennium also indicates a network of shared conventions and notions between Jews and Christians. To understand them,, we must reexamine one of the calculations of the End for the year 1240 presented earlier.

According to one of those calculations, the time elapsed from the giving of the Torah until the birth of Jesus needed to equal the amount of time that would elapse from Jesus's Crucifixion until the coming of the Messiah. Nor is this the only Jewish text that calculates the End on the basis of the birth or Crucifixion of Jesus. A similar calculation was presented by Rabbi Shemaiah of Troyes, a student of Rashi, in a text recently published by Abraham Grossman and again by Simha Emmanuel, giving the date for the Redemption as 1102.[97] But our text, concerning 1240, is unique in that it grants Jesus a status ostensibly equal to that of Moses. In other messianic calculations, the birth of Jesus is used to mark the beginning of the Exile and the subjugation, but Jesus himself plays no positive role; here, however, Jesus bears a new teaching that receives at least partial recognition.

History is here divided into three periods and three persons: Moses, Jesus, and the Messiah. How are we to imagine a Jew, at the height of the Middle Ages, coming up with such a notion? There seems to be an indirect connection between this view and another division of history presented in the

---

97. Avraham Grossman, *Hakhmei Tzarfat ha-Rishonim; Koroteihem, darkam be-hanhagat ha-tzibbur, yetziratam ha-ruhanit* (Jerusalem, 1995), 357; Simha Emanuel, "Calendrical Calculation and Eschatological Calculation: a Jewish-Christian Polemic in 1100" [in Hebrew], *Zion* 63 (1998): 143–55.

Jerusalem Talmud, according to which Balaam lived in the midpoint of history: "Rabbi Hanina son of Rabbi Abahu said: That Evil One [Balaam] arose at half the days of the world."[98] This Talmudic saying served as the basis for a messianic calculation made by Rabbi Judah al-Bargeloni,[99] and by Maimonides in the *Epistle to Yemen:*

> By this method of cryptic allusion it was transmitted to me that Balaam's statement: "Jacob is told at once *[ka'et]*, yea Israel, what God has planned" [Num 23:23], contains a veiled hint as to the date of the restoration of prophecy to Israel. The sentence means that after the lapse of an interval equal to the time that passed from the six days of creation to Balaam's day, seers will again tell Israel what God has planned."[100]

Since Balaam lived in the year 2486 of the Creation, Maimonides believed that prophecy would be renewed in the year 4972 from the Creation, that is, in 1211–1212 C.E. Comparison between these two calculations indicates a possible similarity between them: according to the Rabbinic Sages/ Maimonides, we find the sequence Creation—Balaam—Messiah; according to the French calculation we have Moses—Jesus—Messiah.

This replacing of Balaam with Jesus is not surprising, since the similarity and possibly even partial identification between the two has ancient roots.[101] It is therefore possible, that, in wake of this change, placing Moses within the schema, as a figure of parallel importance to Jesus and the Messiah, may have been called for.

98. *j. Shabbat* 6.9 (8d).

99. Judah al-Bargeloni (n. 6, p. 259), 239. According to this calculation, the end will come in 1214.

100. See n. 33 above; English: 122.

101. For a discussion of the identification of Jesus with Balaam, see Louis Ginzberg, *Legends of the Jews,* 6 (Philadelphia, 1968), 123–24 n. 722; E. E. Urbach, "Rabbinic Homilies on the Prophets of the Nations and the Balaam Narrative" [in Hebrew] *Tarbiz,* 25 (1956), esp. 281–84; David Berger, "Three Typological Themes in Early Jewish Messianism: Messiah Son of Joseph, Rabbinic Calculations, and the Figure of Armilus," *AJS Review* 10 (1985): 162 n. 78. Berger has reservations about the possibility that Balaam served as a typological figure for Jesus, even though many typologies mentioned by him can easily explain how the figure of Balaam was exchanged with that of Jesus. Balaam is identified typologically with Armilus— the former is the great enemy of the first deliverer (Moses), while the latter is the great enemy of the last savior (Messiah)—and with Romulus, the founder of Rome, that is, Edom. It is therefore natural that the Jewish "Antichrist" (Balaam, Armilus) would assume the identity of Jesus, so that the Second Coming of Jesus (Parousia), awaited by Christians, would

There may also be another explanation for placing Jesus as a key figure in a Jewish messianic calculation, alongside Moses and the Messiah. It may reflect an indirect Jewish absorption of the messianic teaching of Joachim de Fiore, in which history is divided into three eras, or *status,* parallel to the Holy Trinity: the era of the Father/the Old Testament (from Moses to Jesus); the era of the Son/the New Testament (from Jesus to the time of Joachim); and the future era of the Holy Spirit, in which the Parousia, the Second Coming of Jesus, will take place. Jews and Muslims will then convert to Christianity, the Holy Roman Empire will be destroyed, and the earthly Church will be transformed into the spiritual one. According to Joachim's calculation, the third, messianic era will be at the end of forty-two generations after Jesus, that is, about 1260.[102] My hypothesis is that, under the influence of the Joachimist doctrine of the three eras, the Jewish messianic calculation put Moses in the place of the Father, Jesus in that of the Son, and the Messiah in place of the Holy Spirit; hence, it was willing to grant Jesus a place of honor alongside Moses within universal history.[103]

The Jewish messianic calculation of the End is articulated as follows: "Likewise the nations will adhere to the Nazarene and his teaching for 1,276 years, and thereafter they will be eliminated at the end of 5000 years." Joachim was not interested beyond that point. He also depicted the world through the opposition of pairs marking the first two eras: Jews versus Gen-

---

be considered by the Jews as the appearance of the "Antichrist" (Armilus). Indeed, in several places the identification of Balaam with Jesus is clearly called for (e.g., in *b. Sanhedrin* 106b), while other sources clearly speak of two distinct figures (as in *b. Gittin* 57a—in the uncensored version the reading there is "Jesus" rather than "the sinners of Israel," as in the Vilna edition.)

102. Morton W. Bloomfield, "Joachim of Fiora: A Critical Survey of His Canon, Teachings, Sources, Biography and Influence," *Traditio* 13 (1957): 249–311; Bloomfield, "Recent Scholarship on Joachim of Fiore and his Influence," in *Prophecy and Millenarianism. Essays in Honour of Marjorie Reeves,* ed. A. Williams (Suffolk, 1980), 21–52; Marjorie Reeves, *The Influence of Prophecy in the Later Middle Ages: A Study of Joachimism* (Oxford, 1969; repr. Notre Dame, 1993), 3–27.

103. On the possible influence of Joachim's teaching on the Kabbalistic doctrine of *shemitot,* see Gerschom Scholem, *Major Trends in Jewish Mysticism* (New York, 1954), 179. On parallels between views that were commonly held in Joachimist circles and the *Ra'ya Mehemna,* see Yitzhak Baer, "The Historical Background of the *Ra'ya Mehemna*" [in Hebrew], *Zion* 5 (1940), 1–44 (reprinted in his *Mehkarim u-Masot* [n. 84, p. 285], 2:306–49). Isaiah Tishby dissented from the parallels noted by Baer in his *Mishnat ha-Zohar* (Jerusalem, 1982), 2:692–702. On the issue of the relation between Joachim and the Jewish sources, cf. Beatrice Hirsh-Reich, "Joachim von Fiore und das Judentum," in *Judentum im Mittelalter,* ed. P. Wilpert (Miscellanea Medievalia. 4; Berlin 1966), 228–63.

tiles, the kings of Israel versus the emperors of Rome, the Synagogue versus the Church. Just as the Jewish author speaks of the destruction of Edom at the beginning of the third era, so does Joachim talk of the destruction of the Holy Roman Empire, which is the new Babylon. Joachim's position implies that the New Testament is not the final revelation. And indeed, the spiritualist Franciscans—the radical element among the Joachimists— compared Saint Francis with Jesus and Moses, since each of them opened a new era. As noted by Marjorie Reeves,[104] Joachim's messianic thinking combines three factors: the idea of the millennium,[105] the conception of history as a reflection of the Six Days of Creation,[106] and the tripartite division of history.[107] All three of these components are found in the Jewish reckoning.

This Jewish messianic text constitutes yet another example of the ability of Jewish society to undergo a profound process of acculturation to the milieu in which they lived, even when that milieu was engaged in a mortal struggle. The shared but invisible framework of Jewish-Christian language

104. Marjorie Reeves, "Joachimist Influences on the Idea of a Last World Emperor," *Traditio* 17 (1961): 323–70.

105. According to Revelation 20:4–5.

106. Auguste Luneau, *L'histoire du salut chez les pères de l'Eglise. La doctrine des âges du monde* (Paris, 1964); R. Schmidt, "Aetates mundi: Die Weltalter als Gliederungsprinzip der Geschichte," *Zeitschrift für Kirchengeschichte* 67 (1955–56): 288–317. In the fourth century, Julian of Toledo wrote *De comprobatione aetatis sextae,* in which he attempted to prove that the sixth millennium, according to his calculations, had already come to an end and that the Messiah had not yet come. By this he sought to refute the Jewish argument that Jesus could not have been the Messiah since he lived before the end of the sixth millennium. On this essay and its author, see Bernhard Blumenkranz, *Les auteurs chrétiens latins du moyen âge sur les juifs et le judaïsme* (Paris, 1963), 119–26.

107. The Jewish division (*b. Sanhedrin* 97a) of six thousand years into three aeons– of chaos, Torah, and Messiah—also appears in ancient Eastern Christian literature, and it spread to the West in the fourth century. The Christian division is into *chaos, logos, christus.* This is discussed by J. Stevenson, *The "Laterculus Malalianus" and the School of Archbishop Theodore* (Cambridge, 1995), 23–25, 122. Cf. Oded Irshai, "Dating the Eschaton: Jewish and Christian Apocalyptic Calculations in Late Antiquity," in *Apocalyptic Time*, ed. A. I. Baumgarten (Leiden, 2000), 113–53. This Talmudic division into three periods also parallels the division of history according to Pauline doctrine, into the period of natural law that prevailed before the giving of the Torah to Moses (chaos), the period of the Law after the giving of the Torah (Torah), and the period of grace following the birth of Jesus (Messiah). In accordance with that, the three watches of the night in Luke 12:35–40 are parallel to the three periods: *tria tempora sunt, ante legem, sub lege et sub gratia* ("these are three times: before the Law, under the Law, and under Grace). See Schmidt, "Aetates mundi," 300.

was the foundation on which the overt polemic between Jews and Christians could be carried out. Thus, traditional society did quietly and in a hidden manner what modern society does consciously and openly: to live history, to be part of it, and to exploit its limited possibilities wisely.

It seems fitting to conclude this book with the cogent remarks of Yitzhak Baer written in 1940, during the darkest period of Jewish history in Germany:

> In studying the history of the Jews in the Middle Ages, as in studying
> that of the Talmudic period, scientific principles which, regarding earlier
> periods, have long been accepted as general conventions, were abandoned.
> To this day, certain prejudices and preconceptions which, regarding the
> relations between Jews and Islam, have already been rejected in large mea-
> sure, have remained in force regarding the intimate contact between Jewish
> and Christian society, serving as obstacles in the way towards true knowl-
> edge of the past. It is customary to summarize these preconceptions by
> using slogans: the "ghetto," the profound hatred between Jews and Chris-
> tians, the profound chasm separating Jewish teaching from Christian
> religion, the total immanence of the development of the Jewish religious
> tradition. To these generalizations, whose truth cannot be entirely denied,
> the historian needs to add according to his own experience, his own as-
> sumptions based upon facts: the everyday contact between Jewish and
> Christian society, the interrelations between them in politics and econ-
> omics, the shared use of various concepts and approaches to public and
> private life, the shared root of the religious-historical heritage . . . surpris-
> ing parallels in the history of the religious ideals, in their existence and
> failures in history. . . . This approach to research sets out, not only to illu-
> minate one period in detail, but to teach about the whole, on the basis of
> the thrust of the inner tendency of all of our history.[108]

With these words, Baer paved the way for historical research in our time; and even if he himself strayed from this path later on,[109] we remain his students and the students of his students.

---

108. Baer (n. 103, p. 293), 3 (= *Mehkarim u-Masot*, 307–8).

109. For Baer's revisionism regarding Christianity after the Holocaust and the establish-ment of the State of Israel, see I. J. Yuval, "Yitzhak Baer and the Search for Authentic Ju-daism," in *The Jewish Past Revisited: Reflections on Modern Jewish Historians*, ed. D. N. Myers and D. B. Ruderman, (New Haven, 1998), 77–87.

Index

France, 39, 56, 80n120, 94, 98, 109, 114–15, 123, 129n106, 132, 138n8, 282n70, 286, 287n90; and immigration to Israel, 264, 267, 270–74, 275–76, 288; millenarian calculation in, 259–65, 267–68, 272, 279, 283, 292; ritual murder libel in, 165n65, 170–72. *See also names of specific towns*

Franciscans, 294

Frankfurt, 128, 175, 204n151, 239, 242, 266, 278, 287–88

Freimann, A. H., 121, 122, 123

Friedmann, M., 38

Friedrich II, 278–82, 288

Fulda, 168n71, 278–83

Galatians, 116

Gamaliel, Rabbi, 62, 63n77, 65, 67, 72, 74–76, 80n121, 89

Garment, divine. *See* Porphyrion

Garsiel, Moshe, 4n1

Genesis, 4–9, 13n20, 24n36, 85, 160, 212, 230, 257, 261–63

Genesis Rabbah, 76

Genghis Khan, 284

Gentiles: conversion of, 94, 109–15; cursing of, 115–34; destruction of, 45n39, 58, 93–111, 115, 133n111, 174, 182, 185, 216, 275, 281n69, 283, 293–94

Germany, 2, 56, 59, 93, 94, 109, 114, 128, 138n8, 160, 286–89, 295; and ritual murder libel, 165n65, 168–70, 168n71, 171, 172, 278–83, 288. *See also names of specific towns*

Gershom Meor ha-Golah, Rabbi, 94n5, 102

Gesta Treverorum, 277

Gilead, 7n7

Ginzberg, Louis, 33–34

Gittin, 25n37, 43n36, 45, 49, 287, 293n101

Gnat, 44, 46, 49, 50, 55

God: and Acts of the Apostles, 82; and Binding of Isaac, 160; and deliverance from Egypt, 80–82; and Jacob and Esau's story, 3–6; and matzah symbolism, 206. *See also* Vengeance, divine

Gog, 109, 112, 141, 226, 267, 284

Goitein, S. D., 273

Goldenberg, R., 51n50

Goldschmidt, Daniel, 62n76, 63n77, 69, 70, 78n116, 81n122, 91, 121, 122

Gombiner, Rabbi Abraham, 245

Goodblatt, David, 146n23

Good Friday, 70, 172, 244

Goshen, 9

Gow, Andrew, 274, 288

Grayzel, Solomon, 281

Great light, 149–51

Great Roman War, 15

Great Sabbath, 188n112, 209–29, 237, 256

Great Week, 59, 211–13, 215, 220–22, 226–29

Gregory IX, 282

Gregory of Tours, 188

Grossman, Avraham, 94n6, 120n83, 140, 160n54

Guibert de Nogent, 165n65, 285n84

Hadad, 9–10

Hadrian, 11

Haeusler, Martin, 260n9

Haftarah, 98n22, 188n112, 213, 215, 219, 223–28

Haggadah: and *afikoman,* 239, 242, 245, 247; and anti-Christian polemic, 75, 80n121, 90, 124; and Christian exegesis, 84–85, 87–88; and Christian liturgy, 70–73, 89; and cursing of Gentiles, 124; and *Dayyenu* prayer, 70–72; and Egyptian plagues, 58, 129; and Exodus from Egypt, 62, 66, 79, 245; and Jacob and Esau's story, 14; and Last Supper of Jesus, 72–73; and Midrash, 63n77, 77, 82, 85, 211; and Redemption, 124, 129; and Temple period, 63–64n77; and vengeful redemption, 98, 100, 101; and *Vindicta Dei,* 52

Haharishu mimeni, 104

Al Haharot Sefarad, 110

Hai Gaon, Rabbi, 109

Hakim, Rabbi, 106

Halakha, 78, 139, 140, 160, 206, 217, 223, 229, 231, 238, 239, 240, 246, 253, 271, 273

and Passover, 58, 77, 79, 88; and *por-phyrion*, 198; and Rachel, grand-daughter of Shuthelah, 252–53; and Talmud, 51; and Torah, 24, 153; and vengeful redemption, 98–99, 101

Midrash Tehillim, 37

Milhemet Mitzvah, 93–94, 109

Millenarian calculation, 257–68, 272, 279, 283, 291–94

Minty, Mary, xiv, 180

Mirsky, A., 199n141

Mishael, 191

Mishnah, 62, 65, 66n84, 73, 74, 77, 88, 90n140, 229

Mi yiten roshi mayim, 105

Moab, 24n36

Moers, 162

Mongols, 284–88

Monogamy, 4n2

Morning prayer, 62, 117, 118, 119, 199

Moses, 9–10, 30, 72n100, 77, 79, 80, 84, 130–31n107, 248–49, 265, 291–93

Moses ben Maimon, Rabbi, 266

Moses of Coucy, Rabbi, 263, 273–74, 288

Moshe ben Eleazar, Rabbi, 289

Mother religion, Judaism as, 27, 69

Mühlhausen, Yom Tov Lipmann, 132, 133, 182, 232, 257

Muslims, 2, 23, 25, 110, 264, 270, 293

Mysterium, 75, 86, 90n140

Nahmanides, 112, 290

Nahum, 107

Narbonne, 173, 174, 282n70

Nasi, 55

Nathan ben Yehudah, Rabbi, 121

Nazis, 20

Nehemiah, 4n3

Nero, 50, 52–53, 55

Nestorianism, 26

Neuss, 175–77, 180

Neustadt, Rabbi Shalom, 238

New Testament, 2, 18, 23n33, 24, 26, 40, 75, 81, 90–91, 131n107, 152, 253, 293–94. *See also names of specific books*

Nicean Council, 60–61, 211

Nirenberg, David, 233

Noah, 260

Norwich, 167–68, 170–71, 173–74, 181–82, 189, 203, 282n70

Numbers, 11, 107, 261, 292

Nuremberg, 137

Obadiah, 212, 231

Obadiah ben Makhir, 194

Ofer, Joseph, 225

Old Testament, 24, 86, 293. *See also names of specific books*

Ometz gevuratekha, 124

Onai Fitrei, 218

Onkelos, 50, 55–56

Oral Law, 24–25, 90

Origen, 14, 40, 48–49, 51, 54, 68, 207n6

Original sin, 32, 46

Orosius, 42

Orthodox Judaism, 29, 30

Or Zaru'a, 223–27, 232, 253n140

Other, Jews as, 22, 30

Otto the Great, 114

Paganism, 10–11, 15, 42, 47, 48n44, 49n47, 57n62, 60, 70, 114n72, 141, 250

Palm Sunday, 211, 221, 227–29

Parallels, Christian-Jewish: and Acts of the Apostles, 64; and *afikoman,* 90–91, 241–42, 244–48; and birth of Jesus, 248–49, 291; and birth of Moses, 248–49; and bread, 207, 229–30; and chronology, 69; and Crucifixion of Jesus, 59, 60, 79, 86–87, 89, 129, 229–30, 244; and deliverance, 2, 60, 65, 68, 71n98, 72, 83, 89, 129; and Destruction of the Temple, 50; and dialogical affinity, 21; and Easter, 57, 68, 90, 205, 207–9; and *eruv,* 237–38; and exegetical practices, 87; and Exodus, 79–87; and *haroset,* 254; and Host, 240–42, 244–48; and human sacrifice, 248–52; and Jacob and Esau's story, 14–16; and martyrdom, 139, 189, 190, 196–203; and messianism, 36, 70, 90, 152, 229, 291–95; and Midrash, 79–89, 198, 248–49, 252; and millenarian calculation, 291–94;

Pogroms: in Austria, 130n107, 133n111, 186n109; chronicles of, 28, 40, 131–32, 135, 139–40, 143, 154, 157, 161, 164, 175, 181, 189; in Frankfurt, 287–88; in Koblenz, 186n109; in Mainz, 144–45, 149n33, 197n134; in Narbonne, 282n70; in Rindfleisch, 137, 289; and ritual murder libel, 169, 170, 181, 182; sacrificial response to, 155n42, 159; in Spain, 113; in Speyer, 179n99; vengeful redemption for, 95, 99, 100, 102–4, 106; in Worms, 181

Polycarp, 210n10

Polygamy, 4n2

Pompey, 58n63

Porphyrion, 95–97, 99, 114n72, 135, 138n7, 197–98

"Pour Out Thy Wrath," 123–24, 128, 129n104, 134, 175, 239

Prayer: *Alenu le-shabeah,* 119, 129n104, 133n111, 192–93, 198–202; *Amidah,* 100, 117, 118, 198n139; *Dayyenu,* 70–72; *Improperia,* 70–72; Morning, 62, 117, 118, 119, 199; *Te Deum laudamus,* 198–202

Prayer of Rashbi, 279

Promised Land, 8, 71, 274

Prophecy of Tripoli, 285

Proselytizing redemption, 94, 109–15

Provence, 94, 109, 232, 259, 272

Proverbs, 187

Psalms, 37, 63n77, 71, 107, 108, 118, 150, 175, 218, 219, 261

Pseudo-Hippolyte, 79

Purim, 120n83, 130–31n107, 165–67, 169, 174, 230, 283

Qamza, 50–52

Quartodecimani, 60–61, 66, 68, 88, 211

Qumran sect, 35, 116

Rachel, 3, 13n20, 34

Rachel, granddaughter of Shuthelah, 252–53

Rashi, 80n121, 217, 247n125

Rebecca, 3, 5, 7, 8, 13, 19, 212

Redemption, xii, 2, 39, 56–58, 72n99, 80, 84, 89, 124, 125, 127, 147, 161, 206,

207, 211, 226, 228, 231–32, 239, 246, 248, 252, 269, 271; and millenarian calculation, 257, 258, 260, 265, 266, 279, 291; proselytizing, 94, 109–15; vengeful, 93–109, 112–15, 127, 134, 136, 138, 140, 141, 143, 173–74, 213

"Red Jew," legend of, 274–75

Red Sea, 57n63, 70, 125

Reeves, Marjorie, 294

Regensburg, 179, 184

Reiner, Elchanan, 28, 271, 272

Resurrection, 111n64, 229, 244

Revelation, 96, 100n26, 152

Rigord's chronicle, 172

Rindfleisch, 137, 289

Ritual murder libel: and baptism, 175–78, 181–82, 184–85, 192n119, 196; in Blois, 170–72, 183–84, 190–96, 198, 203; in Bristol, 190, 196, 198, 200; and children as victims, 164, 165n65, 166, 167–68, 170, 171, 178, 179–80, 183, 185, 186n109, 187–89, 196–98, 203, 279, 282n70; and Crucifixion of Jesus, 165, 171; and Crusades, 169–70, 185, 279; and desecration of the Host, 208–9; dissemination of, 165n65, 167, 168, 170–72; distinguished from blood libel, 168n71; and divine vengeance, 127, 134, 173–74, 185; and Easter, 171–72, 181, 182, 183, 185, 190, 191; and Frederick II's protection of Jews, 278–83; in Fulda, 278–83; and *haroset,* 254; and Jewish martyrdom, xii–xiii, 2, 164, 170, 173, 175, 185–86, 188–89, 190–96, 203; and messianism, 164, 173–75, 185; and Passover, 166–67, 171, 172, 179, 181, 182, 185, 190, 197, 254; and pogroms, 169, 170, 181, 182; and Purim, 165–67, 169, 174; and Simon of Trent's murder, 128, 129n104, 174–75; and Talmud, 280, 281, 283; water associated with, 171, 175–85; and William of Norwich's murder, 167–68, 170–71, 173–74, 181–82, 189, 203, 282n70; and women as murderers, 187–89; in Worms, 181, 182; in Würzburg, 168–69, 182, 189

Text:	11.25/13.5 AGaramond
Display:	Adobe Garamond
Compositor:	Integrated Composition Systems
Indexer:	Andrew Joron

Lightning Source UK Ltd.
Milton Keynes UK
UKOW02f0945171116

287832UK00002B/58/P

9 780520 258181